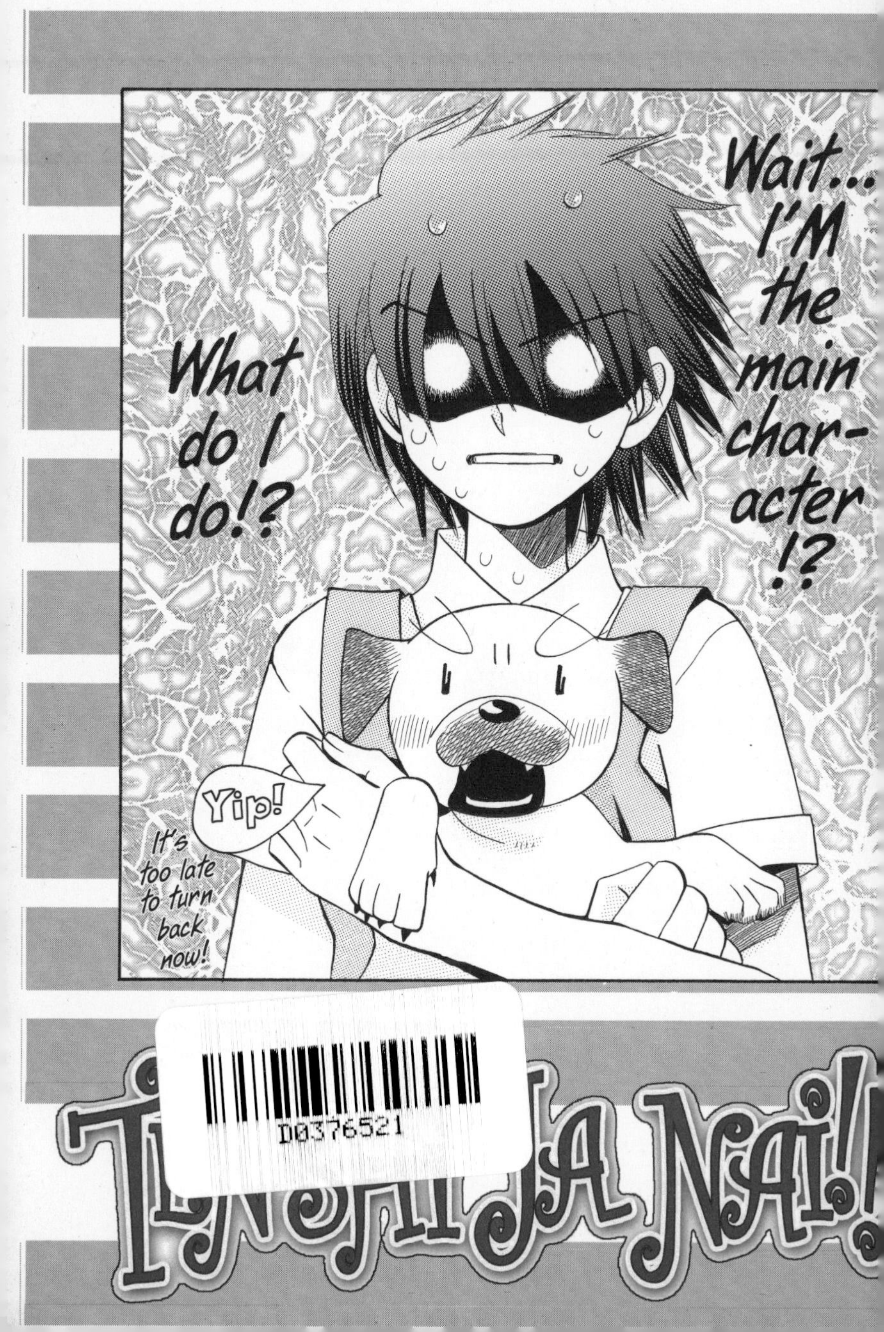
Wait... I'M the main character!?
What do I do!?
Yip!
It's too late to turn back now!

T[illegible]NSHI JA NAI!

Translation –Akira Tsubasa
Lettering – Jake Forbes
Touch-Up – Team Pokopen
Cover Design – Mediaslam

Editor – Jake Forbes

A Go! Comi manga

Published by Go! Media Entertainment, LLC

This edition is struck from the original Japanese film for the best possible reproduction. Absolutely no artwork has been censored.

This book is a work of fiction. Names, places and incidents are either a product of the author's imagination or are used fictitiously.

Visit us online at www.gocomi.com
e-mail: info@gocomi.com

ISBN 0-9768957-1-4

First printed in October 2005

1 2 3 4 5 6 7 8 9

Manufactured in the United States of America

TENSHI JA NAI!!
I'm No Angel!

Volume 1

Story and Art by
Takako Shigematsu

go!comi

Concerning Honorifics

At Go! Comi, we do our best to ensure that our translations read seamlessly in English while respecting the original Japanese language and culture. To this end, the original honorifics (the suffixes found at the end of characters' names) remain intact. In Japan, where politeness and formality are more integrated into every aspect of the language, honorifics give a better understanding of character relationships. They can be used to indicate both respect and affection. Whether a person addresses someone by first name or last name also indicates how close their relationship is.

Here are some of the honorifics you might encounter in this book:

-san: This is the most common and neutral of honorifics. The polite way to address someone you're not on close terms with is to use "-san." It's kind of like Mr. or Ms., except you can use "-san" with first or last names as easily as family names.

-chan: Used for friendly familiarity, mostly applied towards young women and girls.

-kun: Like "-chan," it's an informal suffix for friends and classmates, only "-kun" is usually associated with boys. It can also be used in a professional environment by someone addressing a subordinate.

-sama: Indicates a great deal of respect or admiration.

Sempai: In school, "sempai" is used to refer to an upperclassman or club leader. It can also be used in the workplace by a new employee to address a mentor or staff member with seniority.

Sensei: Teachers, doctors, writers or any master of a trade are referred to as "sensei." When addressing a manga creator, the polite thing to do is attach "-sensei" to the manga-ka's name (as in Shigematsu-sensei).

[blank]: Not using an honorific when addressing someone indicates that the speaker has permission to speak intimately with the other person. This relationship is usually reserved for close friends and family.

TENSHI JA NAI!!

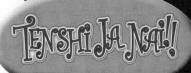

CONTENTS

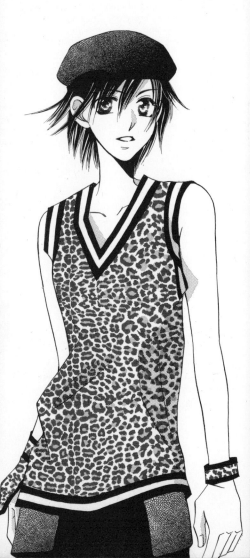

VOL. 1

TENSHI JA NAI!!

I'm No Angel!

WHEN I WAS SEVEN...
...I MODELED FOR A SERIES OF ADS AS A FAVOR TO MY MOM'S PHOTOGRAPHER FRIEND.
"HIKARU-CHAN, DON'T YOU LOO CUTE!"
"TURN AROUND."
"HIKARU-CHAN, YOU LOOK JUST LIKE AN ANGEL!"
RIIIP
DIE!
"YOU THINK YOU'RE BETTER THAN US JUST BECAUSE YOU WERE A MODEL? YOU'RE NOTHING SPECIAL!"
DIE
STUPID
THERE'S NO SUCH THING AS ANGELS.

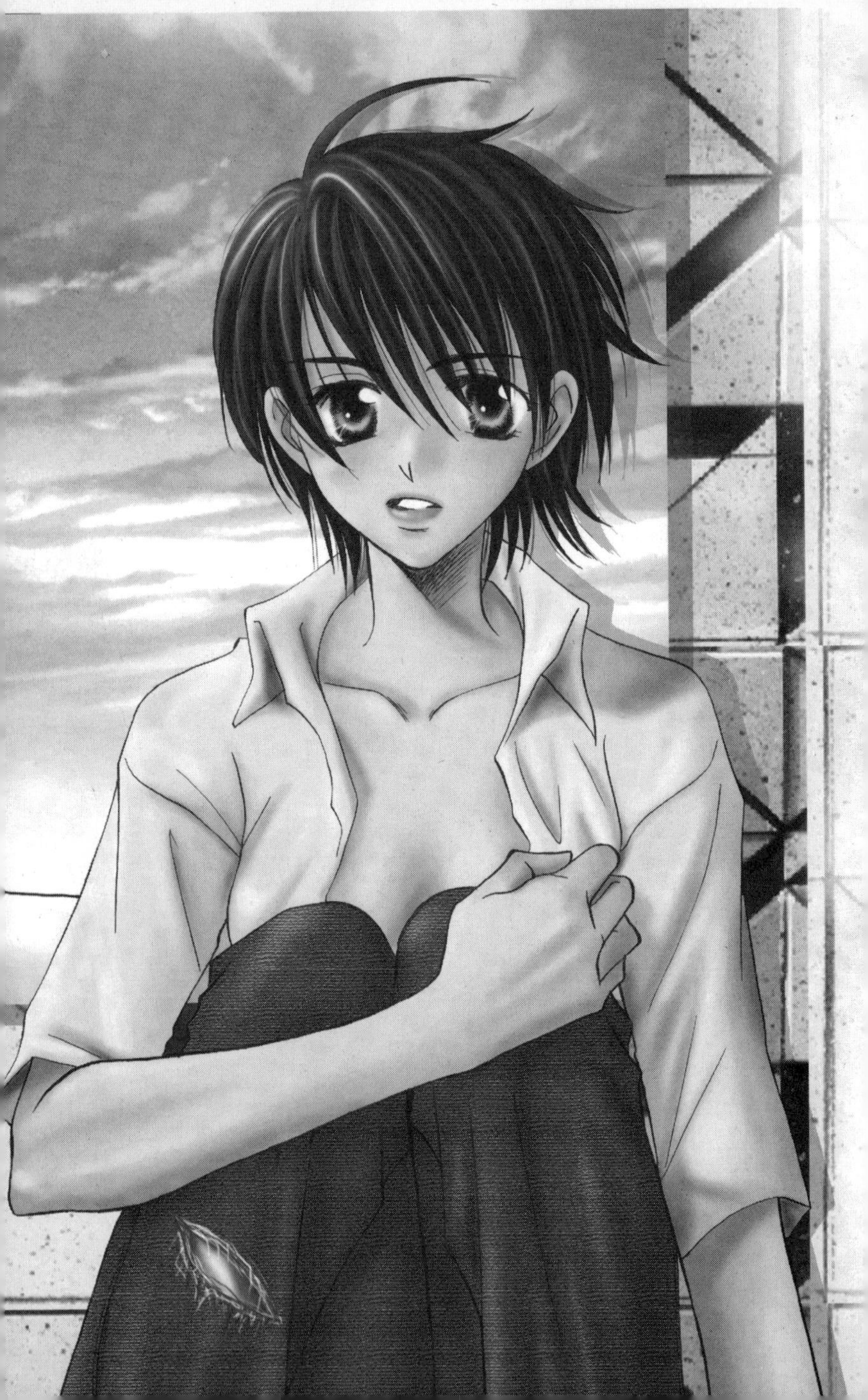

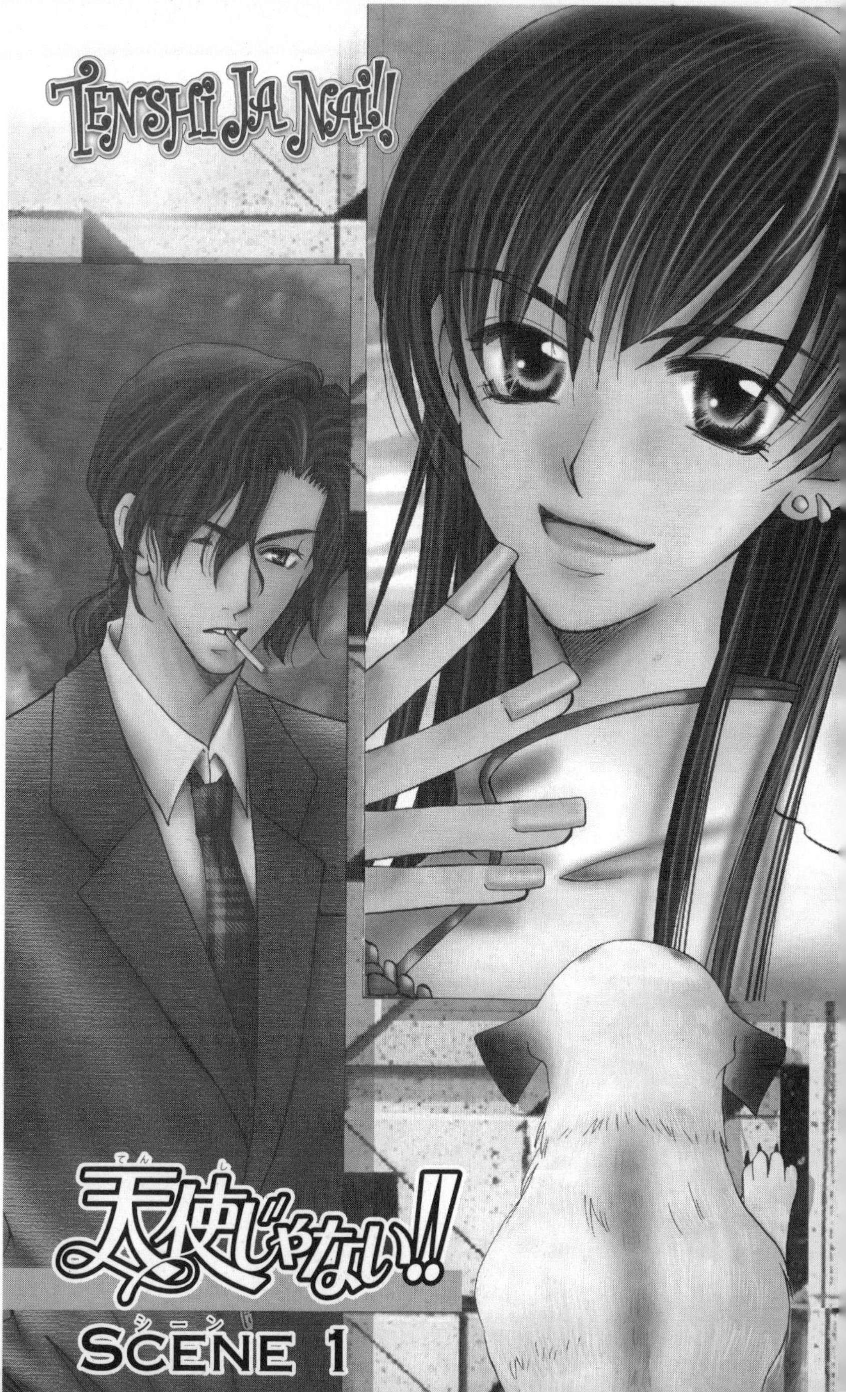
TENSHI JA NAI!!
天使じゃない!!
SCENE 1

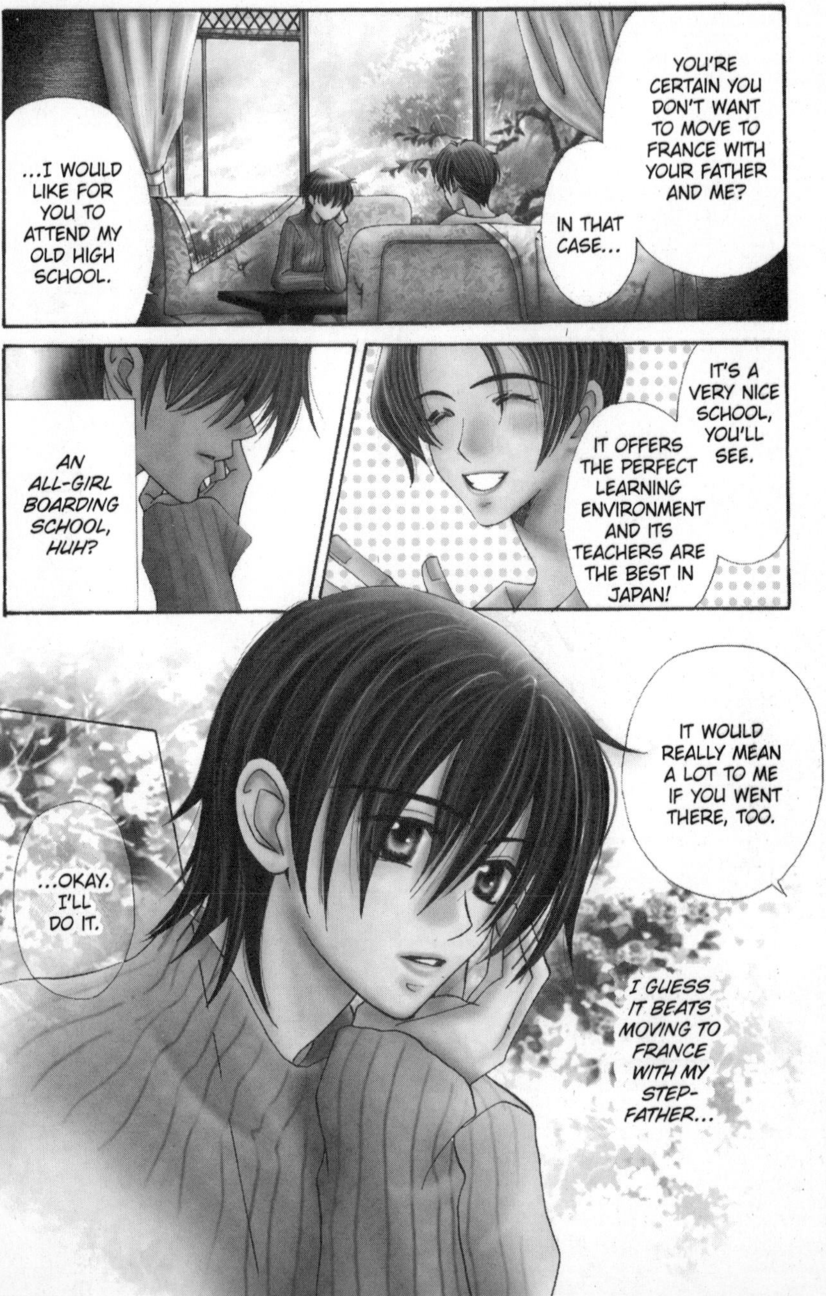
YOU'RE CERTAIN YOU DON'T WANT TO MOVE TO FRANCE WITH YOUR FATHER AND ME?
IN THAT CASE...
...I WOULD LIKE FOR YOU TO ATTEND MY OLD HIGH SCHOOL.
IT'S A VERY NICE SCHOOL, YOU'LL SEE.
IT OFFERS THE PERFECT LEARNING ENVIRONMENT AND ITS TEACHERS ARE THE BEST IN JAPAN!
AN ALL-GIRL BOARDING SCHOOL, HUH?
IT WOULD REALLY MEAN A LOT TO ME IF YOU WENT THERE, TOO.
...OKAY. I'LL DO IT.
I GUESS IT BEATS MOVING TO FRANCE WITH MY STEP-FATHER...

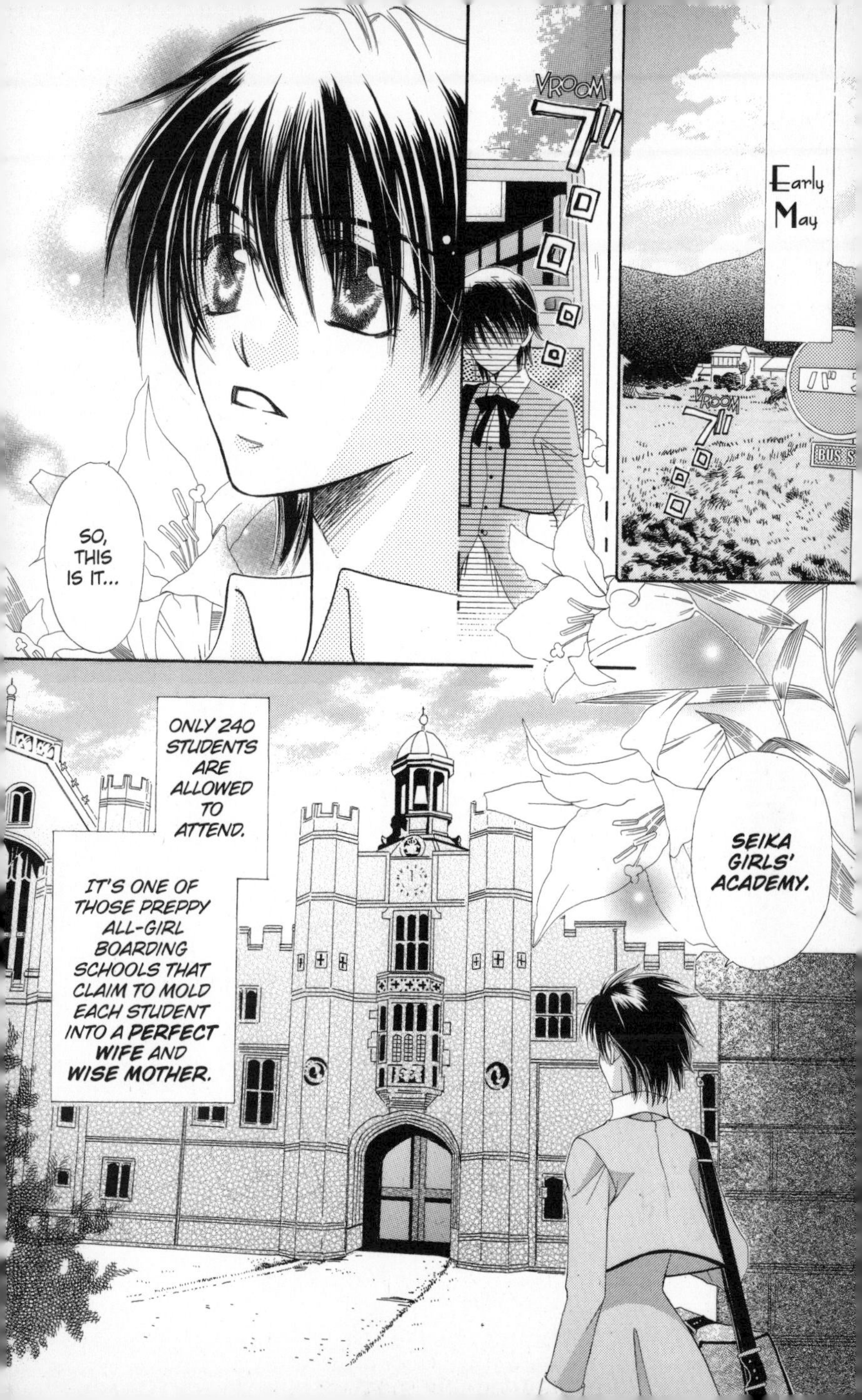
Early May
VROOM
VROOM
SO, THIS IS IT...
SEIKA GIRLS' ACADEMY.
ONLY 240 STUDENTS ARE ALLOWED TO ATTEND.
IT'S ONE OF THOSE PREPPY ALL-GIRL BOARDING SCHOOLS THAT CLAIM TO MOLD EACH STUDENT INTO A **PERFECT WIFE** AND **WISE MOTHER**.

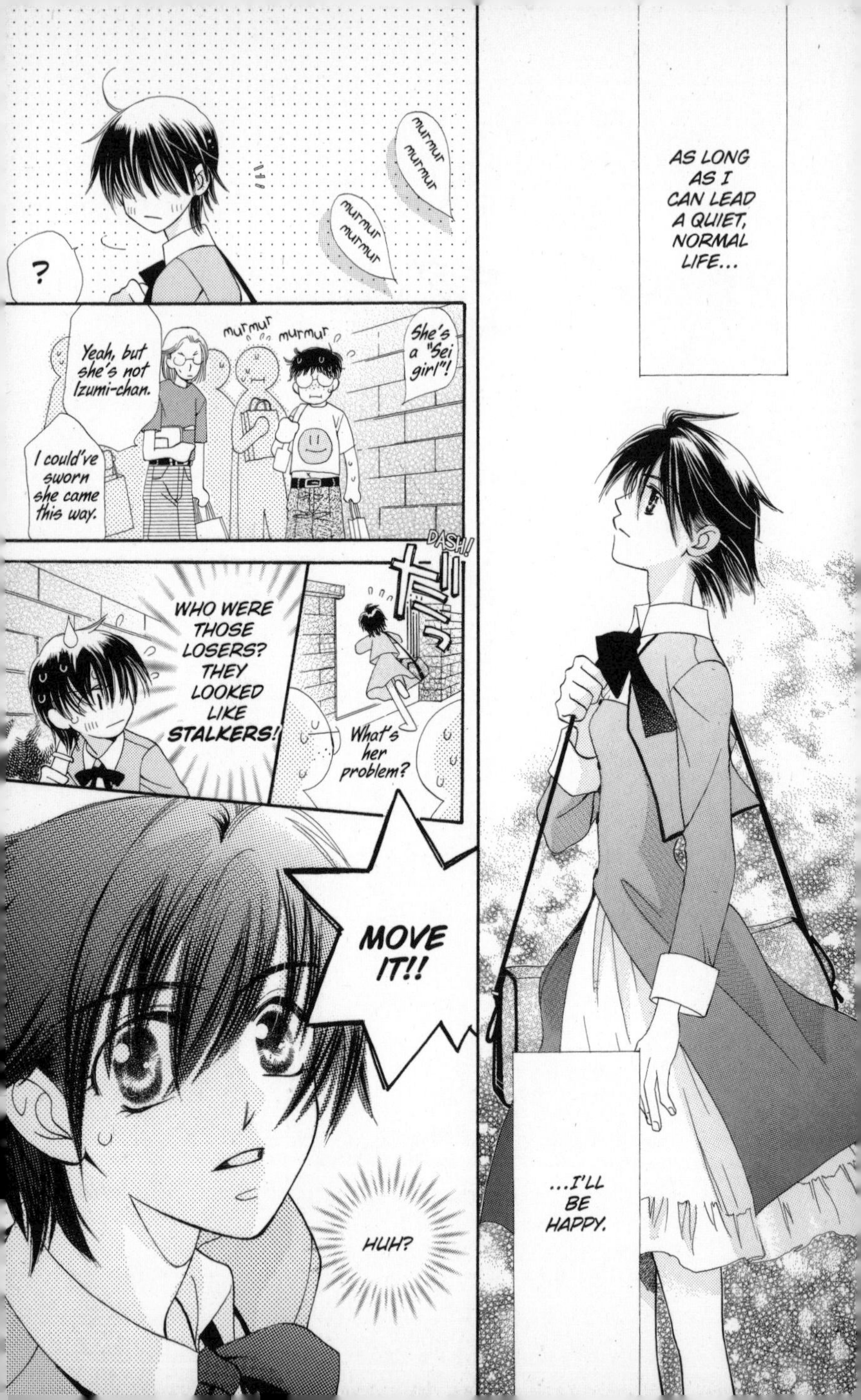
AS LONG AS I CAN LEAD A QUIET, NORMAL LIFE...
...I'LL BE HAPPY.
murmur murmur
murmur murmur
?
She's a "Sei girl"!
murmur murmur
Yeah, but she's not Izumi-chan.
I could've sworn she came this way.
DASH!
What's her problem?
WHO WERE THOSE LOSERS? THEY LOOKED LIKE STALKERS!
MOVE IT!!
HUH?

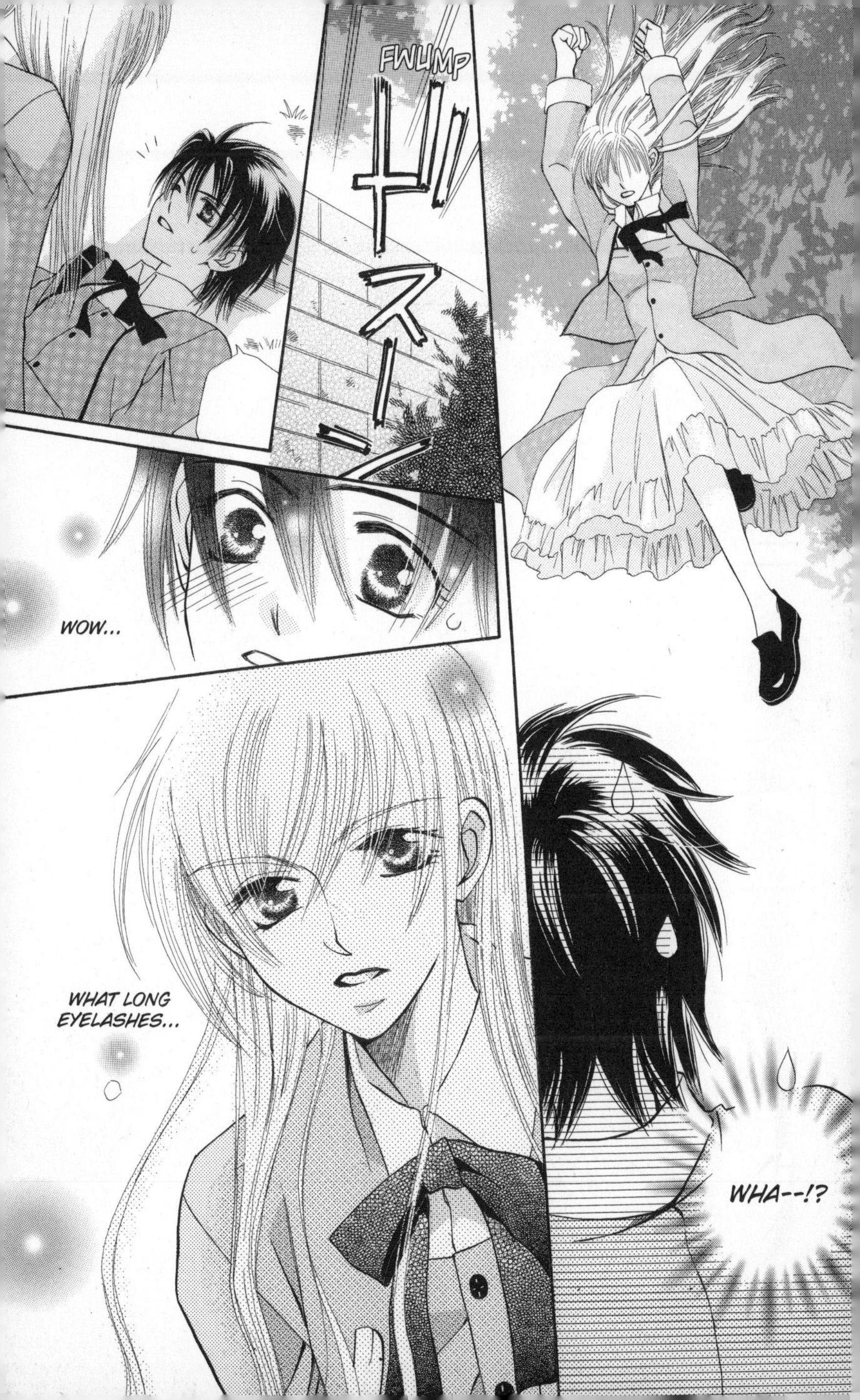
FWUMP
WOW...
WHA--!?
WHAT LONG EYELASHES...

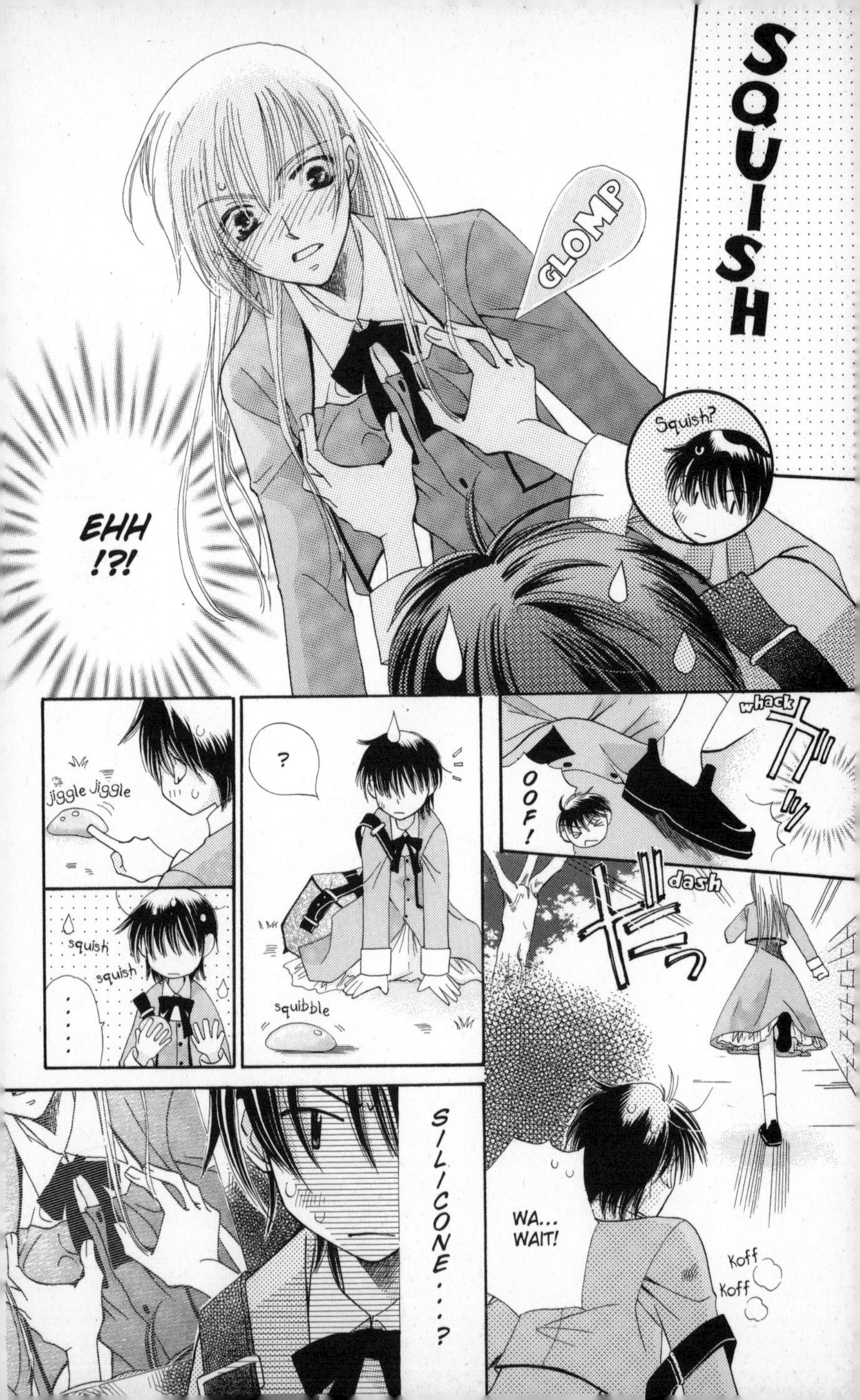
SQUISH
GLOMP
Squish?
EHH !?!
whack
OOF!
?
squibble
jiggle jiggle
squish
squish
.....
dash
WA... WAIT!
Koff
Koff
SILICONE...?

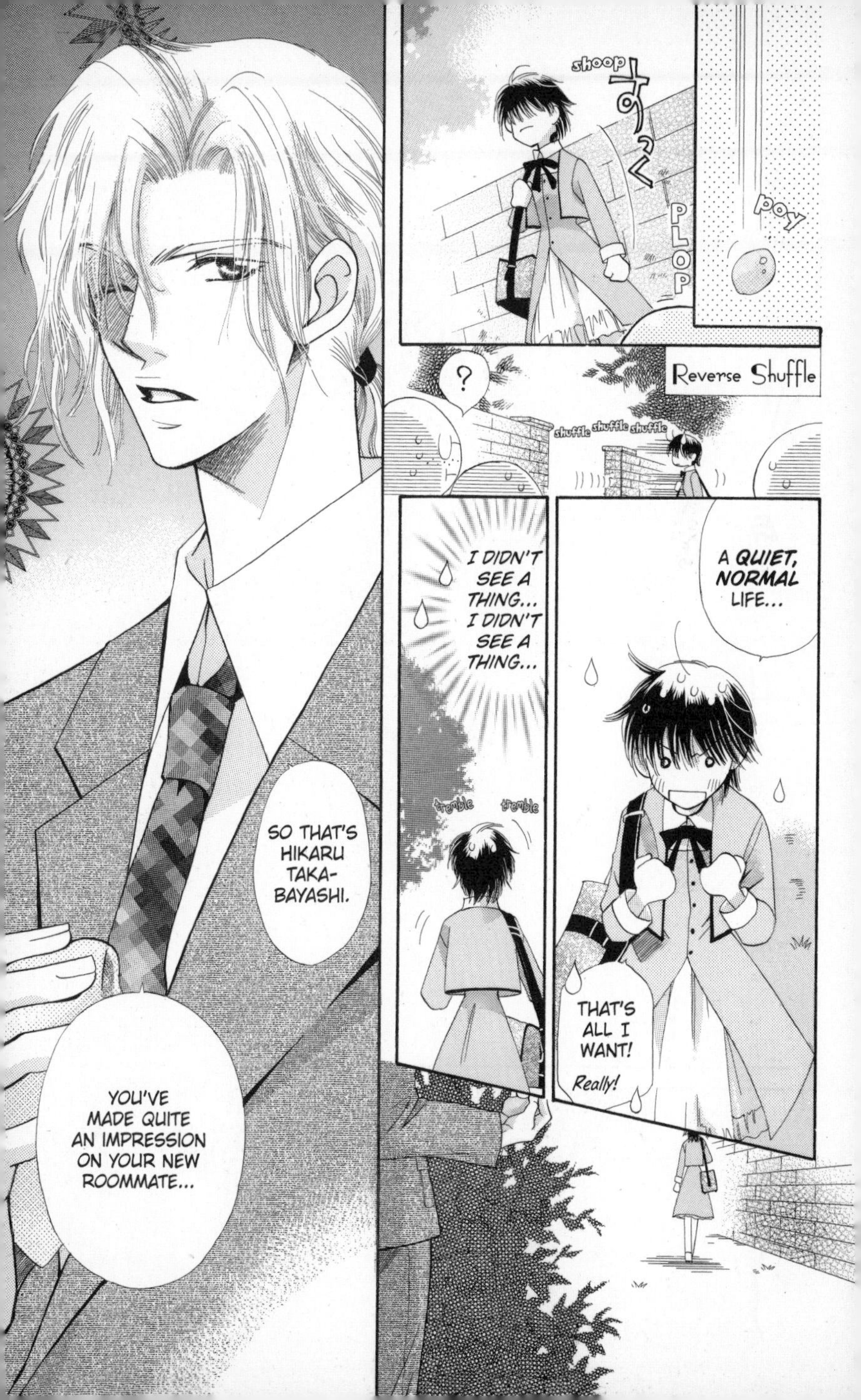

poy
shoop すっく
PLOP PLOP
Reverse Shuffle
?
shuffle shuffle shuffle
A QUIET, NORMAL LIFE...
THAT'S ALL I WANT!
Really!
I DIDN'T SEE A THING... I DIDN'T SEE A THING...
tremble tremble
SO THAT'S HIKARU TAKA-BAYASHI.
YOU'VE MADE QUITE AN IMPRESSION ON YOUR NEW ROOMMATE...

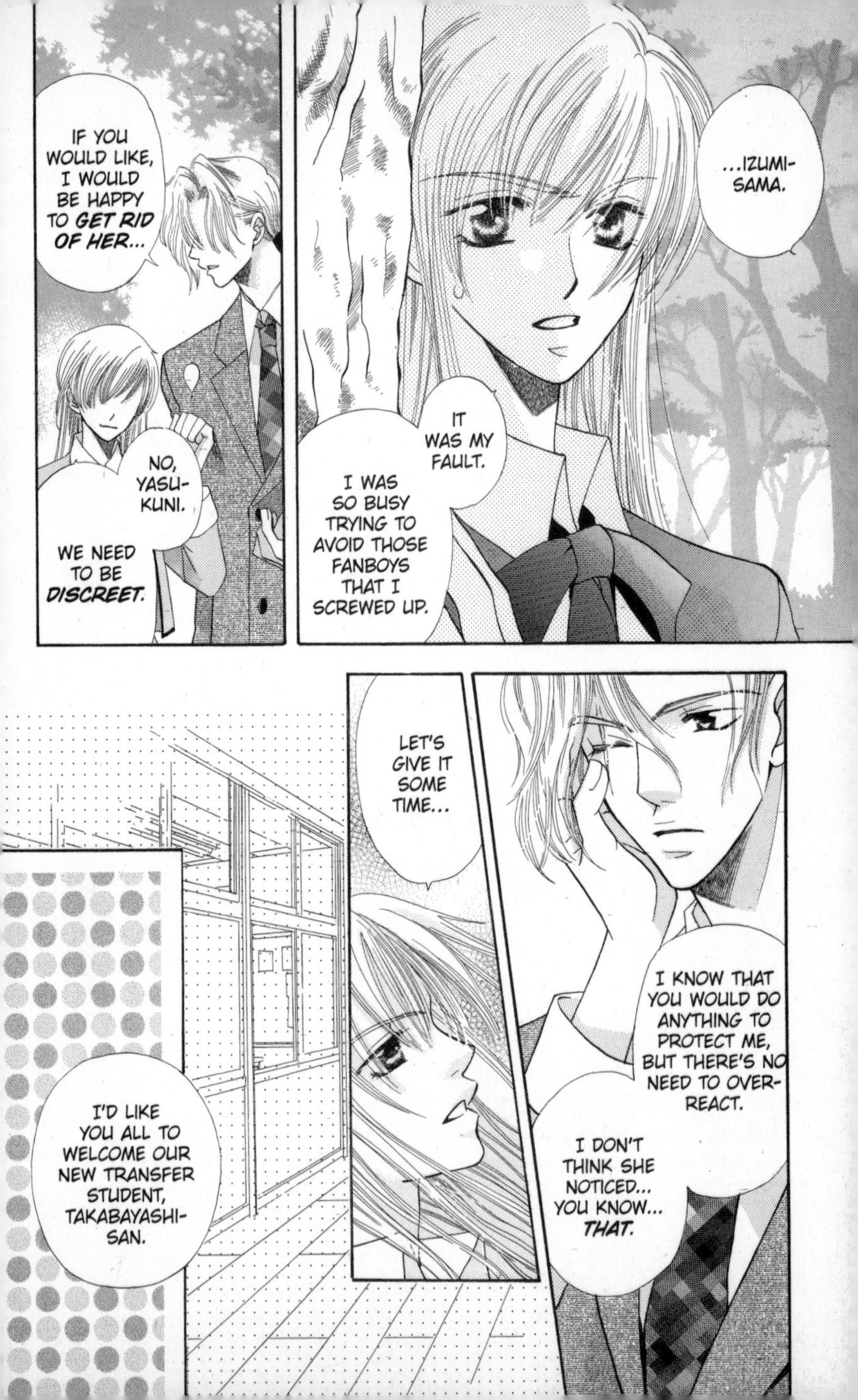

...IZUMI-SAMA.
IT WAS MY FAULT.
I WAS SO BUSY TRYING TO AVOID THOSE FANBOYS THAT I SCREWED UP.
IF YOU WOULD LIKE, I WOULD BE HAPPY TO **GET RID OF HER...**
NO, YASU-KUNI.
WE NEED TO BE ***DISCREET.***
I KNOW THAT YOU WOULD DO ANYTHING TO PROTECT ME, BUT THERE'S NO NEED TO OVER-REACT.
I DON'T THINK SHE NOTICED... YOU KNOW... ***THAT.***
LET'S GIVE IT SOME TIME...
I'D LIKE YOU ALL TO WELCOME OUR NEW TRANSFER STUDENT, TAKABAYASHI-SAN.

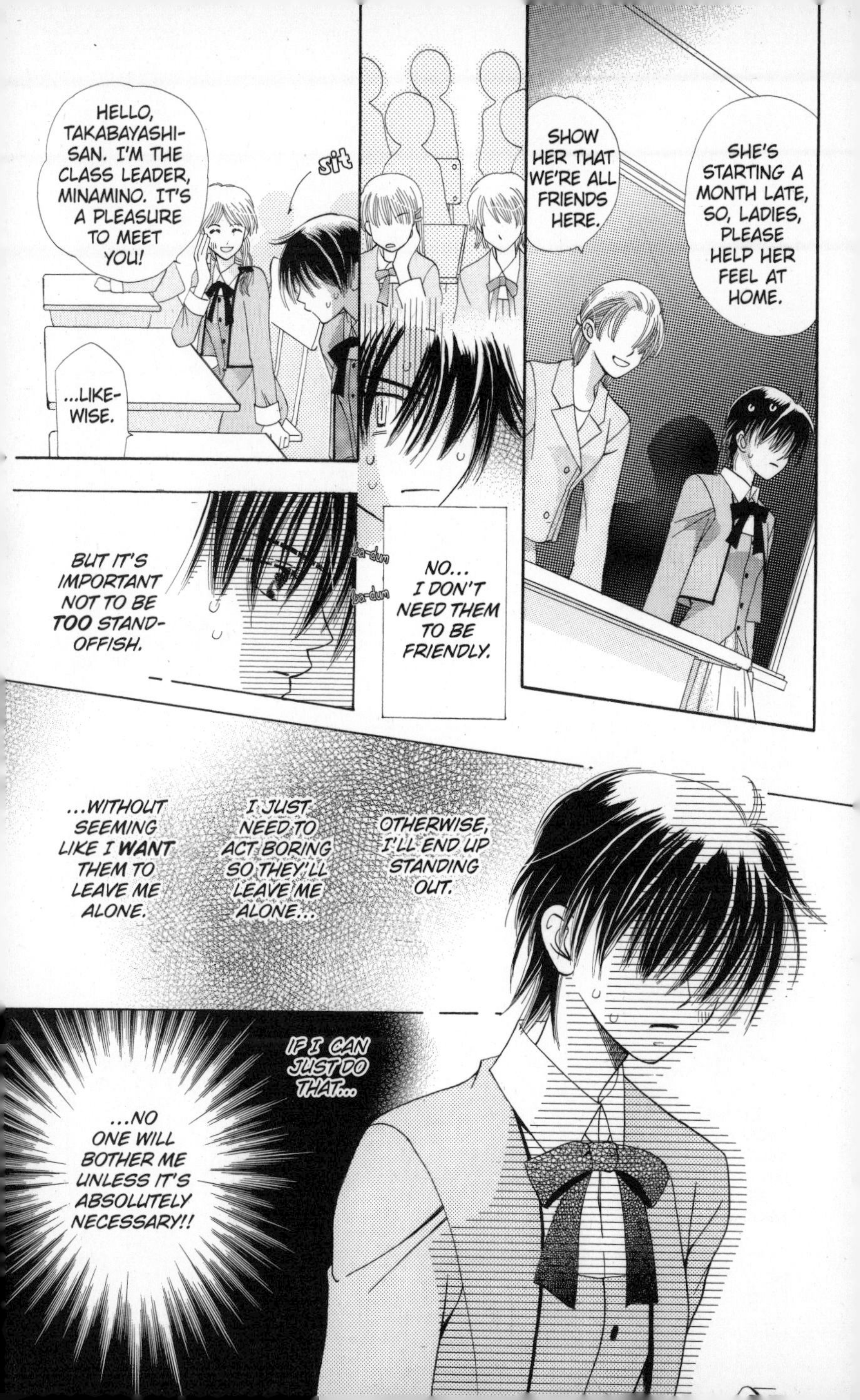
SHE'S STARTING A MONTH LATE, SO, LADIES, PLEASE HELP HER FEEL AT HOME.
SHOW HER THAT WE'RE ALL FRIENDS HERE.
NO... I DON'T NEED THEM TO BE FRIENDLY.
HELLO, TAKABAYASHI-SAN. I'M THE CLASS LEADER, MINAMINO. IT'S A PLEASURE TO MEET YOU!
sit
...LIKE-WISE.
ba-dum
ba-dum
BUT IT'S IMPORTANT NOT TO BE TOO STAND-OFFISH.
OTHERWISE, I'LL END UP STANDING OUT.
I JUST NEED TO ACT BORING SO THEY'LL LEAVE ME ALONE...
...WITHOUT SEEMING LIKE I WANT THEM TO LEAVE ME ALONE.
IF I CAN JUST DO THAT...
...NO ONE WILL BOTHER ME UNLESS IT'S ABSOLUTELY NECESSARY!!

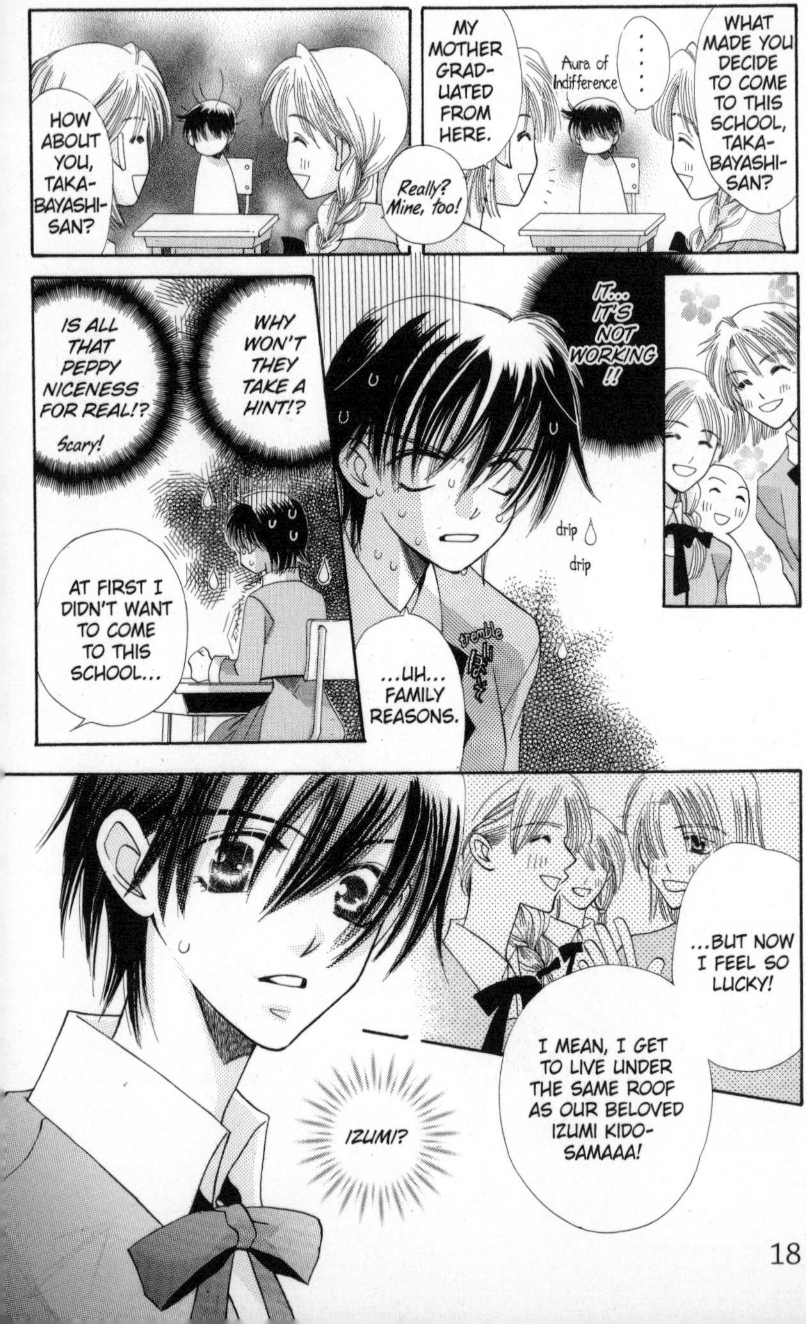
WHAT MADE YOU DECIDE TO COME TO THIS SCHOOL, TAKA-BAYASHI-SAN?
......
Aura of Indifference
MY MOTHER GRAD-UATED FROM HERE.
Really? Mine, too!
HOW ABOUT YOU, TAKA-BAYASHI-SAN?
IT... IT'S NOT WORKING!!
drip
drip
tremble
...UH... FAMILY REASONS.
WHY WON'T THEY TAKE A HINT!?
IS ALL THAT PEPPY NICENESS FOR REAL!?
Scary!
AT FIRST I DIDN'T WANT TO COME TO THIS SCHOOL...
...BUT NOW I FEEL SO LUCKY!
I MEAN, I GET TO LIVE UNDER THE SAME ROOF AS OUR BELOVED IZUMI KIDO-SAMAAA!
IZUMI?

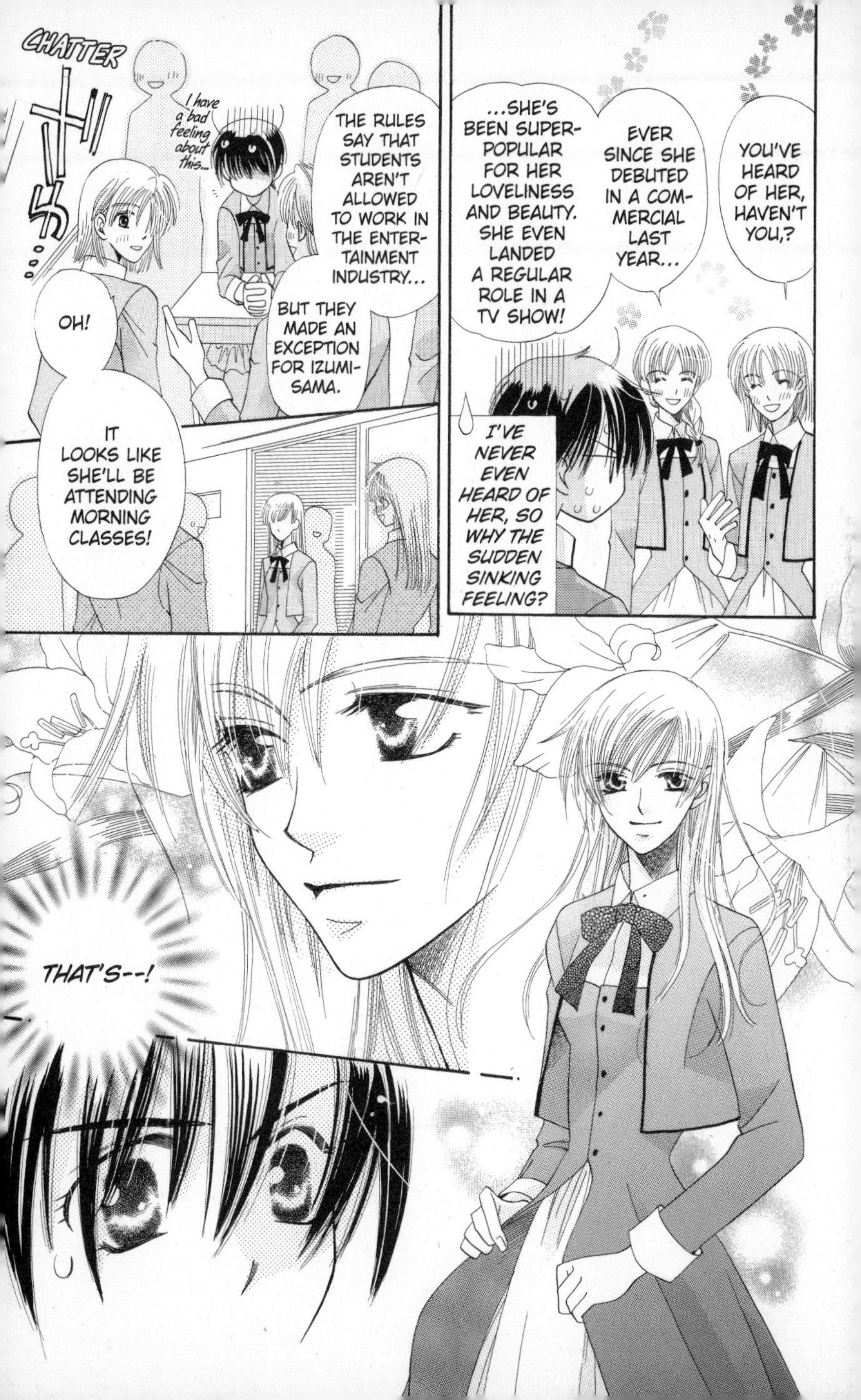
YOU'VE HEARD OF HER, HAVEN'T YOU,?
EVER SINCE SHE DEBUTED IN A COMMERCIAL LAST YEAR...
...SHE'S BEEN SUPER-POPULAR FOR HER LOVELINESS AND BEAUTY. SHE EVEN LANDED A REGULAR ROLE IN A TV SHOW!
I'VE NEVER EVEN HEARD OF HER, SO WHY THE SUDDEN SINKING FEELING?
I have a bad feeling about this...
THE RULES SAY THAT STUDENTS AREN'T ALLOWED TO WORK IN THE ENTERTAINMENT INDUSTRY...
BUT THEY MADE AN EXCEPTION FOR IZUMI-SAMA.
CHATTER
OH!
IT LOOKS LIKE SHE'LL BE ATTENDING MORNING CLASSES!
THAT'S--!

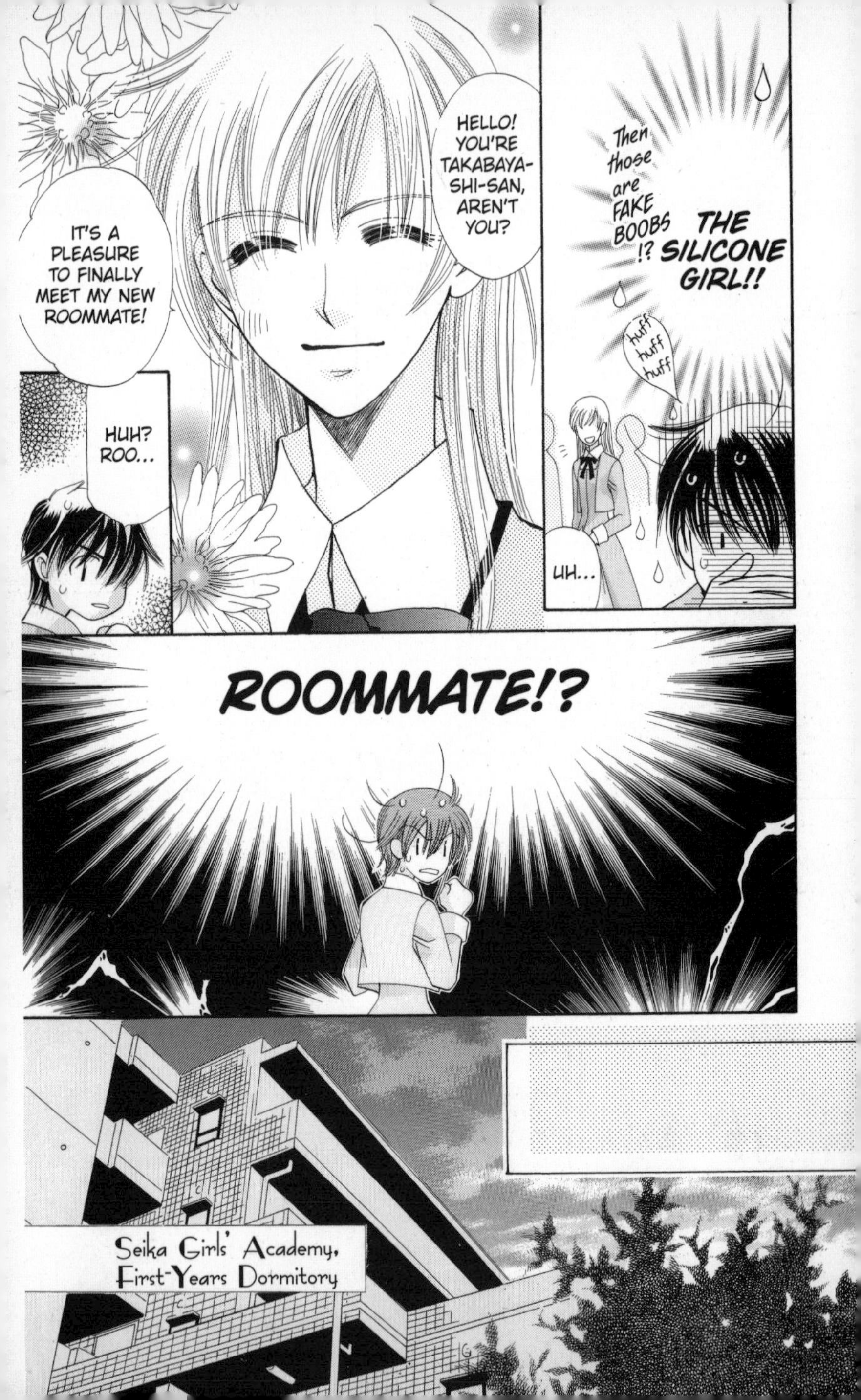

Then those are FAKE BOOBS!?
THE SILICONE GIRL!!
huff huff huff
UH...
HELLO! YOU'RE TAKABAYA-SHI-SAN, AREN'T YOU?
IT'S A PLEASURE TO FINALLY MEET MY NEW ROOMMATE!
HUH? ROO...
ROOMMATE!?
Seika Girls' Academy, First-Years Dormitory

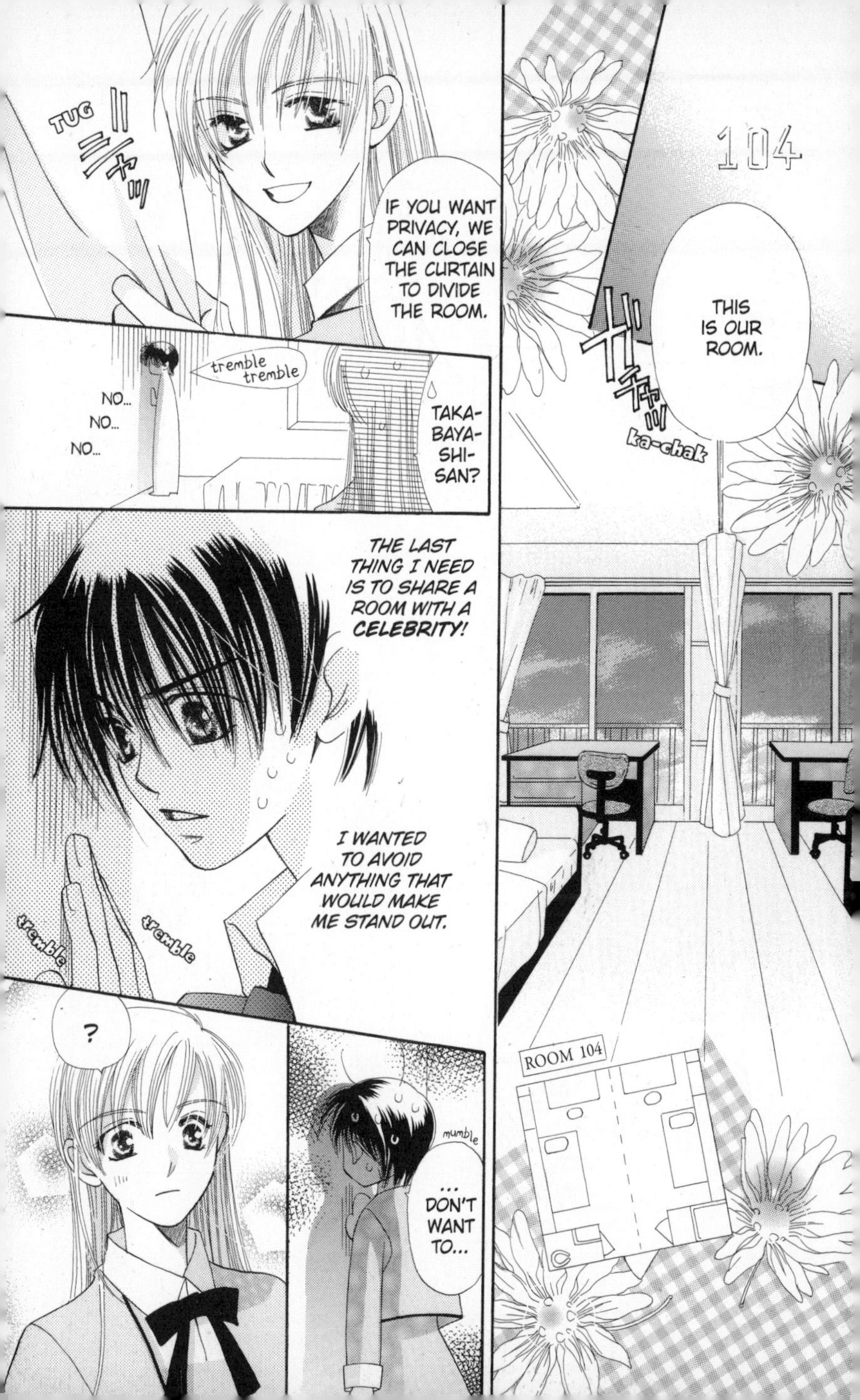

104
ka-chak
THIS IS OUR ROOM.
ROOM 104
TUG
IF YOU WANT PRIVACY, WE CAN CLOSE THE CURTAIN TO DIVIDE THE ROOM.
TAKA-BAYA-SHI-SAN?
tremble tremble
NO... NO... NO...
THE LAST THING I NEED IS TO SHARE A ROOM WITH A CELEBRITY!
I WANTED TO AVOID ANYTHING THAT WOULD MAKE ME STAND OUT.
tremble
tremble
mumble
... DON'T WANT TO...
?

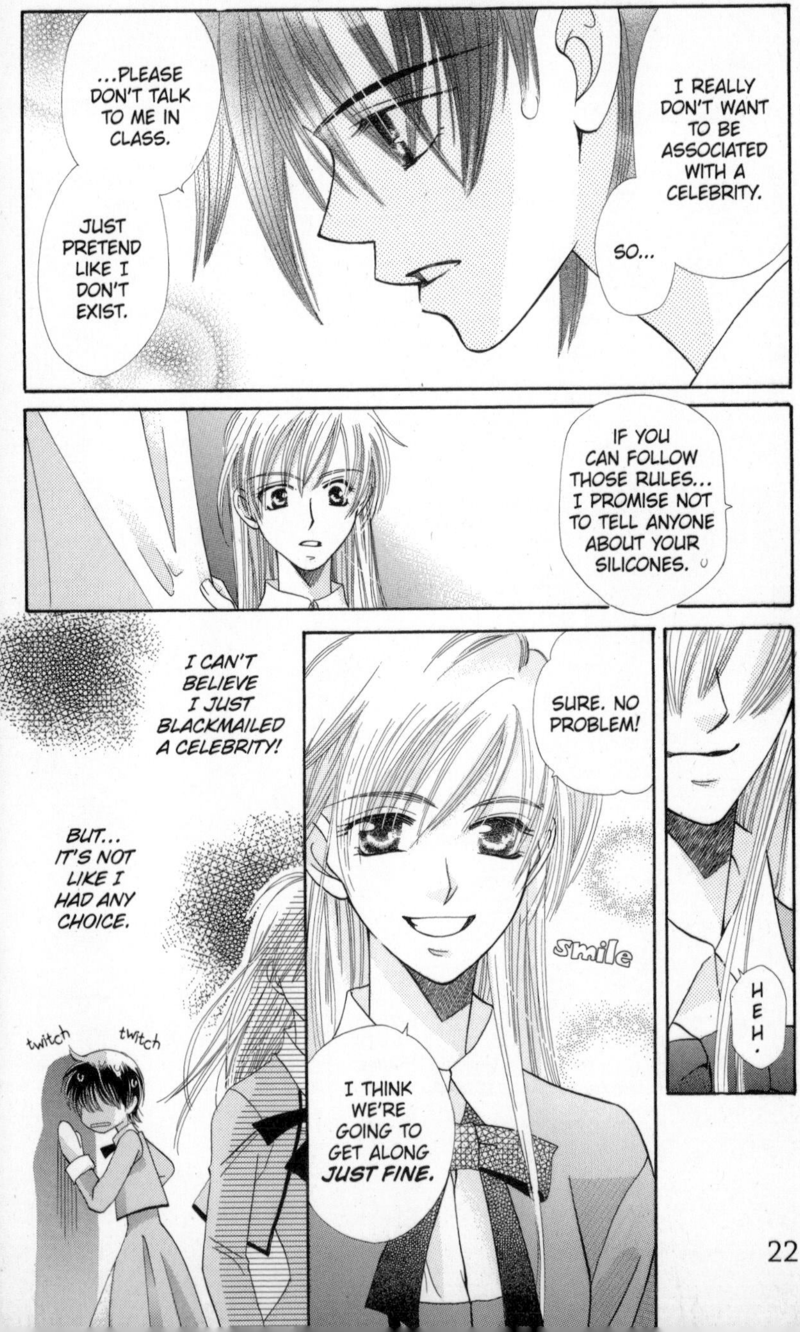
I REALLY DON'T WANT TO BE ASSOCIATED WITH A CELEBRITY.
SO...
...PLEASE DON'T TALK TO ME IN CLASS.
JUST PRETEND LIKE I DON'T EXIST.
IF YOU CAN FOLLOW THOSE RULES... I PROMISE NOT TO TELL ANYONE ABOUT YOUR SILICONES.
HEH.
SURE. NO PROBLEM!
smile
I THINK WE'RE GOING TO GET ALONG *JUST FINE.*
I CAN'T BELIEVE I JUST BLACKMAILED A CELEBRITY!
BUT... IT'S NOT LIKE I HAD ANY CHOICE.
twitch twitch

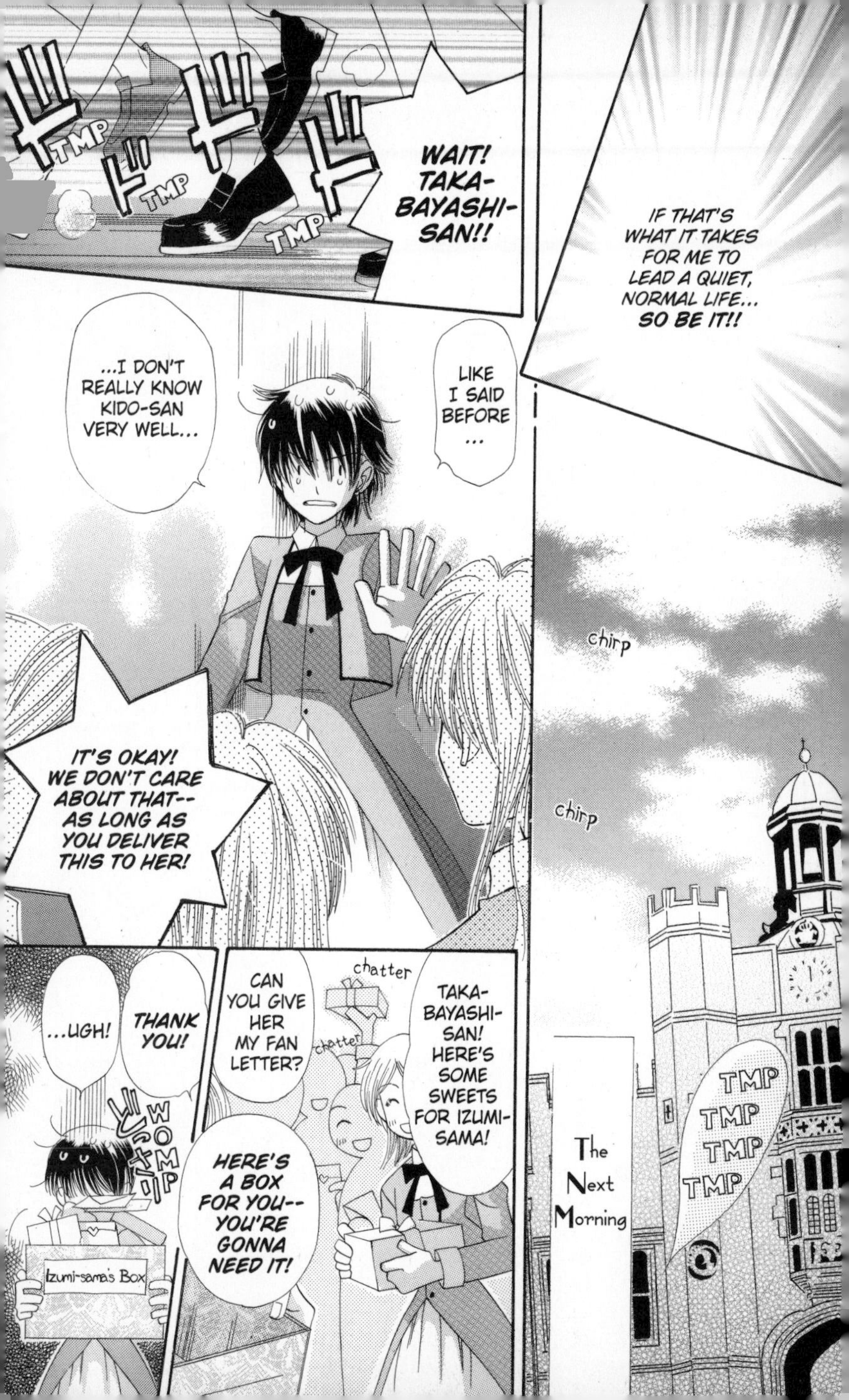
IF THAT'S WHAT IT TAKES FOR ME TO LEAD A QUIET, NORMAL LIFE... SO BE IT!!
chirp
chirp
The Next Morning
TMP TMP TMP TMP
TMP
TMP
TMP
WAIT! TAKA-BAYASHI-SAN!!
LIKE I SAID BEFORE ...
...I DON'T REALLY KNOW KIDO-SAN VERY WELL...
IT'S OKAY! WE DON'T CARE ABOUT THAT-- AS LONG AS YOU DELIVER THIS TO HER!
TAKA-BAYASHI-SAN! HERE'S SOME SWEETS FOR IZUMI-SAMA!
chatter
chatter
CAN YOU GIVE HER MY FAN LETTER?
HERE'S A BOX FOR YOU-- YOU'RE GONNA NEED IT!
THANK YOU!
...UGH!
WOMP
Izumi-sama's Box

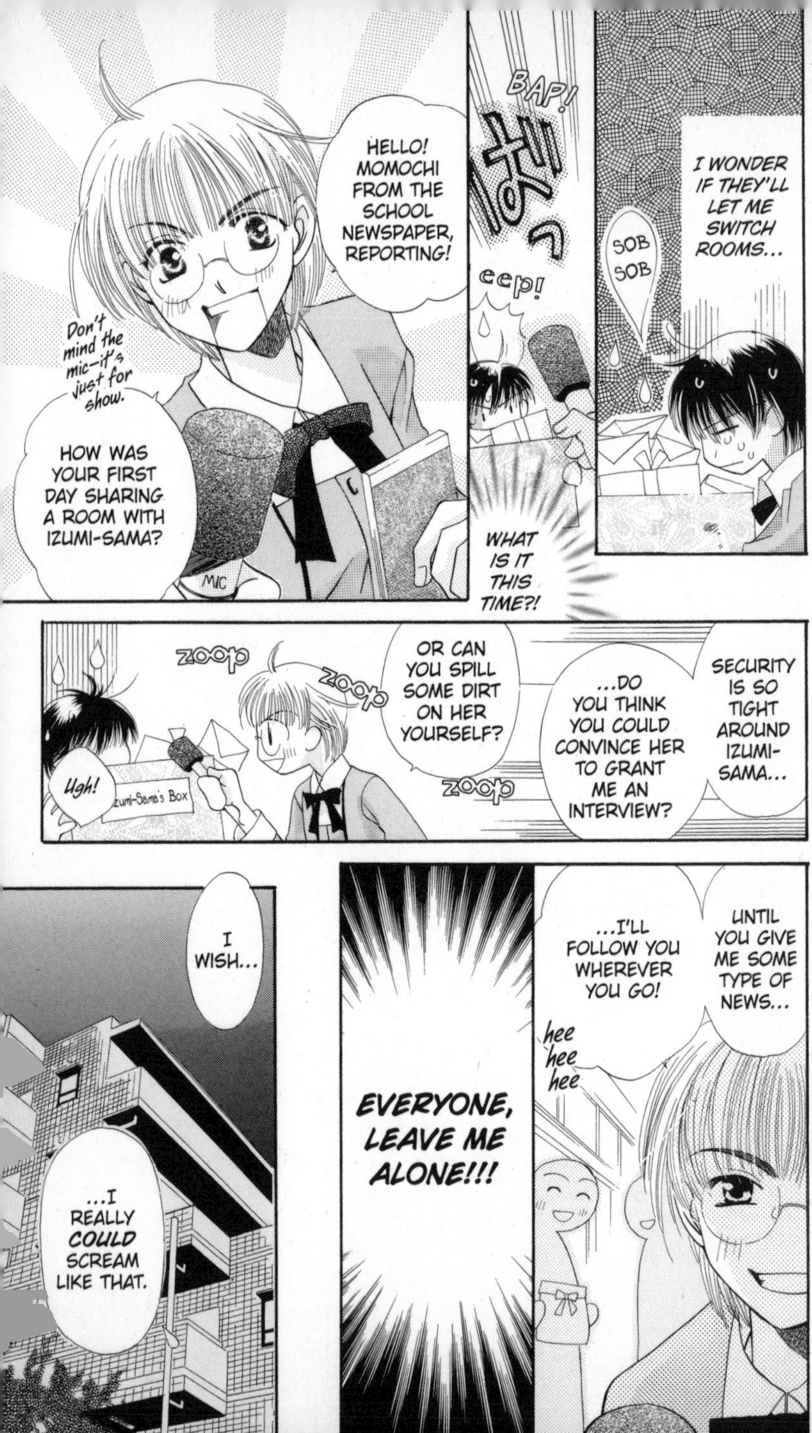

I WONDER IF THEY'LL LET ME SWITCH ROOMS...
SOB SOB
BAP!
ぱっ
eep!
WHAT IS IT THIS TIME?!
HELLO! MOMOCHI FROM THE SCHOOL NEWSPAPER, REPORTING!
Don't mind the mic—it's just for show.
HOW WAS YOUR FIRST DAY SHARING A ROOM WITH IZUMI-SAMA?
MIC
SECURITY IS SO TIGHT AROUND IZUMI-SAMA...
...DO YOU THINK YOU COULD CONVINCE HER TO GRANT ME AN INTERVIEW?
OR CAN YOU SPILL SOME DIRT ON HER YOURSELF?
zoop
zoop
zoop
Ugh!
Izumi-Sama's Box
UNTIL YOU GIVE ME SOME TYPE OF NEWS...
...I'LL FOLLOW YOU WHEREVER YOU GO!
hee hee hee
EVERYONE, LEAVE ME ALONE!!!
I WISH...
...I REALLY COULD SCREAM LIKE THAT.

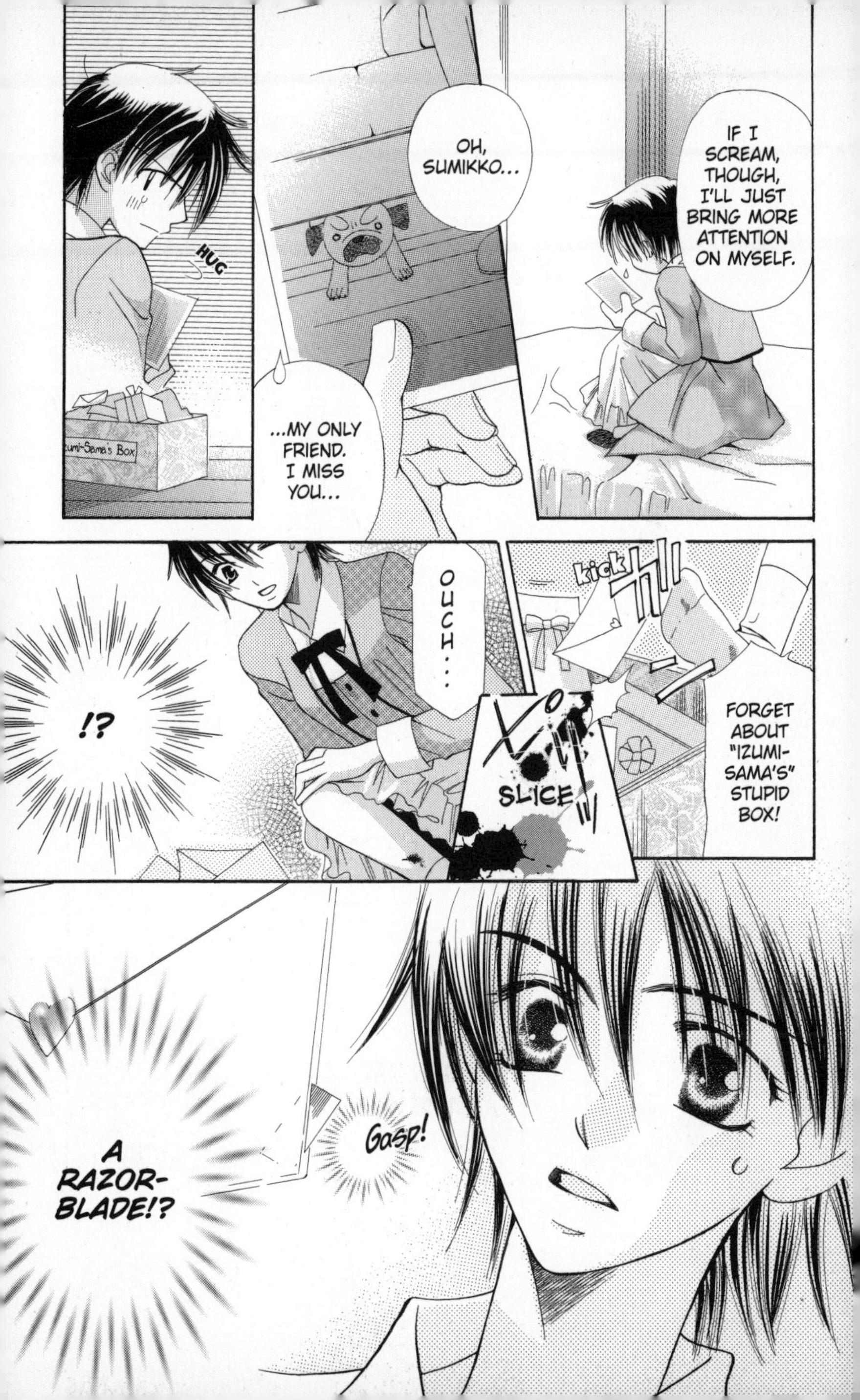
IF I SCREAM, THOUGH, I'LL JUST BRING MORE ATTENTION ON MYSELF.
OH, SUMIKKO...
...MY ONLY FRIEND. I MISS YOU...
HUG
zumi-Sama's Box
kick
FORGET ABOUT "IZUMI-SAMA'S" STUPID BOX!
SLICE
OUCH...
!?
Gasp!
A RAZOR-BLADE!?

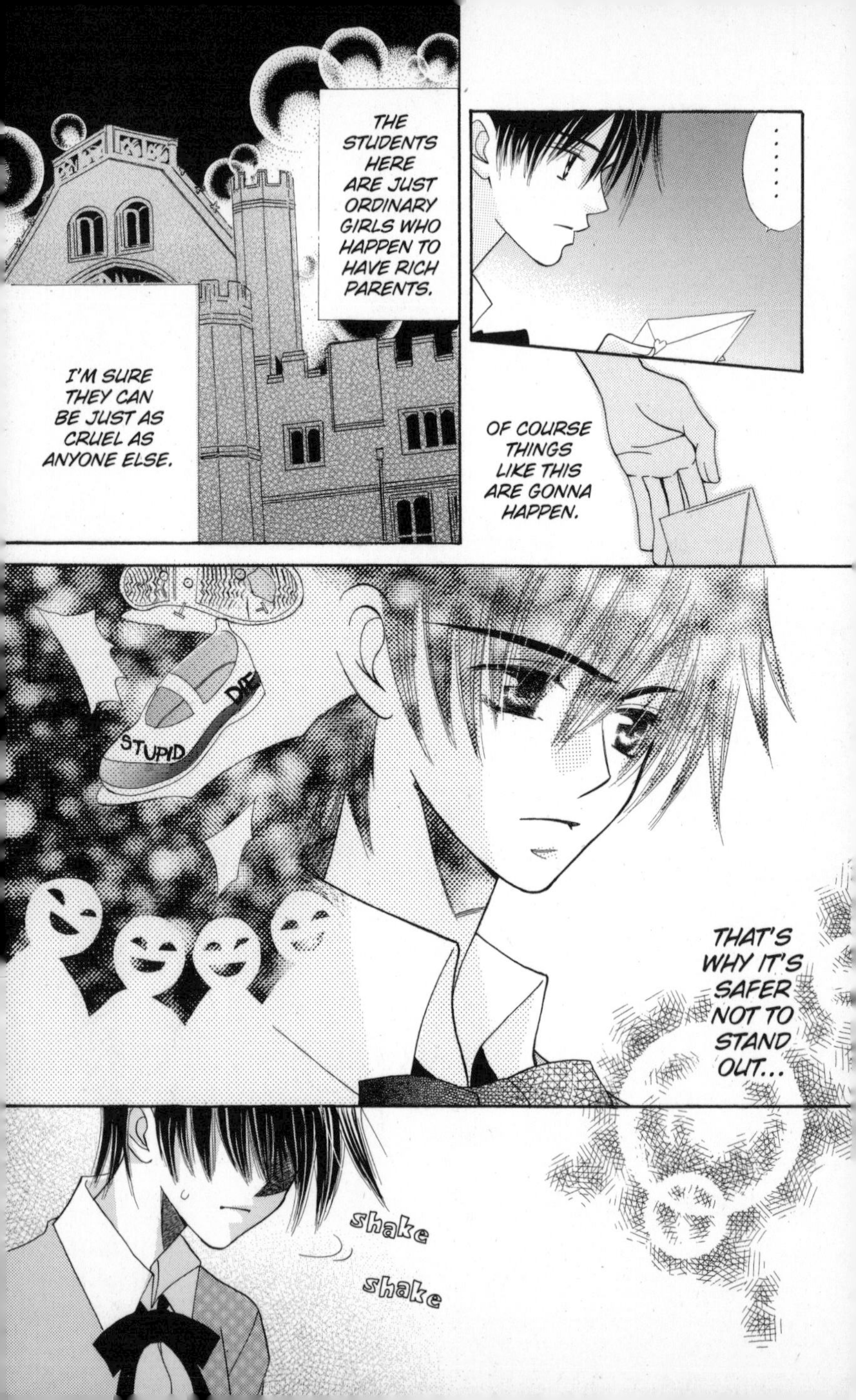
......
OF COURSE THINGS LIKE THIS ARE GONNA HAPPEN.
THE STUDENTS HERE ARE JUST ORDINARY GIRLS WHO HAPPEN TO HAVE RICH PARENTS.
I'M SURE THEY CAN BE JUST AS CRUEL AS ANYONE ELSE.
DIE
STUPID
THAT'S WHY IT'S SAFER NOT TO STAND OUT...
shake
shake

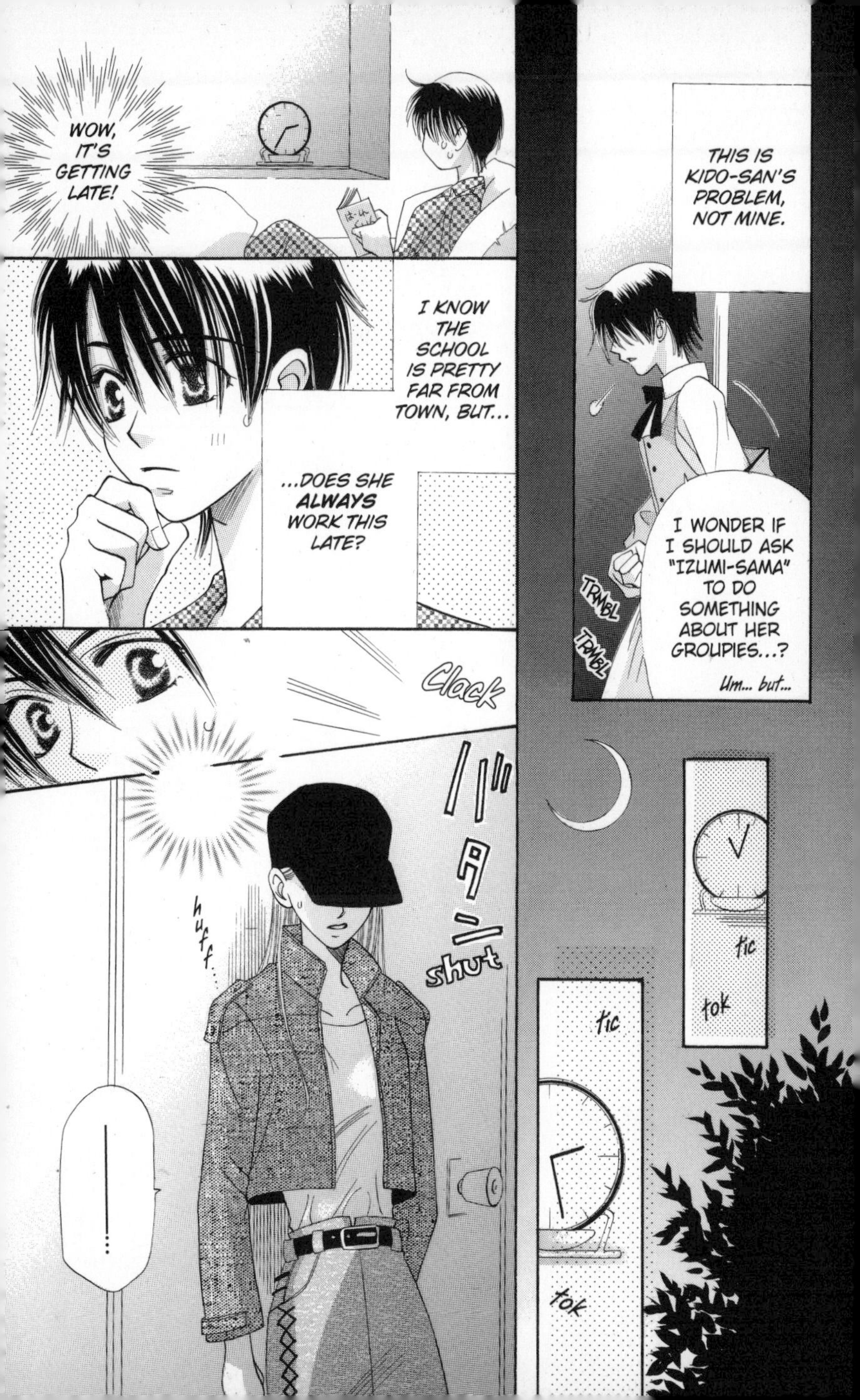
THIS IS KIDO-SAN'S PROBLEM, NOT MINE.
TRMBL TRMBL
I WONDER IF I SHOULD ASK "IZUMI-SAMA" TO DO SOMETHING ABOUT HER GROUPIES...?
Um... but...
tic
tok
tic
tok
WOW, IT'S GETTING LATE!
I KNOW THE SCHOOL IS PRETTY FAR FROM TOWN, BUT...
...DOES SHE **ALWAYS** WORK THIS LATE?
Clack
バタン
shut
huff...
—......

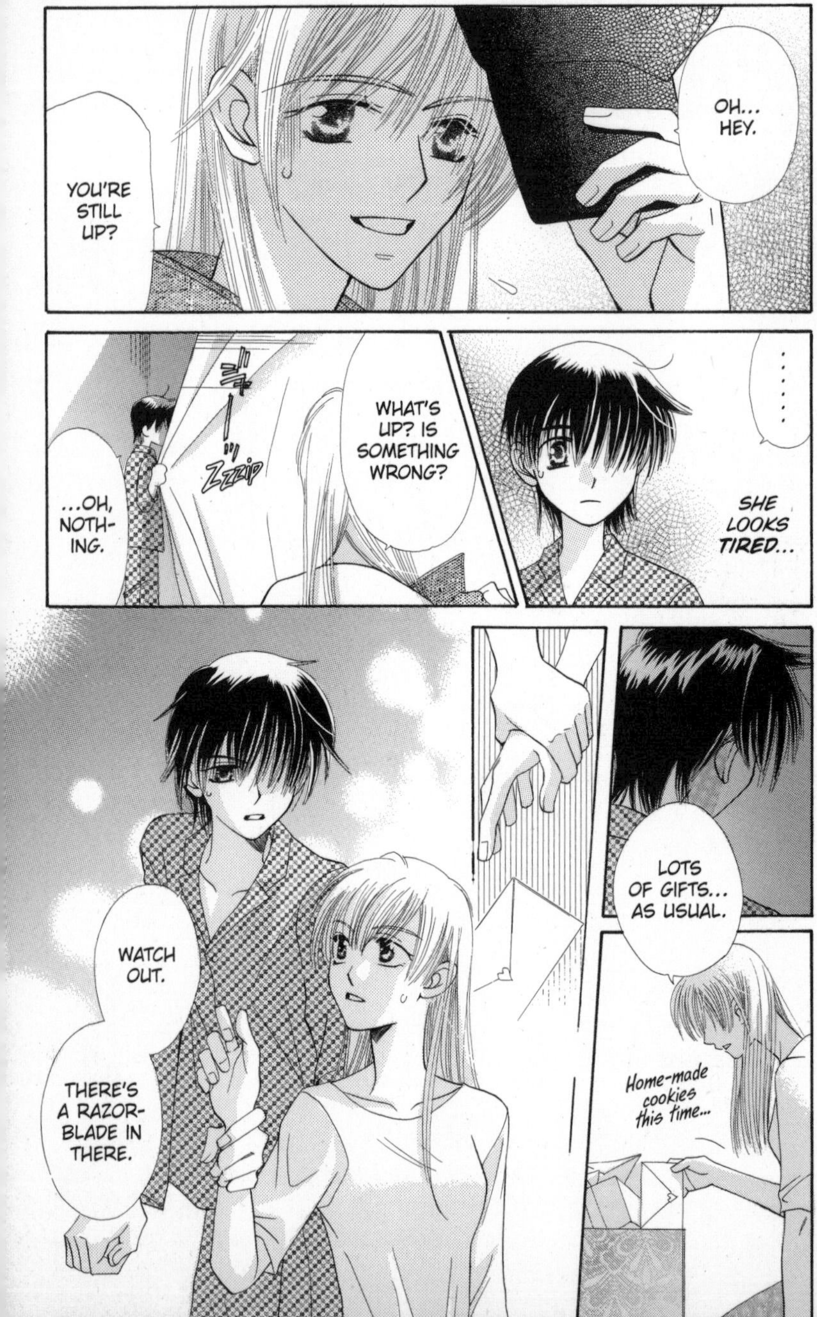

OH... HEY.
YOU'RE STILL UP?
......
SHE LOOKS TIRED...
WHAT'S UP? IS SOMETHING WRONG?
ZZZIP
...OH, NOTH-ING.
LOTS OF GIFTS... AS USUAL.
Home-made cookies this time...
WATCH OUT.
THERE'S A RAZOR-BLADE IN THERE.

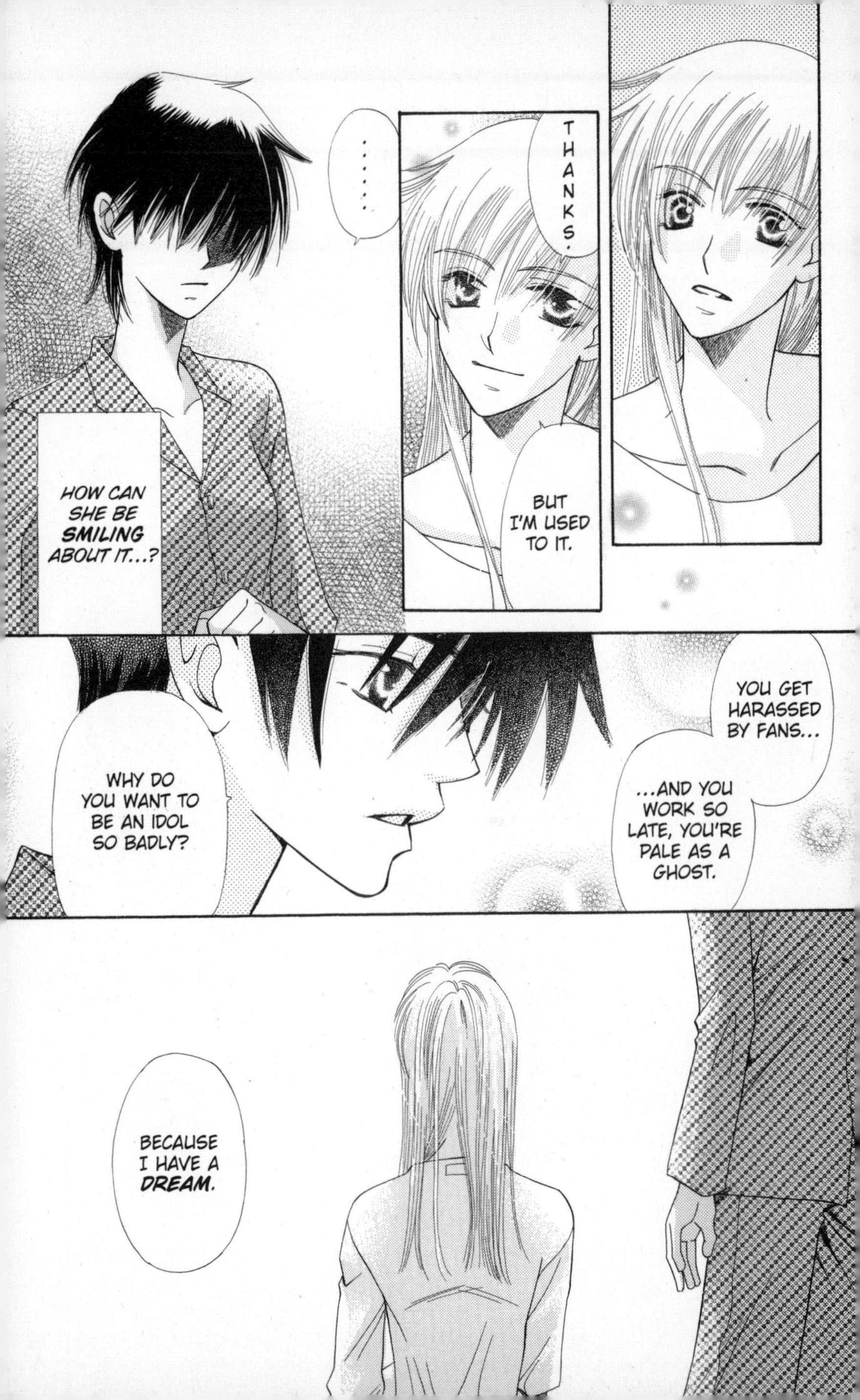
THANKS.
BUT I'M USED TO IT.
......
HOW CAN SHE BE SMILING ABOUT IT...?
YOU GET HARASSED BY FANS...
...AND YOU WORK SO LATE, YOU'RE PALE AS A GHOST.
WHY DO YOU WANT TO BE AN IDOL SO BADLY?
BECAUSE I HAVE A DREAM.

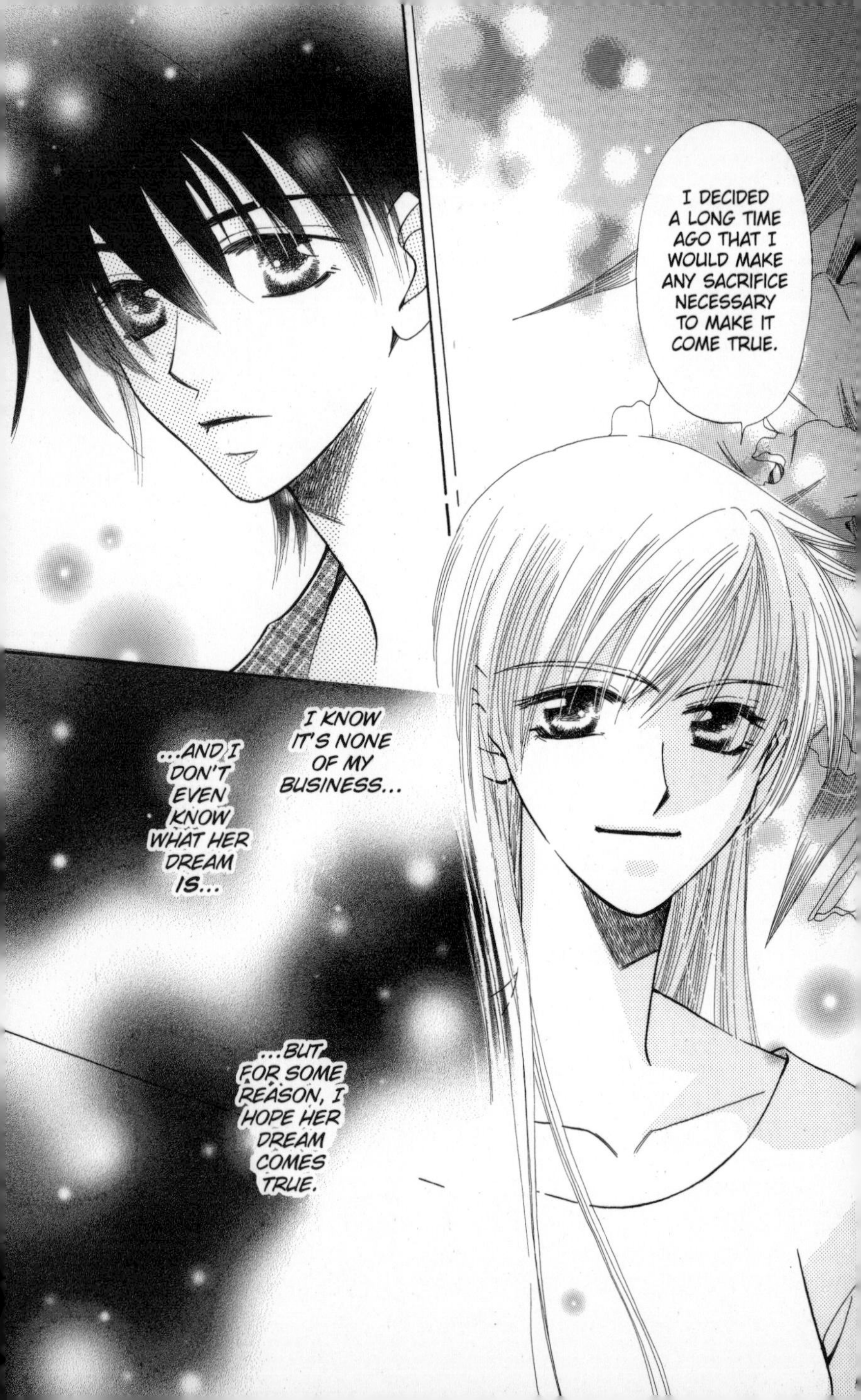
I DECIDED A LONG TIME AGO THAT I WOULD MAKE ANY SACRIFICE NECESSARY TO MAKE IT COME TRUE.
I KNOW IT'S NONE OF MY BUSINESS...
...AND I DON'T EVEN KNOW WHAT HER DREAM IS...
...BUT FOR SOME REASON, I HOPE HER DREAM COMES TRUE.

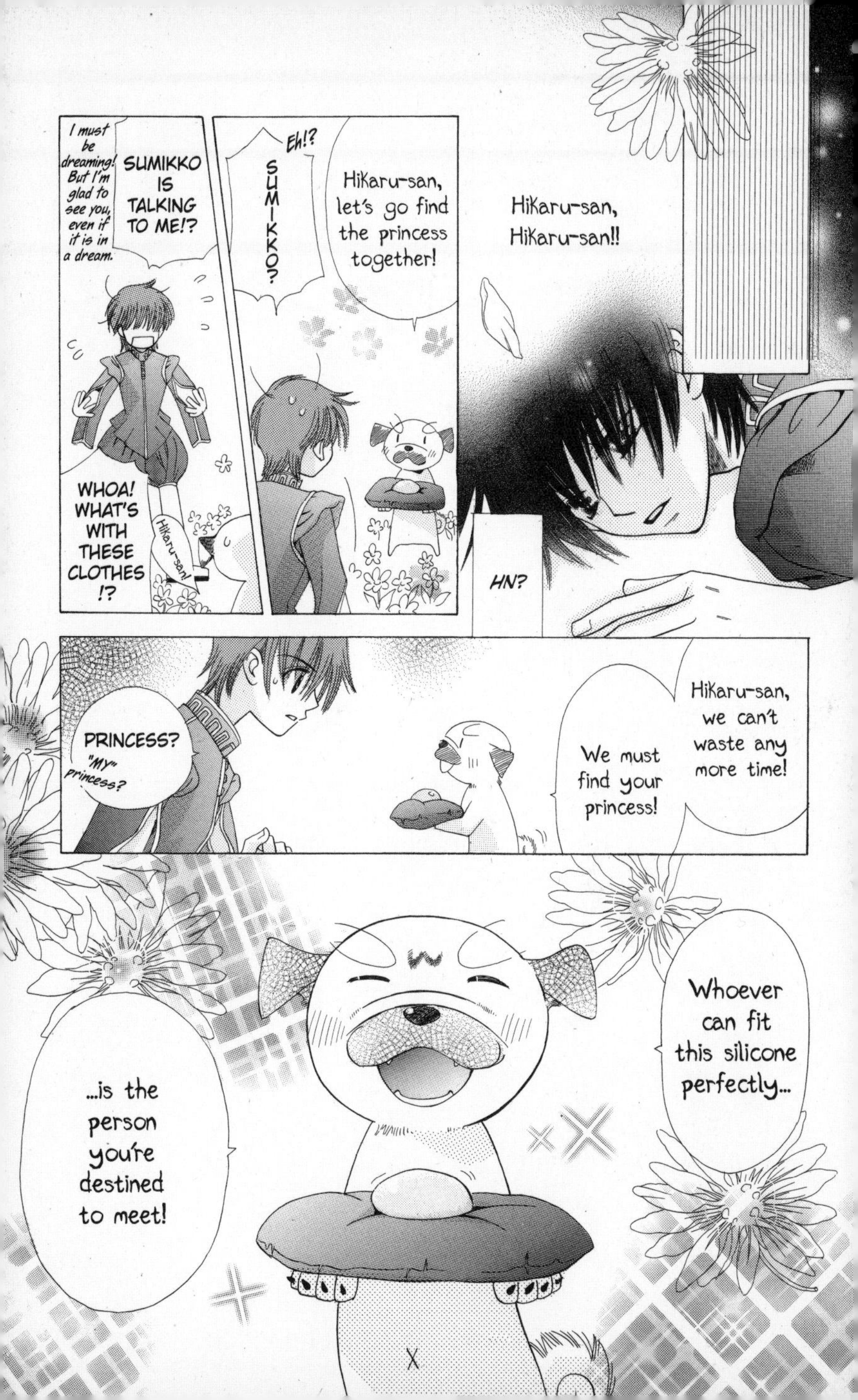

Hikaru-san, Hikaru-san!!
HN?
Hikaru-san, let's go find the princess together!
Eh!?
SUMIKKO?
SUMIKKO IS TALKING TO ME!?
I must be dreaming! But I'm glad to see you, even if it is in a dream.
WHOA! WHAT'S WITH THESE CLOTHES!?
Hikaru-san!
Hikaru-san, we can't waste any more time!
We must find your princess!
PRINCESS?
"MY" princess?
Whoever can fit this silicone perfectly...
...is the person you're destined to meet!

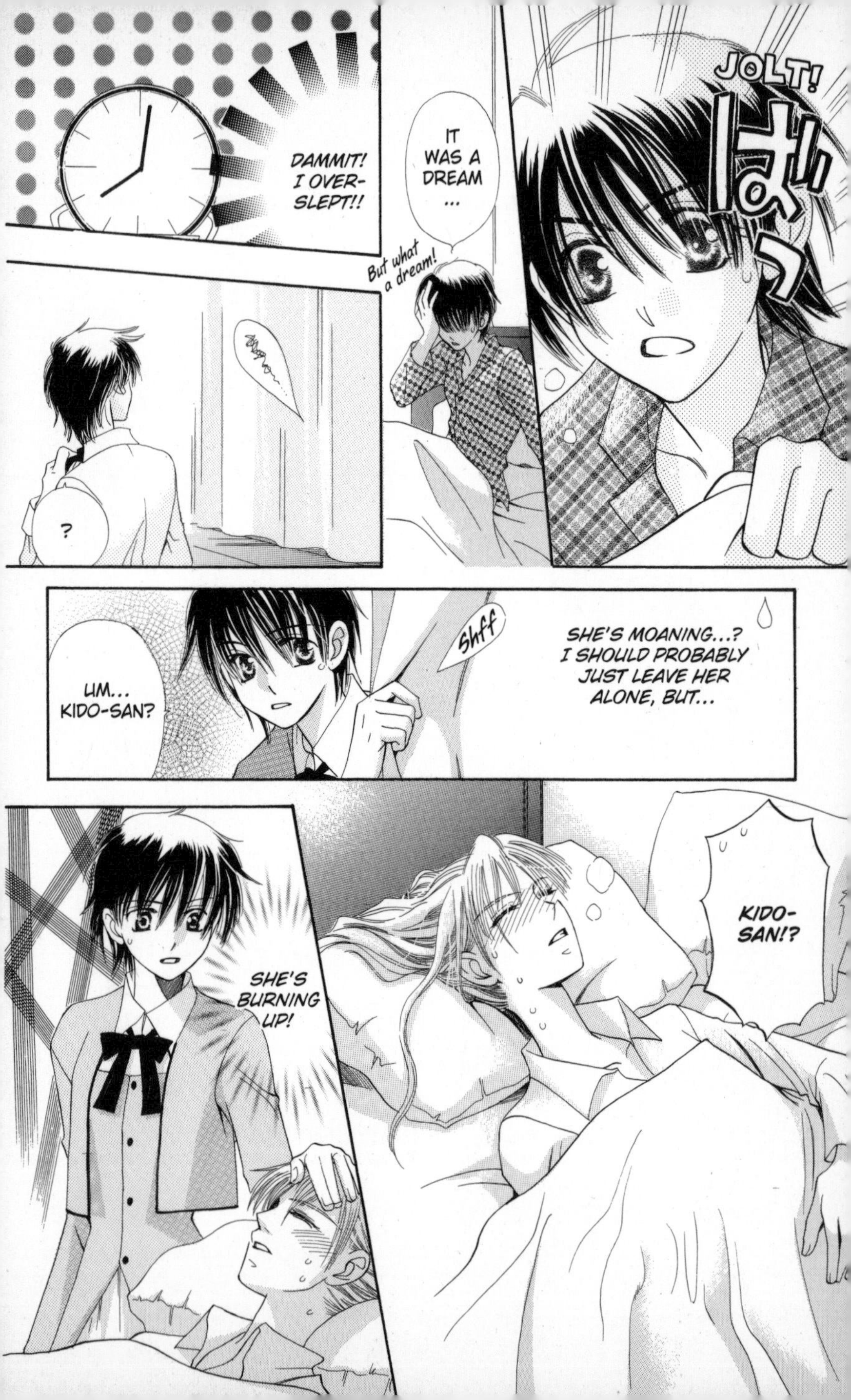

JOLT!
はっ
IT WAS A DREAM ...
But what a dream!
DAMMIT! I OVER-SLEPT!!
?
SHE'S MOANING...? I SHOULD PROBABLY JUST LEAVE HER ALONE, BUT...
Shff
UM... KIDO-SAN?
KIDO-SAN!?
SHE'S BURNING UP!

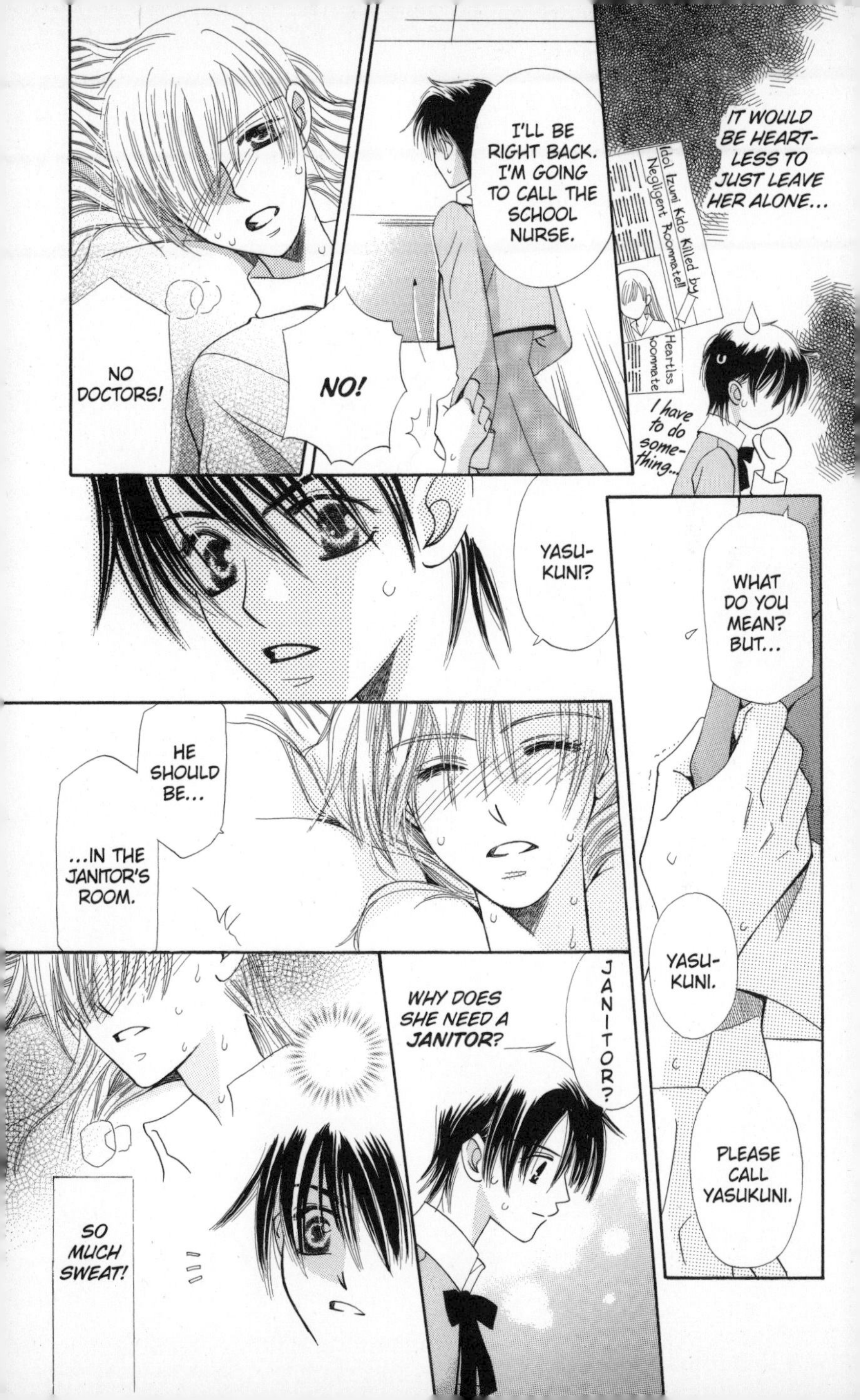
IT WOULD BE HEART-LESS TO JUST LEAVE HER ALONE...
Idol Izumi Kido Killed by Negligent Roommate!!
Heartless Roommate
I have to do something...
I'LL BE RIGHT BACK. I'M GOING TO CALL THE SCHOOL NURSE.
NO!
NO DOCTORS!
WHAT DO YOU MEAN? BUT...
YASU-KUNI.
PLEASE CALL YASUKUNI.
YASU-KUNI?
HE SHOULD BE...
...IN THE JANITOR'S ROOM.
JANITOR?
WHY DOES SHE NEED A JANITOR?
SO MUCH SWEAT!

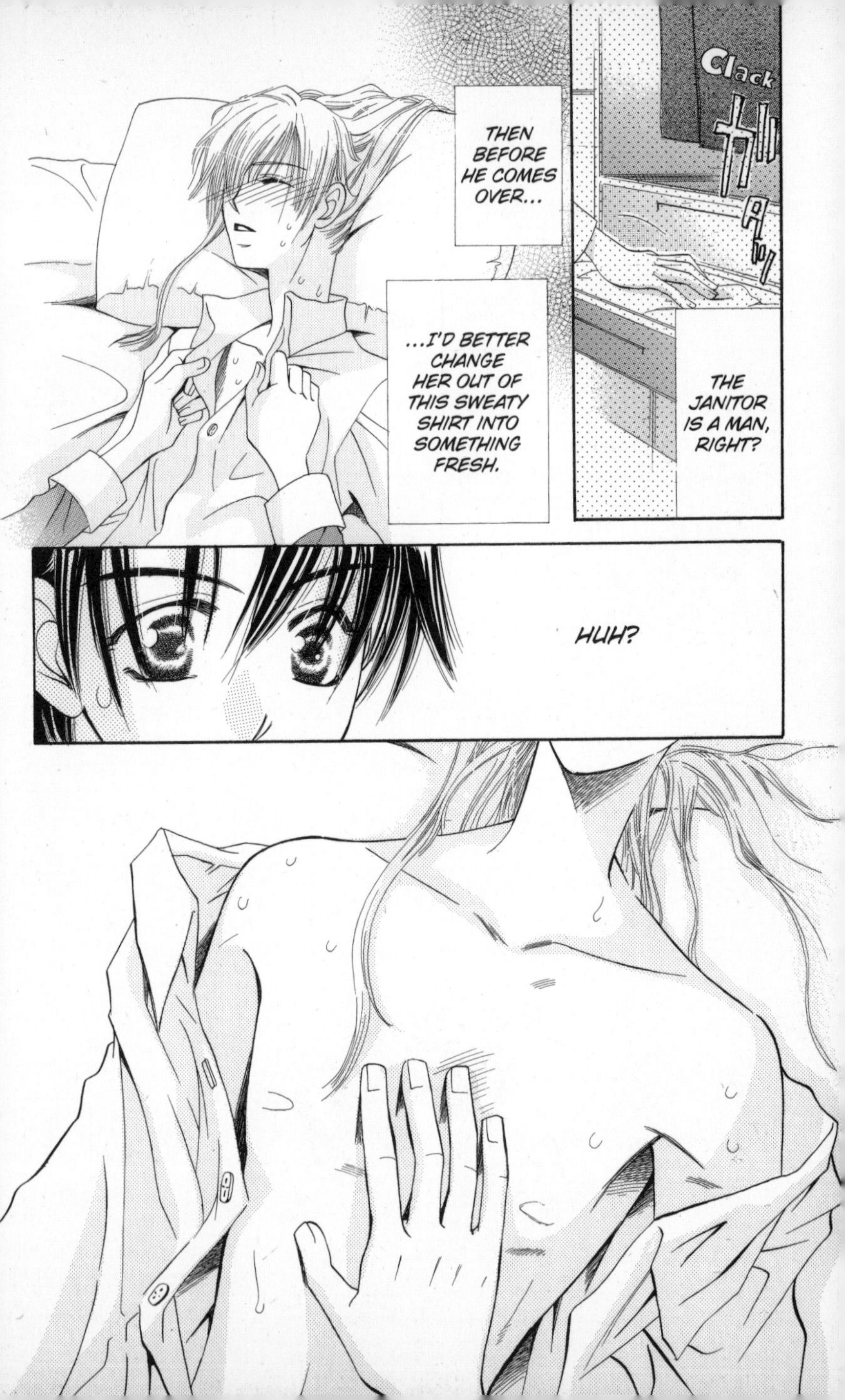
Clack
THE JANITOR IS A MAN, RIGHT?
THEN BEFORE HE COMES OVER...
...I'D BETTER CHANGE HER OUT OF THIS SWEATY SHIRT INTO SOMETHING FRESH.
HUH?

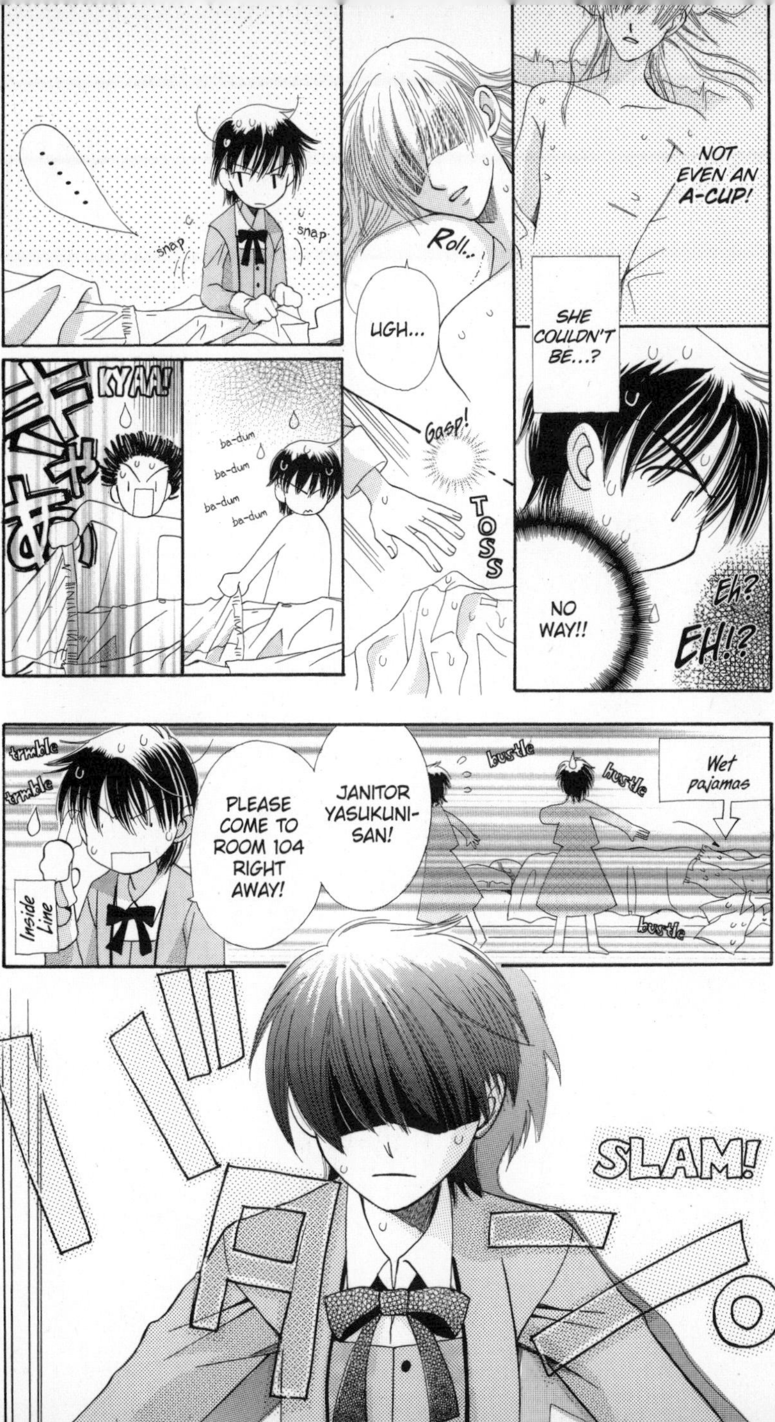
NOT EVEN AN A-CUP!
SHE COULDN'T BE...?
NO WAY!!
Eh?
EH!?
Roll..
UGH...
Gasp!
TOSS
......
snap
snap
ba-dum
ba-dum
ba-dum
ba-dum
KYAA!
きゃあ
Wet pajamas
bustle
hustle
bustle
JANITOR YASUKUNI-SAN!
PLEASE COME TO ROOM 104 RIGHT AWAY!
trmble
trmble
Inside Line
SLAM!

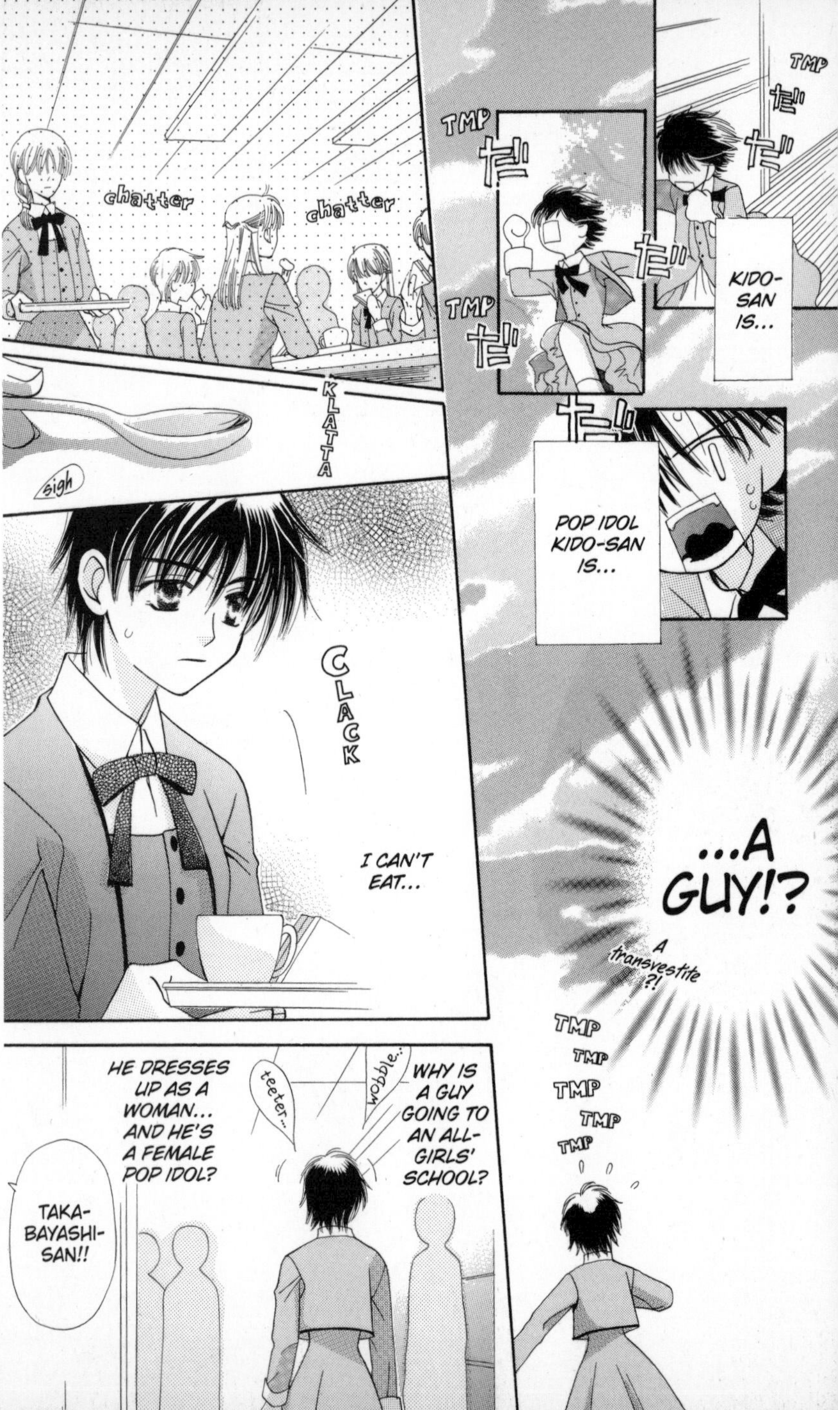
TMP
KIDO-SAN IS...
TMP
TMP
POP IDOL KIDO-SAN IS...
...A GUY!?
A transvestite ?!
TMP
TMP
TMP
TMP
TMP
chatter
chatter
KLATTA
sigh
CLACK
I CAN'T EAT...
WHY IS A GUY GOING TO AN ALL-GIRLS' SCHOOL?
wobble...
teeter...
HE DRESSES UP AS A WOMAN... AND HE'S A FEMALE POP IDOL?
TAKA-BAYASHI-SAN!!

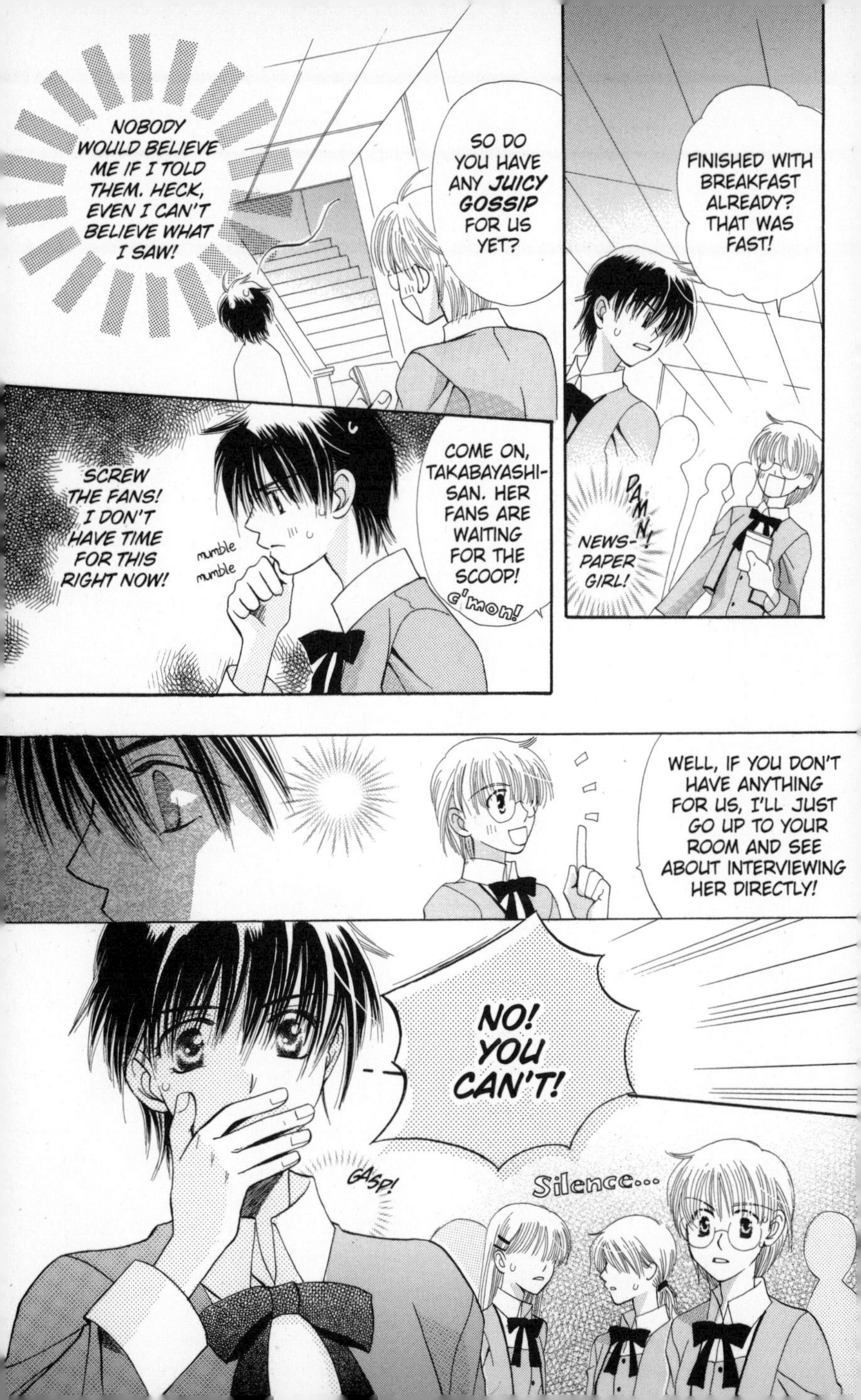
FINISHED WITH BREAKFAST ALREADY? THAT WAS FAST!
DAMN!
NEWS-PAPER GIRL!
SO DO YOU HAVE ANY **JUICY GOSSIP** FOR US YET?
NOBODY WOULD BELIEVE ME IF I TOLD THEM. HECK, EVEN I CAN'T BELIEVE WHAT I SAW!
COME ON, TAKABAYASHI-SAN. HER FANS ARE WAITING FOR THE SCOOP!
c'mon!
mumble mumble
SCREW THE FANS! I DON'T HAVE TIME FOR THIS RIGHT NOW!
WELL, IF YOU DON'T HAVE ANYTHING FOR US, I'LL JUST GO UP TO YOUR ROOM AND SEE ABOUT INTERVIEWING HER DIRECTLY!
NO! YOU CAN'T!
GASP!
Silence...

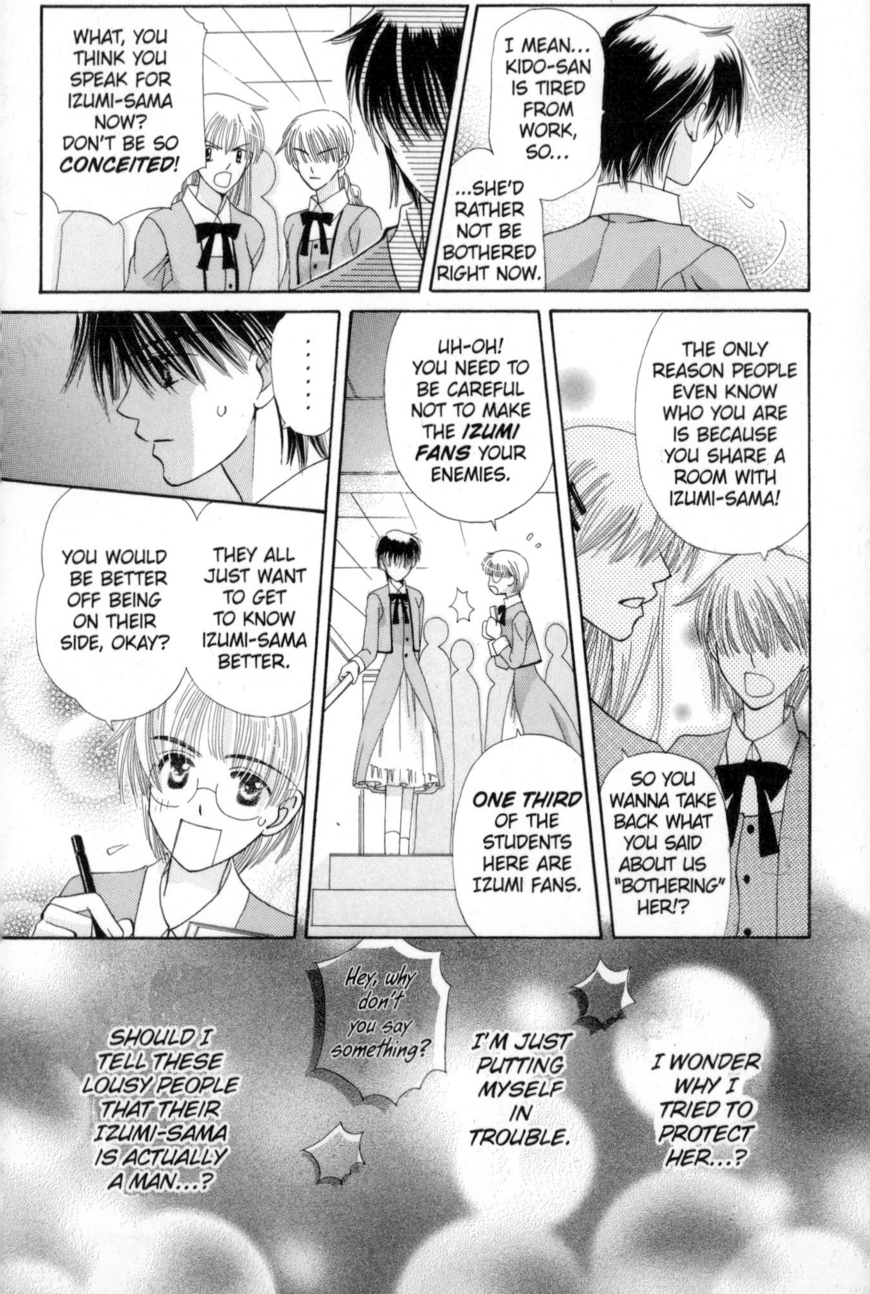
I MEAN... KIDO-SAN IS TIRED FROM WORK, SO...
...SHE'D RATHER NOT BE BOTHERED RIGHT NOW.
WHAT, YOU THINK YOU SPEAK FOR IZUMI-SAMA NOW? DON'T BE SO CONCEITED!
THE ONLY REASON PEOPLE EVEN KNOW WHO YOU ARE IS BECAUSE YOU SHARE A ROOM WITH IZUMI-SAMA!
SO YOU WANNA TAKE BACK WHAT YOU SAID ABOUT US "BOTHERING" HER!?
UH-OH! YOU NEED TO BE CAREFUL NOT TO MAKE THE IZUMI FANS YOUR ENEMIES.
ONE THIRD OF THE STUDENTS HERE ARE IZUMI FANS.
......
THEY ALL JUST WANT TO GET TO KNOW IZUMI-SAMA BETTER.
YOU WOULD BE BETTER OFF BEING ON THEIR SIDE, OKAY?
I WONDER WHY I TRIED TO PROTECT HER...?
Hey, why don't you say something?
I'M JUST PUTTING MYSELF IN TROUBLE.
SHOULD I TELL THESE LOUSY PEOPLE THAT THEIR IZUMI-SAMA IS ACTUALLY A MAN...?

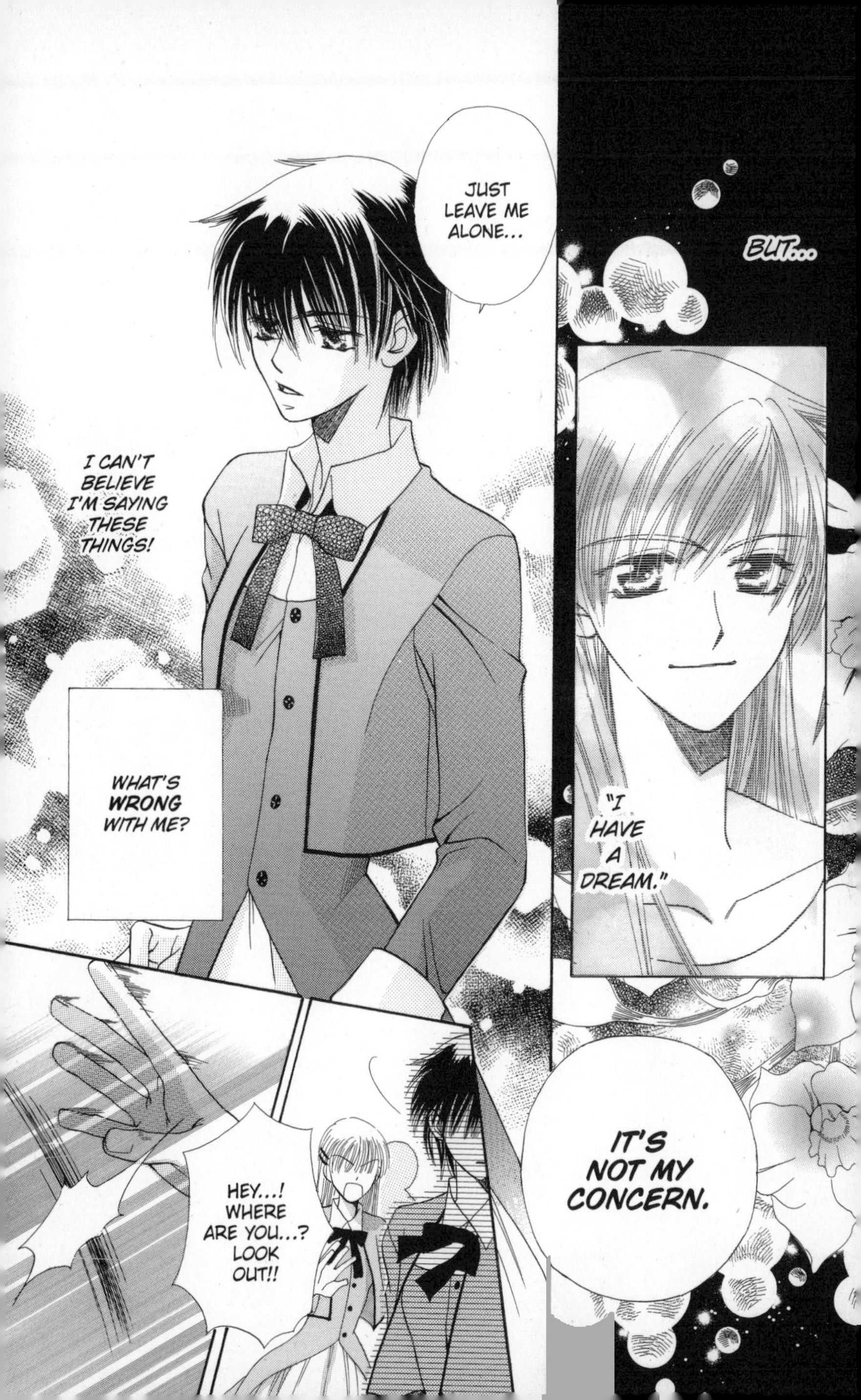
BUT...
"I HAVE A DREAM."
IT'S NOT MY CONCERN.
JUST LEAVE ME ALONE...
I CAN'T BELIEVE I'M SAYING THESE THINGS!
WHAT'S WRONG WITH ME?
HEY...! WHERE ARE YOU...? LOOK OUT!!

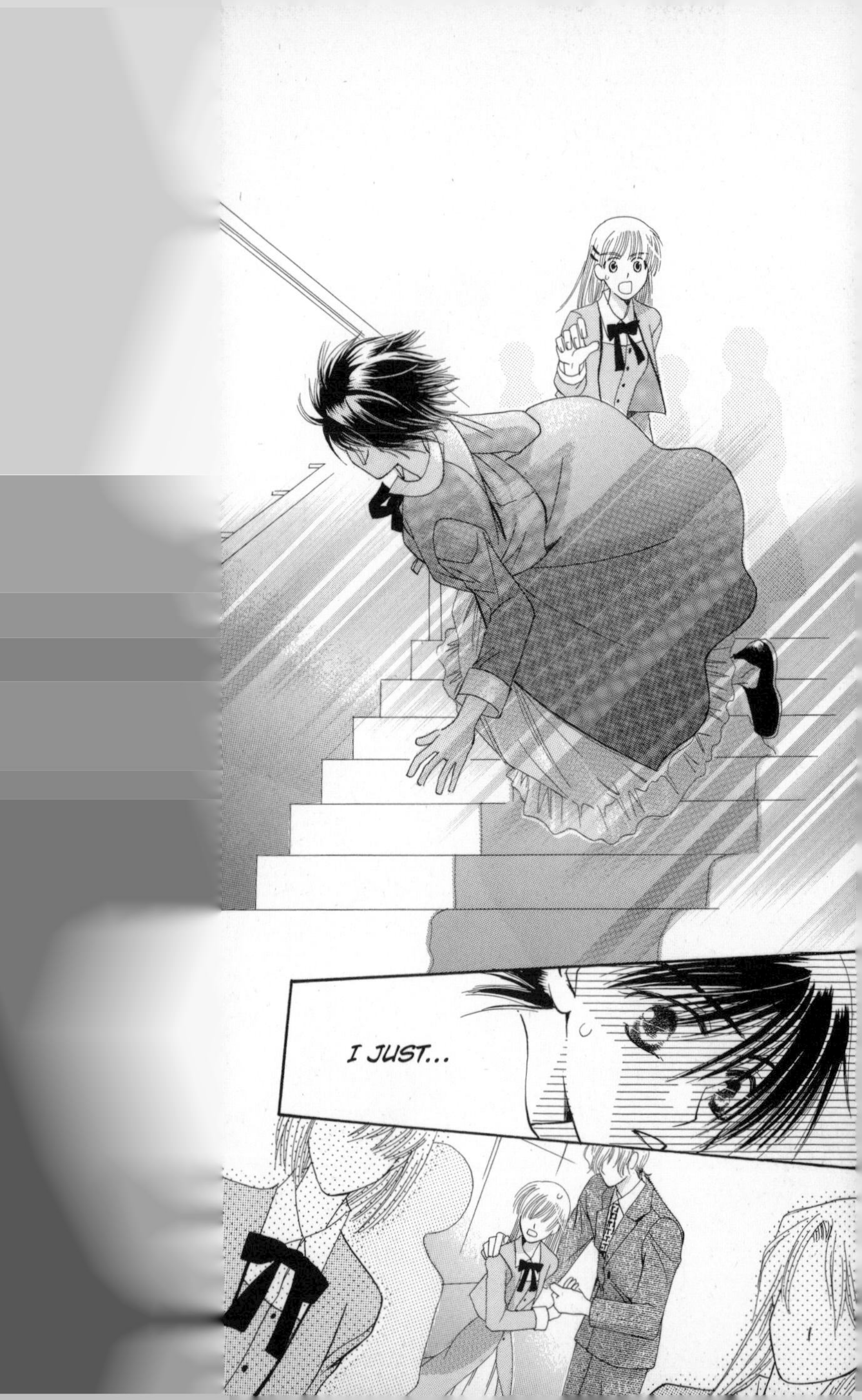
I JUST...

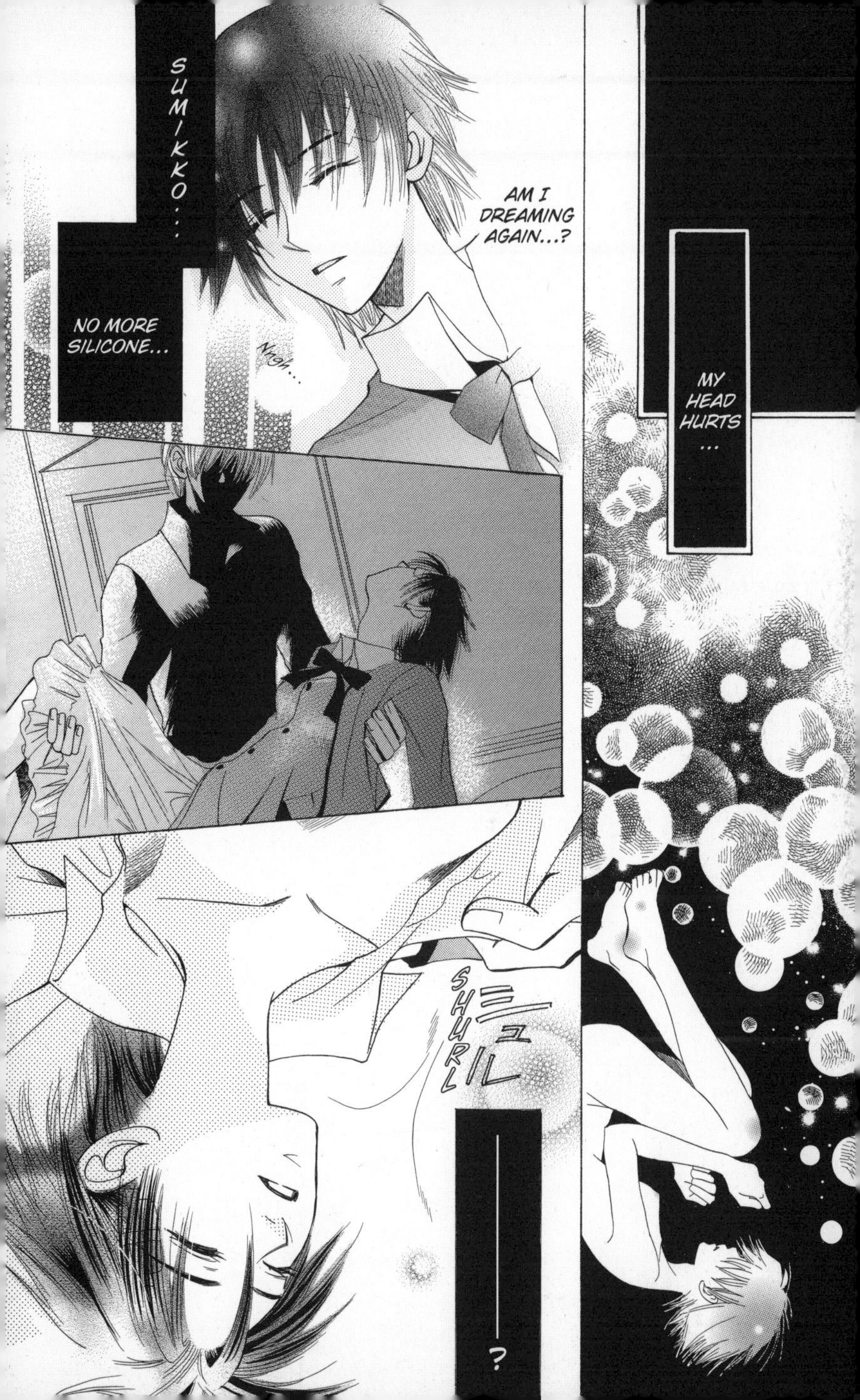
MY HEAD HURTS...
AM I DREAMING AGAIN...?
SUMIKKO...
NO MORE SILICONE...
Nngh...
SHURL
——?

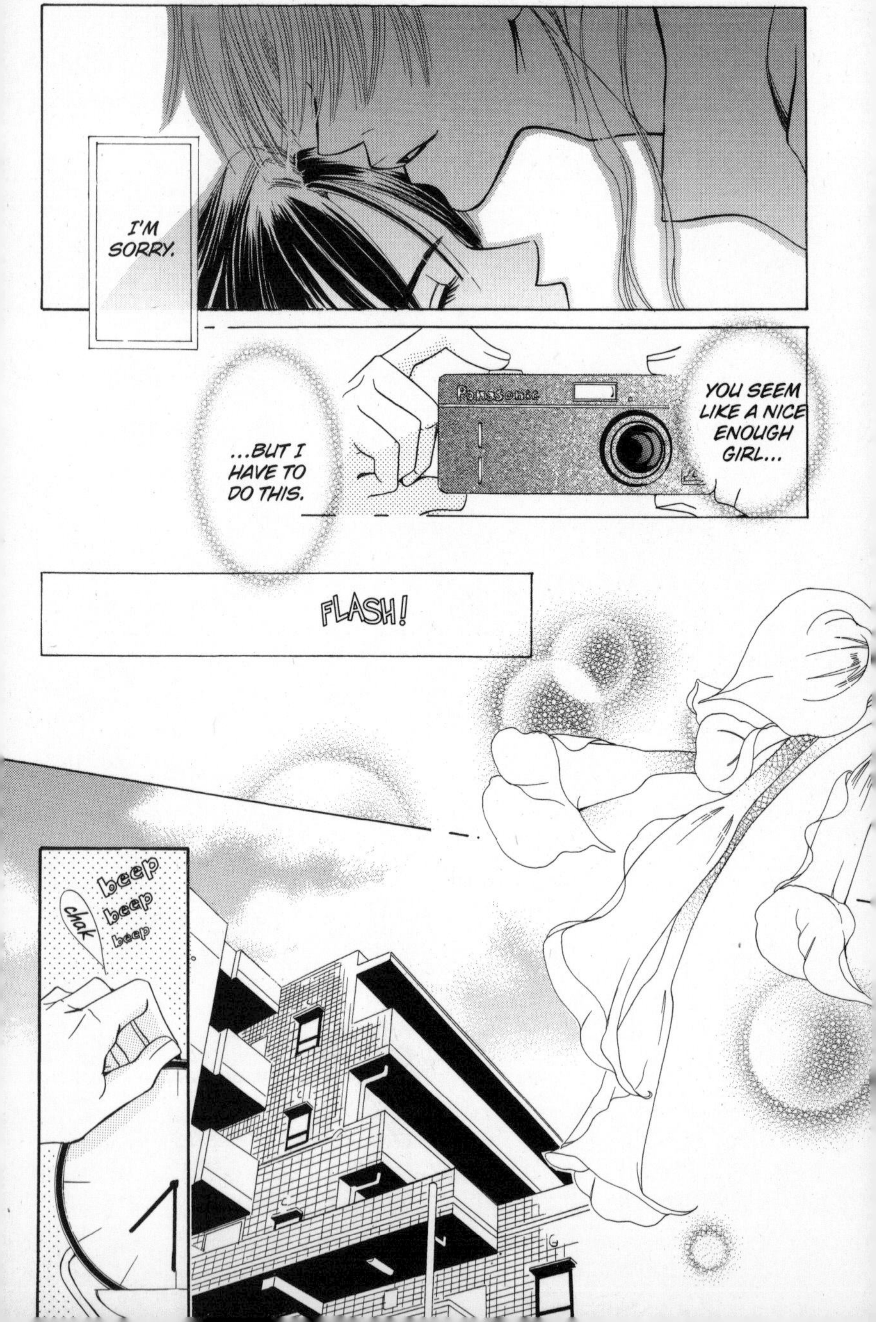
I'M SORRY.
YOU SEEM LIKE A NICE ENOUGH GIRL...
...BUT I HAVE TO DO THIS.
FLASH!
beep beep beep
chak

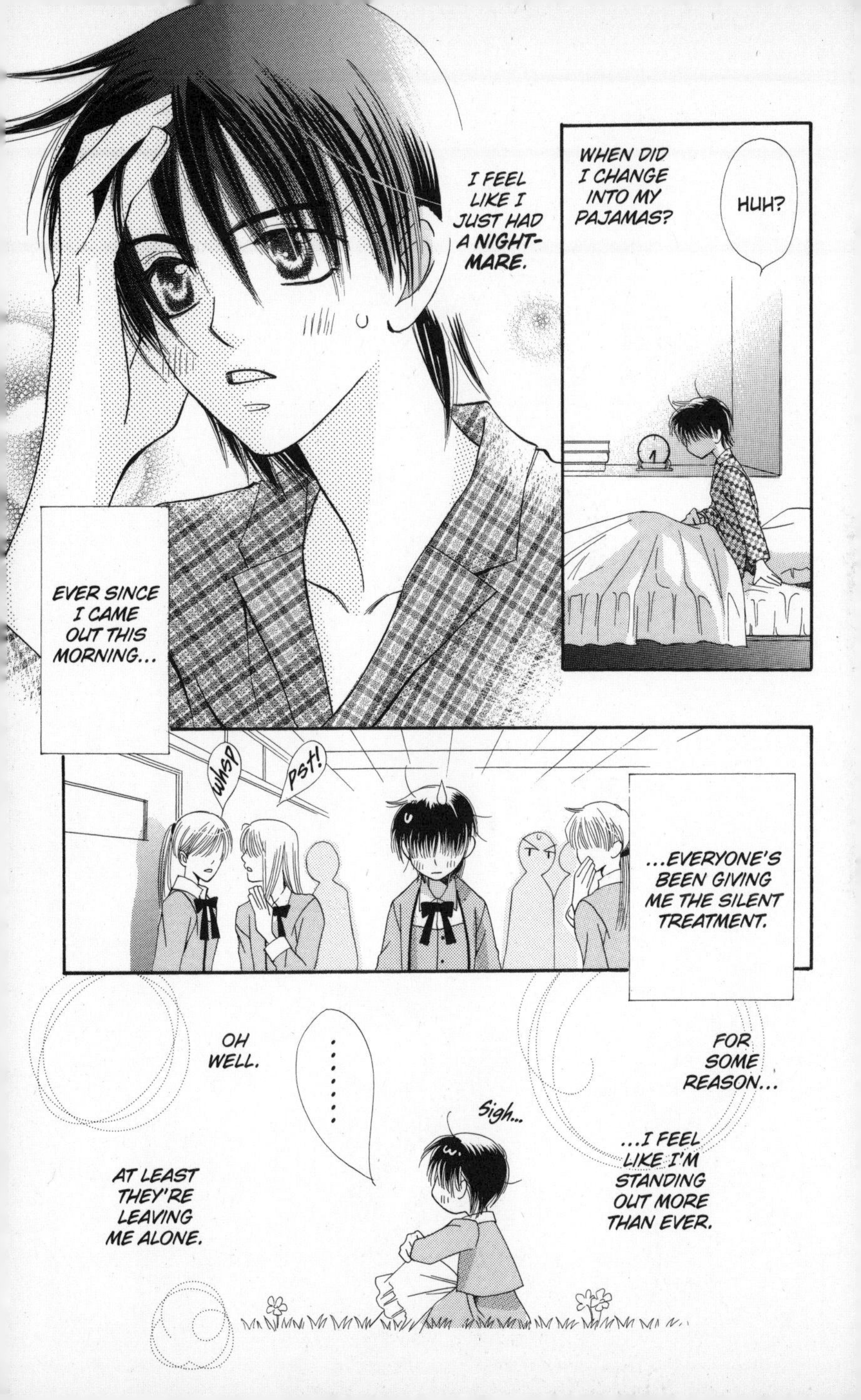
HUH?
WHEN DID I CHANGE INTO MY PAJAMAS?
I FEEL LIKE I JUST HAD A NIGHTMARE.
EVER SINCE I CAME OUT THIS MORNING...
...EVERYONE'S BEEN GIVING ME THE SILENT TREATMENT.
pst!
whsp
FOR SOME REASON...
...I FEEL LIKE I'M STANDING OUT MORE THAN EVER.
Sigh...
....
OH WELL.
AT LEAST THEY'RE LEAVING ME ALONE.

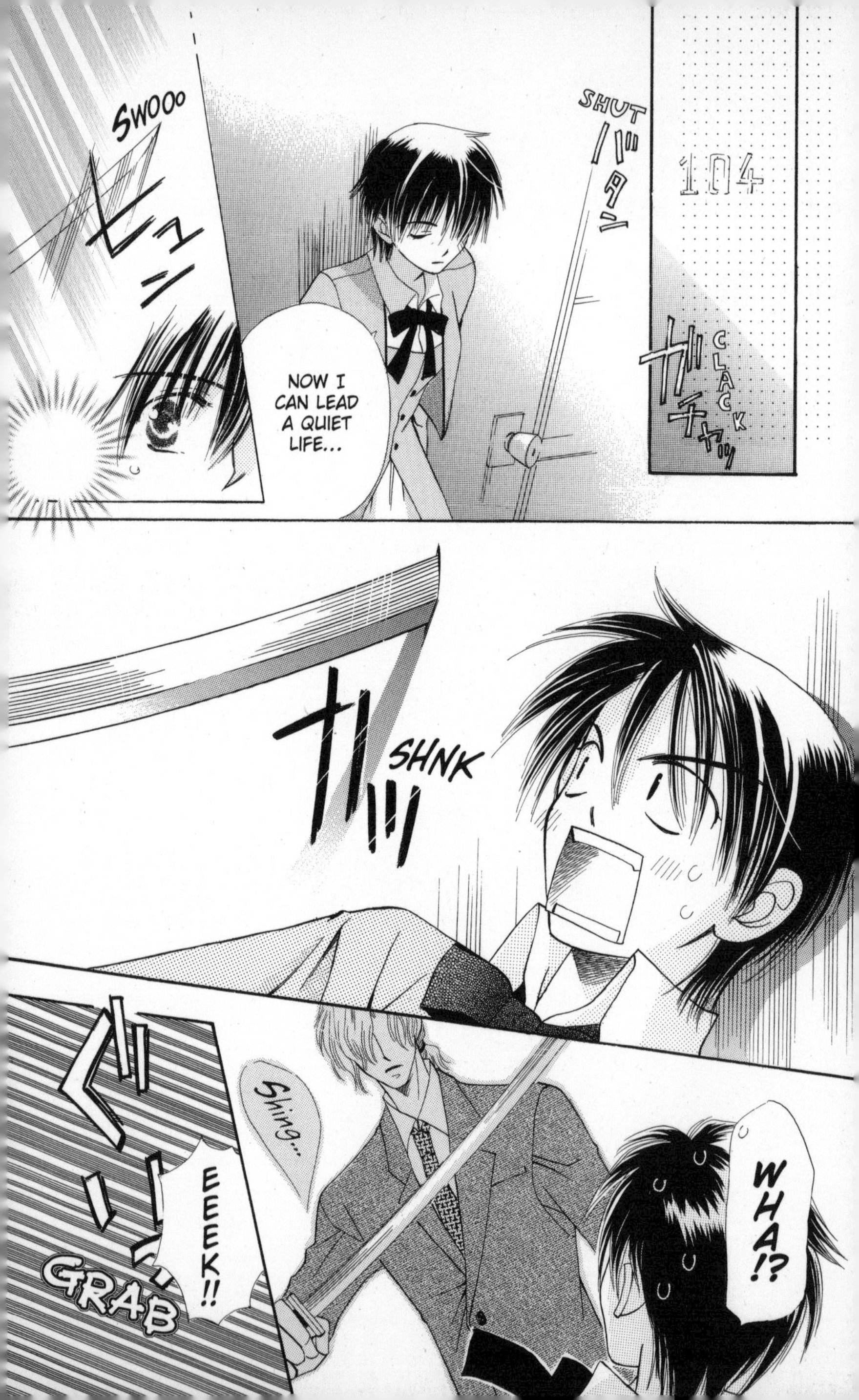
SHUT
104
CLACK
NOW I CAN LEAD A QUIET LIFE...
SWOOO
SHNK
WHA!?
Shing...
EEEK!!
GRAB

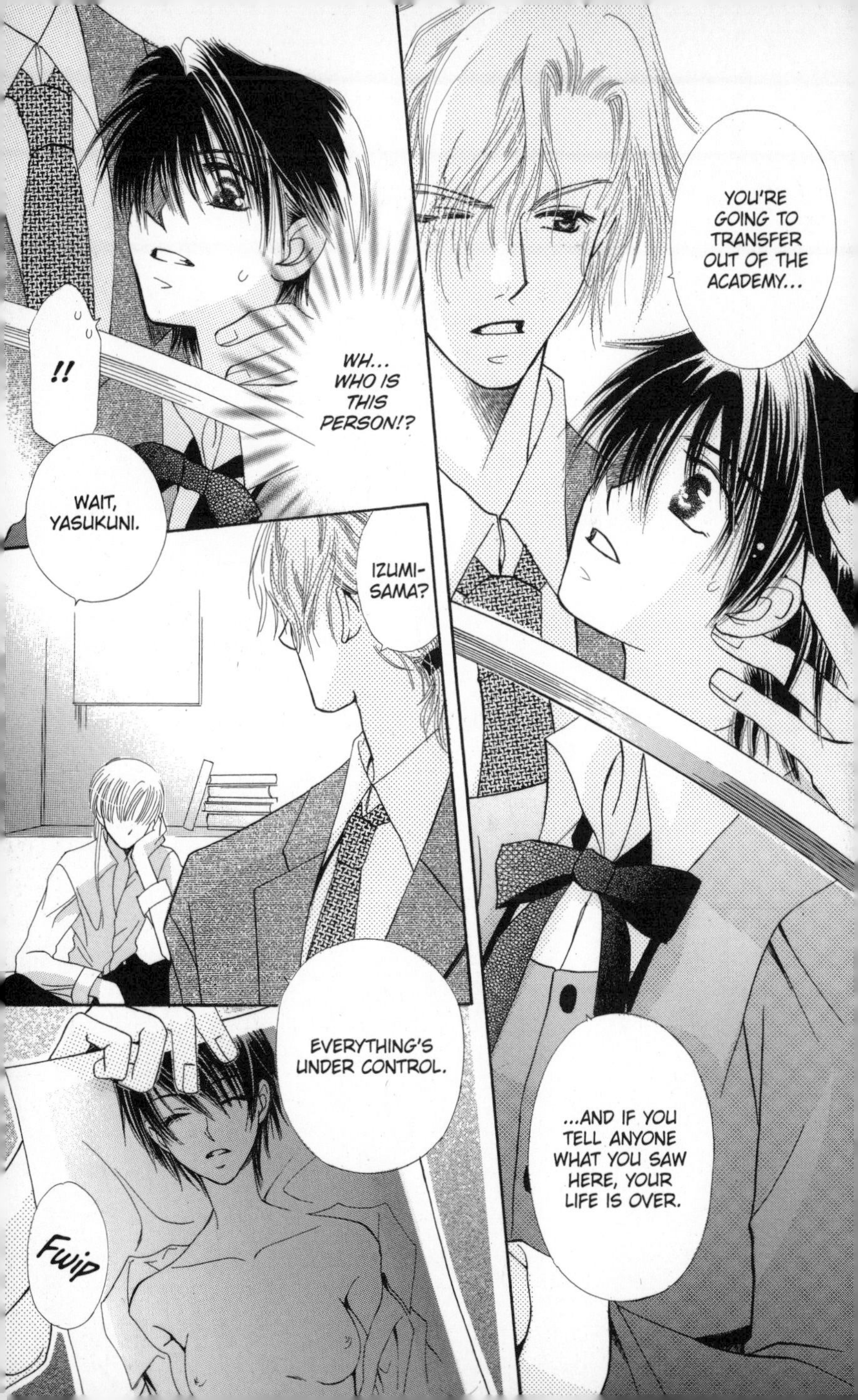
YOU'RE GOING TO TRANSFER OUT OF THE ACADEMY...
...AND IF YOU TELL ANYONE WHAT YOU SAW HERE, YOUR LIFE IS OVER.
WH... WHO IS THIS PERSON!?
!!
WAIT, YASUKUNI.
IZUMI-SAMA?
EVERYTHING'S UNDER CONTROL.
Fwip

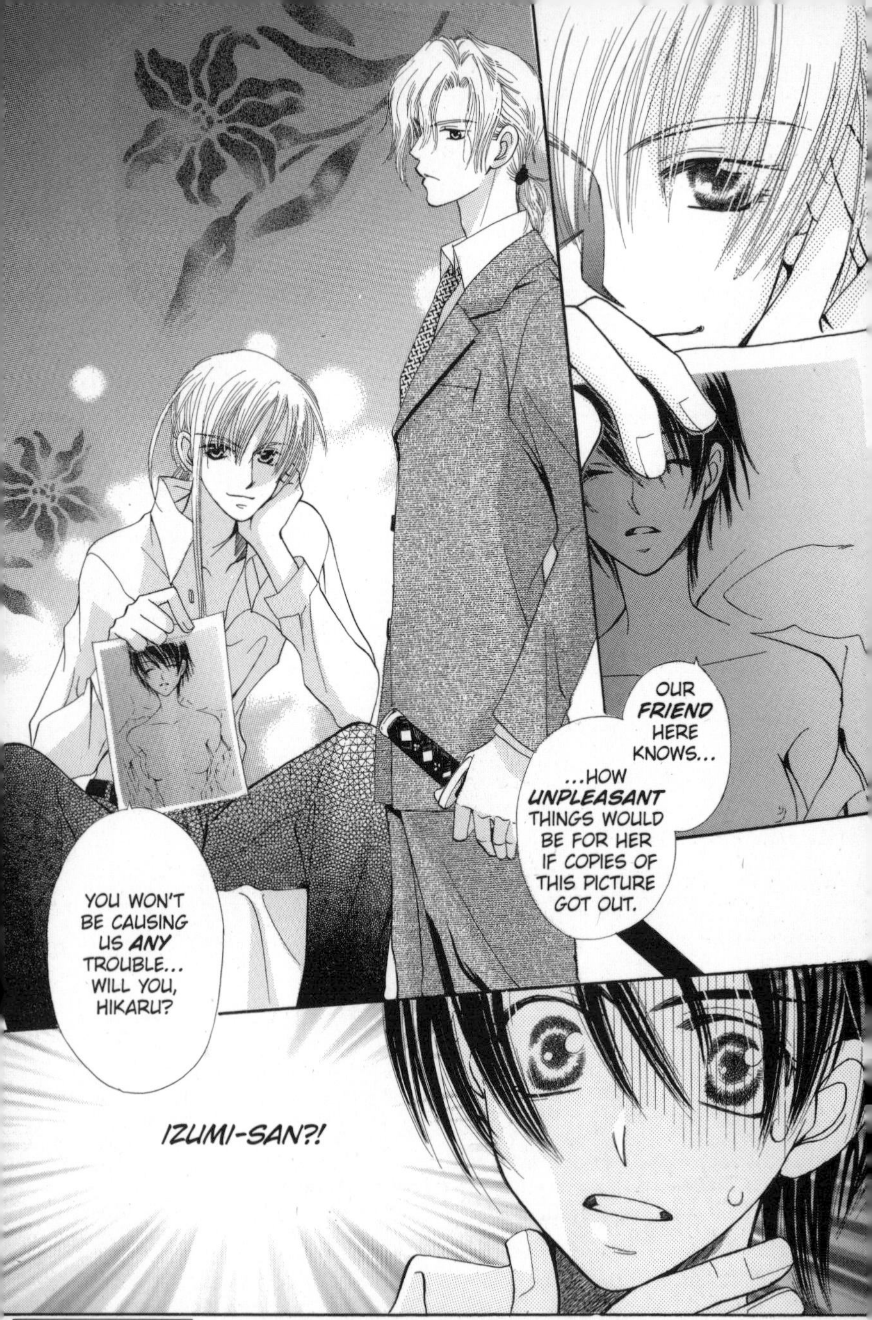
OUR FRIEND HERE KNOWS...
...HOW UNPLEASANT THINGS WOULD BE FOR HER IF COPIES OF THIS PICTURE GOT OUT.
YOU WON'T BE CAUSING US ANY TROUBLE... WILL YOU, HIKARU?
IZUMI-SAN?!

End of Scene 1

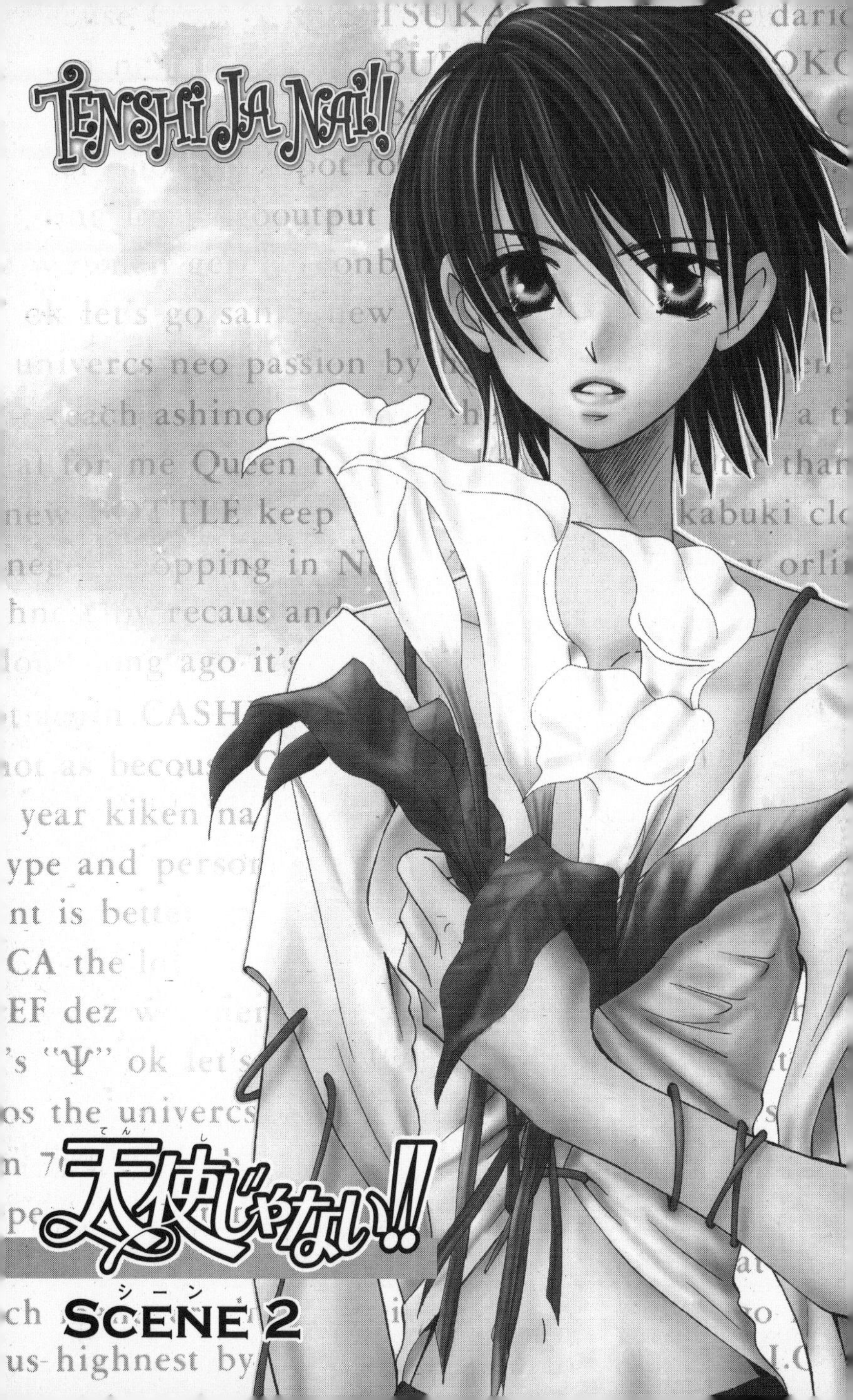
TENSHI JA NAI!!
天使じゃない!!
SCENE 2

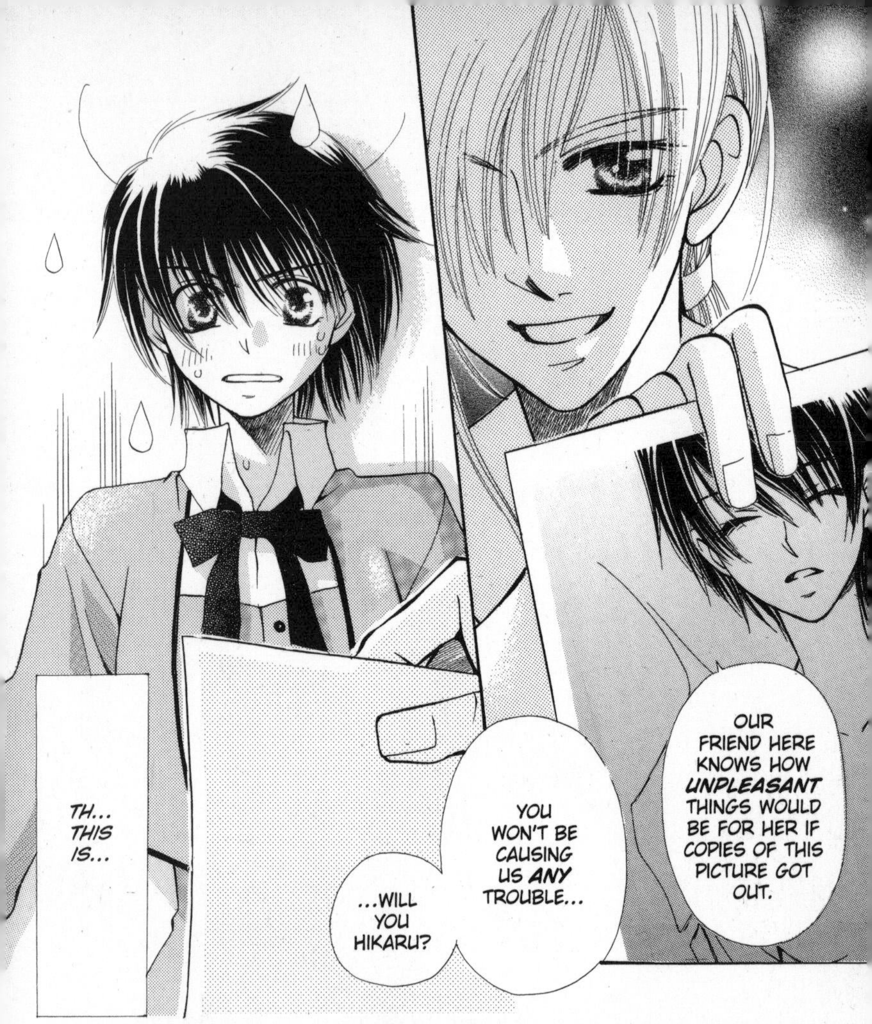
OUR FRIEND HERE KNOWS HOW UNPLEASANT THINGS WOULD BE FOR HER IF COPIES OF THIS PICTURE GOT OUT.
YOU WON'T BE CAUSING US ANY TROUBLE...
...WILL YOU HIKARU?
TH... THIS IS...

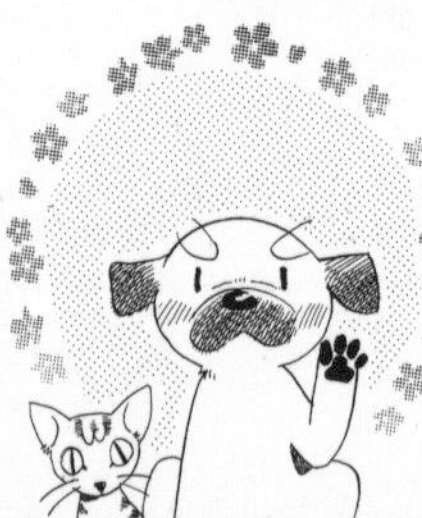

To those who've known me for a while and those meeting me for the first time...

Konnichiwa! Thanks so much for picking up my book. If you're already familiar with my work, thanks for coming back. I hope to see you all again in the next volume!
If any of you are checking out this book in a store, the cashier is right over there. [laugh]

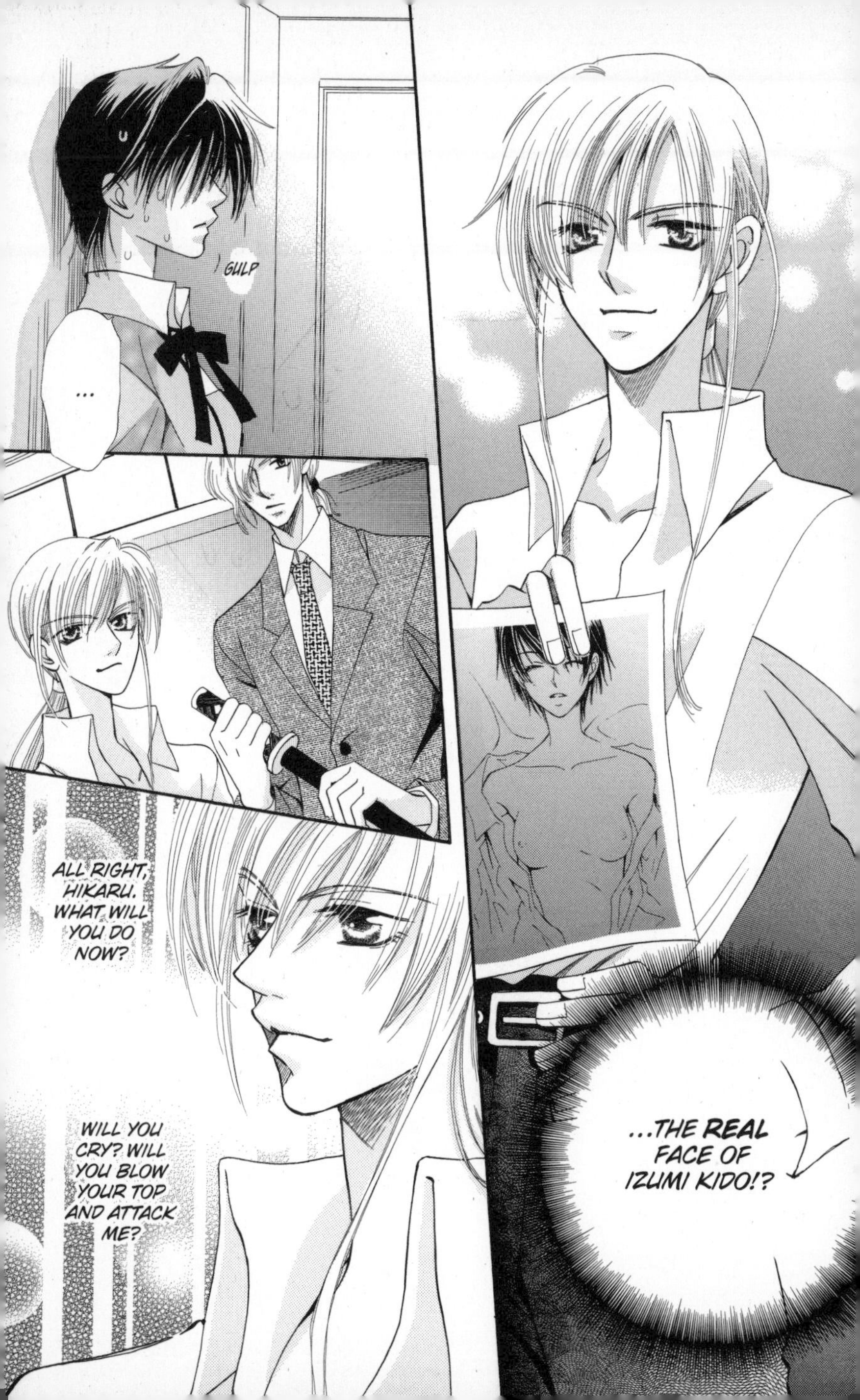
...THE REAL FACE OF IZUMI KIDO!?
GULP
...
ALL RIGHT, HIKARU. WHAT WILL YOU DO NOW?
WILL YOU CRY? WILL YOU BLOW YOUR TOP AND ATTACK ME?

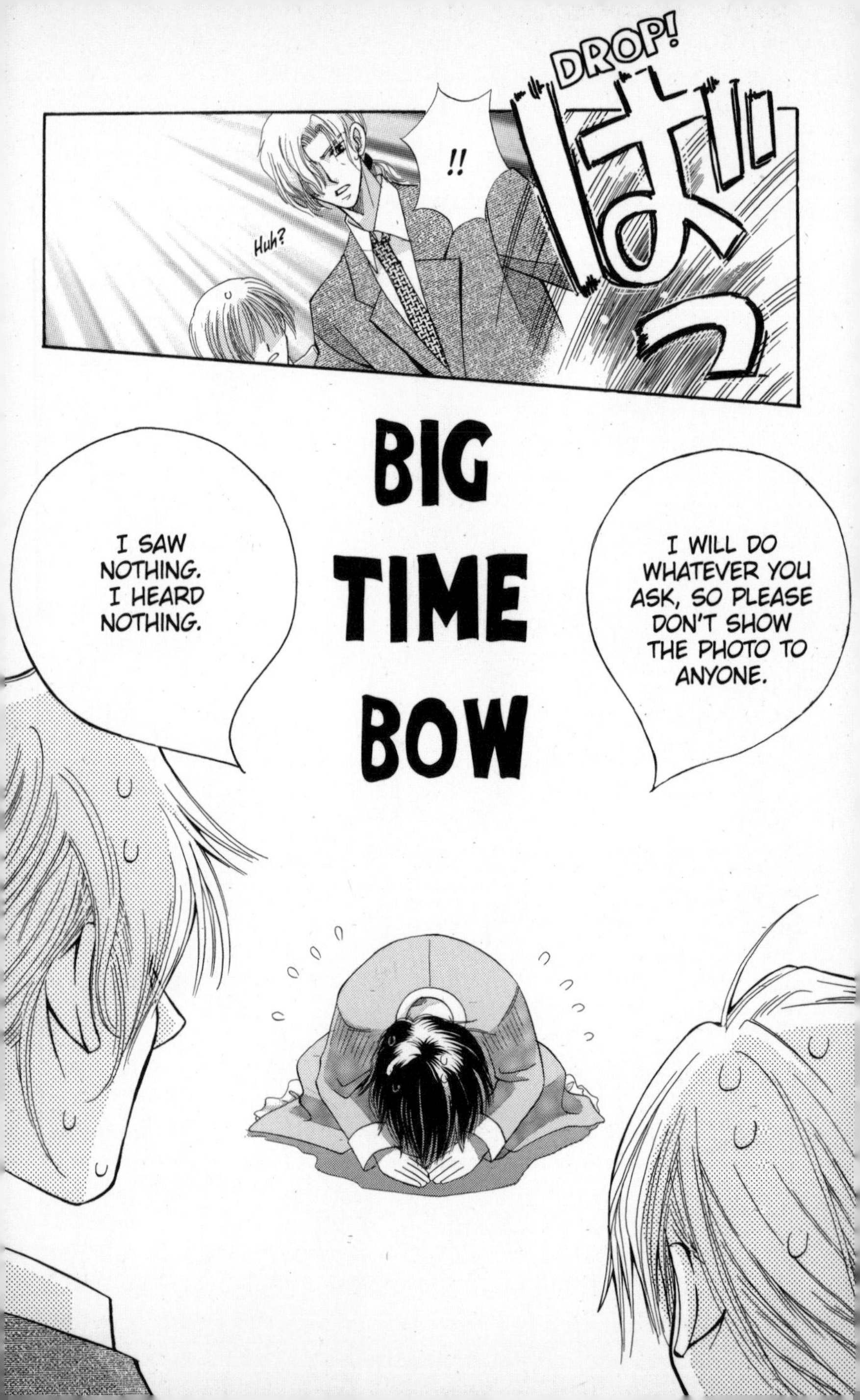
DROP!
ばっ
!!
Huh?
I WILL DO WHATEVER YOU ASK, SO PLEASE DON'T SHOW THE PHOTO TO ANYONE.
BIG TIME BOW
I SAW NOTHING. I HEARD NOTHING.

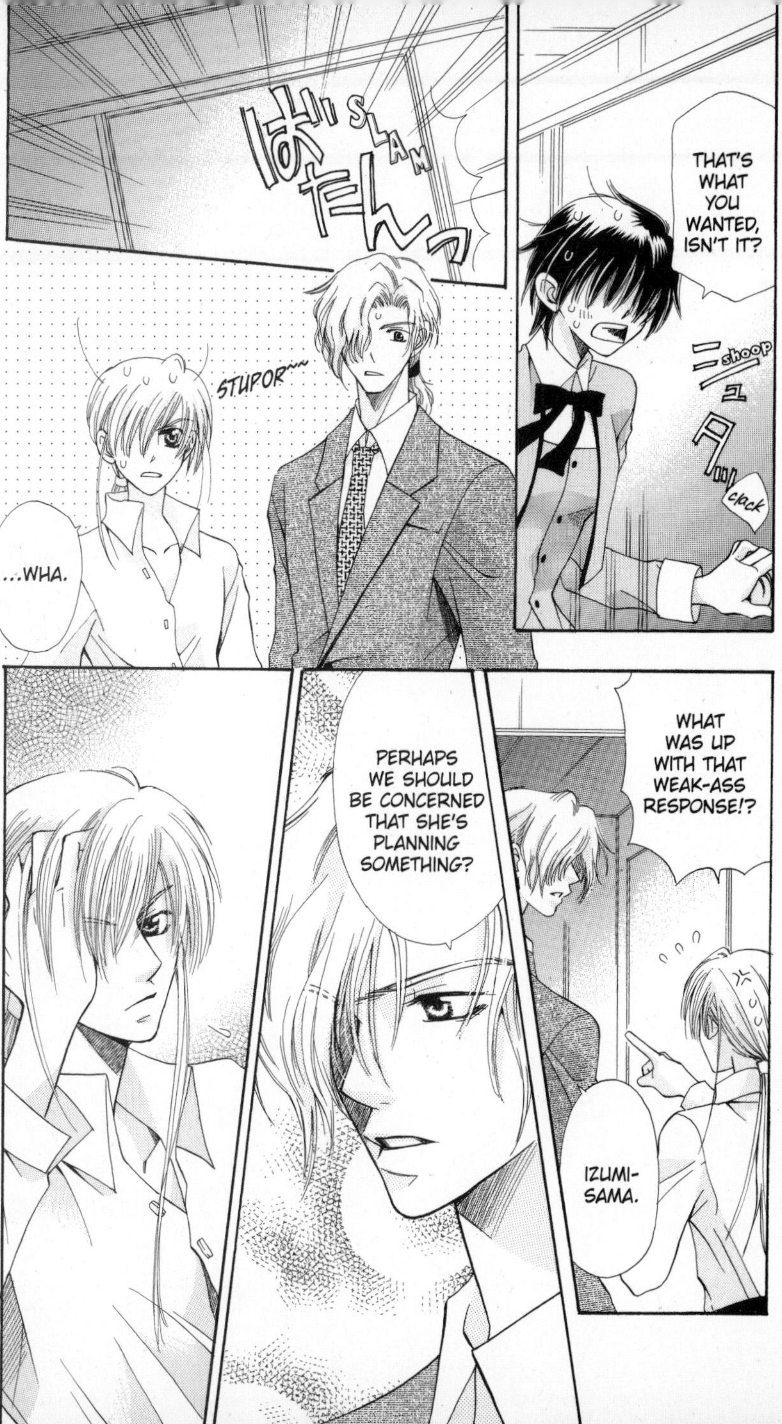

THAT'S WHAT YOU WANTED, ISN'T IT?
ニュタッ SHOOP
CLACK
ばたんっ SLAM
STUPOR~~
...WHA.
WHAT WAS UP WITH THAT WEAK-ASS RESPONSE!?
IZUMI-SAMA.
PERHAPS WE SHOULD BE CONCERNED THAT SHE'S PLANNING SOMETHING?

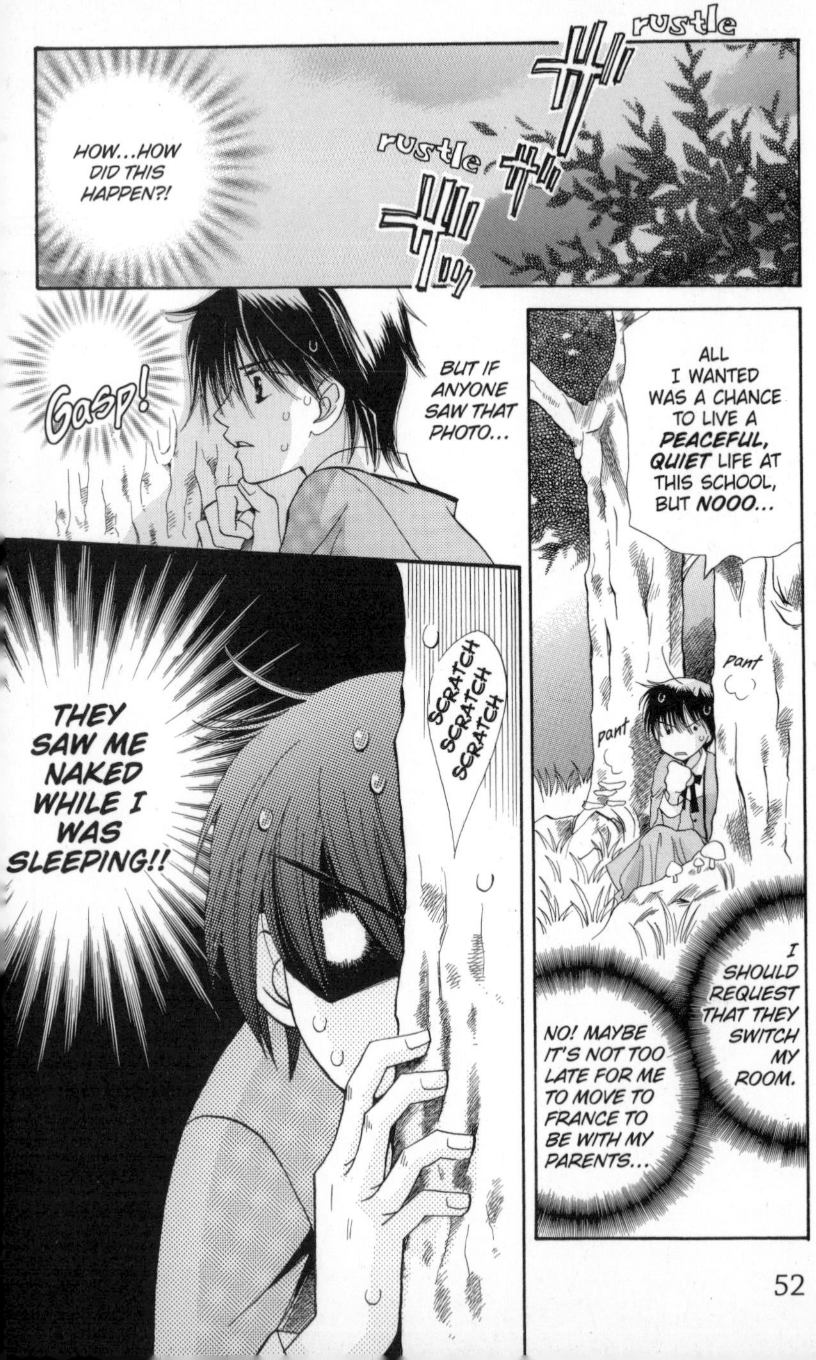
rustle
rustle
HOW...HOW DID THIS HAPPEN?!
ALL I WANTED WAS A CHANCE TO LIVE A **PEACEFUL, QUIET** LIFE AT THIS SCHOOL, BUT **NOOO...**
pant
pant
I SHOULD REQUEST THAT THEY SWITCH MY ROOM.
NO! MAYBE IT'S NOT TOO LATE FOR ME TO MOVE TO FRANCE TO BE WITH MY PARENTS...
Gasp!
BUT IF ANYONE SAW THAT PHOTO...
SCRATCH SCRATCH SCRATCH
THEY SAW ME NAKED WHILE I WAS SLEEPING!!

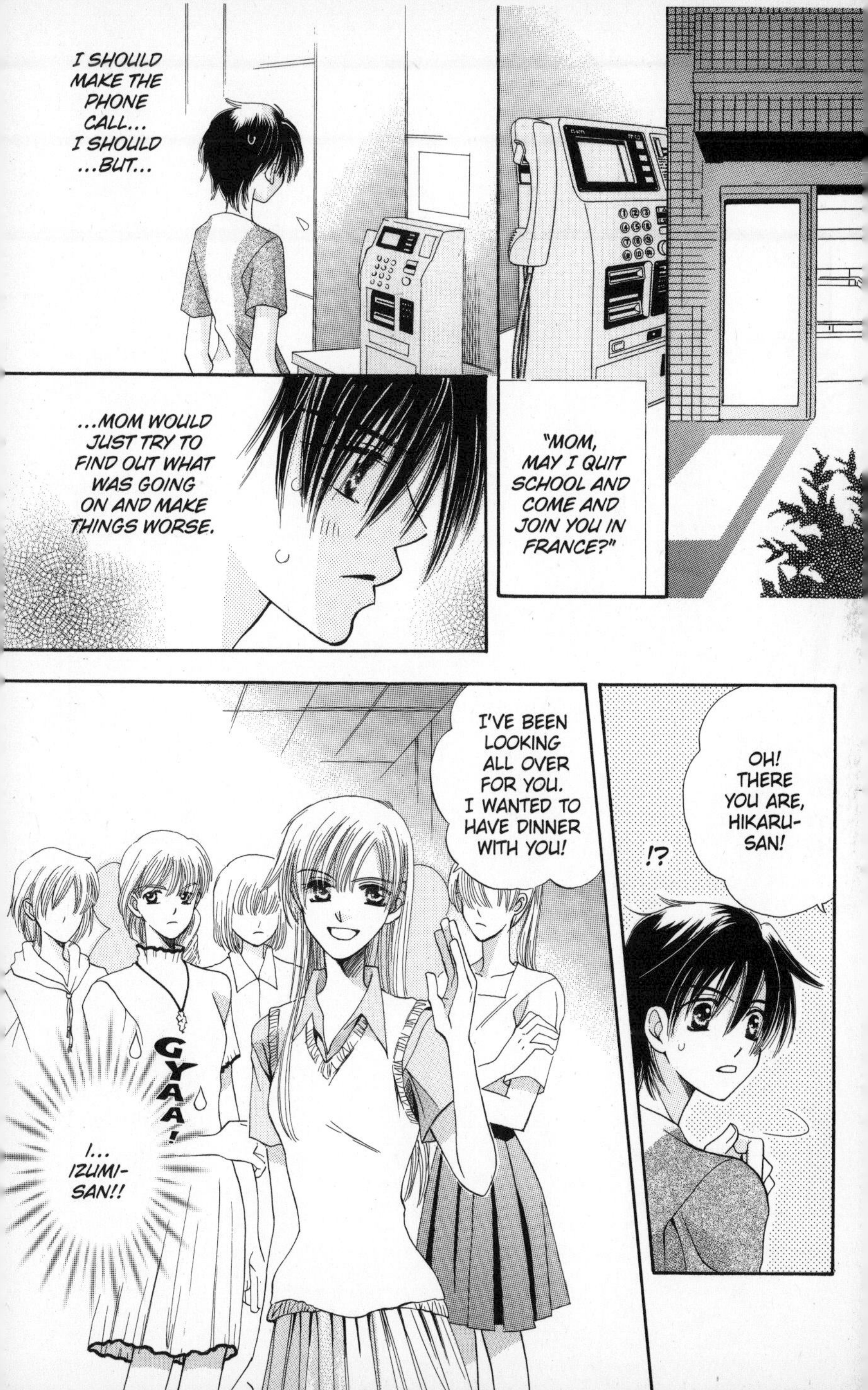
"MOM, MAY I QUIT SCHOOL AND COME AND JOIN YOU IN FRANCE?"
I SHOULD MAKE THE PHONE CALL... I SHOULD ...BUT...
...MOM WOULD JUST TRY TO FIND OUT WHAT WAS GOING ON AND MAKE THINGS WORSE.
OH! THERE YOU ARE, HIKARU-SAN!
!?
I'VE BEEN LOOKING ALL OVER FOR YOU. I WANTED TO HAVE DINNER WITH YOU!
GYAA!
I... IZUMI-SAN!!

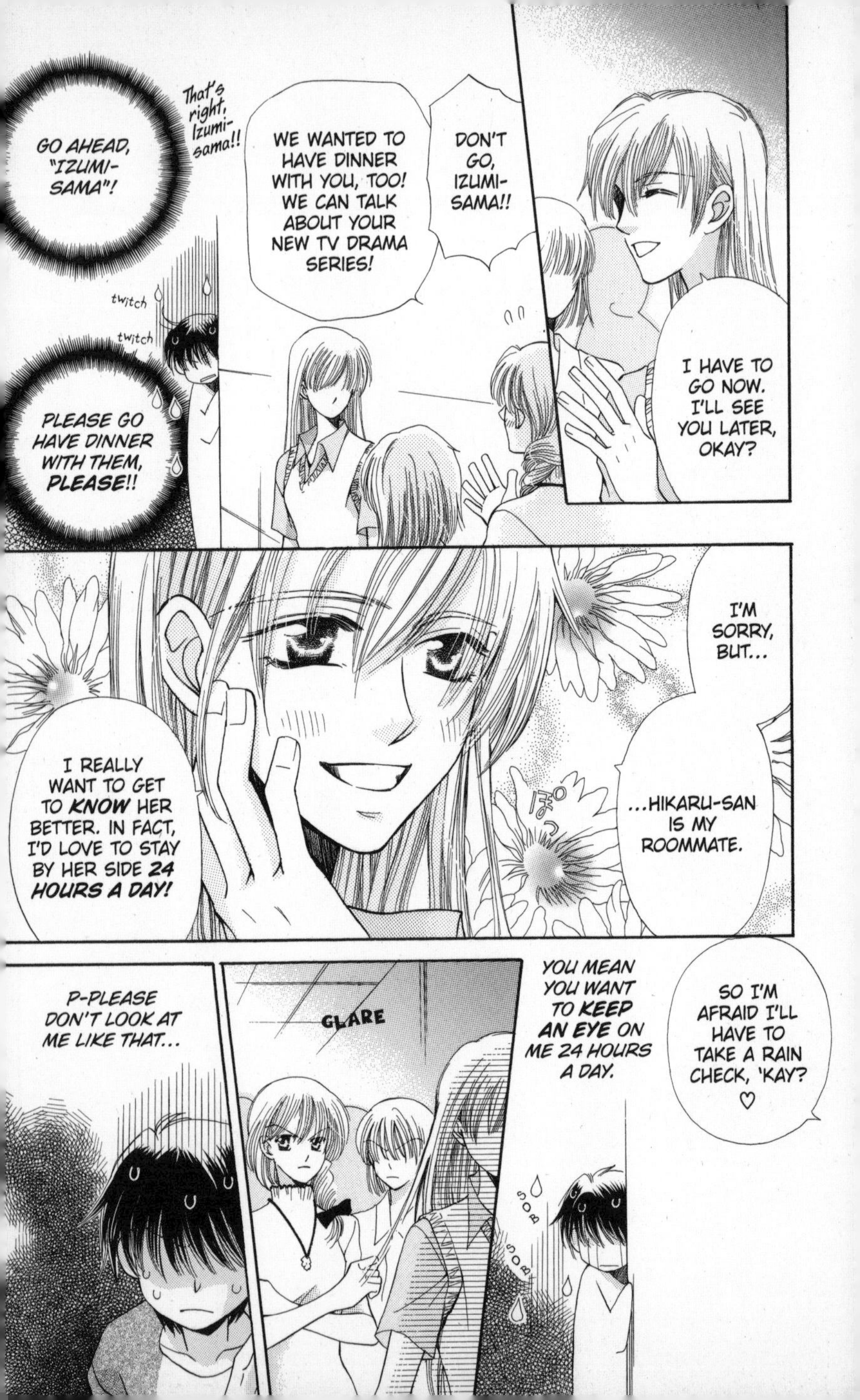
I HAVE TO GO NOW. I'LL SEE YOU LATER, OKAY?
DON'T GO, IZUMI-SAMA!!
WE WANTED TO HAVE DINNER WITH YOU, TOO! WE CAN TALK ABOUT YOUR NEW TV DRAMA SERIES!
That's right, Izumi-sama!!
GO AHEAD, "IZUMI-SAMA"!
twitch
twitch
PLEASE GO HAVE DINNER WITH THEM, **PLEASE**!!
I'M SORRY, BUT...
...HIKARU-SAN IS MY ROOMMATE.
ぽっ
I REALLY WANT TO GET TO **KNOW** HER BETTER. IN FACT, I'D LOVE TO STAY BY HER SIDE **24 HOURS A DAY!**
SO I'M AFRAID I'LL HAVE TO TAKE A RAIN CHECK, 'KAY? ♡
YOU MEAN YOU WANT TO **KEEP AN EYE** ON ME 24 HOURS A DAY.
SOB
SOB
GLARE
P-PLEASE DON'T LOOK AT ME LIKE THAT...

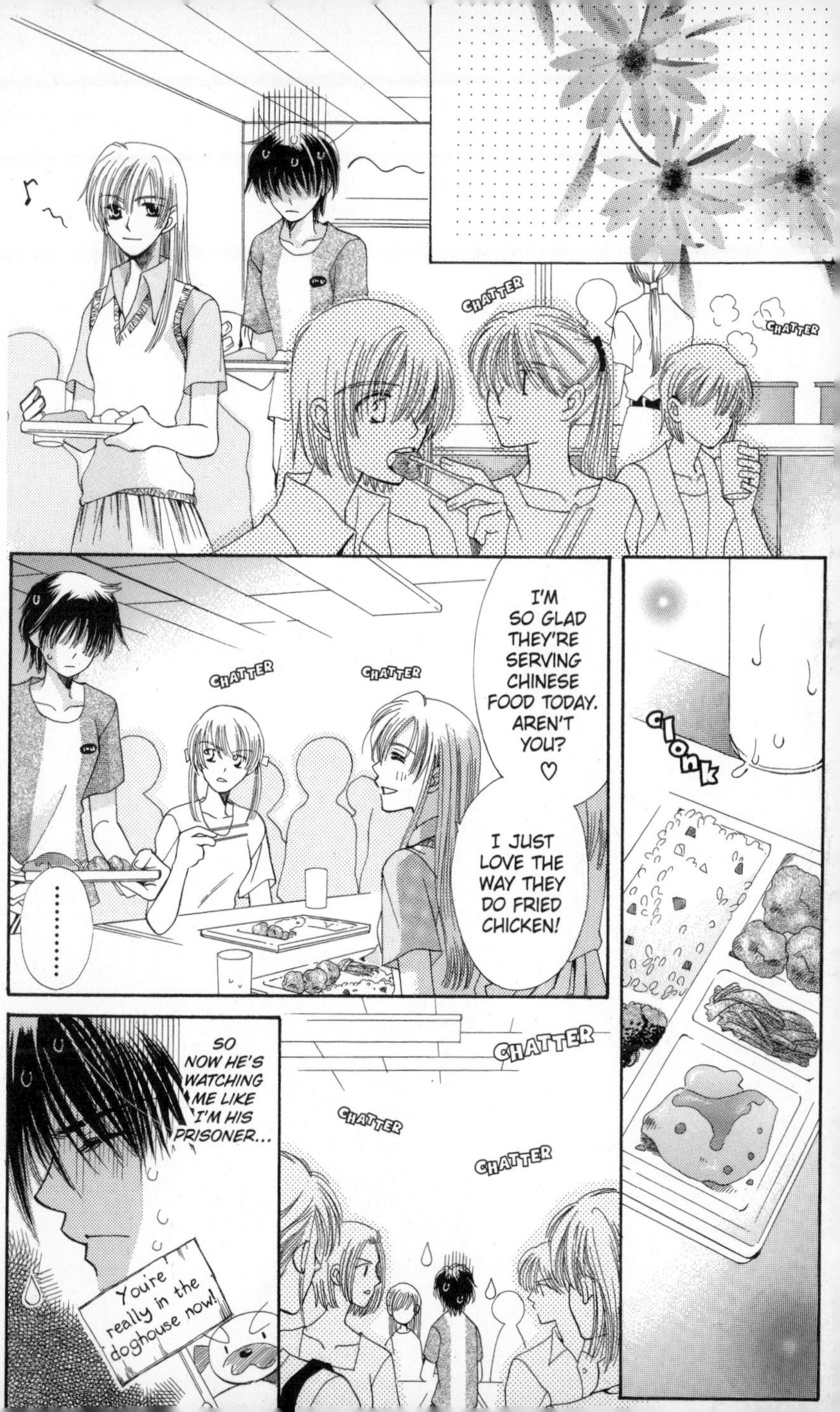
CHATTER
CHATTER
CHATTER
CHATTER
I'M SO GLAD THEY'RE SERVING CHINESE FOOD TODAY. AREN'T YOU? ♡
I JUST LOVE THE WAY THEY DO FRIED CHICKEN!
......
CLONK
CHATTER
SO NOW HE'S WATCHING ME LIKE I'M HIS PRISONER...
CHATTER
CHATTER
You're really in the doghouse now!

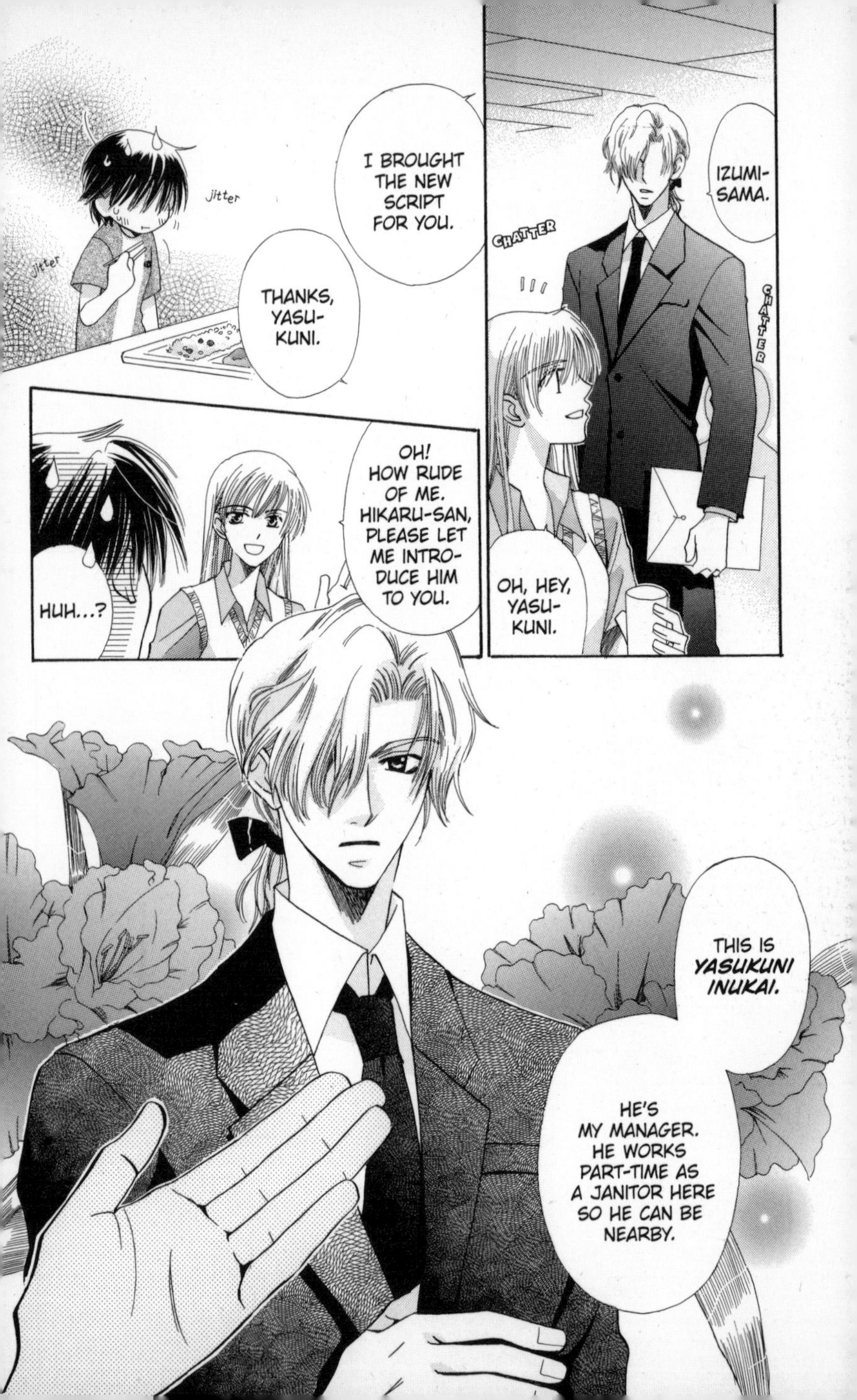
IZUMI-SAMA.
CHATTER
CHATTER
OH, HEY, YASU-KUNI.
I BROUGHT THE NEW SCRIPT FOR YOU.
jitter
THANKS, YASU-KUNI.
jitter
OH! HOW RUDE OF ME. HIKARU-SAN, PLEASE LET ME INTRO-DUCE HIM TO YOU.
HUH...?
THIS IS *YASUKUNI INUKAI.*
HE'S MY MANAGER. HE WORKS PART-TIME AS A JANITOR HERE SO HE CAN BE NEARBY.

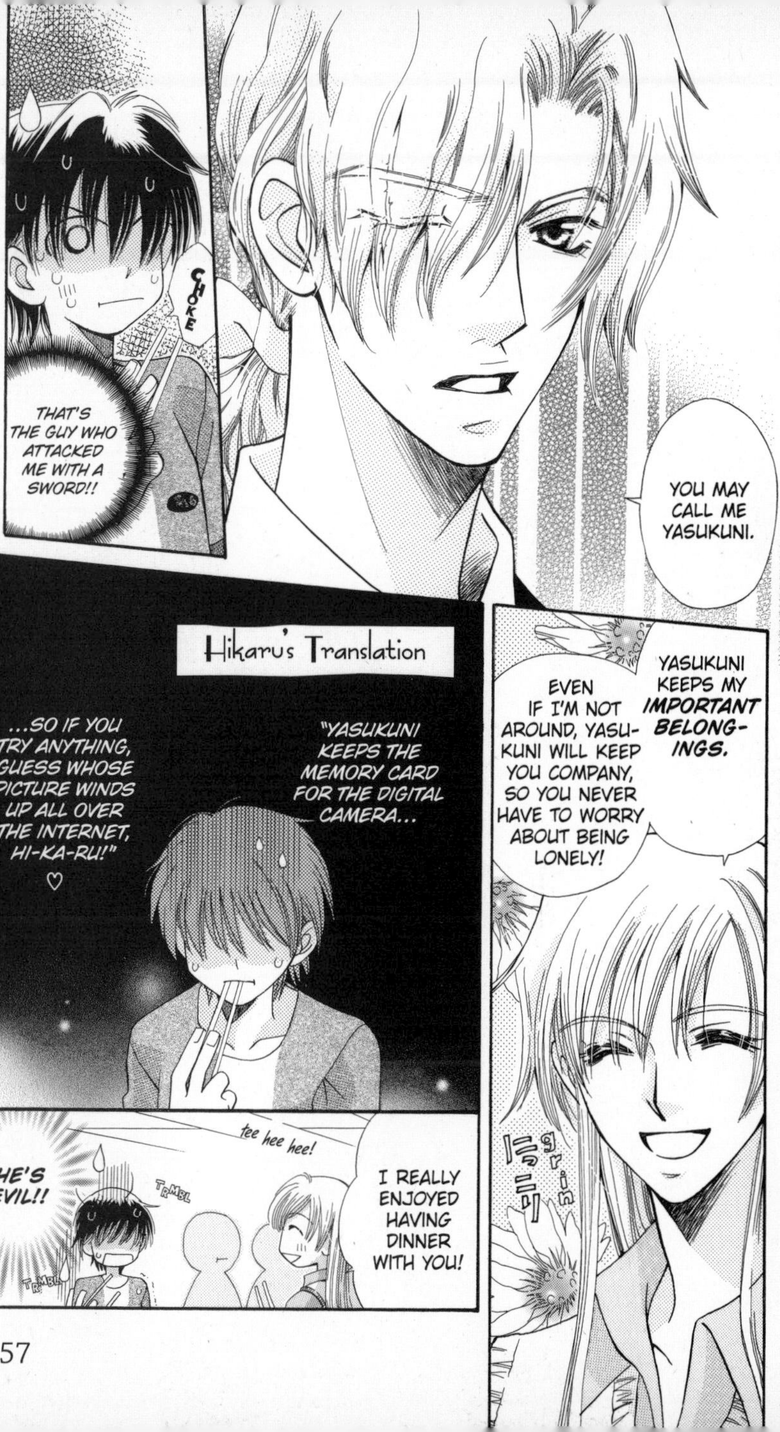
YOU MAY CALL ME YASUKUNI.
CHOKE
THAT'S THE GUY WHO ATTACKED ME WITH A SWORD!!
YASUKUNI KEEPS MY ***IMPORTANT BELONGINGS.***
EVEN IF I'M NOT AROUND, YASUKUNI WILL KEEP YOU COMPANY, SO YOU NEVER HAVE TO WORRY ABOUT BEING LONELY!
grin
Hikaru's Translation
"YASUKUNI KEEPS THE MEMORY CARD FOR THE DIGITAL CAMERA...
...SO IF YOU TRY ANYTHING, GUESS WHOSE PICTURE WINDS UP ALL OVER THE INTERNET, HI-KA-RU!" ♡
I REALLY ENJOYED HAVING DINNER WITH YOU!
tee hee hee!
TRMBL
HE'S EVIL!!
TRMBL

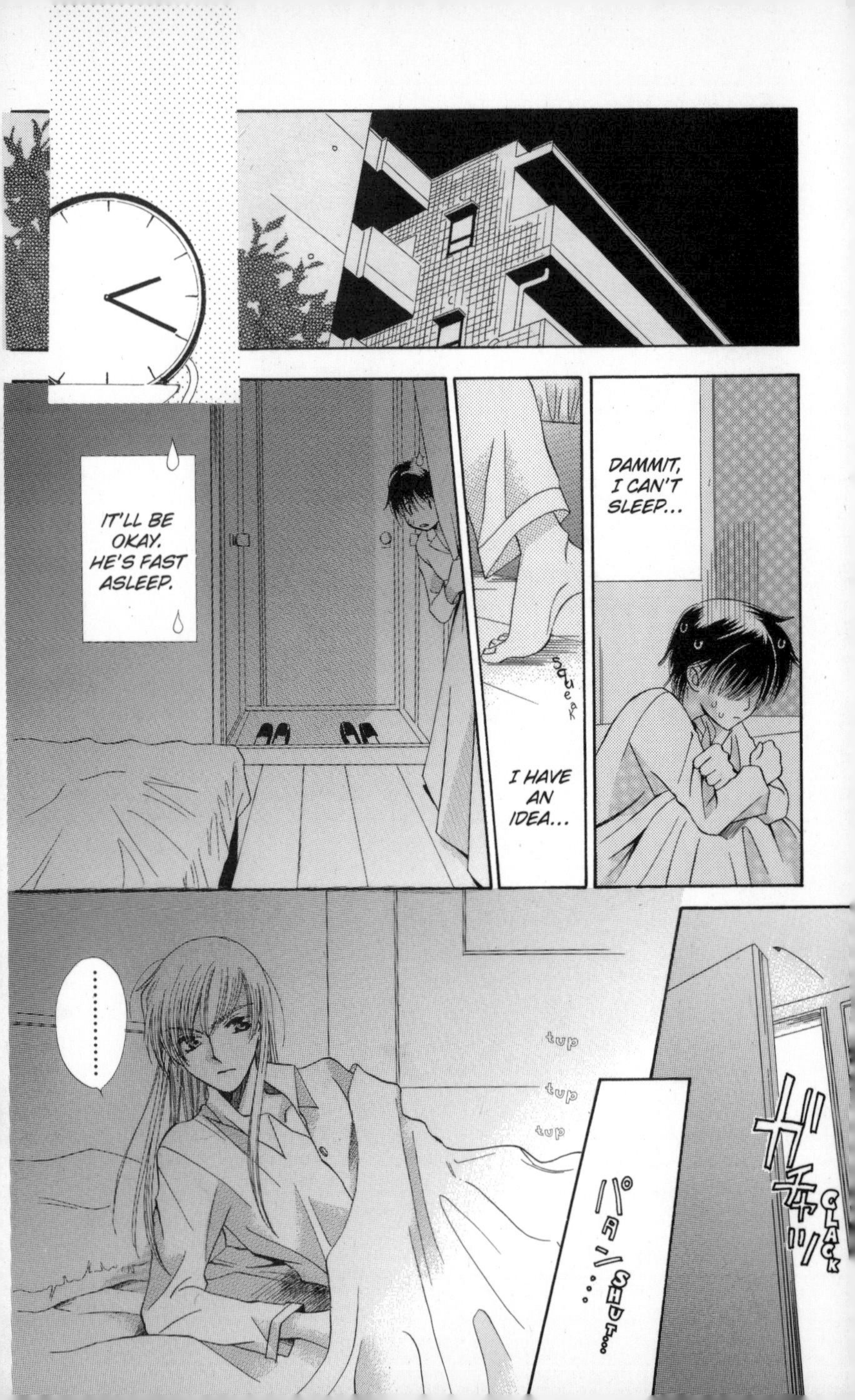
DAMMIT, I CAN'T SLEEP...
squeak
I HAVE AN IDEA...
IT'LL BE OKAY. HE'S FAST ASLEEP.
ガチャッ
CLACK
パタン…
SHUT...
tup
tup
tup
......

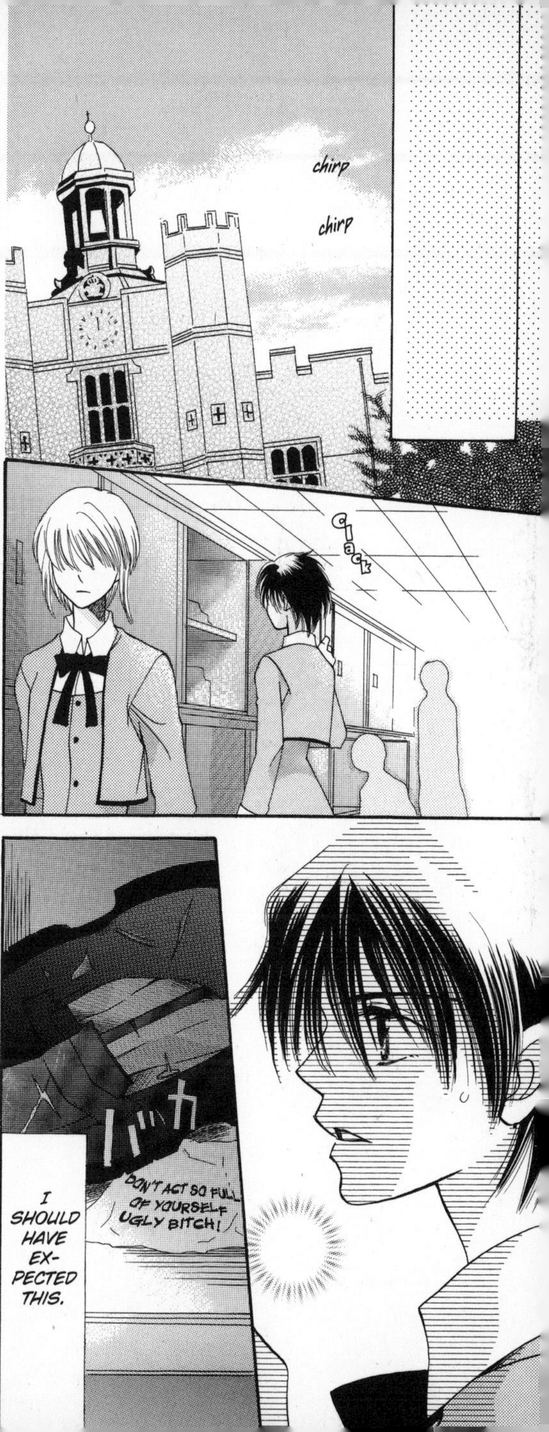
chirp
chirp
clack
DON'T ACT SO FULL OF YOURSELF UGLY BITCH!
I SHOULD HAVE EX-PECTED THIS.

My Favorite Things these days...
Part 1

...Are definitely imported snacks!

A friend of mine, "H," who works as my assistant, finds these snacks for me from somewhere. (Thank you!) "H" and I love orange-flavored snacks. At the moment we are very much into Knusperli Super Crunch. The name of it is difficult to remember. It's an orange and yogurt flavored cereal. It's super good!

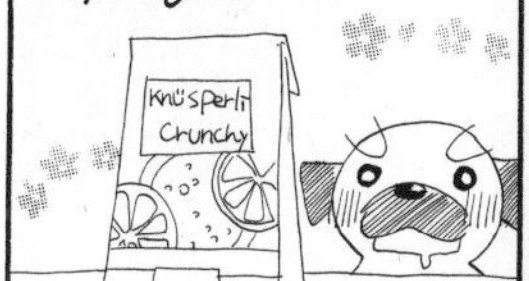
Knüsperli Crunchy

The cereal is made in Austria. Pour milk over it and it tastes the best while the cereal is still crunchy.

Apparently there are other flavors available, such as chocolate, white chocolate, banana, and strawberry.

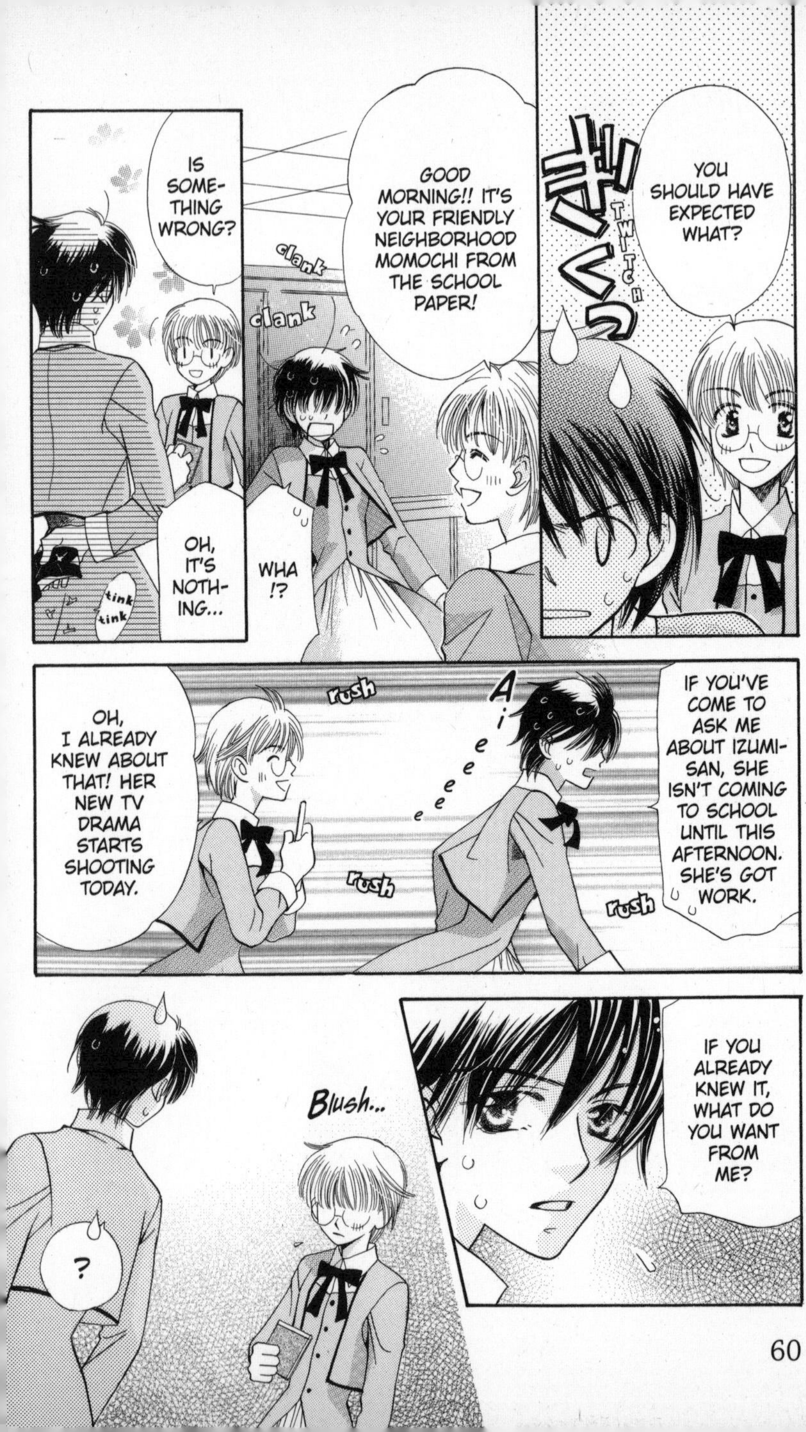
YOU SHOULD HAVE EXPECTED WHAT?
ぎくっ
TWITCH
GOOD MORNING!! IT'S YOUR FRIENDLY NEIGHBORHOOD MOMOCHI FROM THE SCHOOL PAPER!
clank
clank
WHA !?
IS SOME-THING WRONG?
OH, IT'S NOTH-ING...
tink
tink
IF YOU'VE COME TO ASK ME ABOUT IZUMI-SAN, SHE ISN'T COMING TO SCHOOL UNTIL THIS AFTERNOON. SHE'S GOT WORK.
Aieeeeee
rush
rush
rush
OH, I ALREADY KNEW ABOUT THAT! HER NEW TV DRAMA STARTS SHOOTING TODAY.
IF YOU ALREADY KNEW IT, WHAT DO YOU WANT FROM ME?
Blush...
?

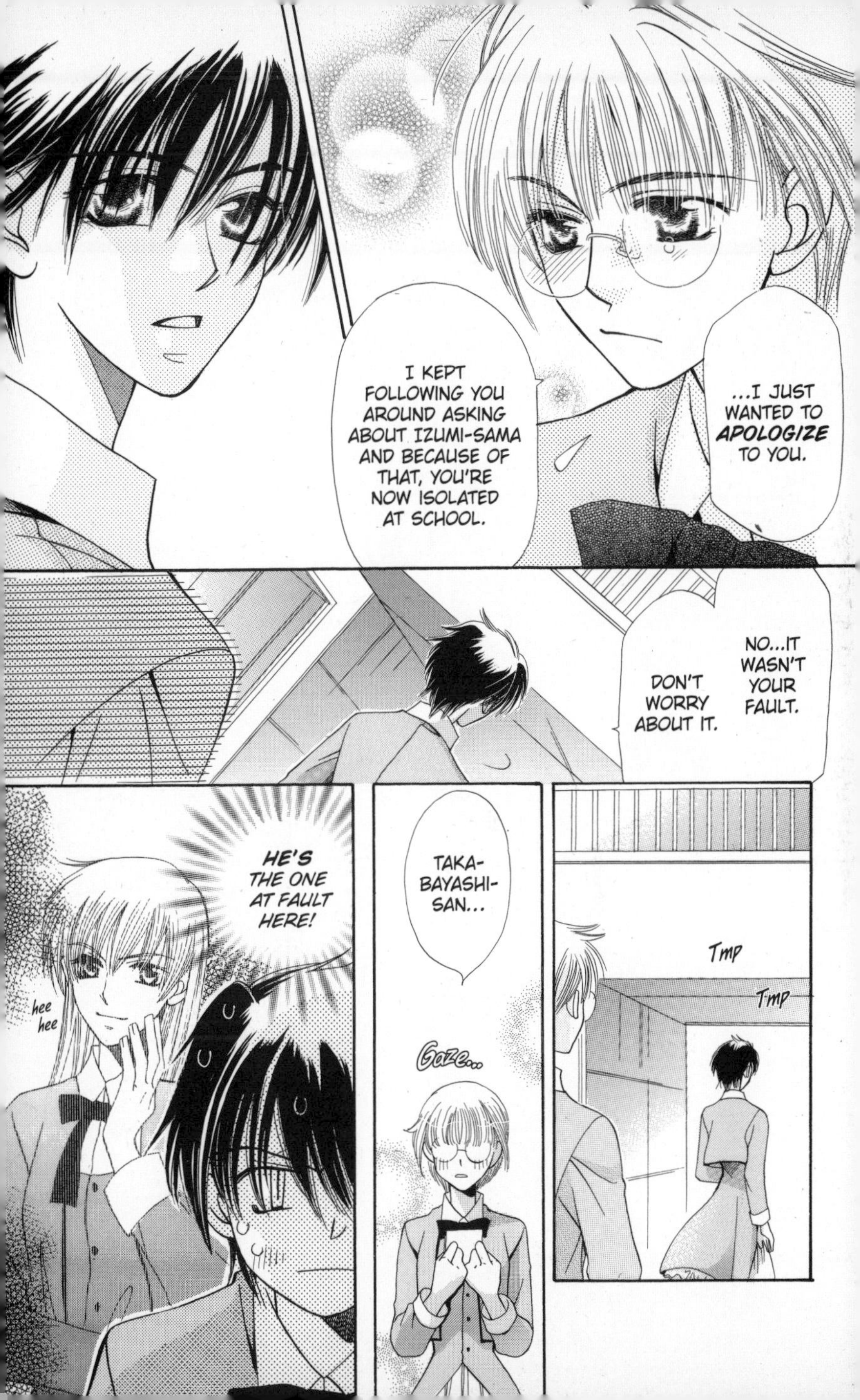
...I JUST WANTED TO **APOLOGIZE** TO YOU.
I KEPT FOLLOWING YOU AROUND ASKING ABOUT IZUMI-SAMA AND BECAUSE OF THAT, YOU'RE NOW ISOLATED AT SCHOOL.
NO...IT WASN'T YOUR FAULT.
DON'T WORRY ABOUT IT.
Tmp
Tmp
TAKA-BAYASHI-SAN...
Gaze...
HE'S THE ONE AT FAULT HERE!
hee hee

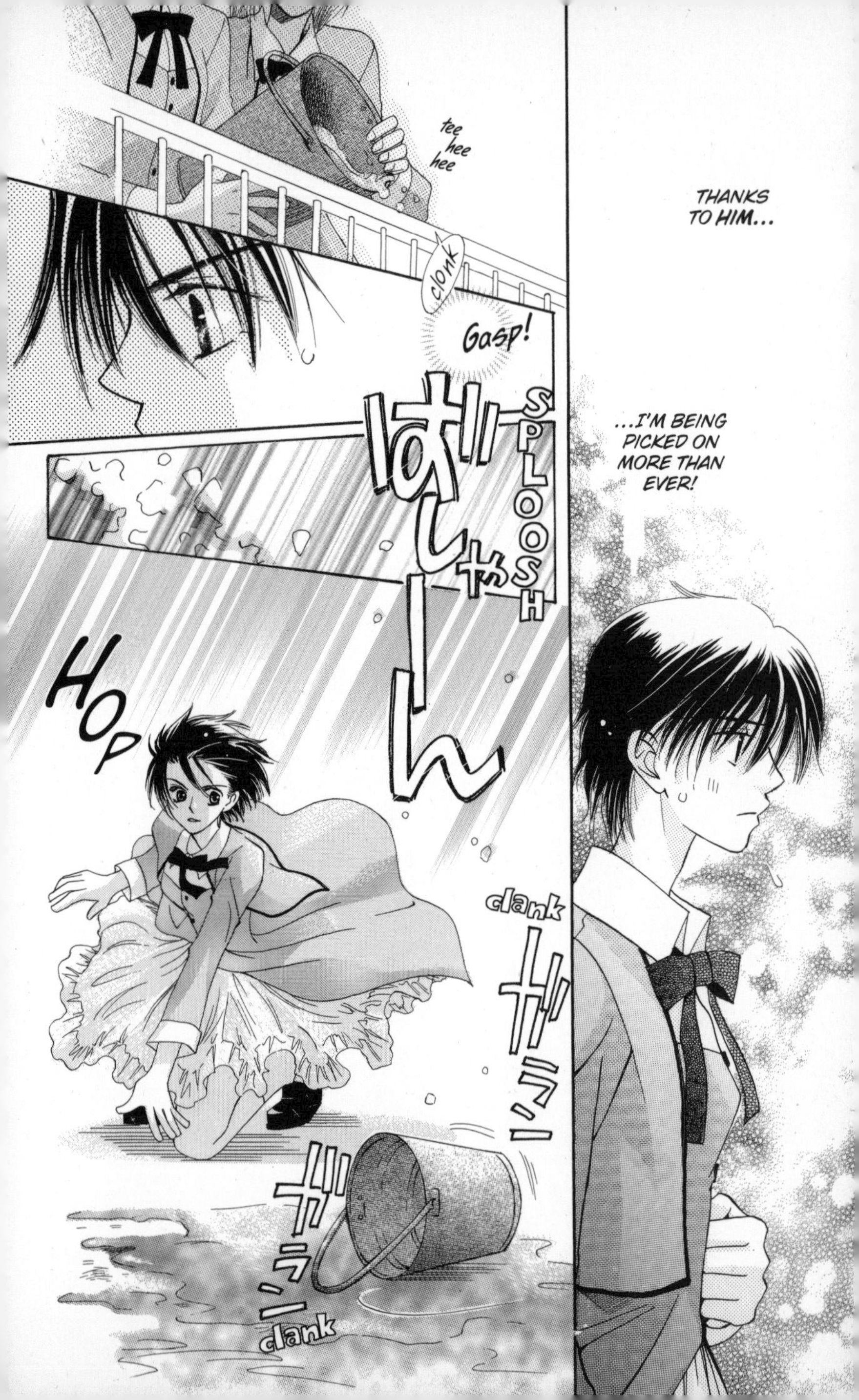
THANKS TO HIM...
...I'M BEING PICKED ON MORE THAN EVER!
tee hee hee
clonk
Gasp!
ばしゃーん
SPLOOSH
HOP
clank
ガラ〜ン
ガラ〜ン
clank

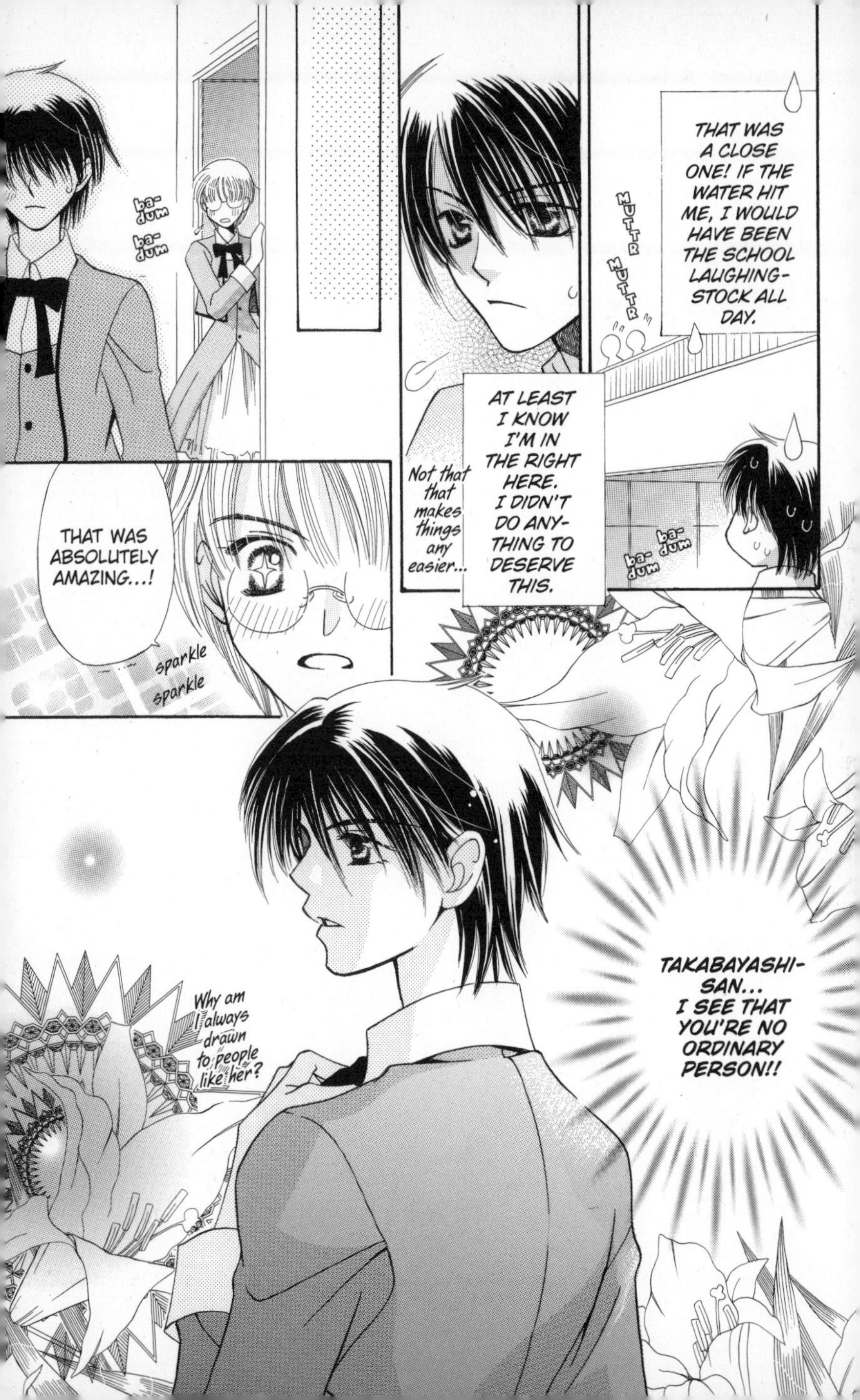
THAT WAS A CLOSE ONE! IF THE WATER HIT ME, I WOULD HAVE BEEN THE SCHOOL LAUGHING-STOCK ALL DAY.
MUTTR MUTTR
ba-dum ba-dum
AT LEAST I KNOW I'M IN THE RIGHT HERE. I DIDN'T DO ANYTHING TO DESERVE THIS.
Not that that makes things any easier...
ba-dum ba-dum
THAT WAS ABSOLUTELY AMAZING...!
sparkle sparkle
TAKABAYASHI-SAN... I SEE THAT YOU'RE NO ORDINARY PERSON!!
Why am I always drawn to people like her?

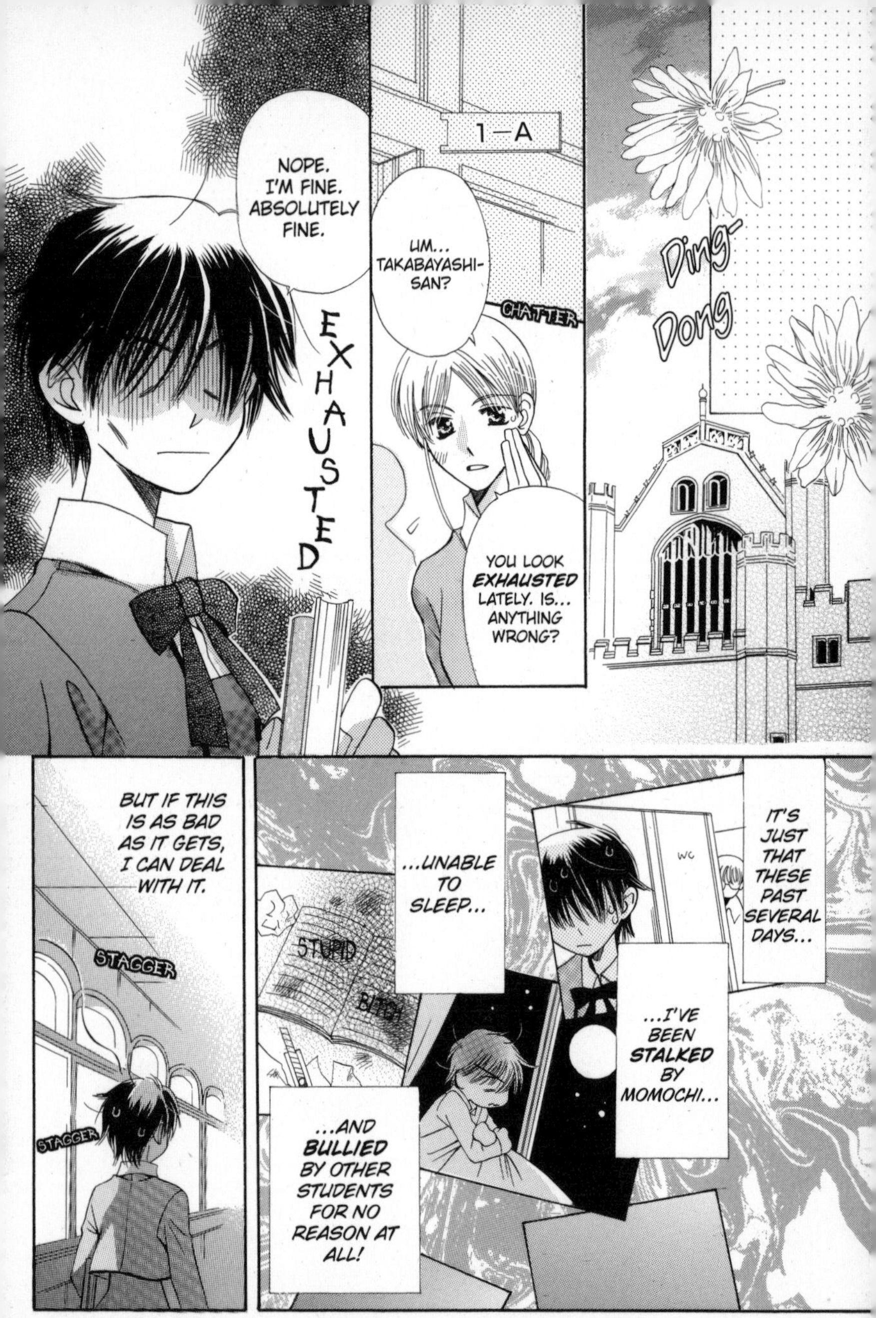
Ding-Dong
UM... TAKABAYASHI-SAN?
CHATTER
YOU LOOK EXHAUSTED LATELY. IS... ANYTHING WRONG?
1-A
NOPE. I'M FINE. ABSOLUTELY FINE.
EXHAUSTED
IT'S JUST THAT THESE PAST SEVERAL DAYS...
...I'VE BEEN STALKED BY MOMOCHI...
WC
...UNABLE TO SLEEP...
STUPID
BITCH
...AND BULLIED BY OTHER STUDENTS FOR NO REASON AT ALL!
BUT IF THIS IS AS BAD AS IT GETS, I CAN DEAL WITH IT.
STAGGER
STAGGER

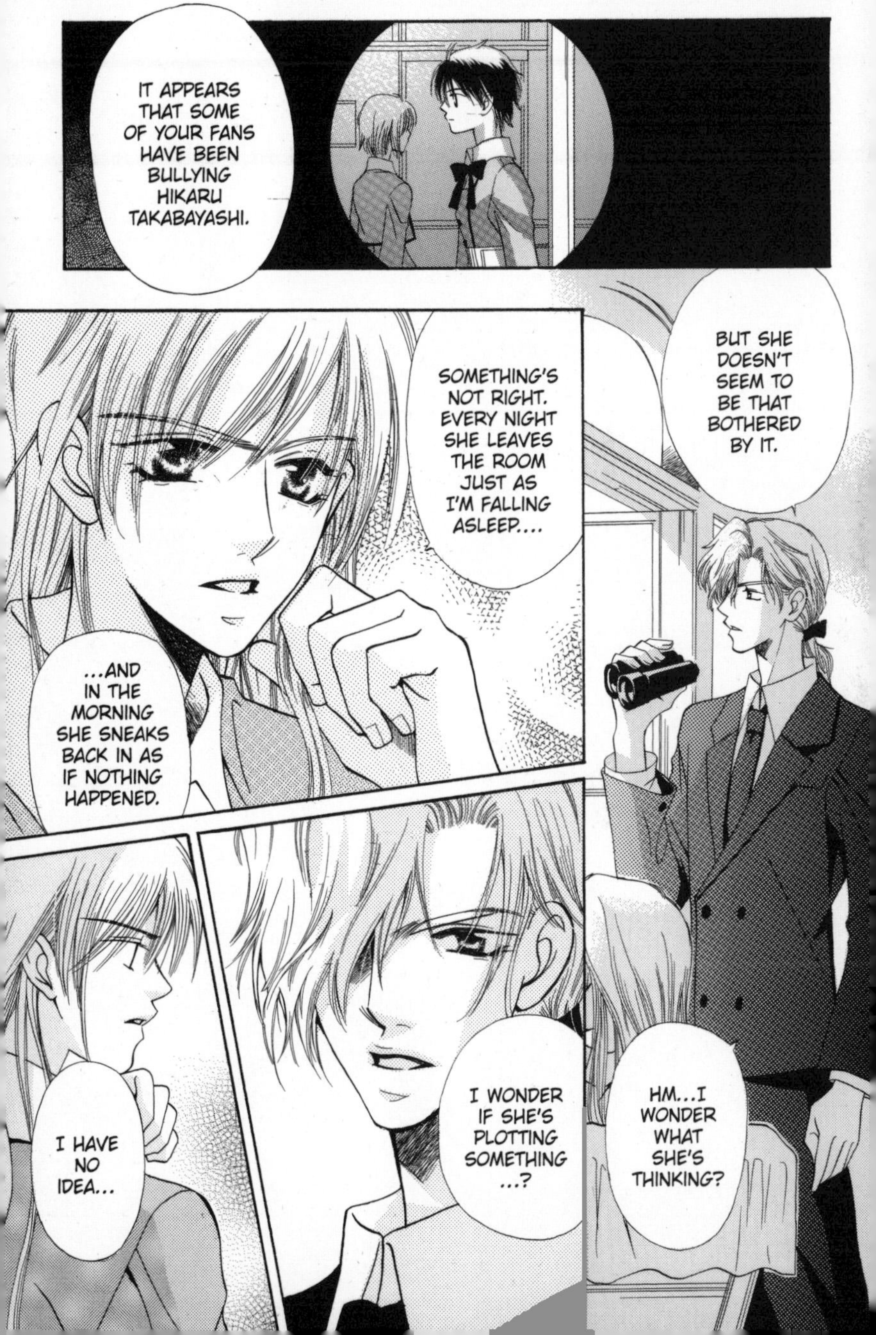
IT APPEARS THAT SOME OF YOUR FANS HAVE BEEN BULLYING HIKARU TAKABAYASHI.
BUT SHE DOESN'T SEEM TO BE THAT BOTHERED BY IT.
HM...I WONDER WHAT SHE'S THINKING?
SOMETHING'S NOT RIGHT. EVERY NIGHT SHE LEAVES THE ROOM JUST AS I'M FALLING ASLEEP....
...AND IN THE MORNING SHE SNEAKS BACK IN AS IF NOTHING HAPPENED.
I WONDER IF SHE'S PLOTTING SOMETHING ...?
I HAVE NO IDEA...

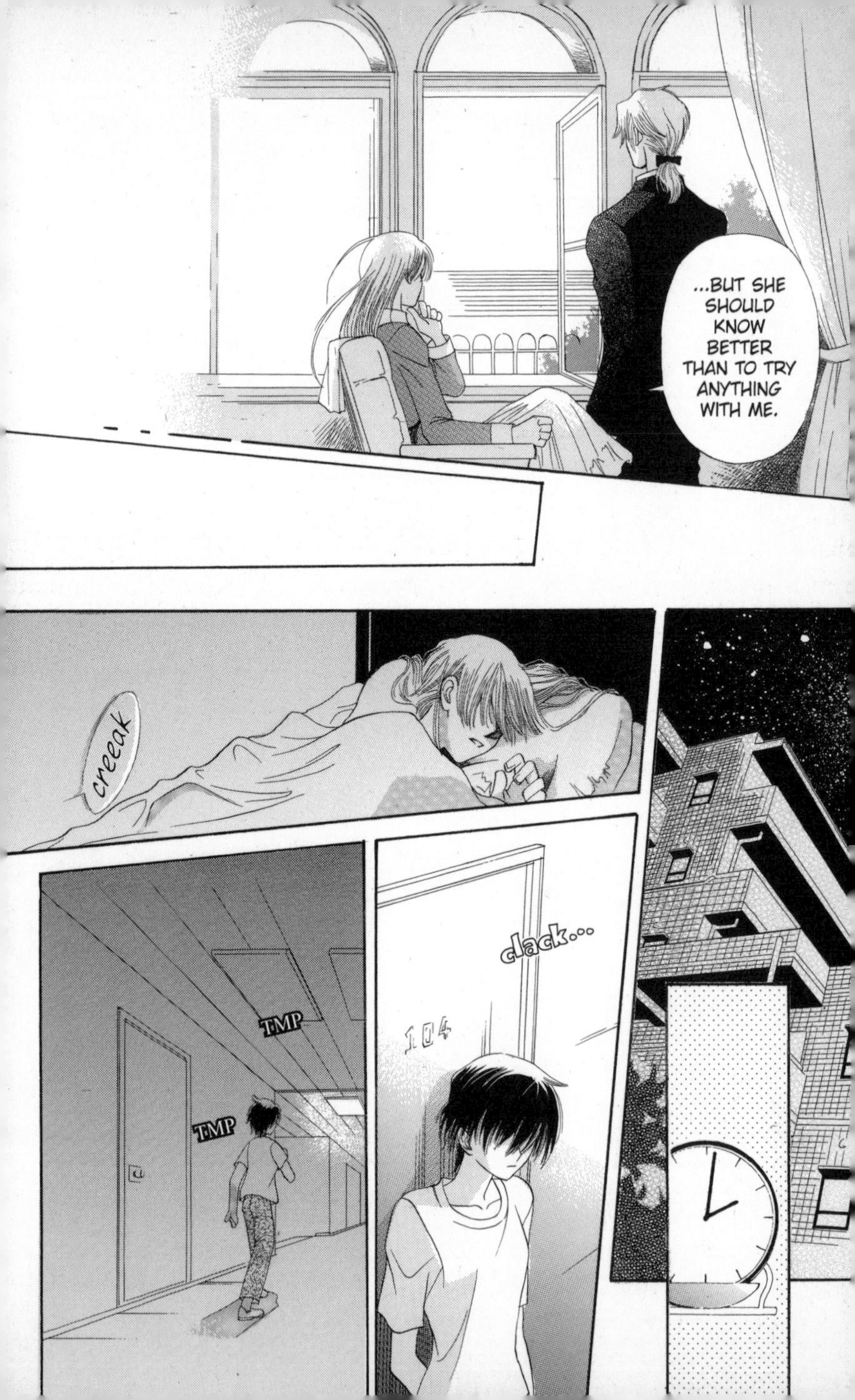
...BUT SHE SHOULD KNOW BETTER THAN TO TRY ANYTHING WITH ME.
creeak
clack...
104
TMP
TMP

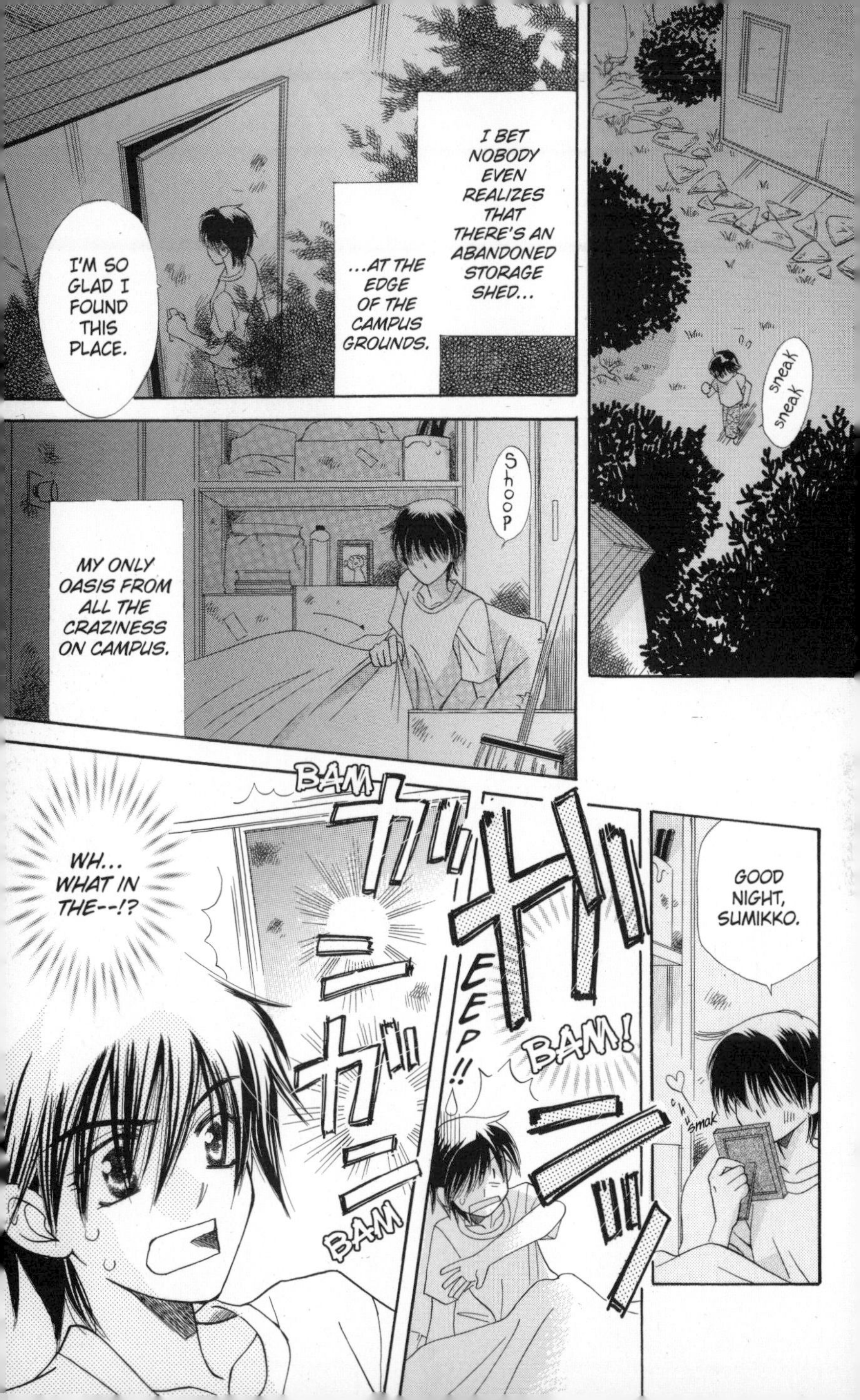
sneak sneak
I BET NOBODY EVEN REALIZES THAT THERE'S AN ABANDONED STORAGE SHED...
...AT THE EDGE OF THE CAMPUS GROUNDS.
I'M SO GLAD I FOUND THIS PLACE.
Shoop
MY ONLY OASIS FROM ALL THE CRAZINESS ON CAMPUS.
GOOD NIGHT, SUMIKKO.
chu smak
BAM
BAM!
EEP!!
WH... WHAT IN THE--!?
BAM

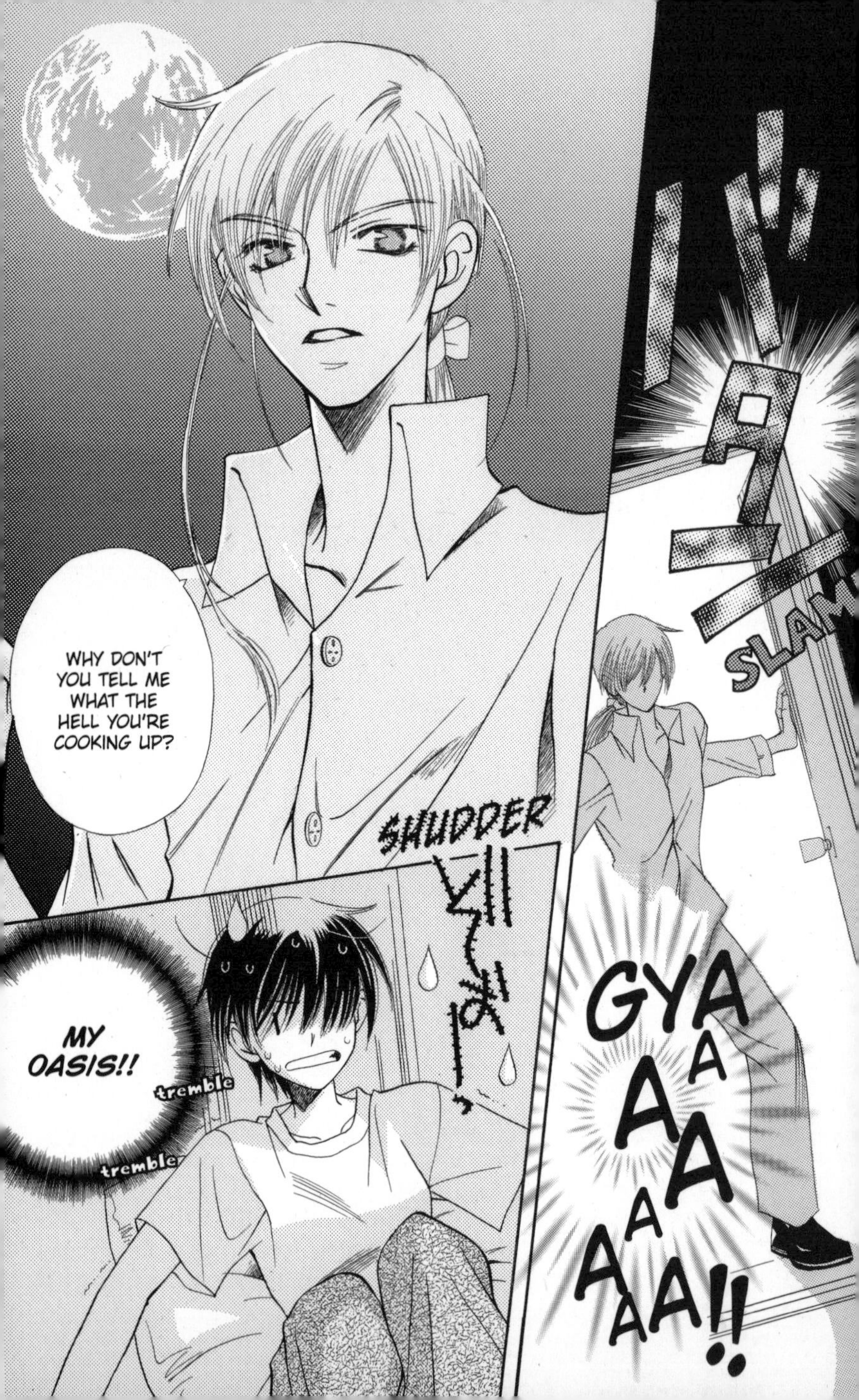
SLAM
GYAAAAAAAAA!!
WHY DON'T YOU TELL ME WHAT THE HELL YOU'RE COOKING UP?
SHUDDER
MY OASIS!!
tremble
tremble

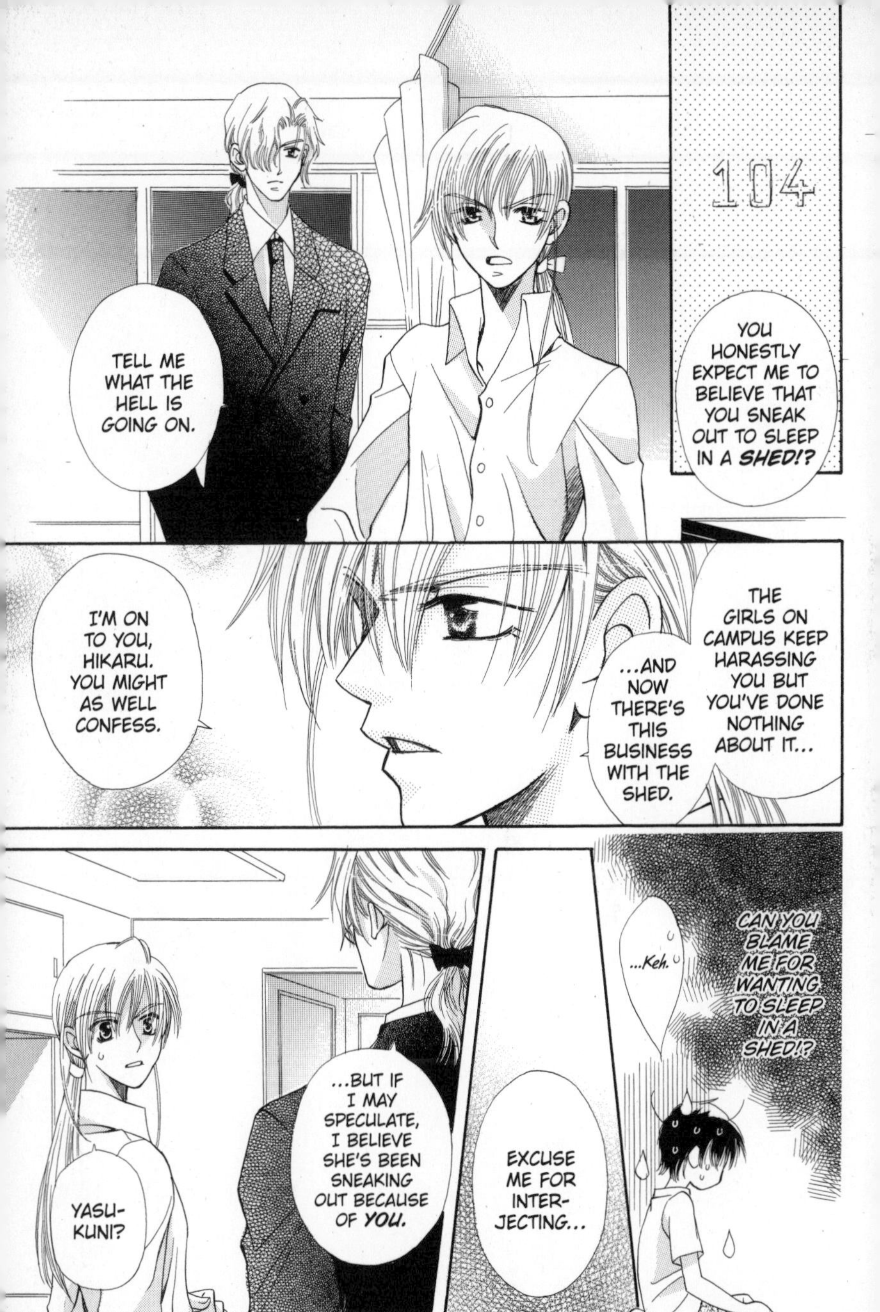
104
YOU HONESTLY EXPECT ME TO BELIEVE THAT YOU SNEAK OUT TO SLEEP IN A *SHED!?*
TELL ME WHAT THE HELL IS GOING ON.
THE GIRLS ON CAMPUS KEEP HARASSING YOU BUT YOU'VE DONE NOTHING ABOUT IT...
...AND NOW THERE'S THIS BUSINESS WITH THE SHED.
I'M ON TO YOU, HIKARU. YOU MIGHT AS WELL CONFESS.
CAN YOU BLAME ME FOR WANTING TO SLEEP IN A SHED!?
...Keh.
EXCUSE ME FOR INTER-JECTING...
...BUT IF I MAY SPECULATE, I BELIEVE SHE'S BEEN SNEAKING OUT BECAUSE OF *YOU.*
YASU-KUNI?

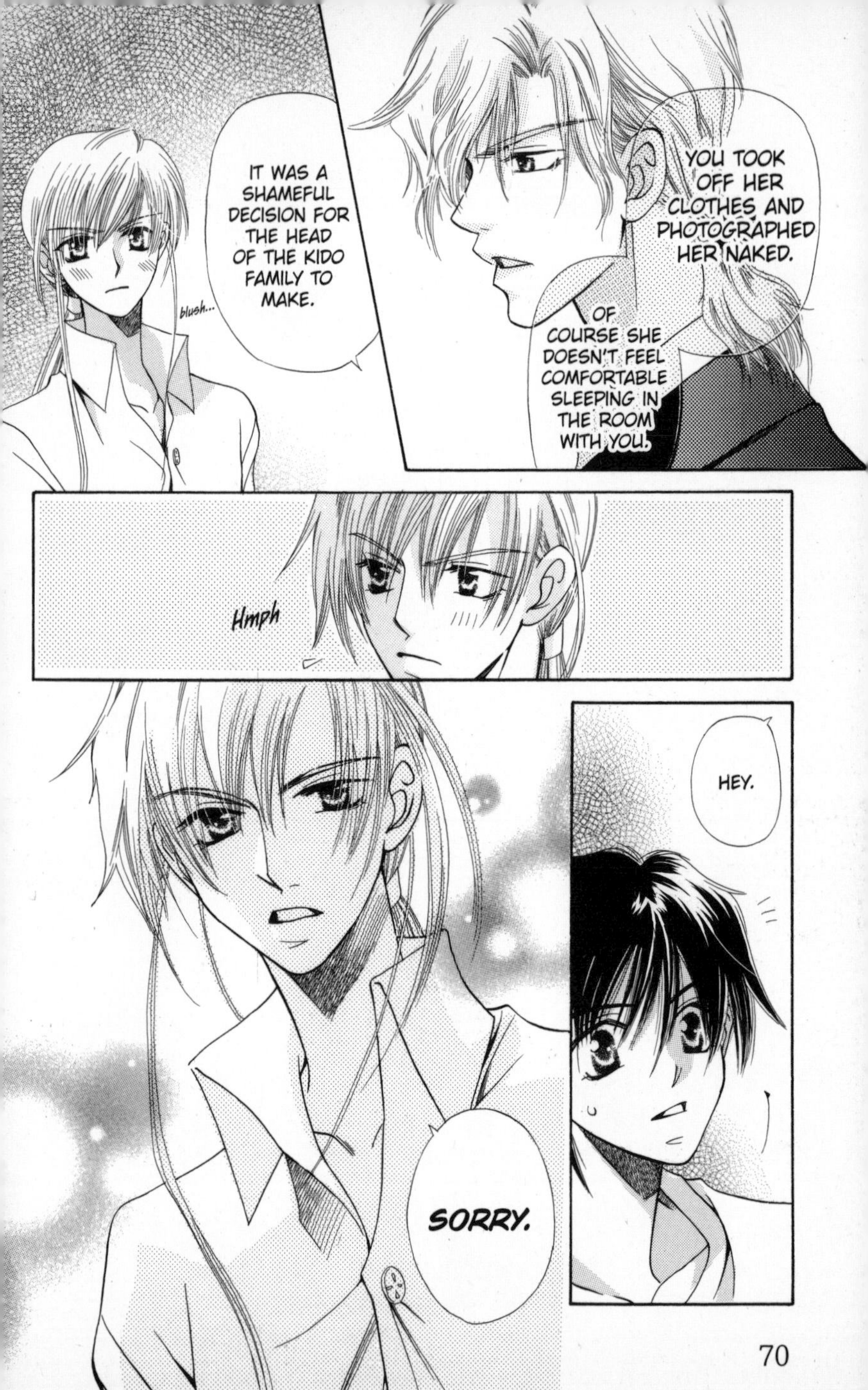
YOU TOOK OFF HER CLOTHES AND PHOTOGRAPHED HER NAKED.
OF COURSE SHE DOESN'T FEEL COMFORTABLE SLEEPING IN THE ROOM WITH YOU.
IT WAS A SHAMEFUL DECISION FOR THE HEAD OF THE KIDO FAMILY TO MAKE.
blush...
Hmph
HEY.
SORRY.

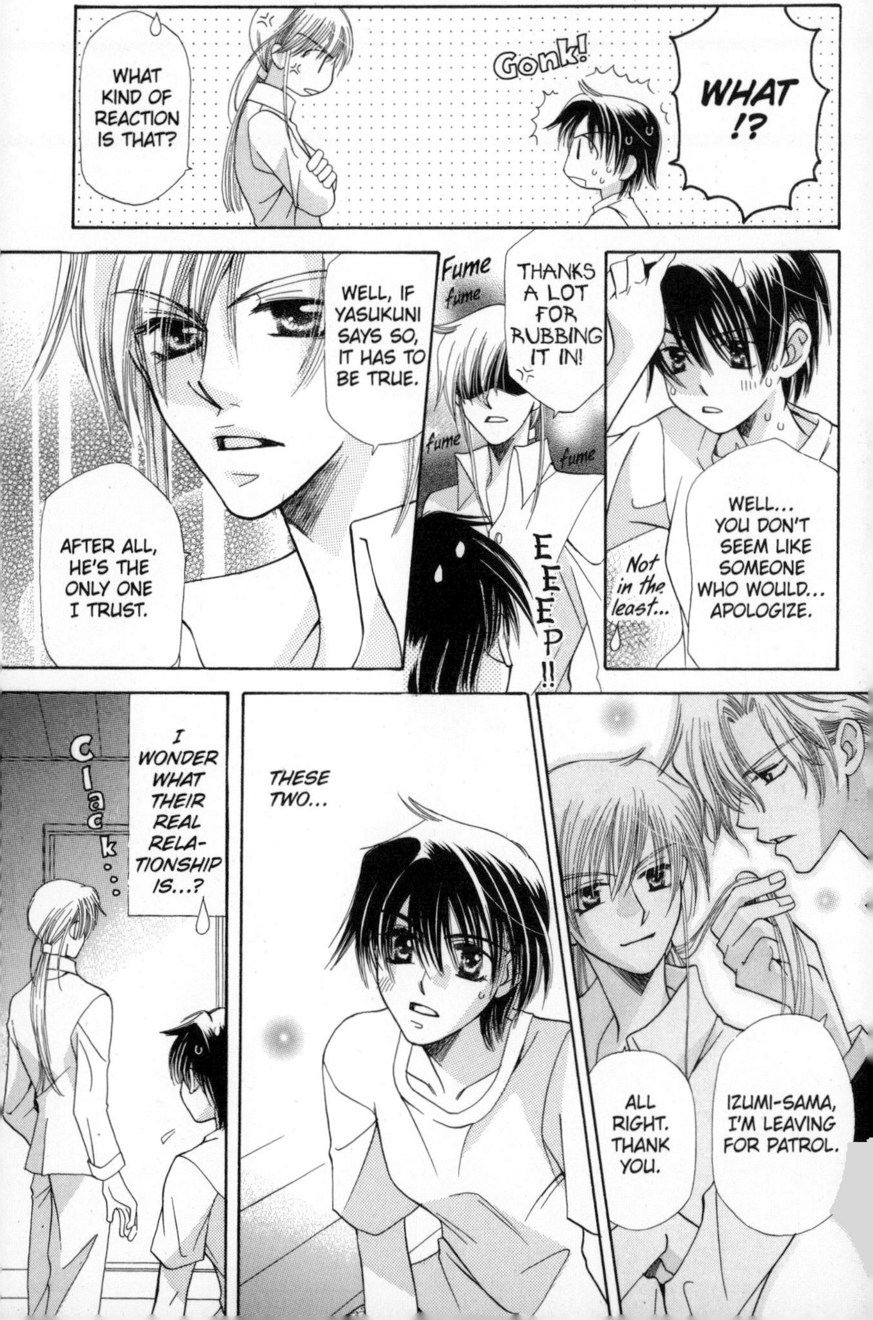
WHAT !?
Gonk!
WHAT KIND OF REACTION IS THAT?
WELL... YOU DON'T SEEM LIKE SOMEONE WHO WOULD... APOLOGIZE.
Not in the least...
THANKS A LOT FOR RUBBING IT IN!
Fume fume
fume
fume
EEEEP!!
WELL, IF YASUKUNI SAYS SO, IT HAS TO BE TRUE.
AFTER ALL, HE'S THE ONLY ONE I TRUST.
IZUMI-SAMA, I'M LEAVING FOR PATROL.
ALL RIGHT. THANK YOU.
THESE TWO...
I WONDER WHAT THEIR REAL RELATIONSHIP IS...?
Clack...

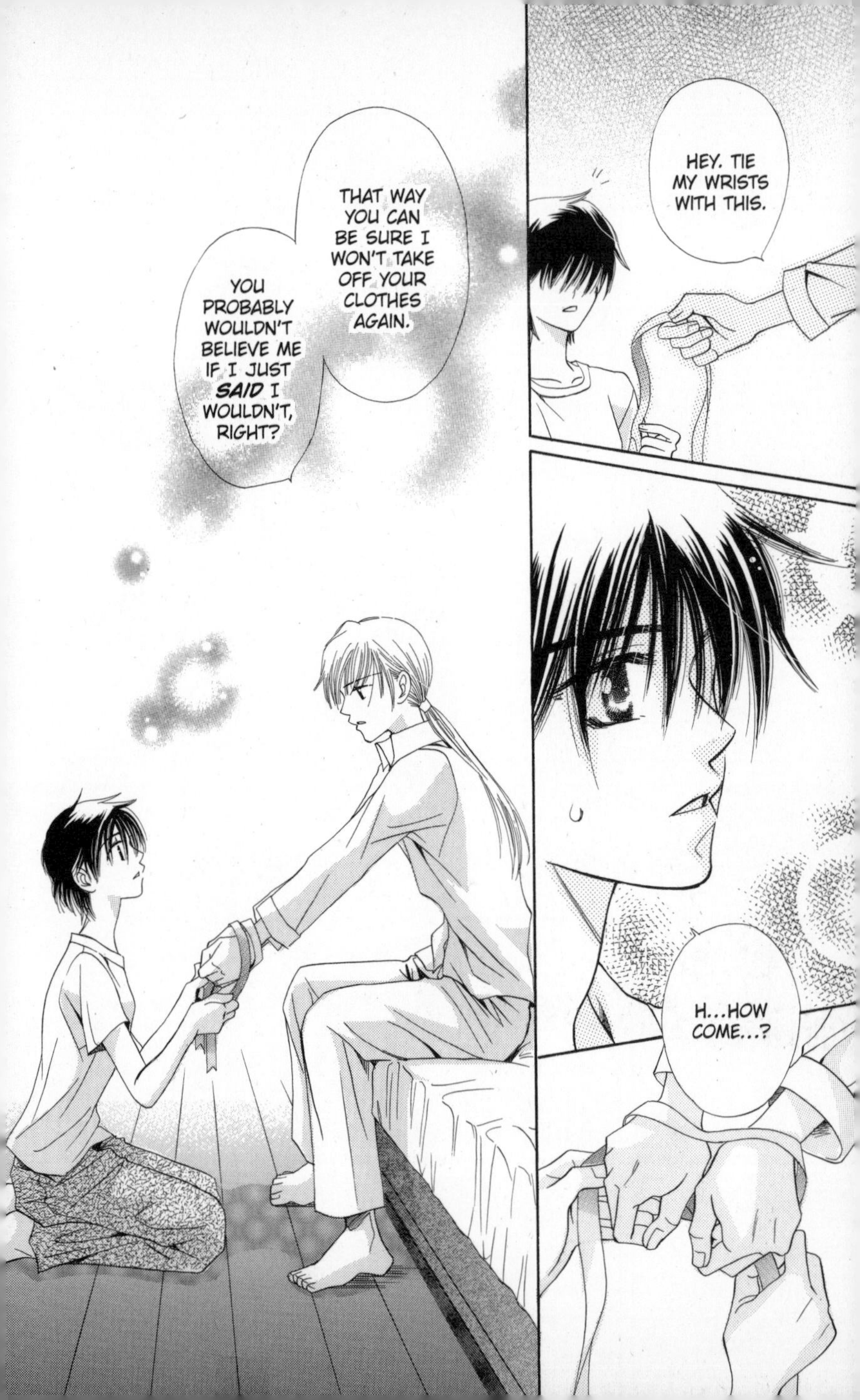
HEY. TIE MY WRISTS WITH THIS.
H...HOW COME...?
THAT WAY YOU CAN BE SURE I WON'T TAKE OFF YOUR CLOTHES AGAIN.
YOU PROBABLY WOULDN'T BELIEVE ME IF I JUST *SAID* I WOULDN'T, RIGHT?

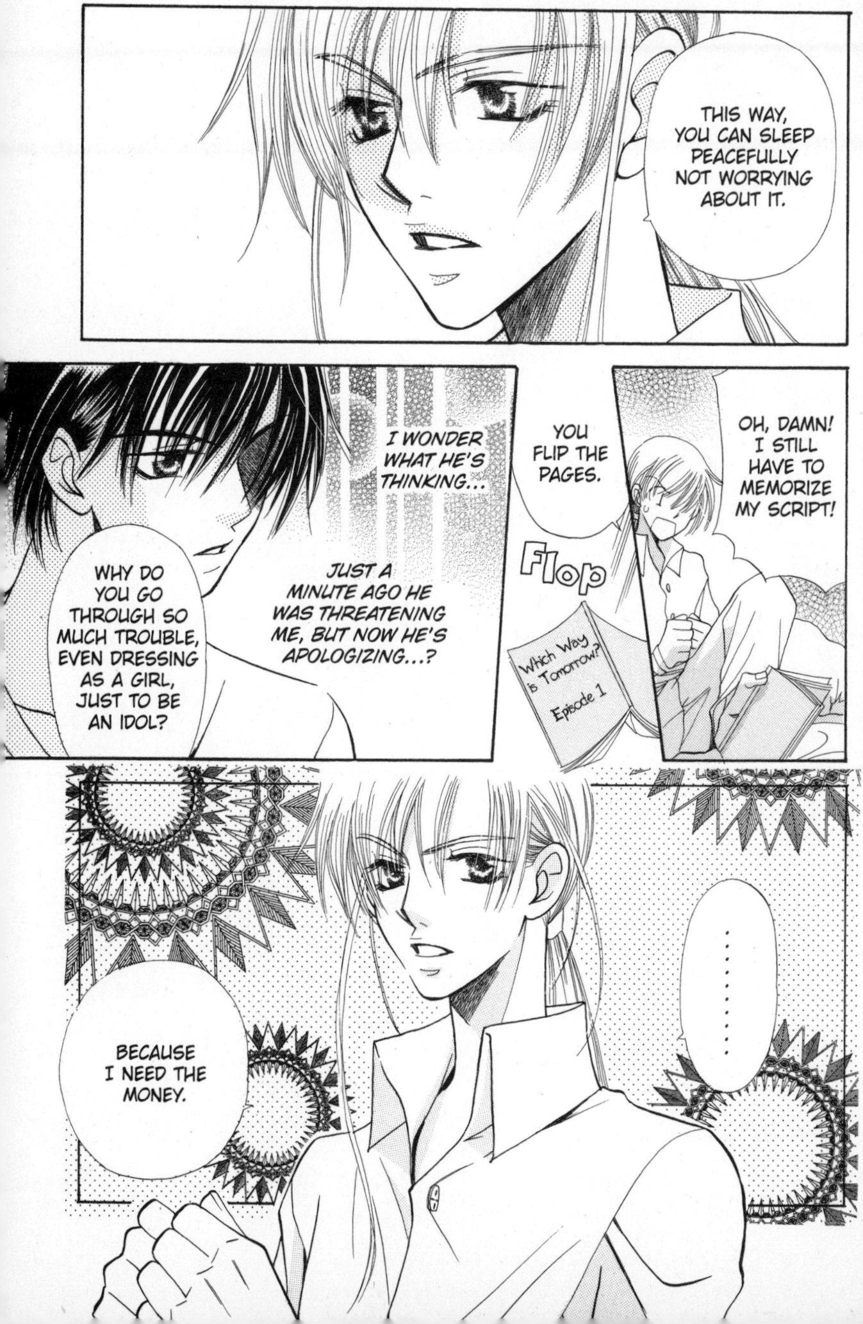
THIS WAY, YOU CAN SLEEP PEACEFULLY NOT WORRYING ABOUT IT.
OH, DAMN! I STILL HAVE TO MEMORIZE MY SCRIPT!
YOU FLIP THE PAGES.
Flop
Which Way is Tomorrow? Episode 1
I WONDER WHAT HE'S THINKING...
JUST A MINUTE AGO HE WAS THREATENING ME, BUT NOW HE'S APOLOGIZING...?
WHY DO YOU GO THROUGH SO MUCH TROUBLE, EVEN DRESSING AS A GIRL, JUST TO BE AN IDOL?
....
BECAUSE I NEED THE MONEY.

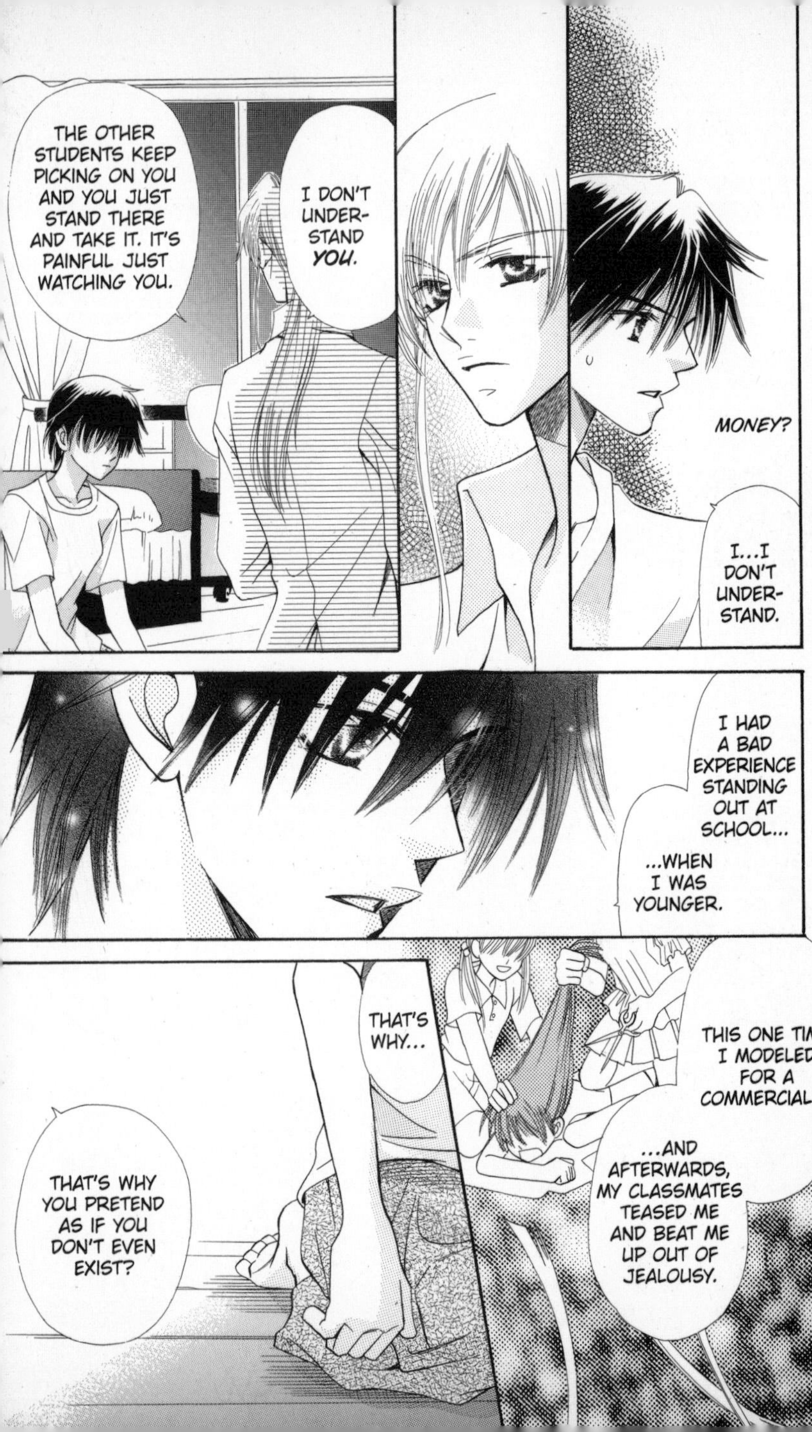
MONEY?
I...I DON'T UNDER-STAND.
I DON'T UNDER-STAND *YOU*.
THE OTHER STUDENTS KEEP PICKING ON YOU AND YOU JUST STAND THERE AND TAKE IT. IT'S PAINFUL JUST WATCHING YOU.
I HAD A BAD EXPERIENCE STANDING OUT AT SCHOOL...
...WHEN I WAS YOUNGER.
THIS ONE TIME I MODELED FOR A COMMERCIAL...
...AND AFTERWARDS, MY CLASSMATES TEASED ME AND BEAT ME UP OUT OF JEALOUSY.
THAT'S WHY...
THAT'S WHY YOU PRETEND AS IF YOU DON'T EVEN EXIST?

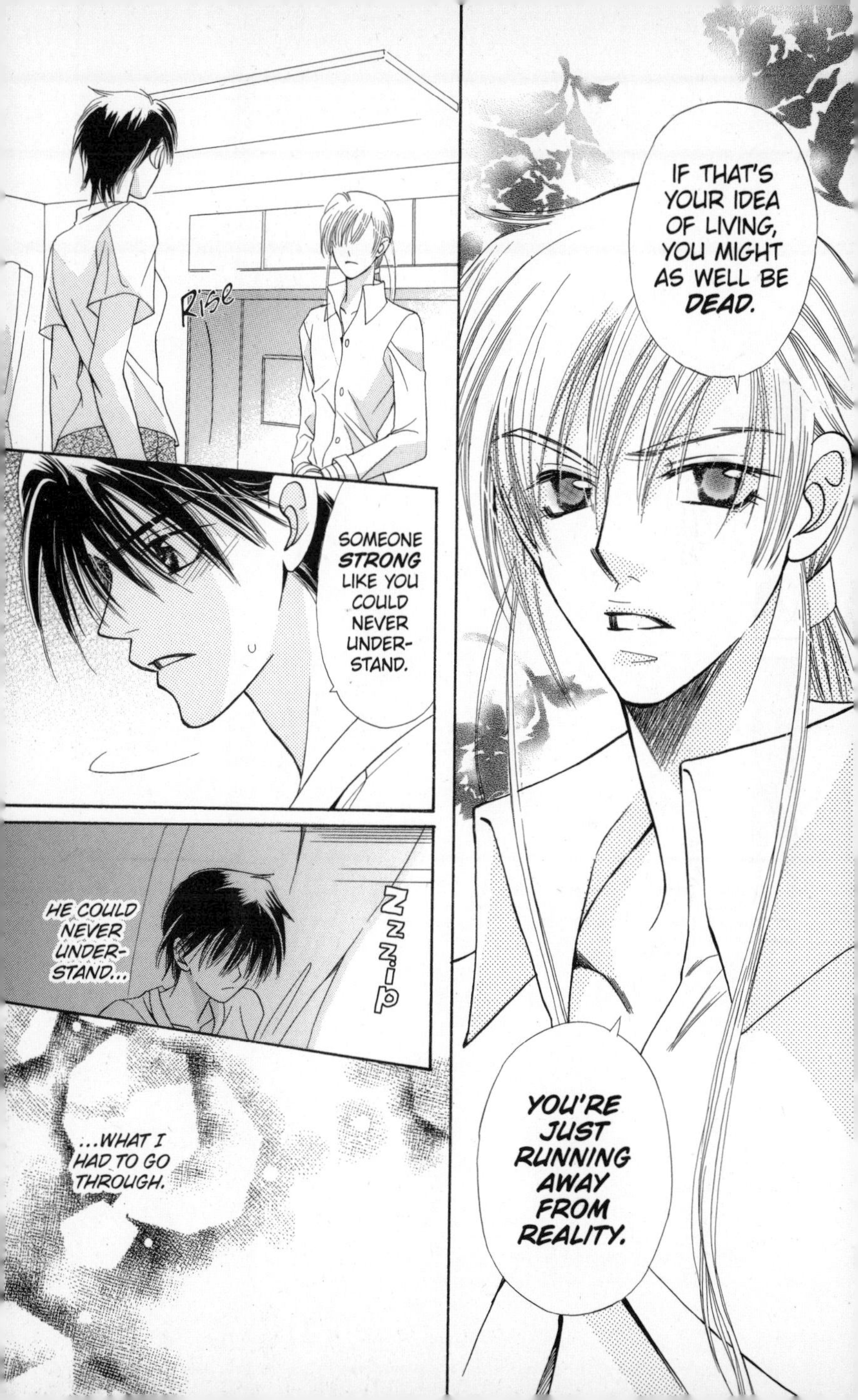
IF THAT'S YOUR IDEA OF LIVING, YOU MIGHT AS WELL BE **DEAD.**
YOU'RE JUST RUNNING AWAY FROM REALITY.
Rise
SOMEONE **STRONG** LIKE YOU COULD NEVER UNDER-STAND.
Zzzip
HE COULD NEVER UNDER-STAND...
...WHAT I HAD TO GO THROUGH.

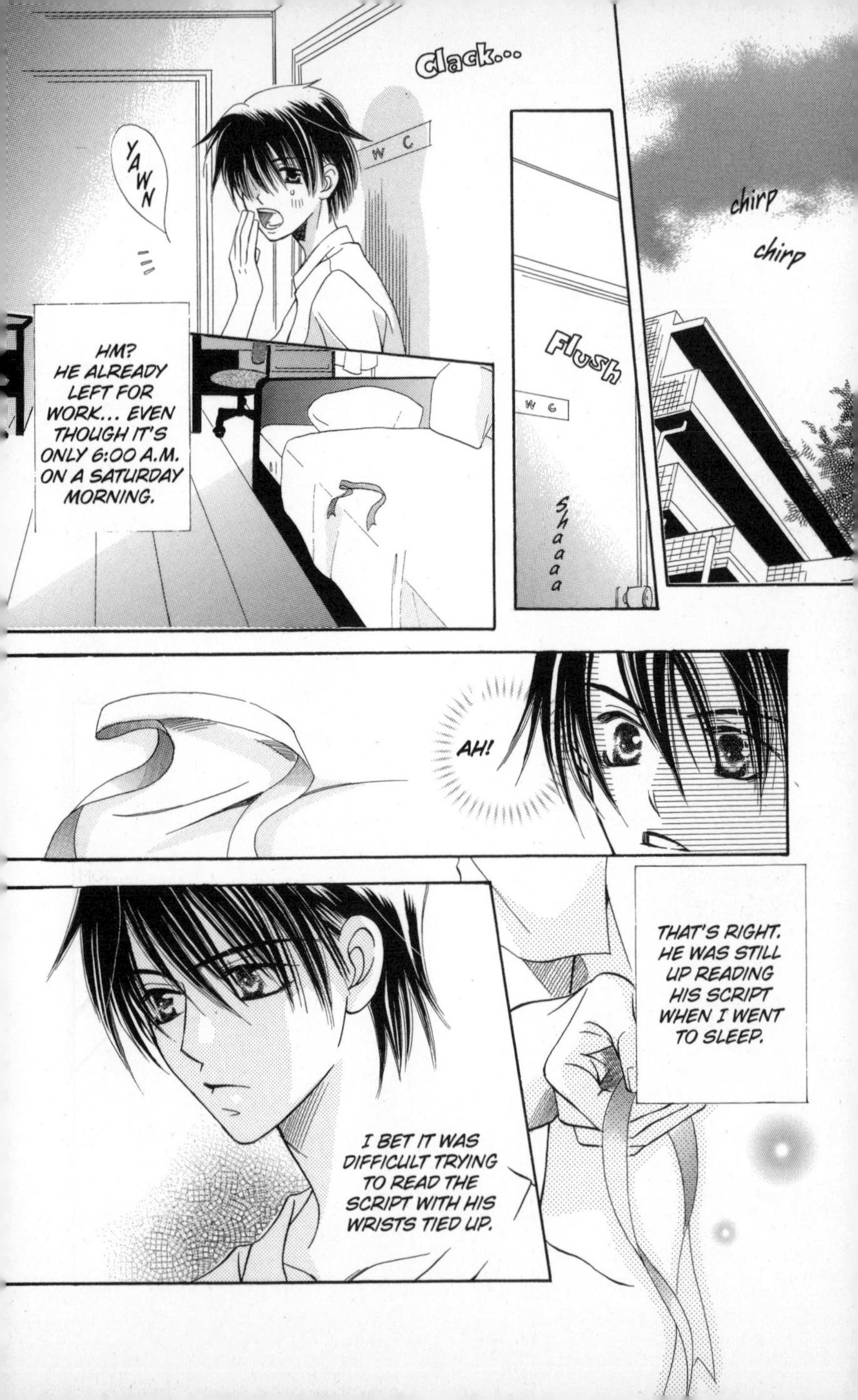
chirp
chirp
Clack...
Flush
W C
Shaaaa
YAWN
W C
HM?
HE ALREADY LEFT FOR WORK... EVEN THOUGH IT'S ONLY 6:00 A.M. ON A SATURDAY MORNING.
AH!
THAT'S RIGHT. HE WAS STILL UP READING HIS SCRIPT WHEN I WENT TO SLEEP.
I BET IT WAS DIFFICULT TRYING TO READ THE SCRIPT WITH HIS WRISTS TIED UP.

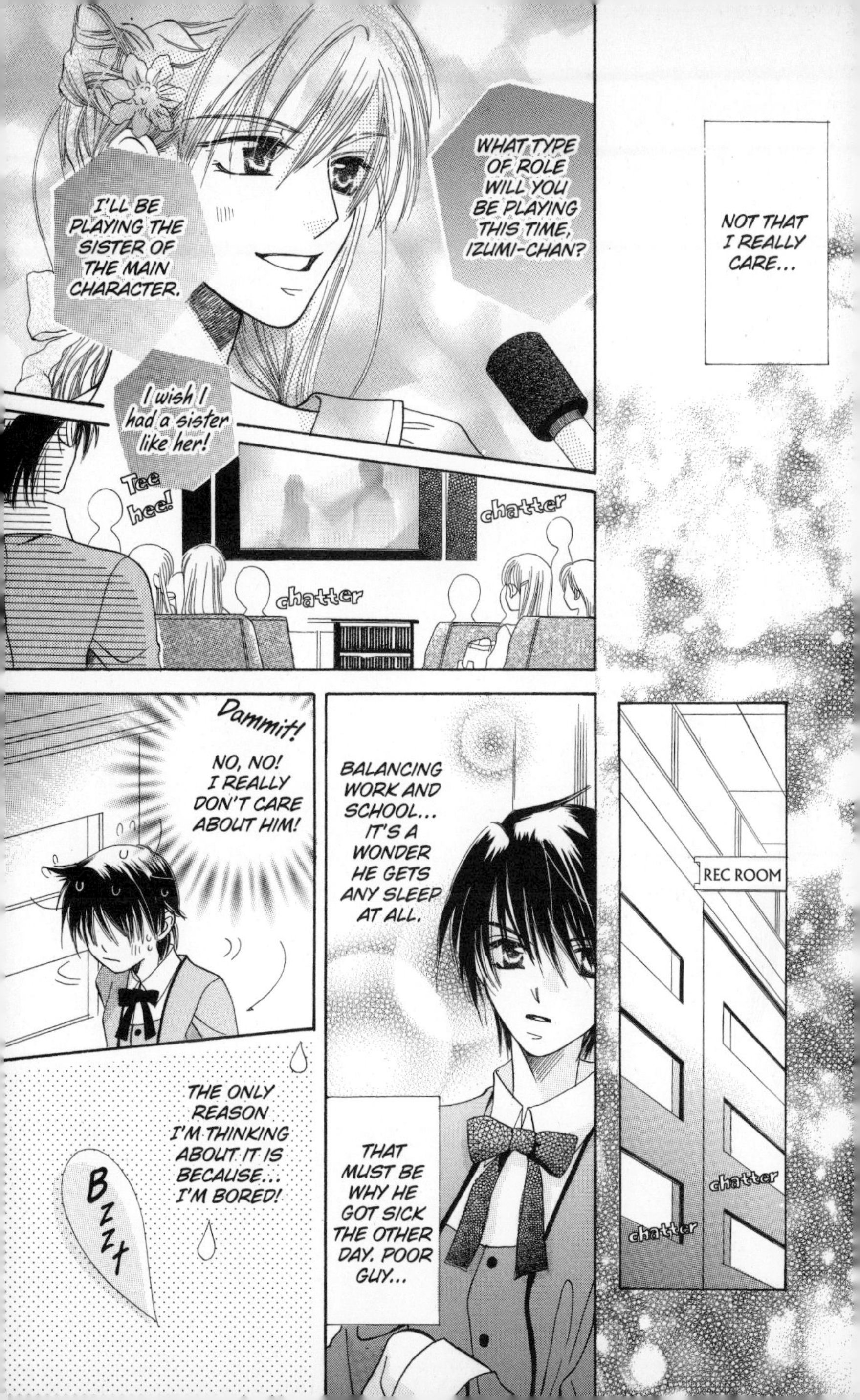
REC ROOM
chatter
chatter
WHAT TYPE OF ROLE WILL YOU BE PLAYING THIS TIME, IZUMI-CHAN?
I'LL BE PLAYING THE SISTER OF THE MAIN CHARACTER.
I wish I had a sister like her!
Tee hee!
chatter
chatter
BALANCING WORK AND SCHOOL... IT'S A WONDER HE GETS ANY SLEEP AT ALL.
THAT MUST BE WHY HE GOT SICK THE OTHER DAY. POOR GUY...
NOT THAT I REALLY CARE...
Dammit!
NO, NO! I REALLY DON'T CARE ABOUT HIM!
THE ONLY REASON I'M THINKING ABOUT IT IS BECAUSE... I'M BORED!
Bzzt

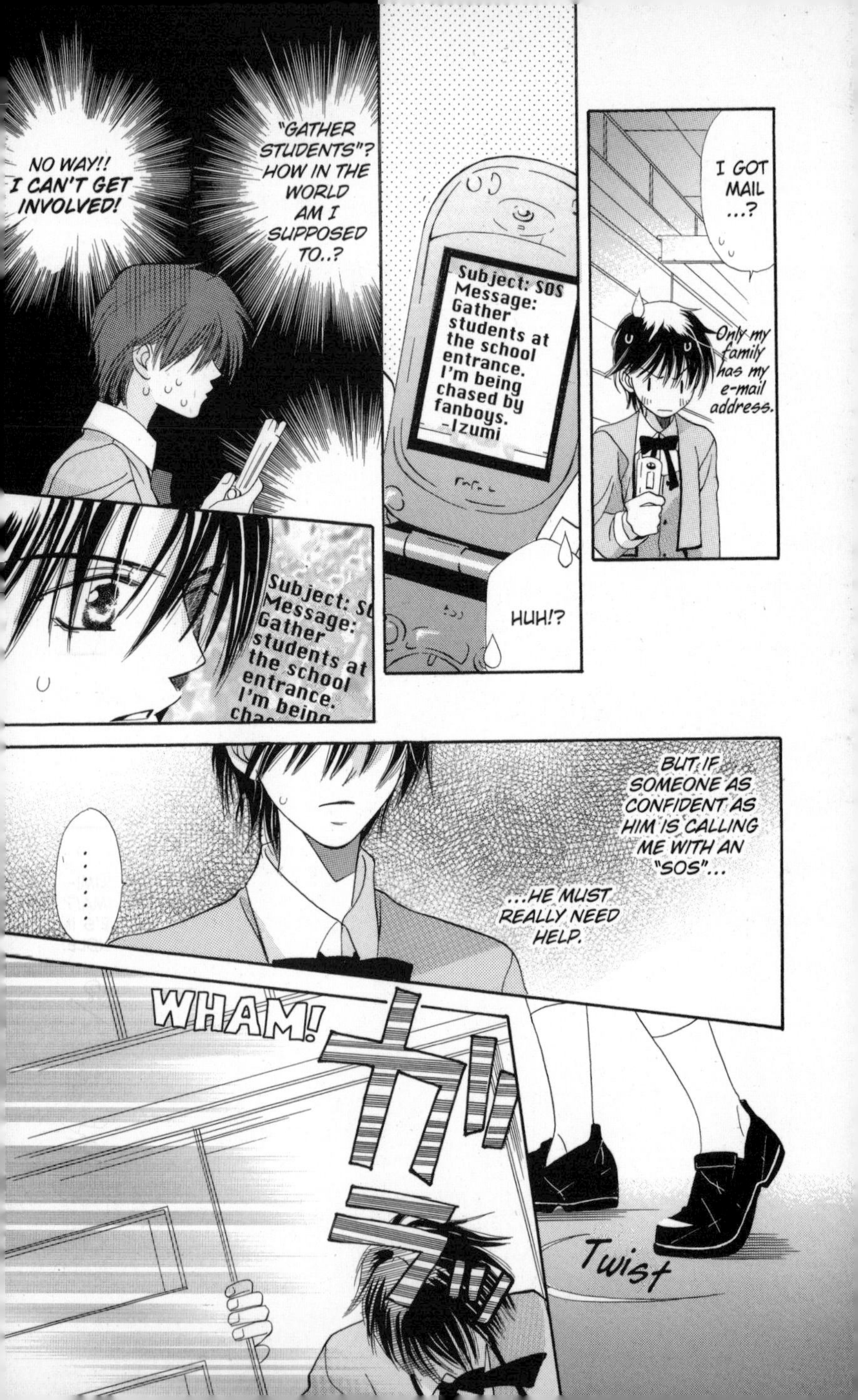
I GOT MAIL ...?
Only my family has my e-mail address.
Subject: SOS Message: Gather students at the school entrance. I'm being chased by fanboys. -Izumi
HUH!?
"GATHER STUDENTS"? HOW IN THE WORLD AM I SUPPOSED TO..?
NO WAY!! I CAN'T GET INVOLVED!
Subject: SO Message: Gather students at the school entrance. I'm being cha
BUT IF SOMEONE AS CONFIDENT AS HIM IS CALLING ME WITH AN "SOS"...
...HE MUST REALLY NEED HELP.
......
WHAM!
Twist

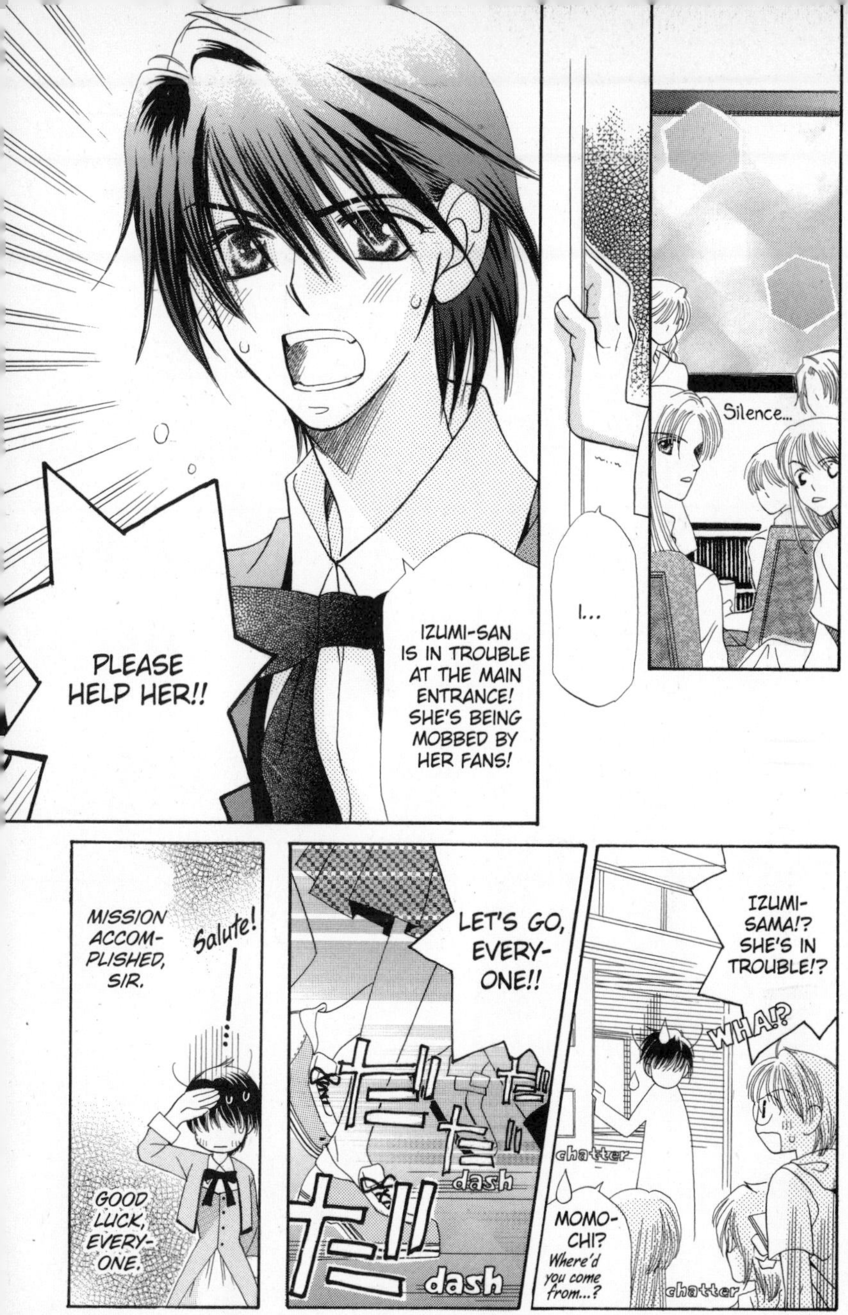
Silence...
I...
IZUMI-SAN IS IN TROUBLE AT THE MAIN ENTRANCE! SHE'S BEING MOBBED BY HER FANS!
PLEASE HELP HER!!
IZUMI-SAMA!? SHE'S IN TROUBLE!?
WHA!?
chatter
MOMO-CHI? Where'd you come from...?
chatter
LET'S GO, EVERY-ONE!!
dash
dash
MISSION ACCOMPLISHED, SIR.
Salute!
GOOD LUCK, EVERY-ONE.

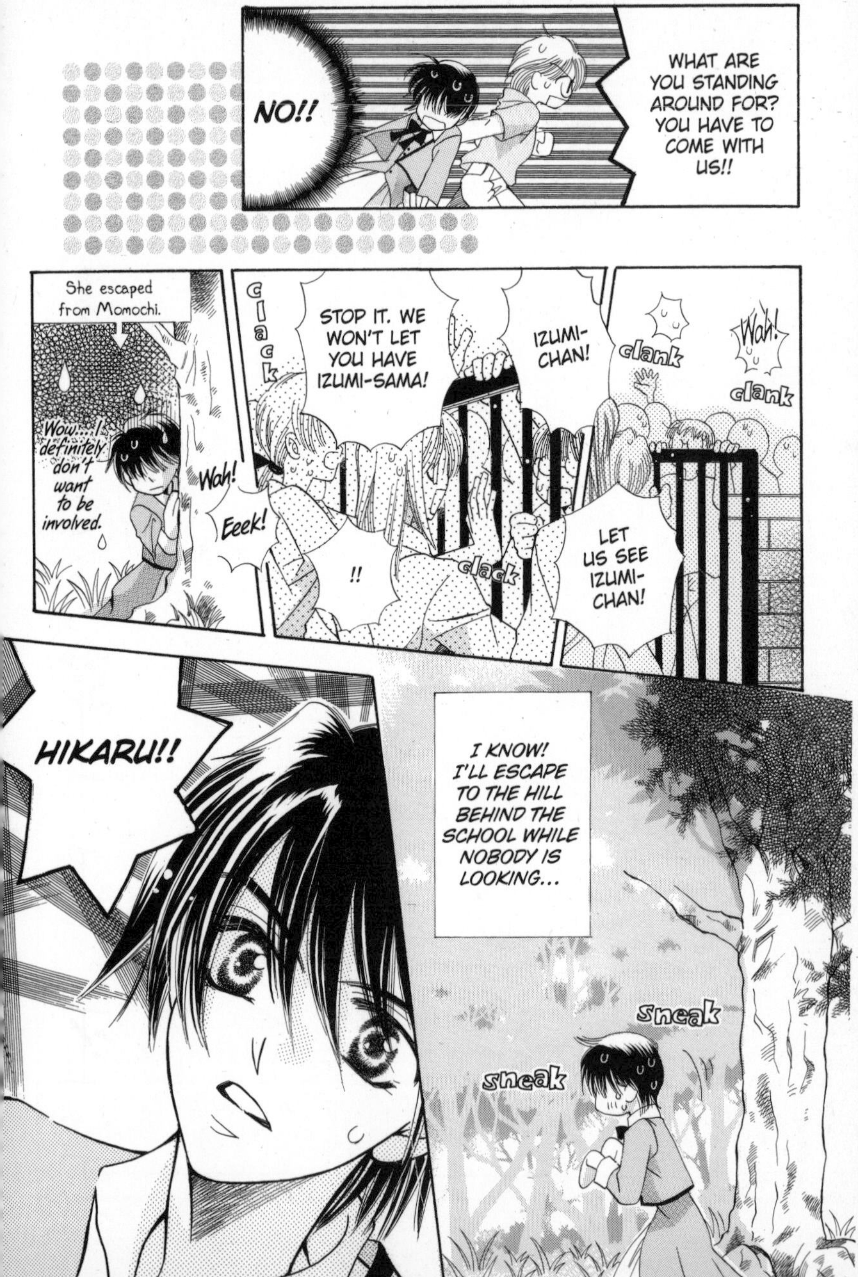
WHAT ARE YOU STANDING AROUND FOR? YOU HAVE TO COME WITH US!!
NO!!
Wah!
clank
clank
LET US SEE IZUMI-CHAN!
IZUMI-CHAN!
STOP IT. WE WON'T LET YOU HAVE IZUMI-SAMA!
clack
clack
!!
Wah!
Eeek!
She escaped from Momochi.
Wow... I definitely don't want to be involved.
I KNOW! I'LL ESCAPE TO THE HILL BEHIND THE SCHOOL WHILE NOBODY IS LOOKING...
sneak
sneak
HIKARU!!

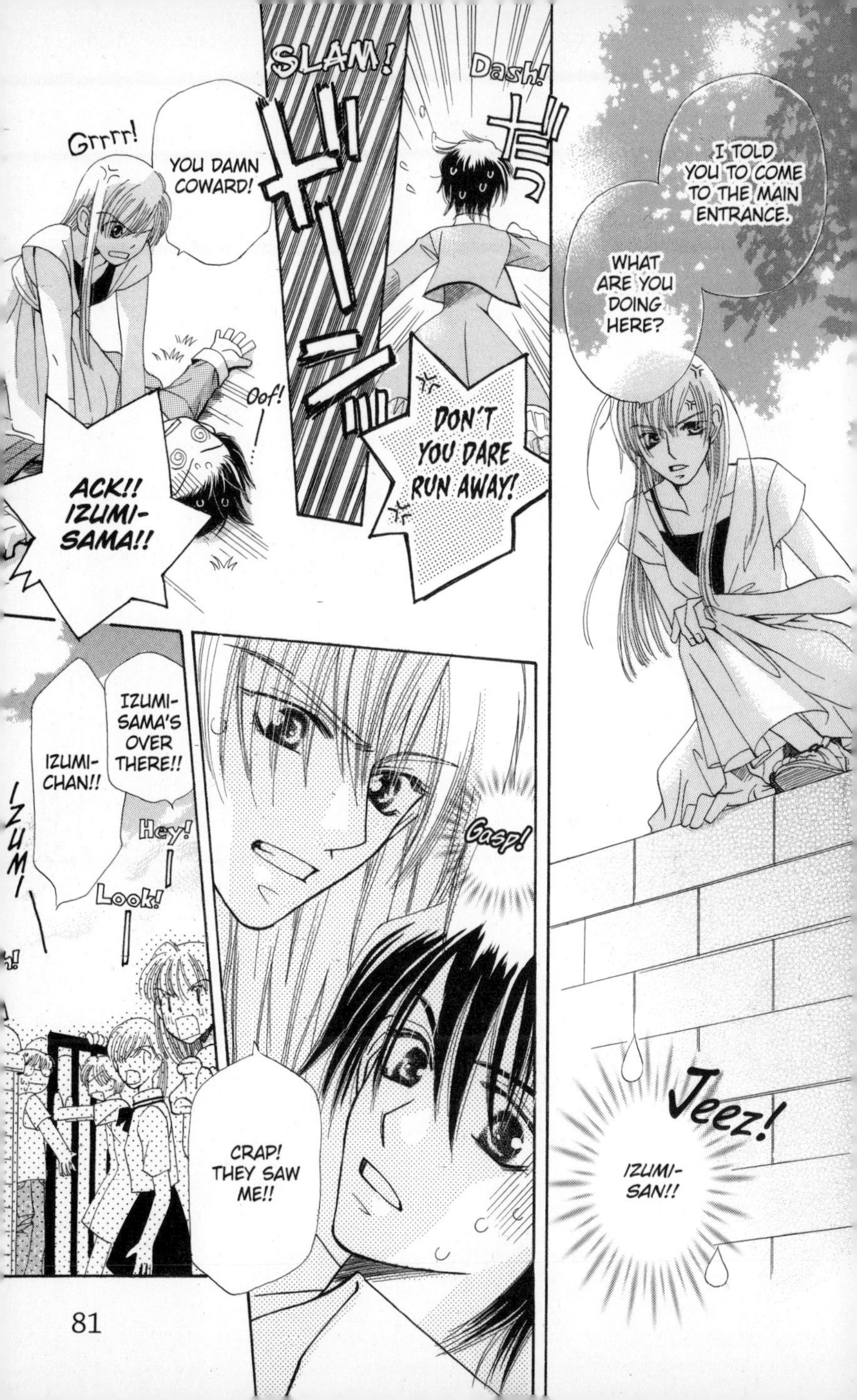

I TOLD YOU TO COME TO THE MAIN ENTRANCE.
WHAT ARE YOU DOING HERE?
Jeez!
IZUMI-SAN!!
Dash!
SLAM!
DON'T YOU DARE RUN AWAY!
Grrrr!
YOU DAMN COWARD!
Oof!
ACK!! IZUMI-SAMA!!
Gasp!
CRAP! THEY SAW ME!!
IZUMI-SAMA'S OVER THERE!!
IZUMI-CHAN!!
Hey!
Look!
IZUMI

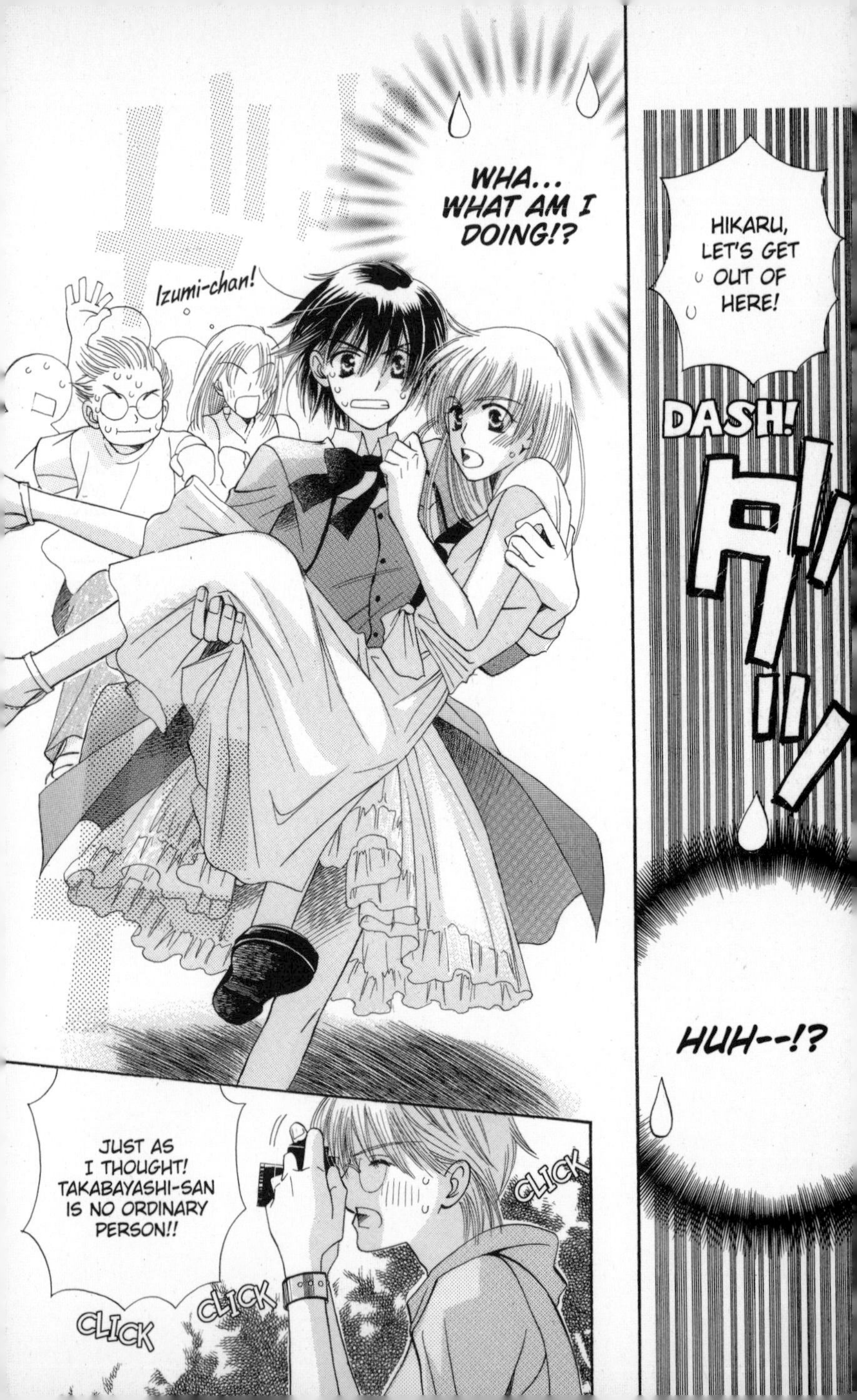
HIKARU, LET'S GET OUT OF HERE!
DASH!
HUH--!?
WHA... WHAT AM I DOING!?
Izumi-chan!
JUST AS I THOUGHT! TAKABAYASHI-SAN IS NO ORDINARY PERSON!!
CLICK
CLICK
CLICK

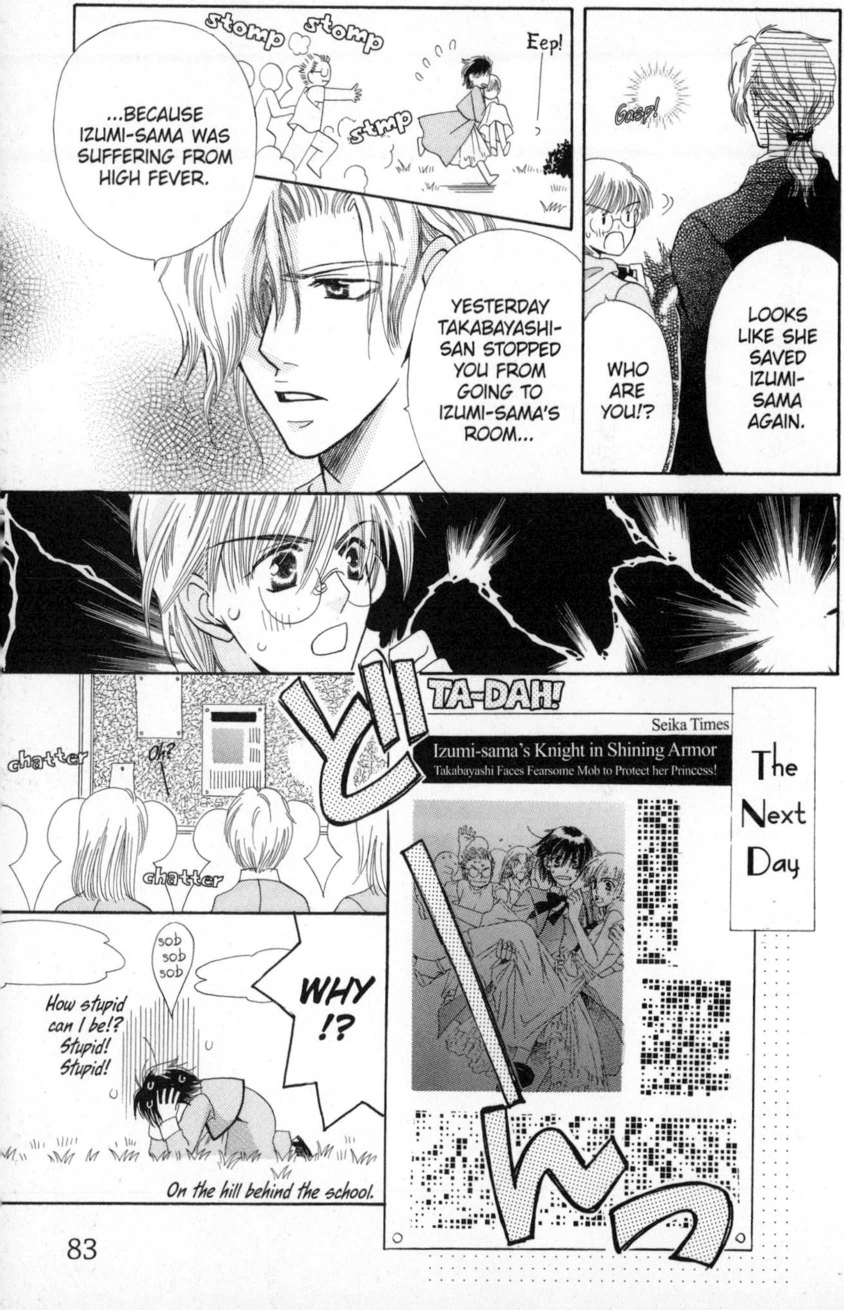
Gasp!
WHO ARE YOU!?
LOOKS LIKE SHE SAVED IZUMI-SAMA AGAIN.
Eep!
stomp stomp
stmp
YESTERDAY TAKABAYASHI-SAN STOPPED YOU FROM GOING TO IZUMI-SAMA'S ROOM...
...BECAUSE IZUMI-SAMA WAS SUFFERING FROM HIGH FEVER.
The Next Day
TA-DAH!
Seika Times
Izumi-sama's Knight in Shining Armor
Takabayashi Faces Fearsome Mob to Protect her Princess!
Oh?
chatter
chatter
WHY!?
sob sob sob
How stupid can I be!? Stupid! Stupid!
On the hill behind the school.

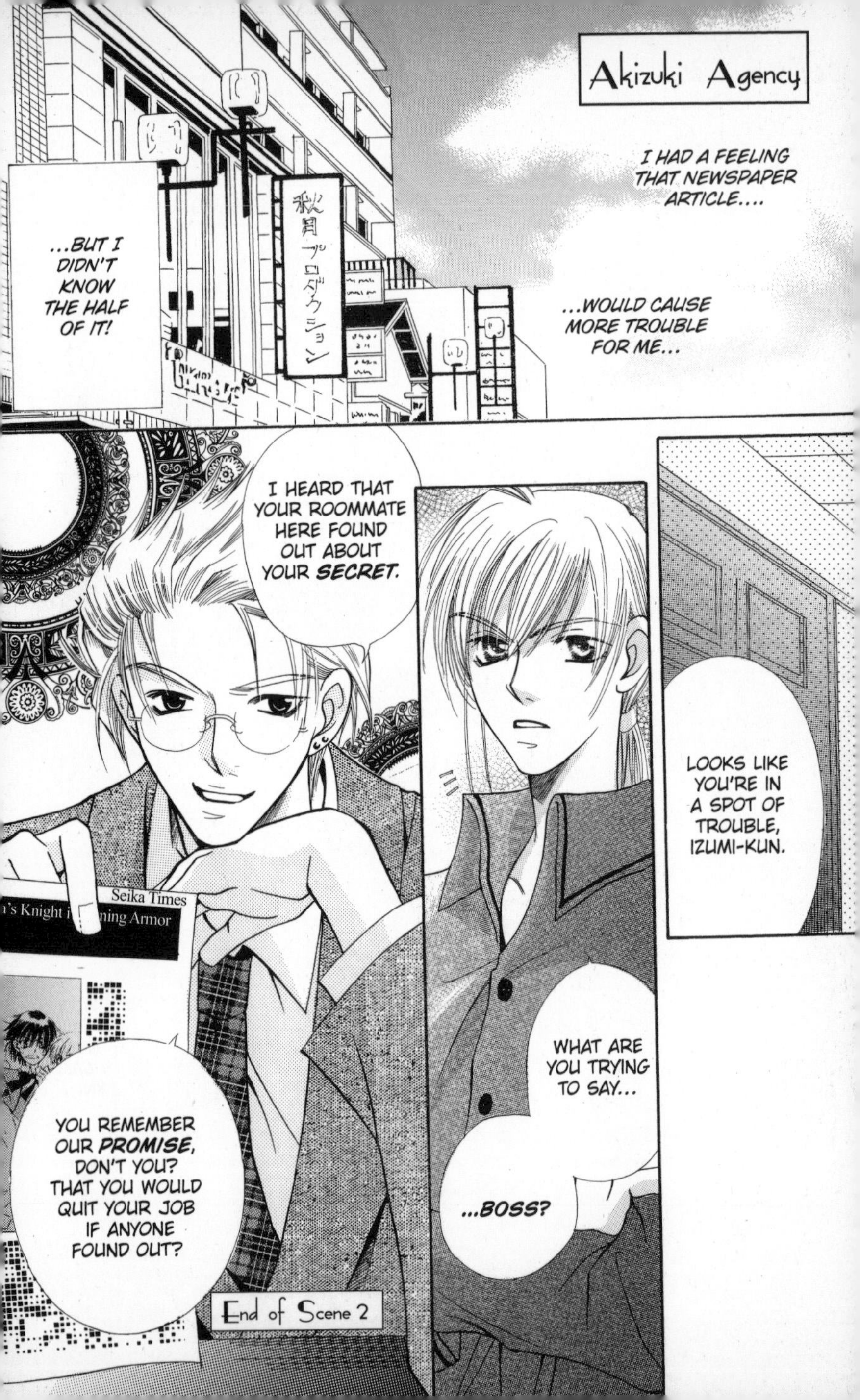

Akizuki Agency
I HAD A FEELING THAT NEWSPAPER ARTICLE....
...WOULD CAUSE MORE TROUBLE FOR ME...
秋月プロダクション
...BUT I DIDN'T KNOW THE HALF OF IT!
LOOKS LIKE YOU'RE IN A SPOT OF TROUBLE, IZUMI-KUN.
I HEARD THAT YOUR ROOMMATE HERE FOUND OUT ABOUT YOUR *SECRET*.
WHAT ARE YOU TRYING TO SAY...
...BOSS?
Seika Times
YOU REMEMBER OUR *PROMISE*, DON'T YOU? THAT YOU WOULD QUIT YOUR JOB IF ANYONE FOUND OUT?
End of Scene 2

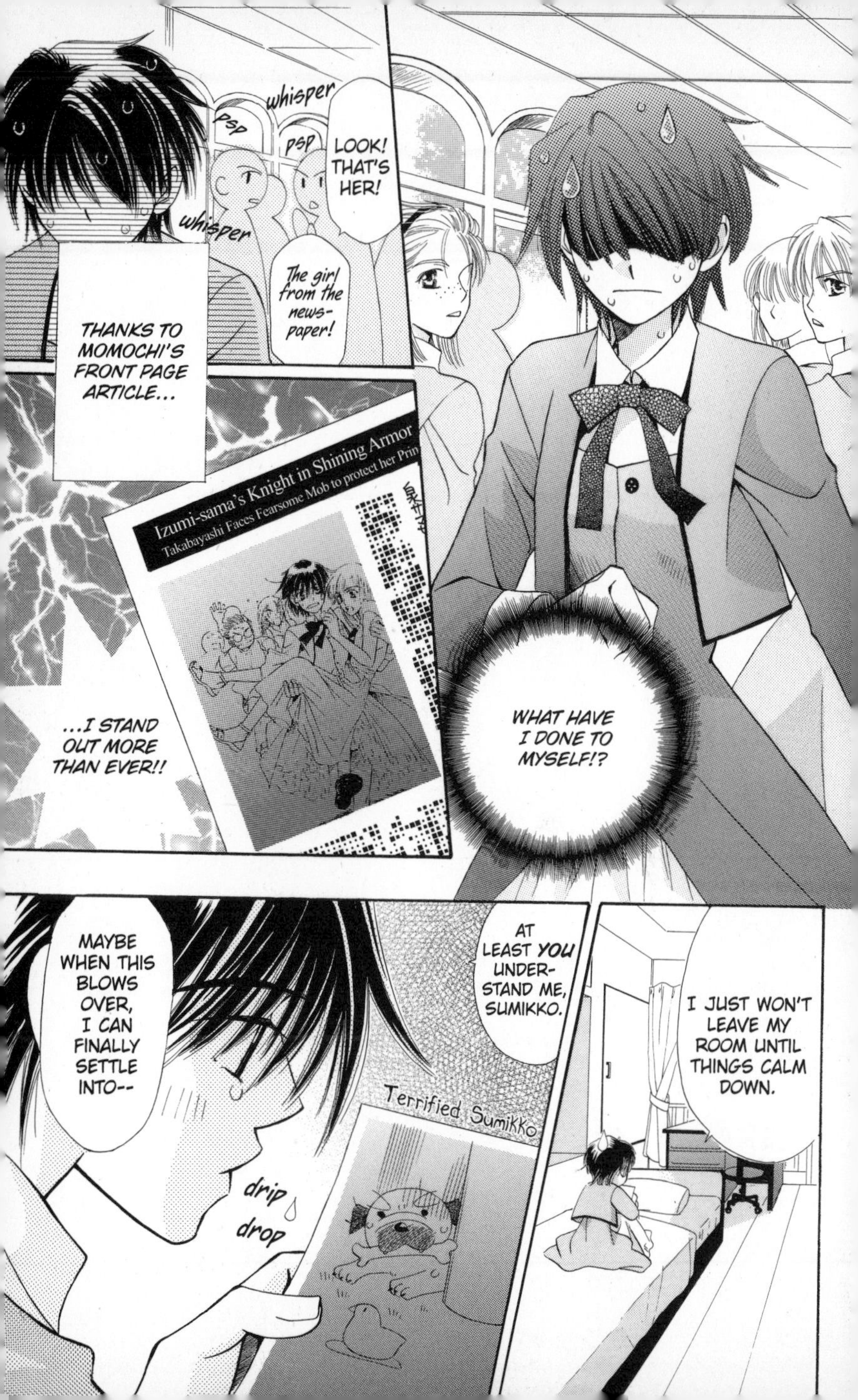
WHAT HAVE I DONE TO MYSELF!?
whisper
psp
psp
LOOK! THAT'S HER!
whisper
The girl from the news-paper!
THANKS TO MOMOCHI'S FRONT PAGE ARTICLE...
Izumi-sama's Knight in Shining Armor
Takabayashi Faces Fearsome Mob to protect her Prin
...I STAND OUT MORE THAN EVER!!
I JUST WON'T LEAVE MY ROOM UNTIL THINGS CALM DOWN.
AT LEAST YOU UNDER-STAND ME, SUMIKKO.
MAYBE WHEN THIS BLOWS OVER, I CAN FINALLY SETTLE INTO--
Terrified Sumikko
drip drop

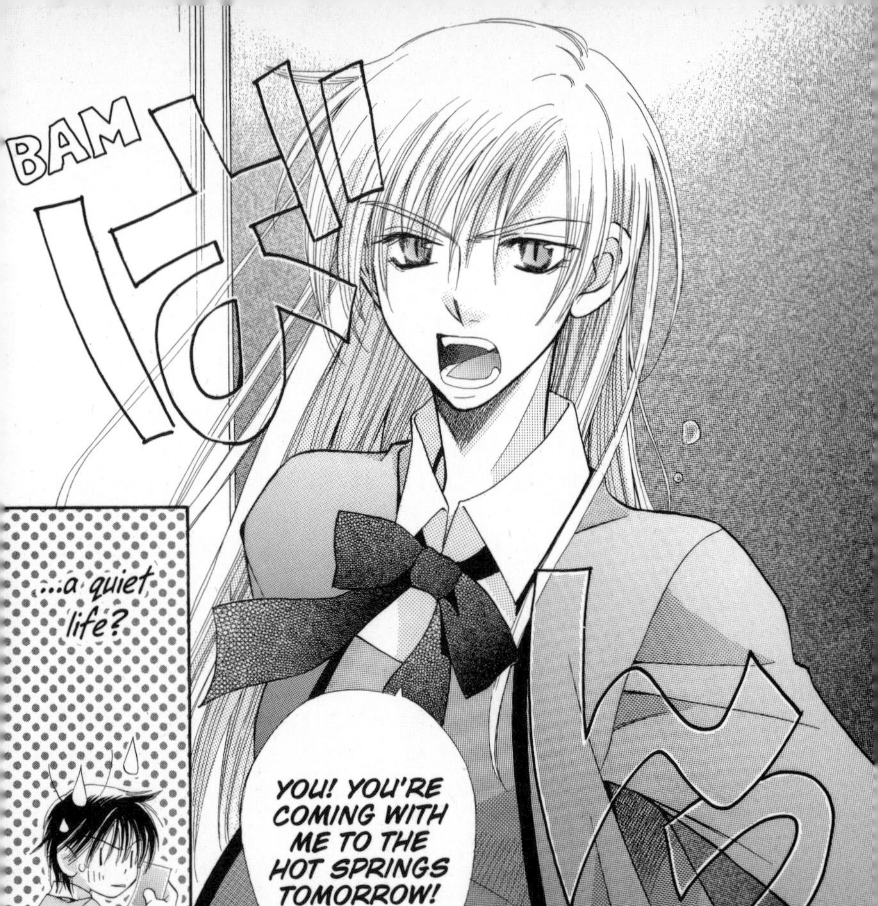
BAM
YOU! YOU'RE COMING WITH ME TO THE HOT SPRINGS TOMORROW!
...a quiet life?

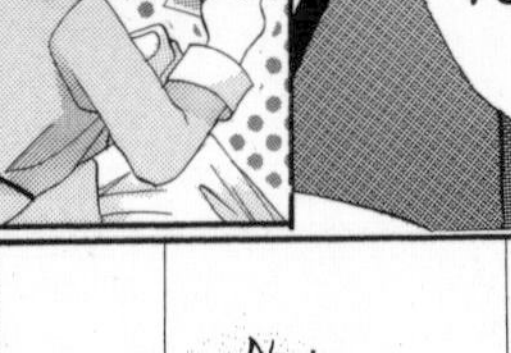
N-nice to meet you...

Hikaru Takabayashi (15 years old)
Birthday: January 1
Blood type: A
Mushroom-type. Extroverted and a little weird. Kind of like something that grew out of overly moist soil--like a rare type of mushroom. Give some fresh air, and some light, and hopefully she can grow out of her mushroom-ness.

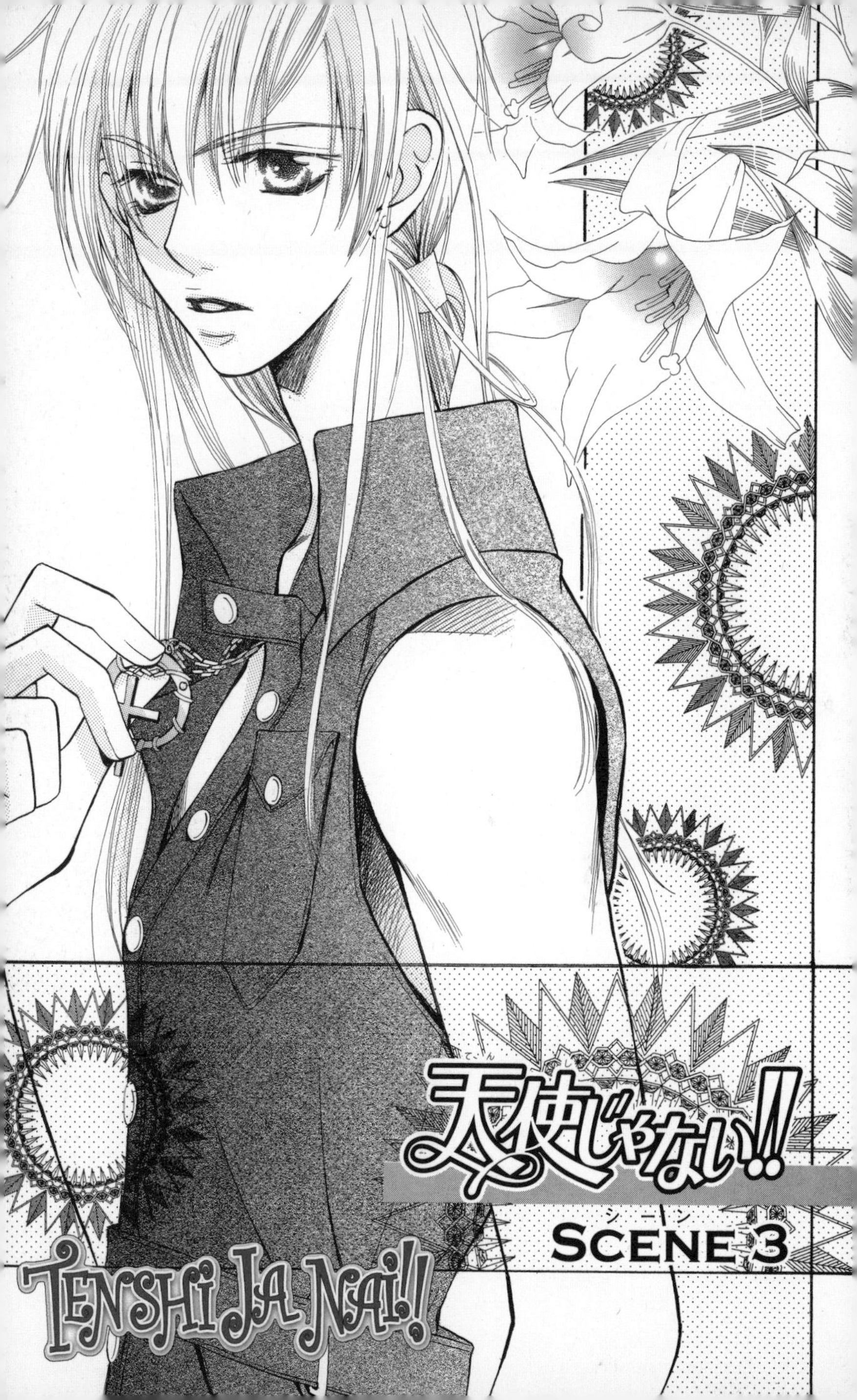
天使じゃない!!
SCENE 3
TENSHI JA NAI!!

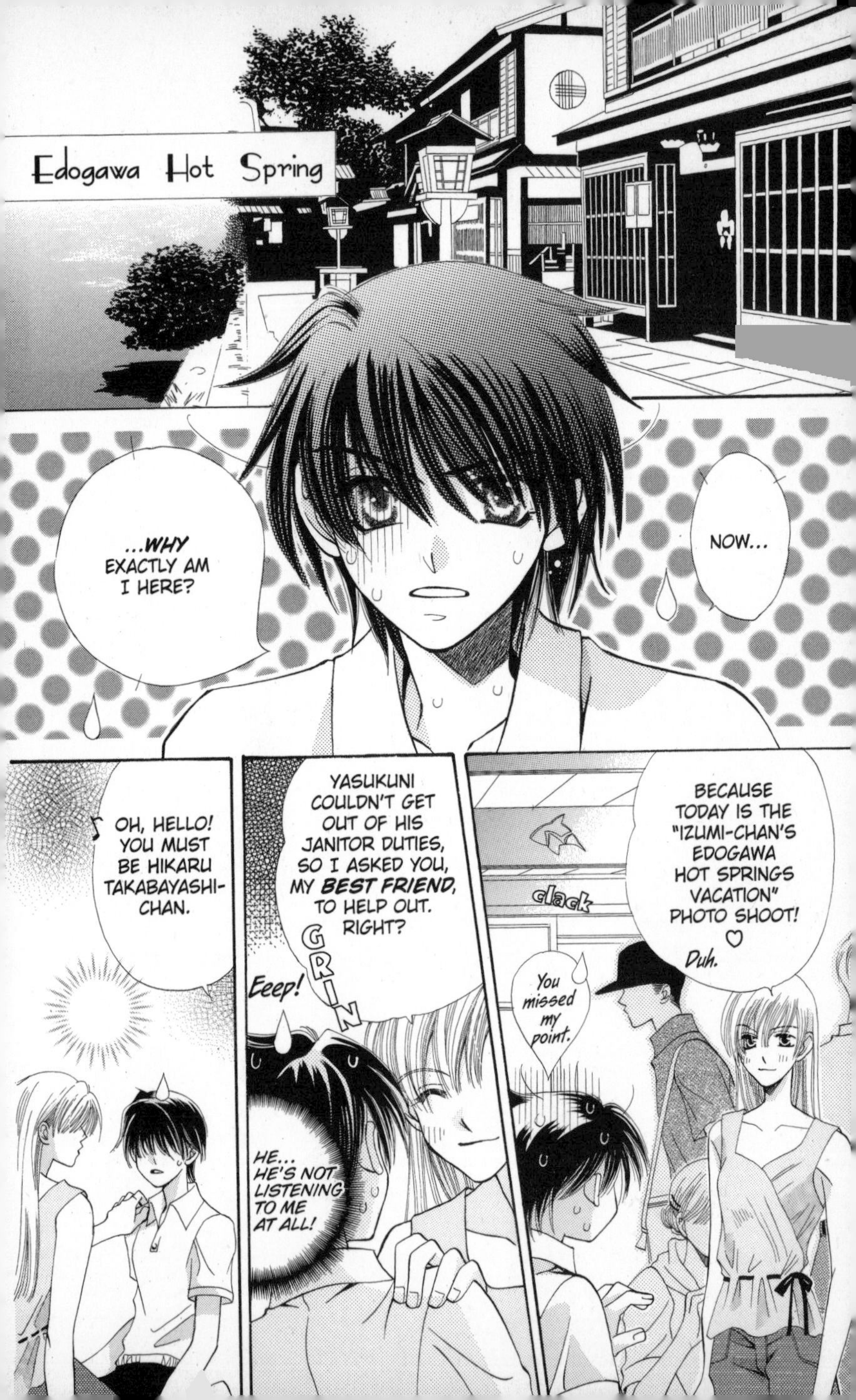
Edogawa Hot Spring
NOW...
...WHY EXACTLY AM I HERE?
BECAUSE TODAY IS THE "IZUMI-CHAN'S EDOGAWA HOT SPRINGS VACATION" PHOTO SHOOT! ♡
Duh.
clack
You missed my point.
YASUKUNI COULDN'T GET OUT OF HIS JANITOR DUTIES, SO I ASKED YOU, MY BEST FRIEND, TO HELP OUT. RIGHT?
GRIN
Eeep!
HE... HE'S NOT LISTENING TO ME AT ALL!
OH, HELLO! YOU MUST BE HIKARU TAKABAYASHI-CHAN.

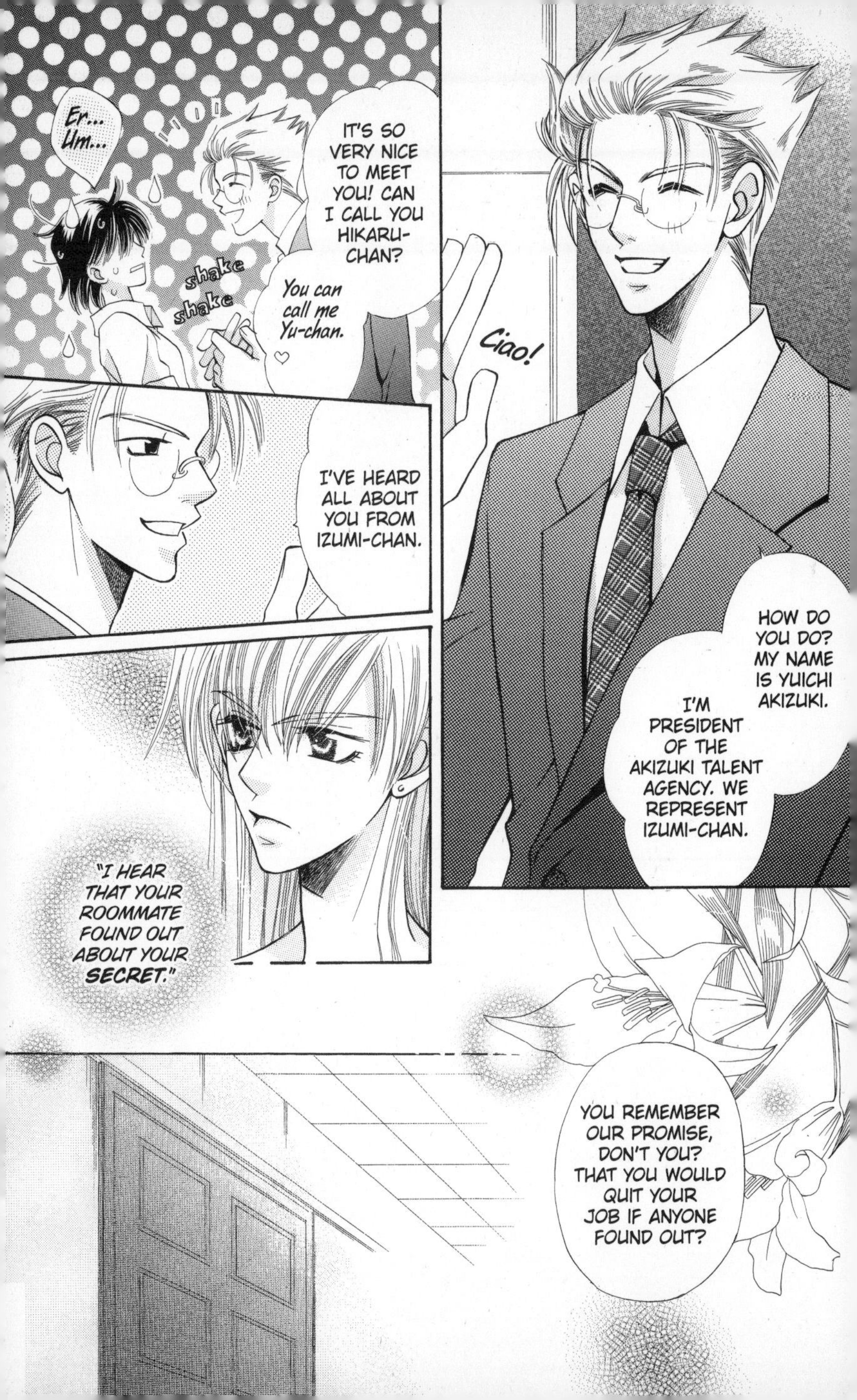
Ciao!
HOW DO YOU DO? MY NAME IS YUICHI AKIZUKI.
I'M PRESIDENT OF THE AKIZUKI TALENT AGENCY. WE REPRESENT IZUMI-CHAN.
IT'S SO VERY NICE TO MEET YOU! CAN I CALL YOU HIKARU-CHAN?
You can call me Yu-chan. ♡
Er... Um...
shake shake
I'VE HEARD ALL ABOUT YOU FROM IZUMI-CHAN.
"I HEAR THAT YOUR ROOMMATE FOUND OUT ABOUT YOUR SECRET."
YOU REMEMBER OUR PROMISE, DON'T YOU? THAT YOU WOULD QUIT YOUR JOB IF ANYONE FOUND OUT?

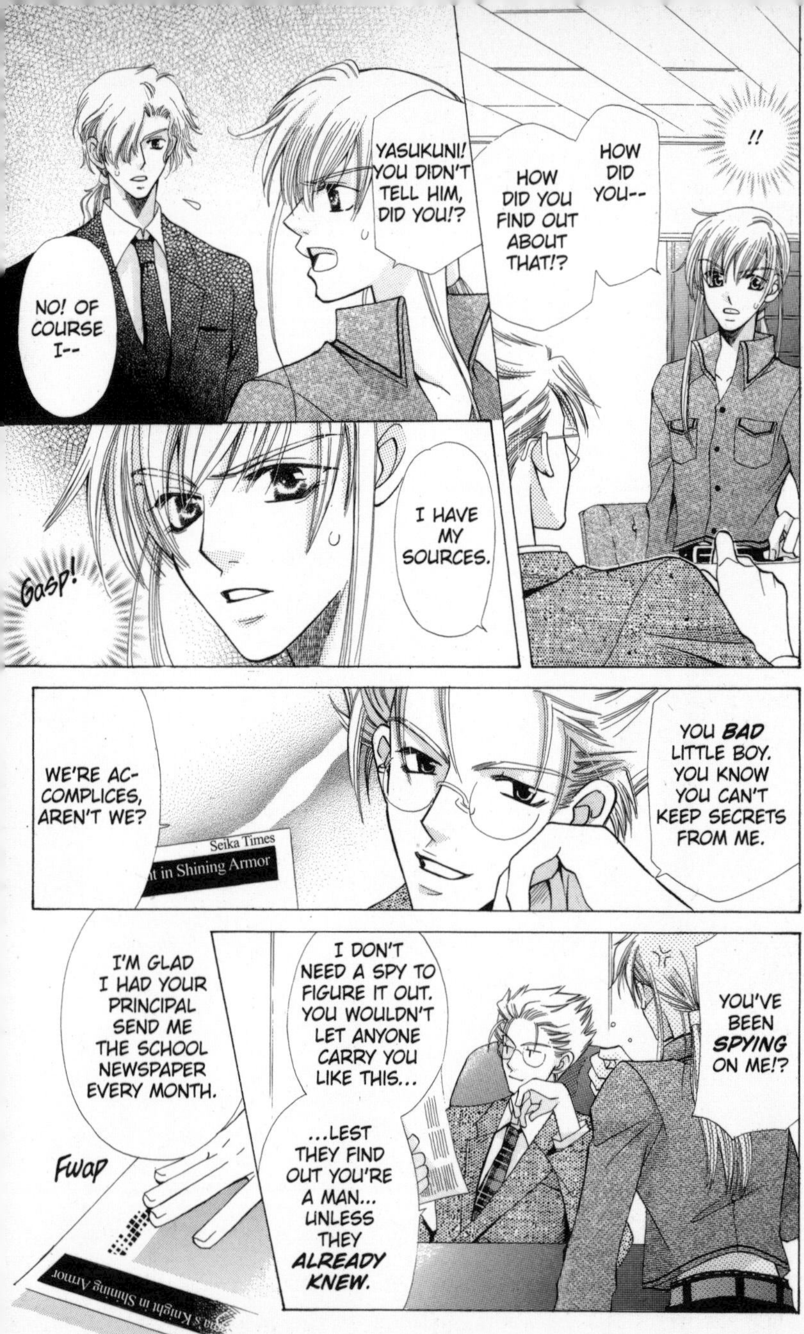
!!
HOW DID YOU--
HOW DID YOU FIND OUT ABOUT THAT!?
YASUKUNI! YOU DIDN'T TELL HIM, DID YOU!?
NO! OF COURSE I--
I HAVE MY SOURCES.
Gasp!
YOU **BAD** LITTLE BOY. YOU KNOW YOU CAN'T KEEP SECRETS FROM ME.
WE'RE AC-COMPLICES, AREN'T WE?
Seika Times
...t in Shining Armor
YOU'VE BEEN ***SPYING*** ON ME!?
I DON'T NEED A SPY TO FIGURE IT OUT. YOU WOULDN'T LET ANYONE CARRY YOU LIKE THIS...
...LEST THEY FIND OUT YOU'RE A MAN... UNLESS THEY ***ALREADY KNEW***.
I'M GLAD I HAD YOUR PRINCIPAL SEND ME THE SCHOOL NEWSPAPER EVERY MONTH.
Fwap
...a's Knight in Shining Armor

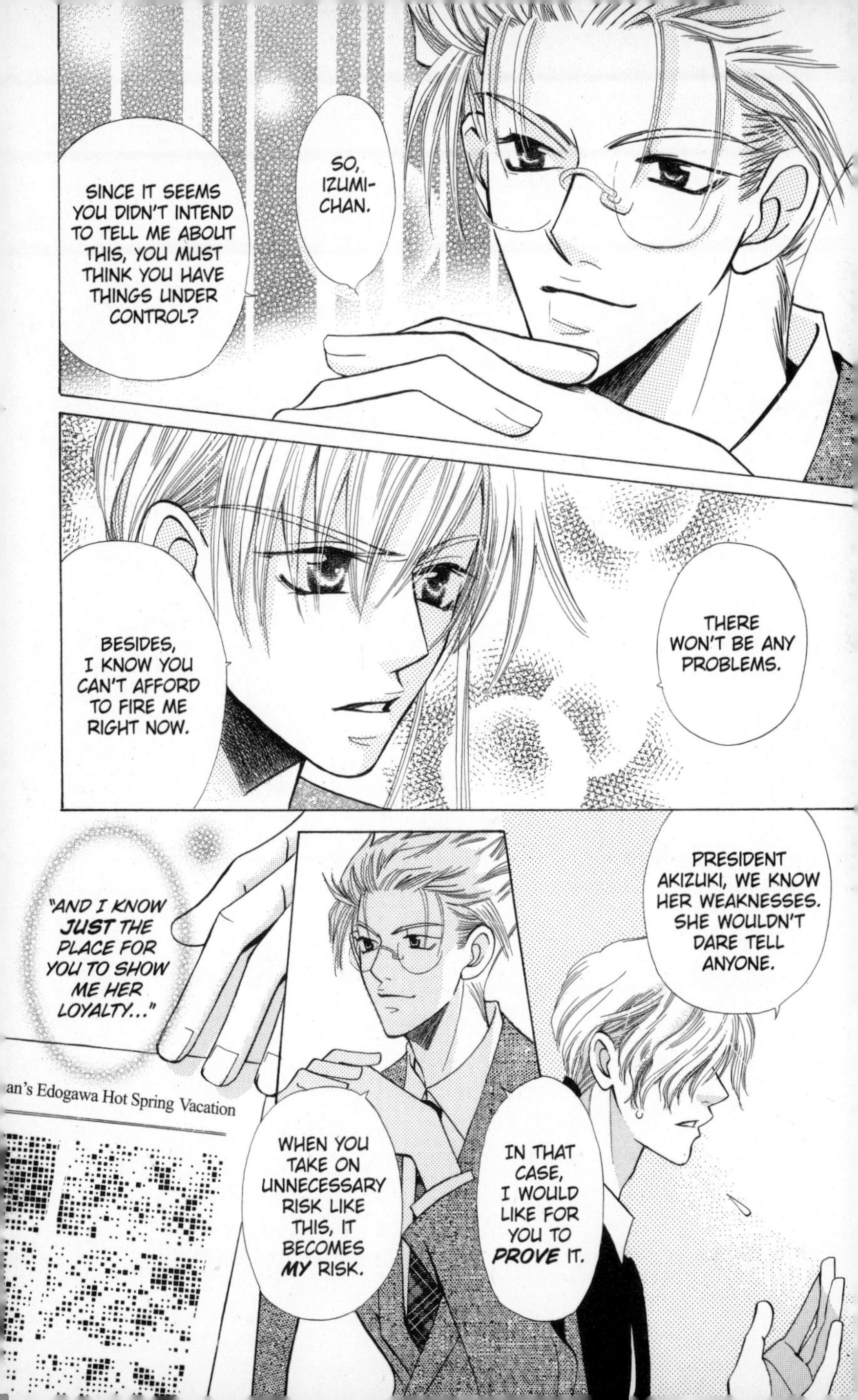
SO, IZUMI-CHAN.
SINCE IT SEEMS YOU DIDN'T INTEND TO TELL ME ABOUT THIS, YOU MUST THINK YOU HAVE THINGS UNDER CONTROL?
THERE WON'T BE ANY PROBLEMS.
BESIDES, I KNOW YOU CAN'T AFFORD TO FIRE ME RIGHT NOW.
PRESIDENT AKIZUKI, WE KNOW HER WEAKNESSES. SHE WOULDN'T DARE TELL ANYONE.
IN THAT CASE, I WOULD LIKE FOR YOU TO ***PROVE*** IT.
WHEN YOU TAKE ON UNNECESSARY RISK LIKE THIS, IT BECOMES ***MY*** RISK.
*"AND I KNOW **JUST** THE PLACE FOR YOU TO SHOW ME HER LOYALTY..."*
an's Edogawa Hot Spring Vacation

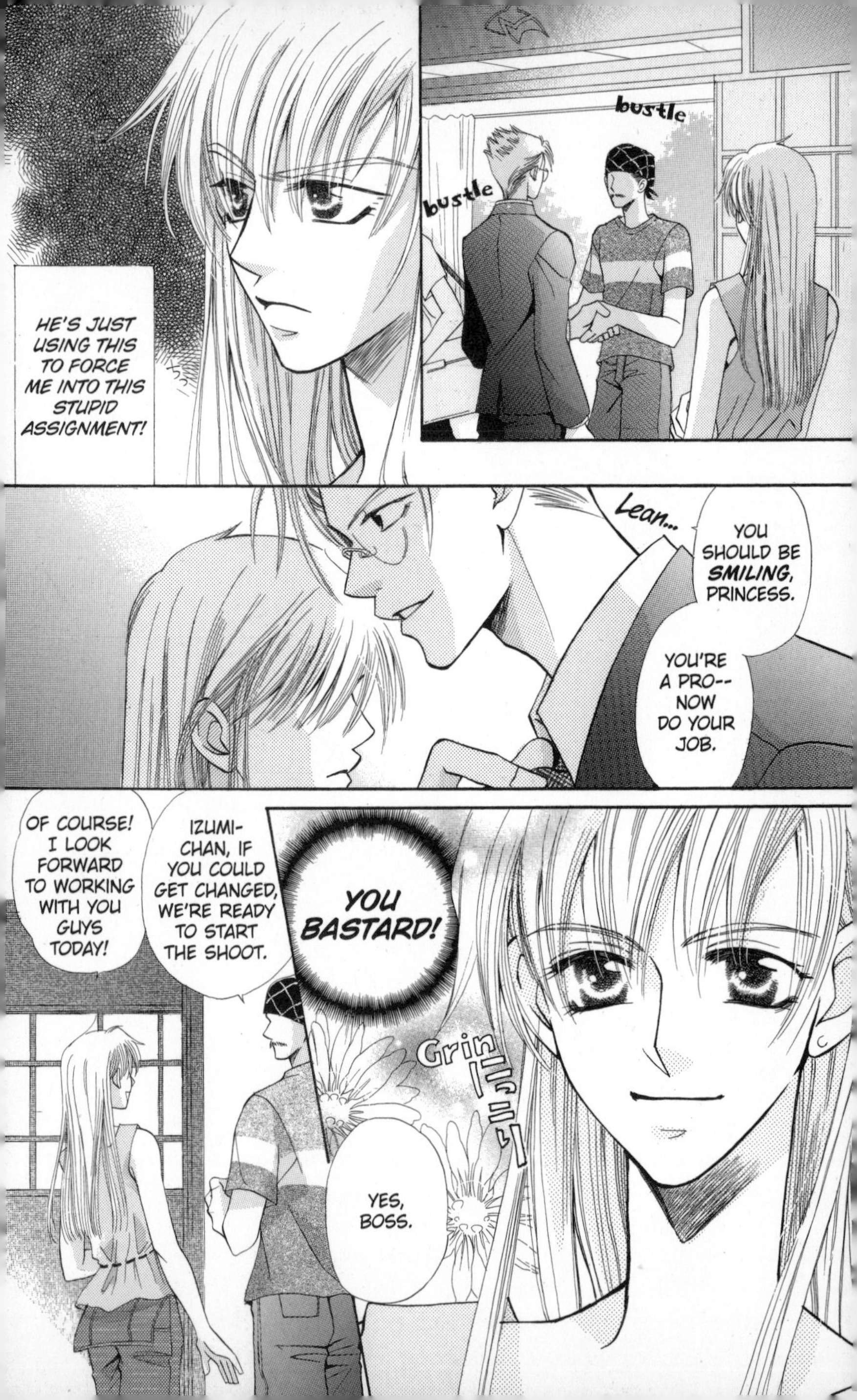
bustle
bustle
HE'S JUST USING THIS TO FORCE ME INTO THIS STUPID ASSIGNMENT!
Lean...
YOU SHOULD BE SMILING, PRINCESS.
YOU'RE A PRO-- NOW DO YOUR JOB.
YOU BASTARD!
Grin
YES, BOSS.
IZUMI-CHAN, IF YOU COULD GET CHANGED, WE'RE READY TO START THE SHOOT.
OF COURSE! I LOOK FORWARD TO WORKING WITH YOU GUYS TODAY!

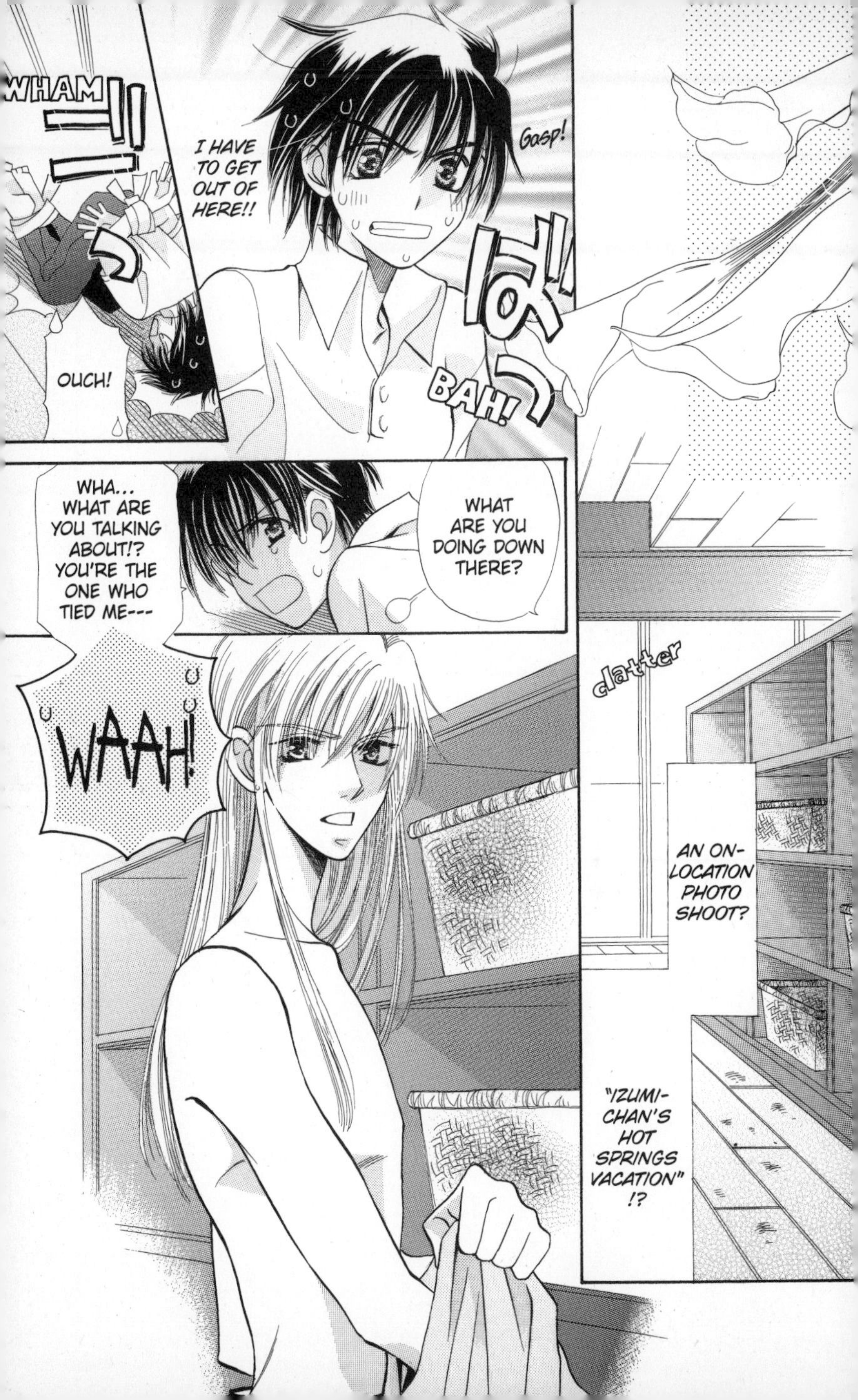
Gasp!
I HAVE TO GET OUT OF HERE!!
BAH!
WHAM
OUCH!
clatter
AN ON-LOCATION PHOTO SHOOT?
"IZUMI-CHAN'S HOT SPRINGS VACATION" !?
WHAT ARE YOU DOING DOWN THERE?
WHA... WHAT ARE YOU TALKING ABOUT!? YOU'RE THE ONE WHO TIED ME---
WAAH!

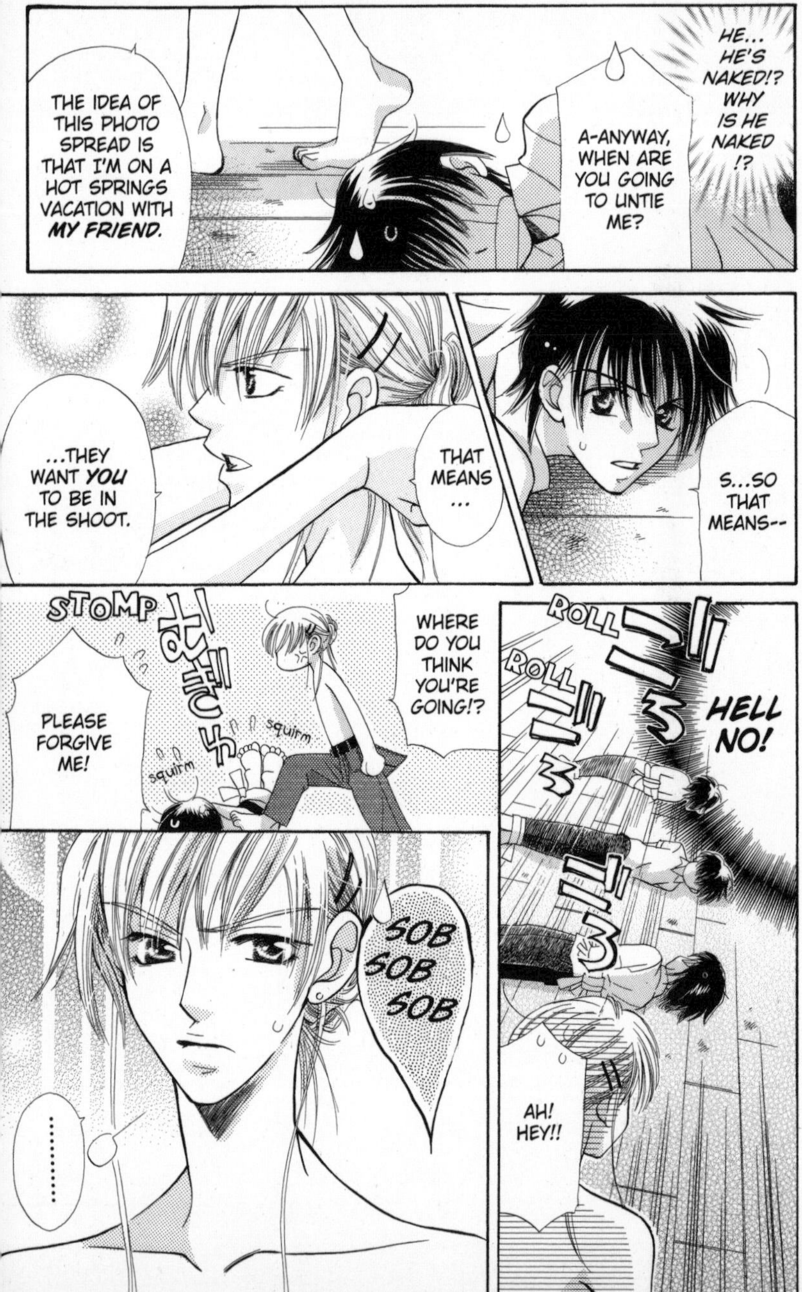
HE... HE'S NAKED!? WHY IS HE NAKED !?
A-ANYWAY, WHEN ARE YOU GOING TO UNTIE ME?
THE IDEA OF THIS PHOTO SPREAD IS THAT I'M ON A HOT SPRINGS VACATION WITH MY FRIEND.
S...SO THAT MEANS--
THAT MEANS ...
...THEY WANT YOU TO BE IN THE SHOOT.
ROLL
ROLL
HELL NO!
AH! HEY!!
WHERE DO YOU THINK YOU'RE GOING!?
STOMP
squirm
squirm
PLEASE FORGIVE ME!
SOB SOB SOB
....

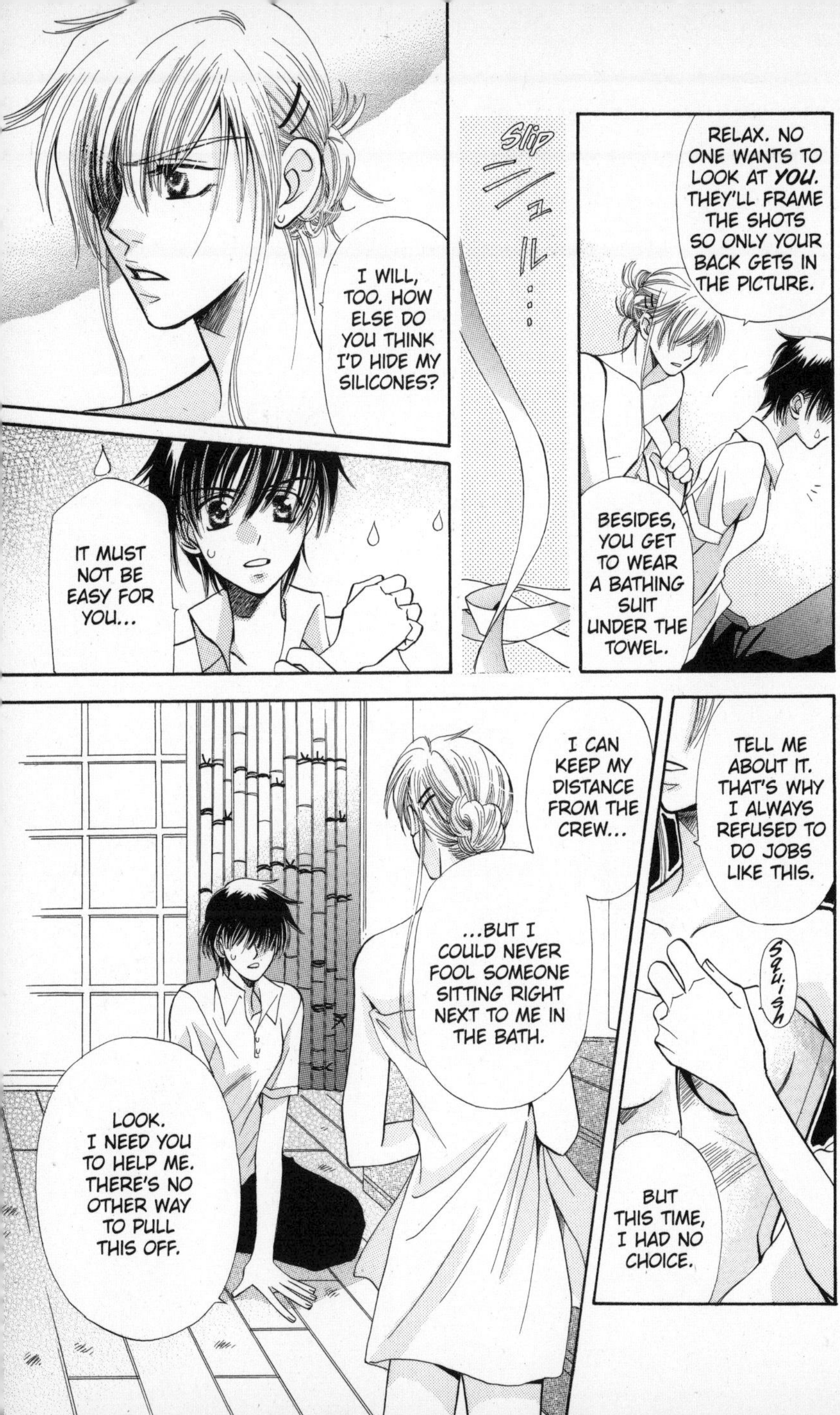

RELAX. NO ONE WANTS TO LOOK AT ***YOU***. THEY'LL FRAME THE SHOTS SO ONLY YOUR BACK GETS IN THE PICTURE.
BESIDES, YOU GET TO WEAR A BATHING SUIT UNDER THE TOWEL.
Slip
I WILL, TOO. HOW ELSE DO YOU THINK I'D HIDE MY SILICONES?
IT MUST NOT BE EASY FOR YOU...
TELL ME ABOUT IT. THAT'S WHY I ALWAYS REFUSED TO DO JOBS LIKE THIS.
SQUISH
BUT THIS TIME, I HAD NO CHOICE.
I CAN KEEP MY DISTANCE FROM THE CREW...
...BUT I COULD NEVER FOOL SOMEONE SITTING RIGHT NEXT TO ME IN THE BATH.
LOOK. I NEED YOU TO HELP ME. THERE'S NO OTHER WAY TO PULL THIS OFF.

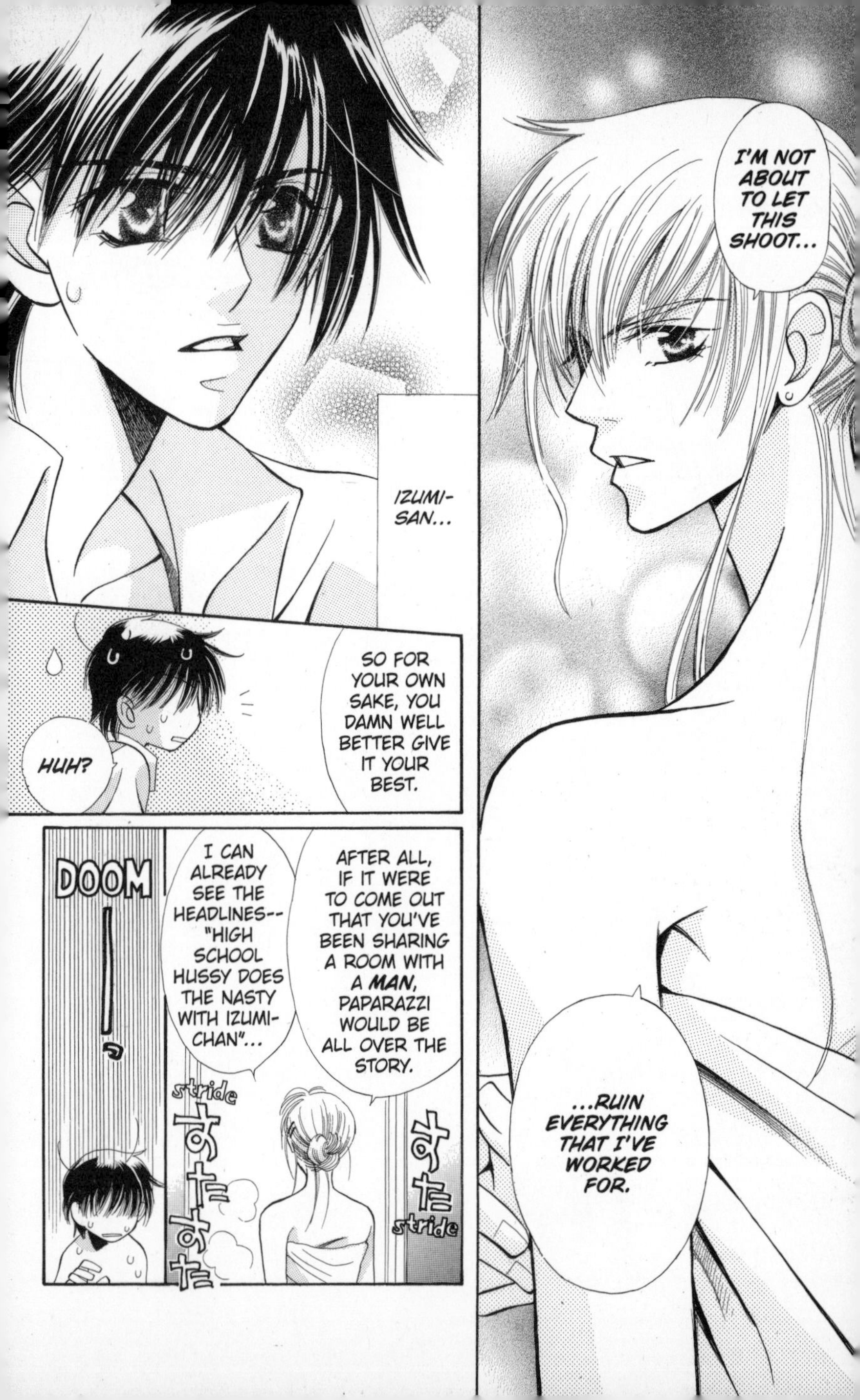
I'M NOT ABOUT TO LET THIS SHOOT...
...RUIN EVERYTHING THAT I'VE WORKED FOR.
IZUMI-SAN...
SO FOR YOUR OWN SAKE, YOU DAMN WELL BETTER GIVE IT YOUR BEST.
HUH?
AFTER ALL, IF IT WERE TO COME OUT THAT YOU'VE BEEN SHARING A ROOM WITH A *MAN*, PAPARAZZI WOULD BE ALL OVER THE STORY.
I CAN ALREADY SEE THE HEADLINES-- "HIGH SCHOOL HUSSY DOES THE NASTY WITH IZUMI-CHAN"...
すた stride
stride すたすた
DOOM

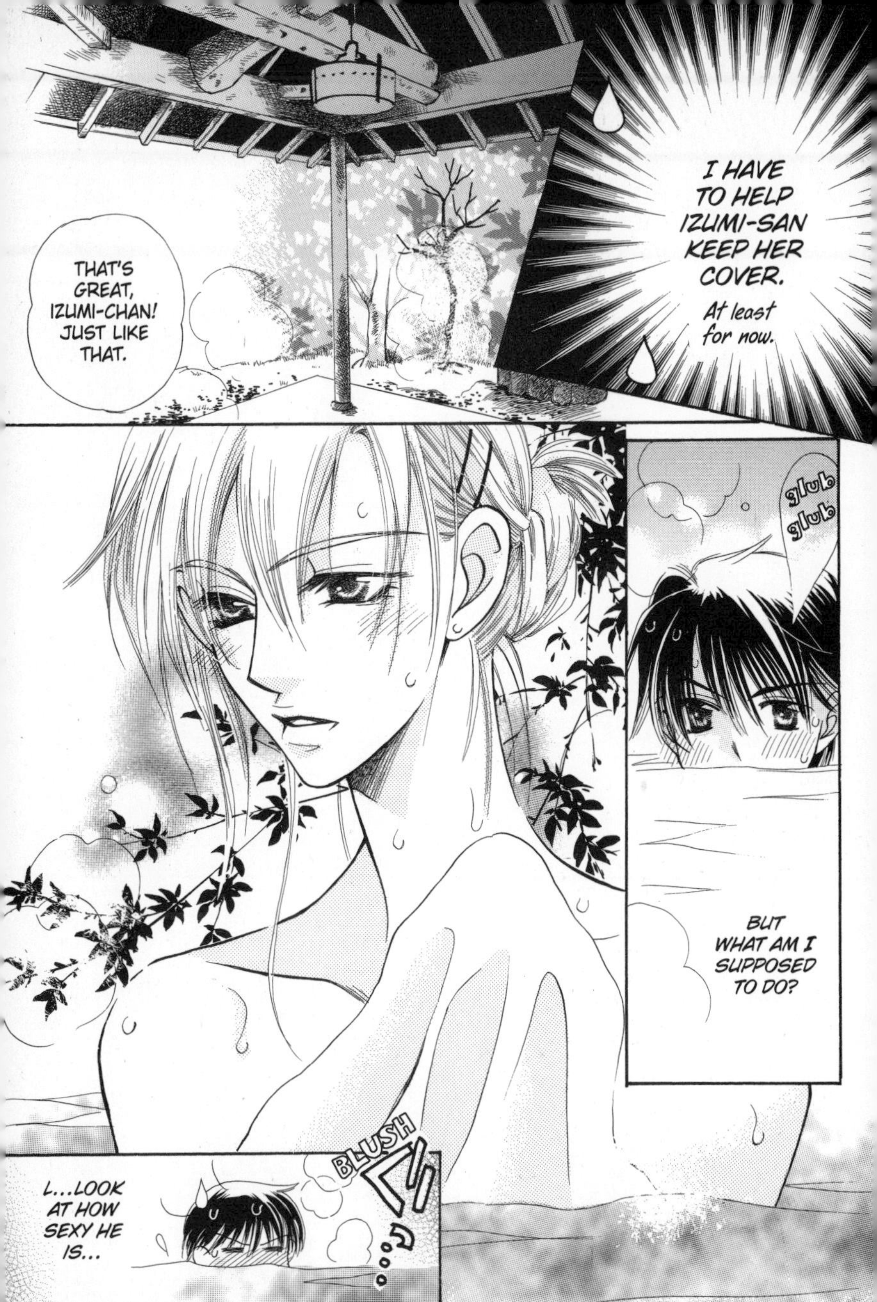

I HAVE TO HELP IZUMI-SAN KEEP HER COVER.
At least for now.
THAT'S GREAT, IZUMI-CHAN! JUST LIKE THAT.
glub glub
BUT WHAT AM I SUPPOSED TO DO?
BLUSH
L...LOOK AT HOW SEXY HE IS...

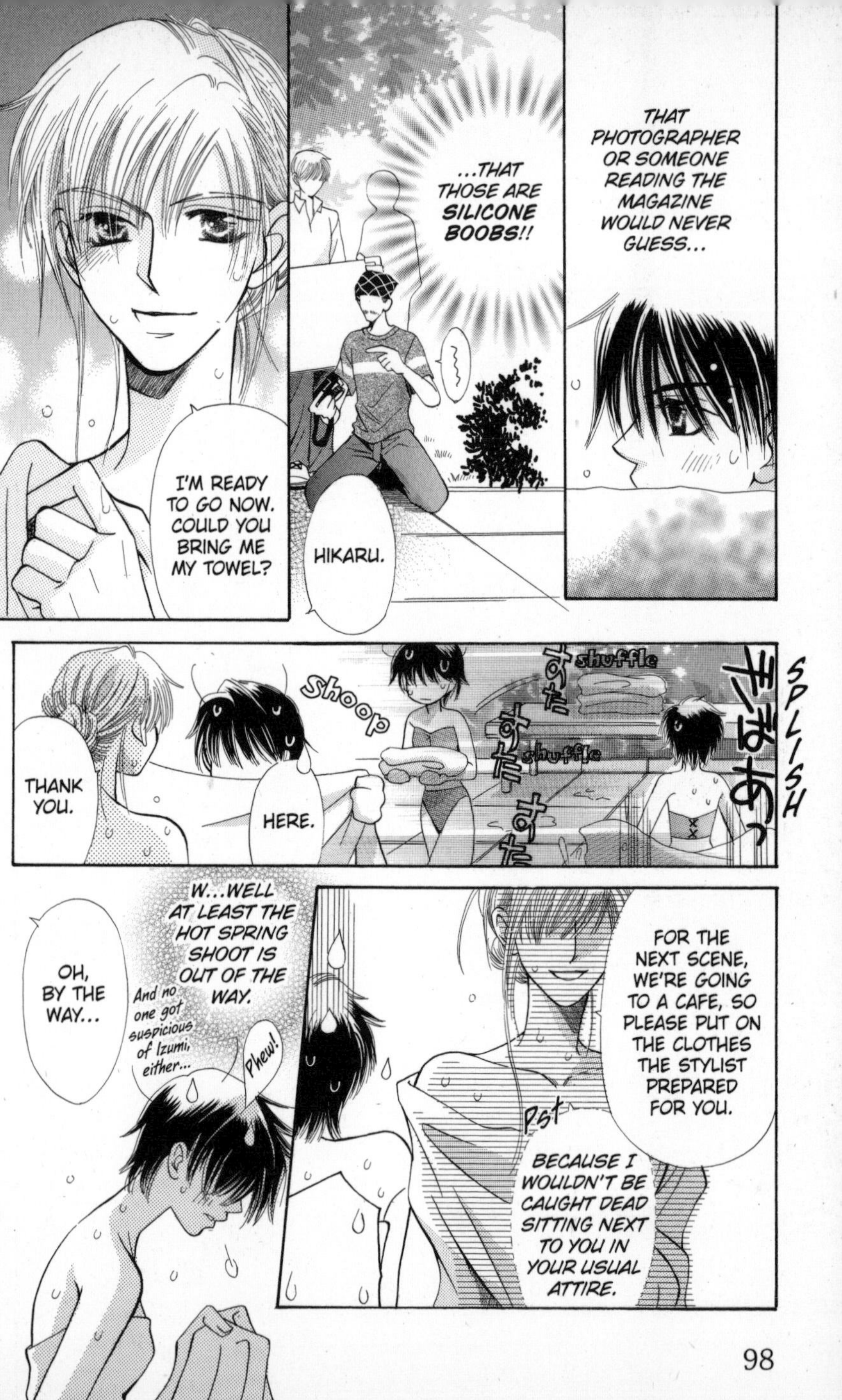
THAT PHOTOGRAPHER OR SOMEONE READING THE MAGAZINE WOULD NEVER GUESS...
...THAT THOSE ARE SILICONE BOOBS!!
HIKARU.
I'M READY TO GO NOW. COULD YOU BRING ME MY TOWEL?
SPLISH
shuffle
shuffle
Shoop
HERE.
THANK YOU.
FOR THE NEXT SCENE, WE'RE GOING TO A CAFE, SO PLEASE PUT ON THE CLOTHES THE STYLIST PREPARED FOR YOU.
Pst
BECAUSE I WOULDN'T BE CAUGHT DEAD SITTING NEXT TO YOU IN YOUR USUAL ATTIRE.
W...WELL AT LEAST THE HOT SPRING SHOOT IS OUT OF THE WAY.
And no one got suspicious of Izumi, either...
Phew!
OH, BY THE WAY...

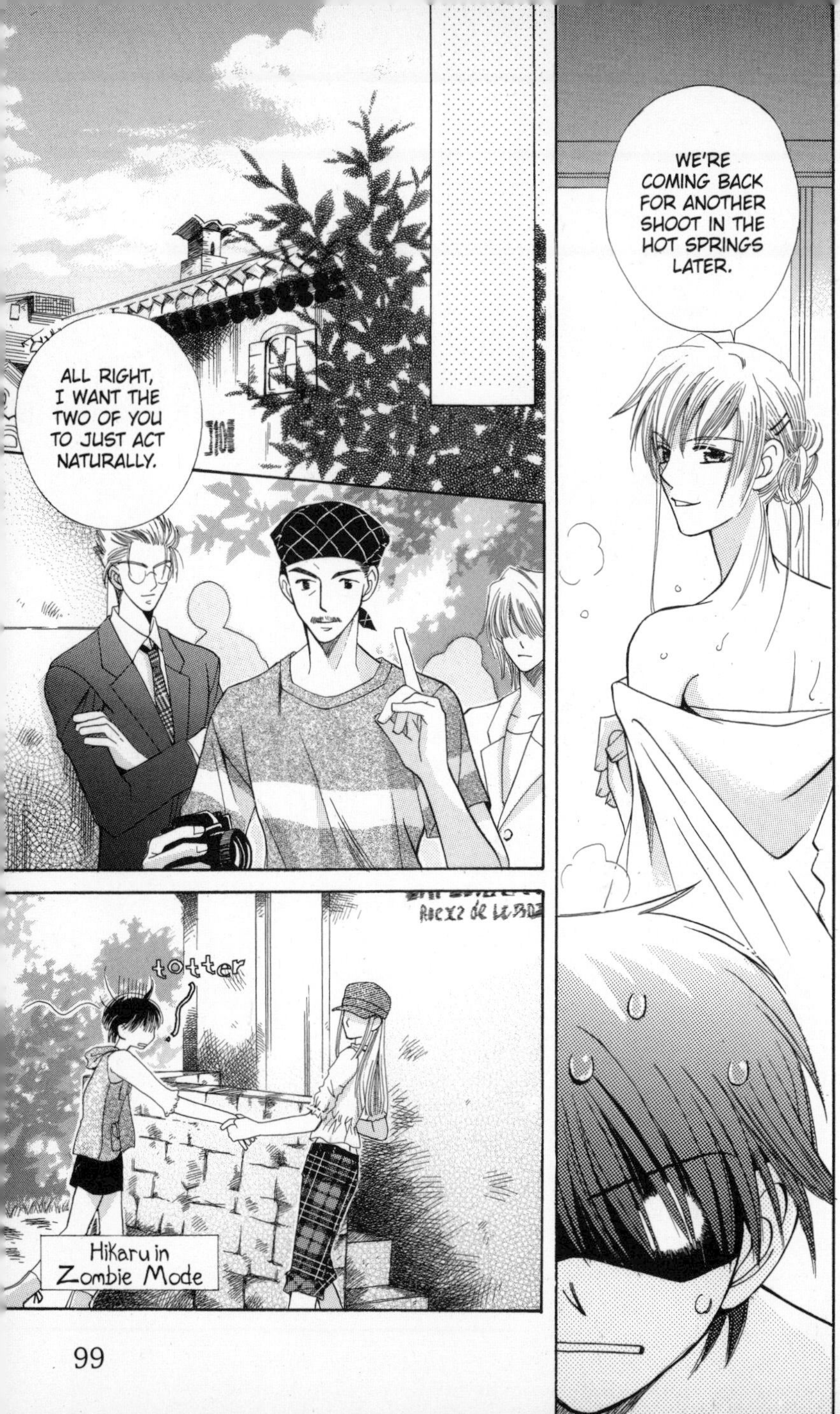

WE'RE COMING BACK FOR ANOTHER SHOOT IN THE HOT SPRINGS LATER.
ALL RIGHT, I WANT THE TWO OF YOU TO JUST ACT NATURALLY.
totter
Hikaru in Zombie Mode

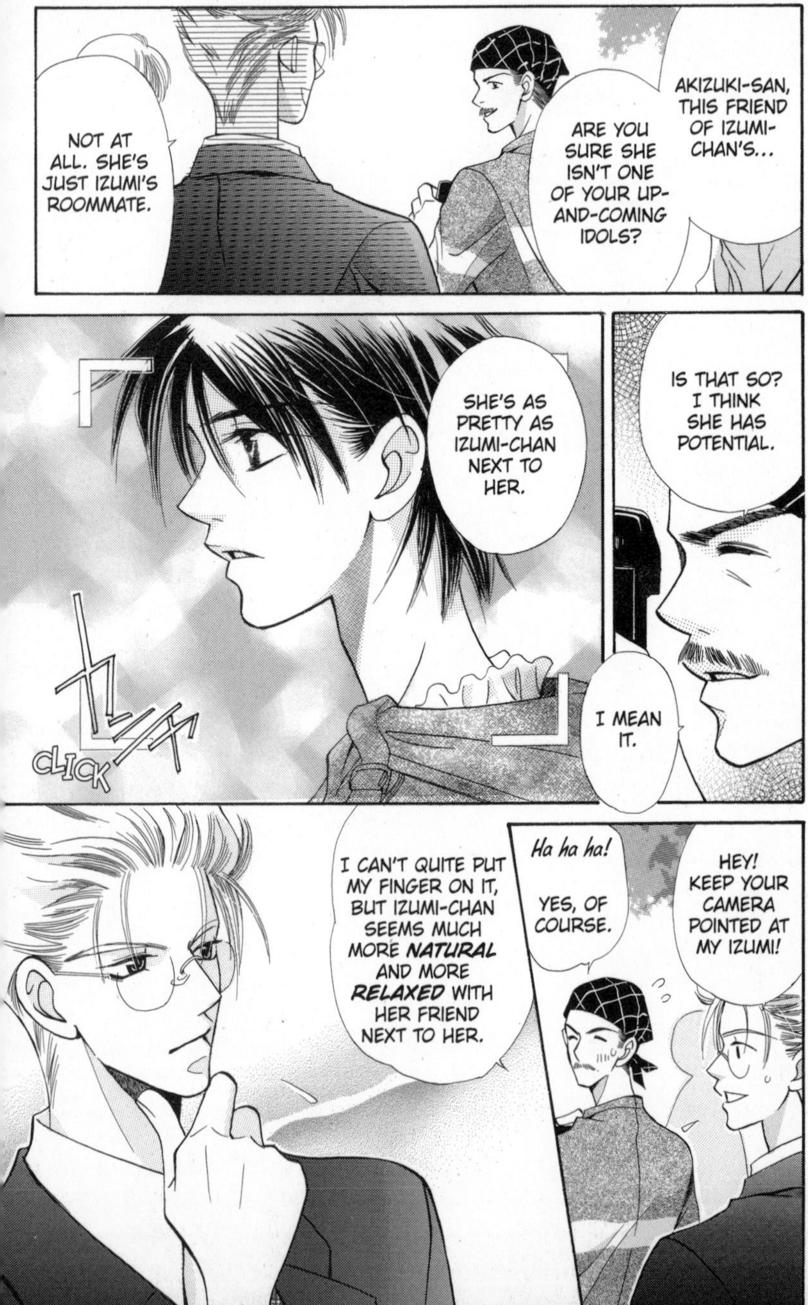
AKIZUKI-SAN, THIS FRIEND OF IZUMI-CHAN'S...
ARE YOU SURE SHE ISN'T ONE OF YOUR UP-AND-COMING IDOLS?
NOT AT ALL. SHE'S JUST IZUMI'S ROOMMATE.
IS THAT SO? I THINK SHE HAS POTENTIAL.
I MEAN IT.
SHE'S AS PRETTY AS IZUMI-CHAN NEXT TO HER.
CLICK
HEY! KEEP YOUR CAMERA POINTED AT MY IZUMI!
Ha ha ha!
YES, OF COURSE.
I CAN'T QUITE PUT MY FINGER ON IT, BUT IZUMI-CHAN SEEMS MUCH MORE NATURAL AND MORE RELAXED WITH HER FRIEND NEXT TO HER.

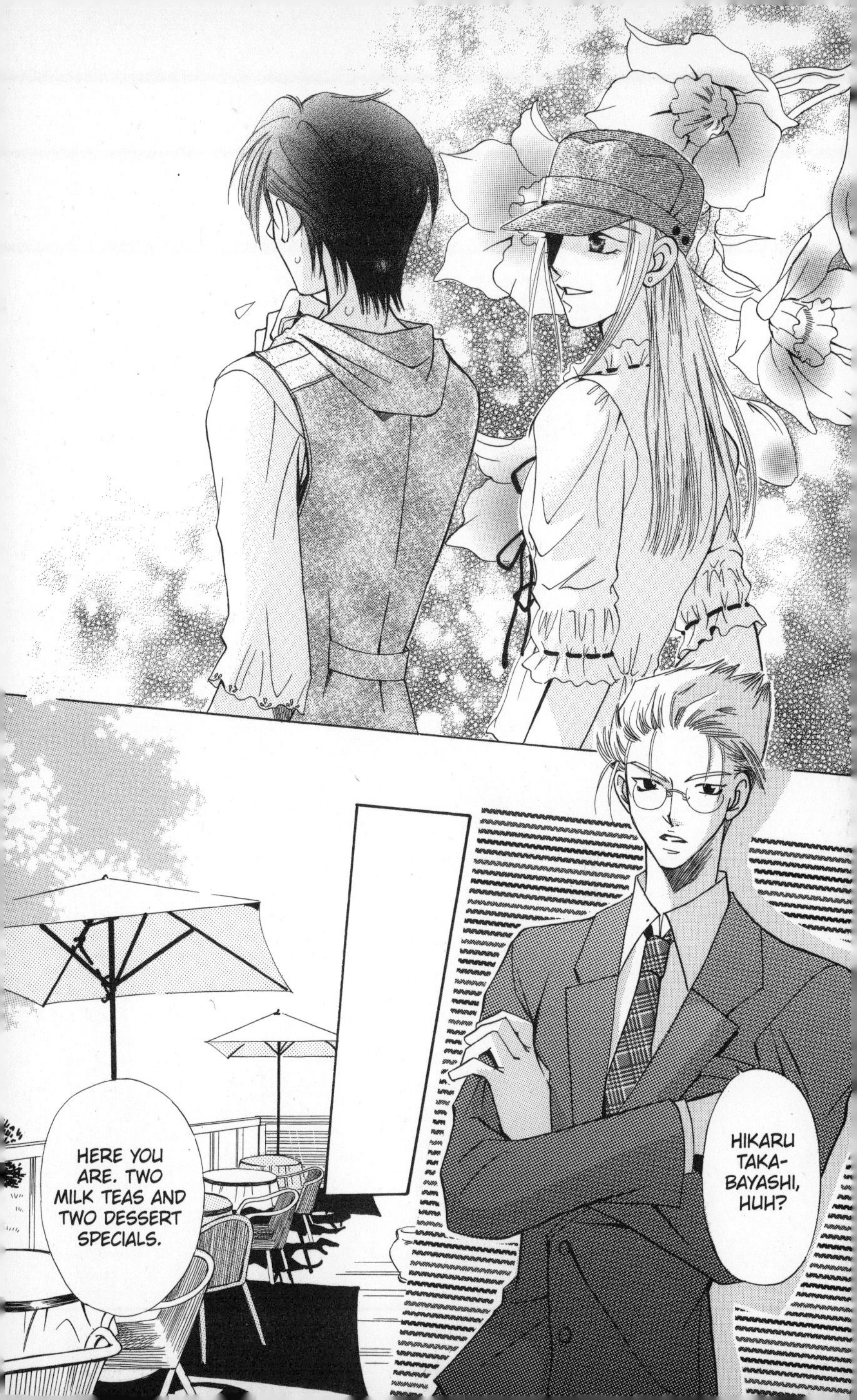
HIKARU TAKA-BAYASHI, HUH?
HERE YOU ARE. TWO MILK TEAS AND TWO DESSERT SPECIALS.

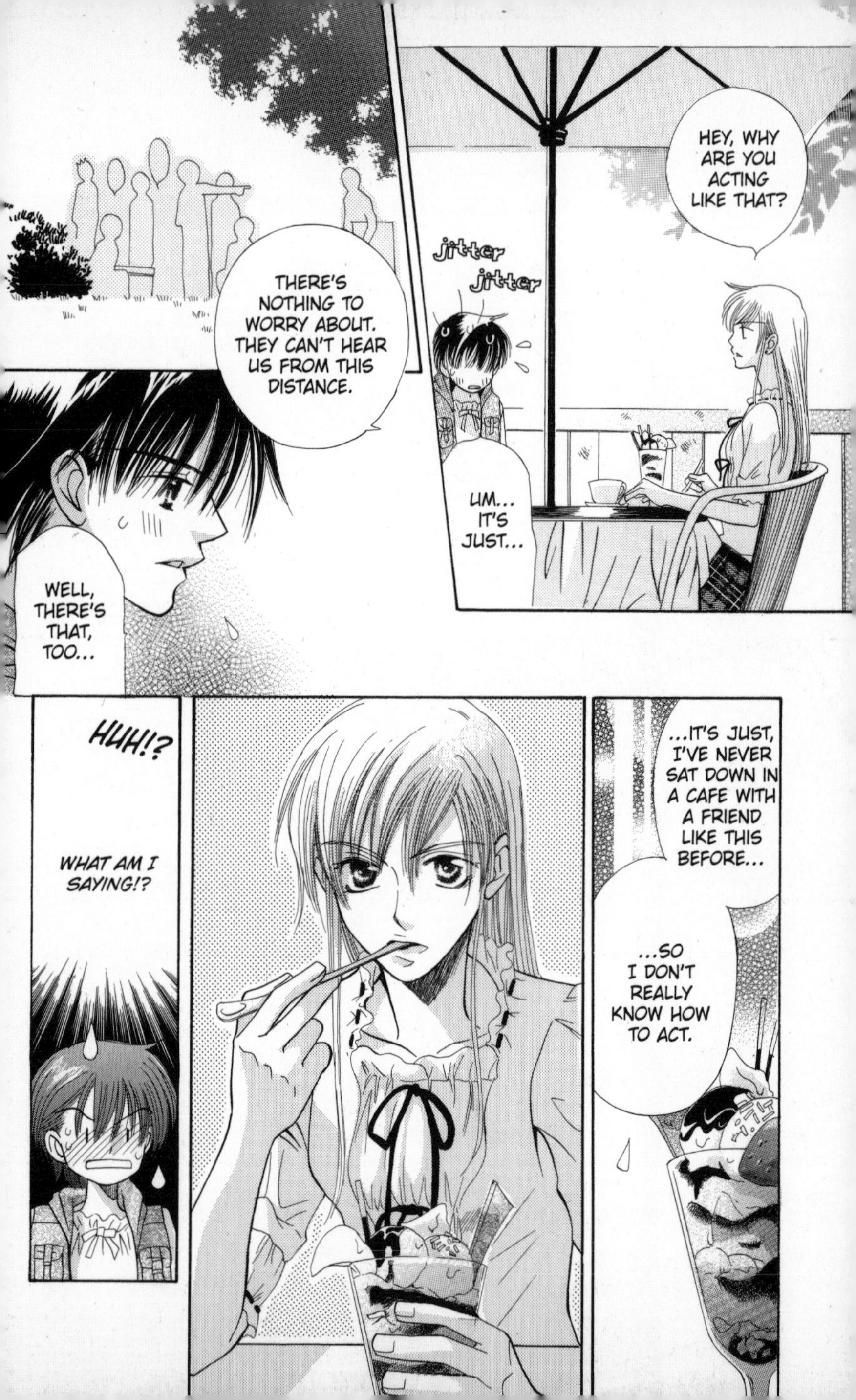
HEY, WHY ARE YOU ACTING LIKE THAT?
jitter
jitter
UM... IT'S JUST...
THERE'S NOTHING TO WORRY ABOUT. THEY CAN'T HEAR US FROM THIS DISTANCE.
WELL, THERE'S THAT, TOO...
...IT'S JUST, I'VE NEVER SAT DOWN IN A CAFE WITH A FRIEND LIKE THIS BEFORE...
...SO I DON'T REALLY KNOW HOW TO ACT.
HUH!?
WHAT AM I SAYING!?

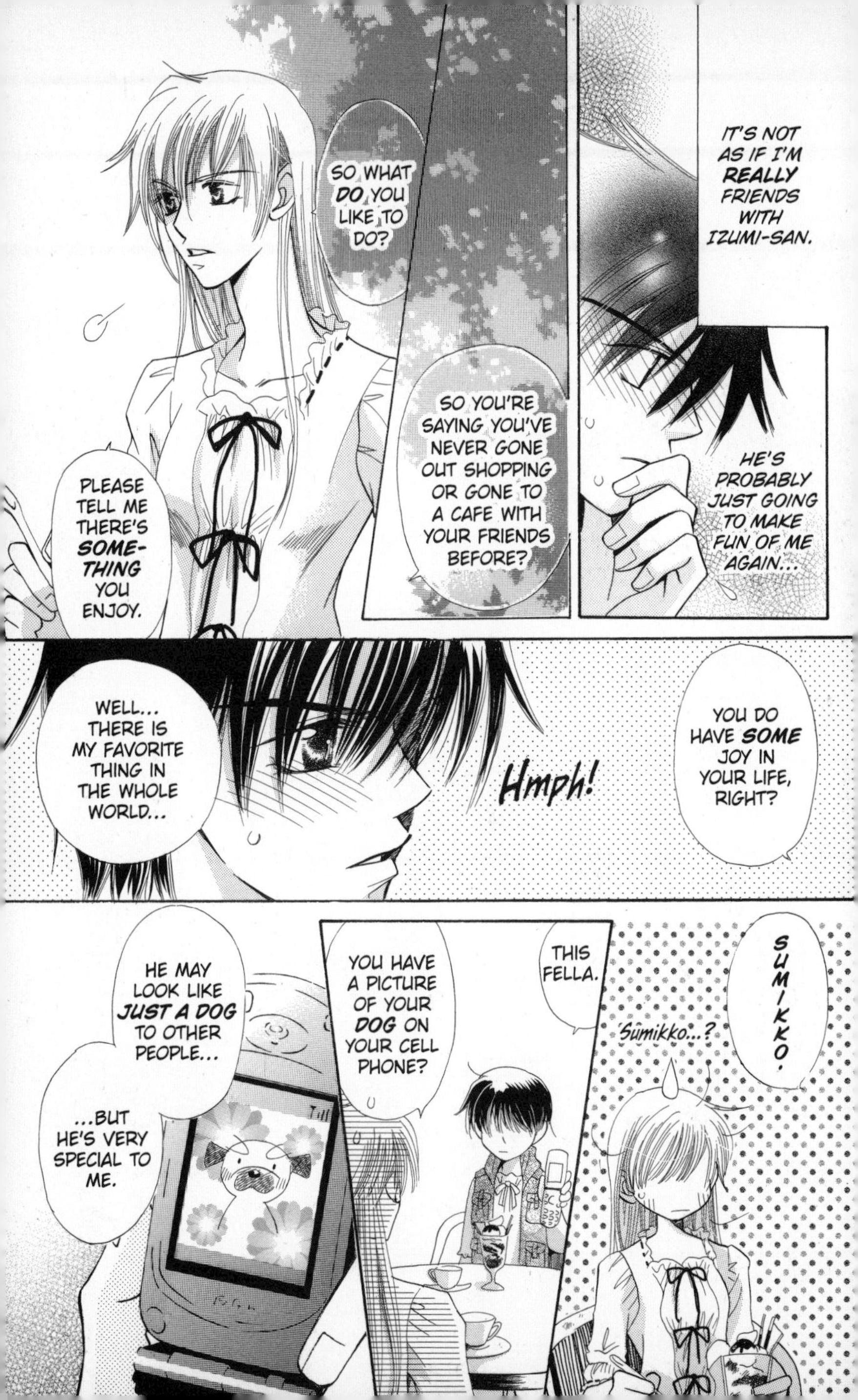

IT'S NOT AS IF I'M REALLY FRIENDS WITH IZUMI-SAN.
HE'S PROBABLY JUST GOING TO MAKE FUN OF ME AGAIN...
SO YOU'RE SAYING YOU'VE NEVER GONE OUT SHOPPING OR GONE TO A CAFE WITH YOUR FRIENDS BEFORE?
SO WHAT DO YOU LIKE TO DO?
PLEASE TELL ME THERE'S SOMETHING YOU ENJOY.
YOU DO HAVE SOME JOY IN YOUR LIFE, RIGHT?
Hmph!
WELL... THERE IS MY FAVORITE THING IN THE WHOLE WORLD...
SUMIKKO.
Sumikko...?
THIS FELLA.
YOU HAVE A PICTURE OF YOUR DOG ON YOUR CELL PHONE?
HE MAY LOOK LIKE JUST A DOG TO OTHER PEOPLE...
...BUT HE'S VERY SPECIAL TO ME.

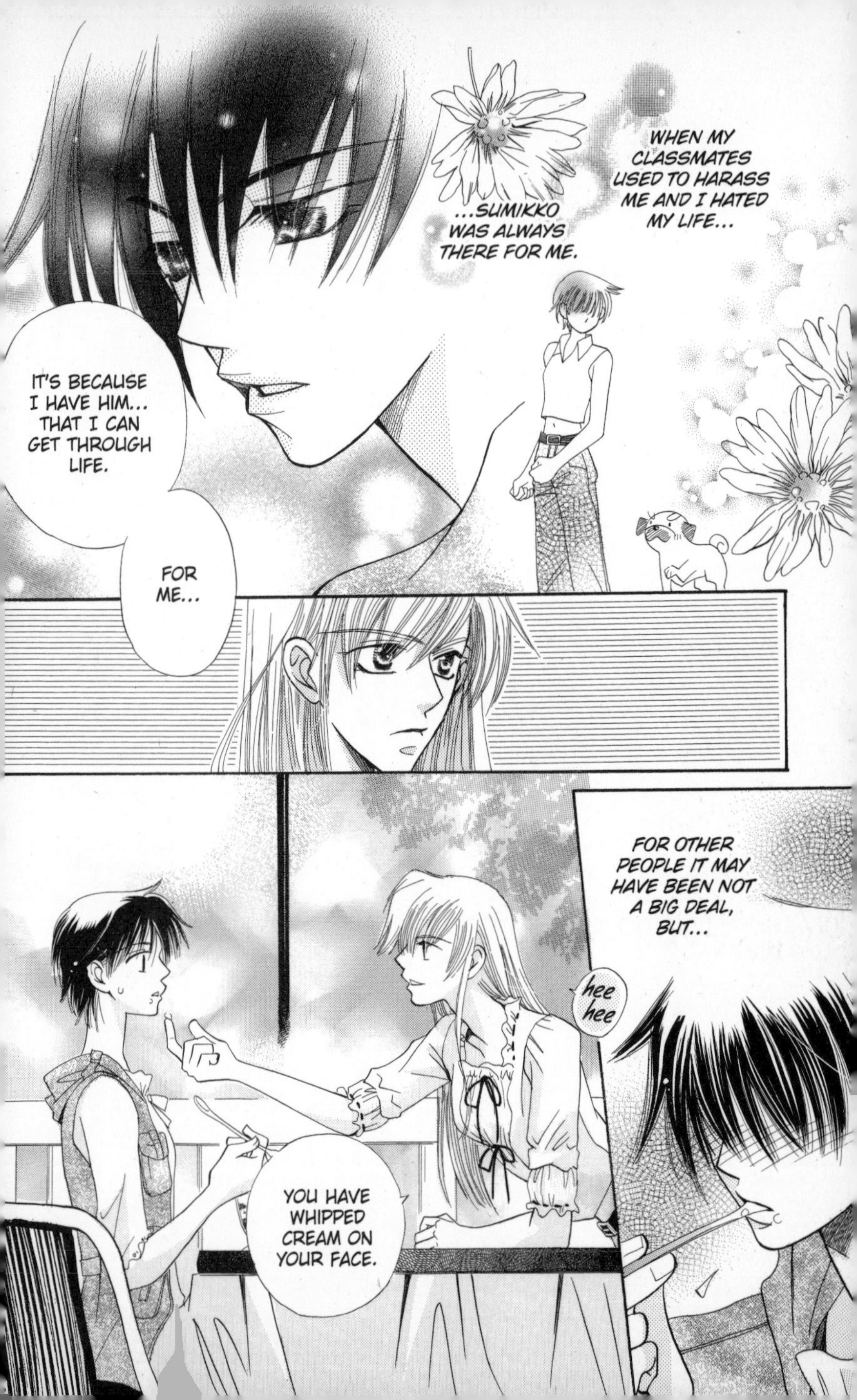
WHEN MY CLASSMATES USED TO HARASS ME AND I HATED MY LIFE...
...SUMIKKO WAS ALWAYS THERE FOR ME.
IT'S BECAUSE I HAVE HIM... THAT I CAN GET THROUGH LIFE.
FOR ME...
FOR OTHER PEOPLE IT MAY HAVE BEEN NOT A BIG DEAL, BUT...
hee hee
YOU HAVE WHIPPED CREAM ON YOUR FACE.

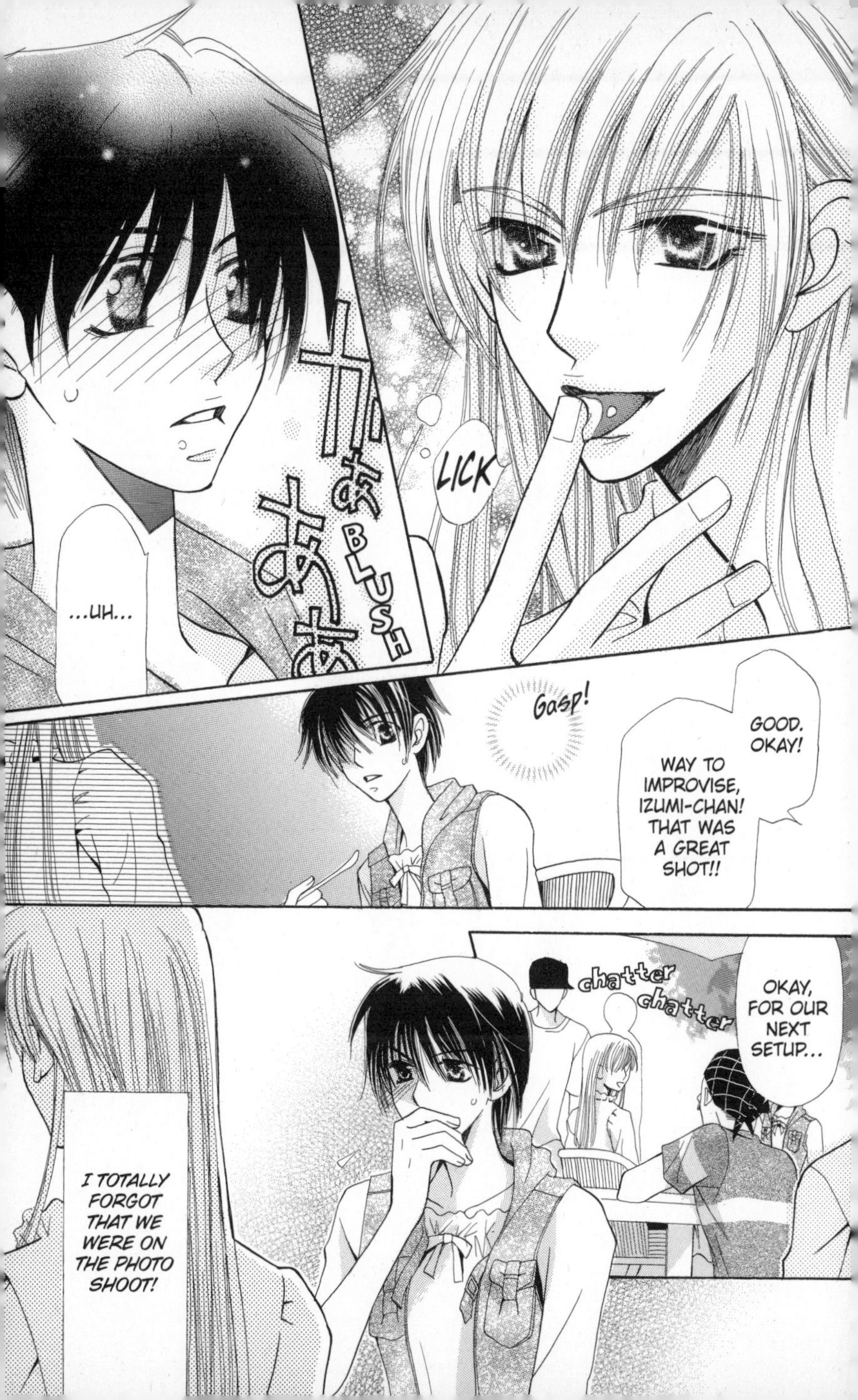

LICK
BLUSH
...UH...
GOOD. OKAY!
WAY TO IMPROVISE, IZUMI-CHAN! THAT WAS A GREAT SHOT!!
Gasp!
OKAY, FOR OUR NEXT SETUP...
chatter chatter
I TOTALLY FORGOT THAT WE WERE ON THE PHOTO SHOOT!

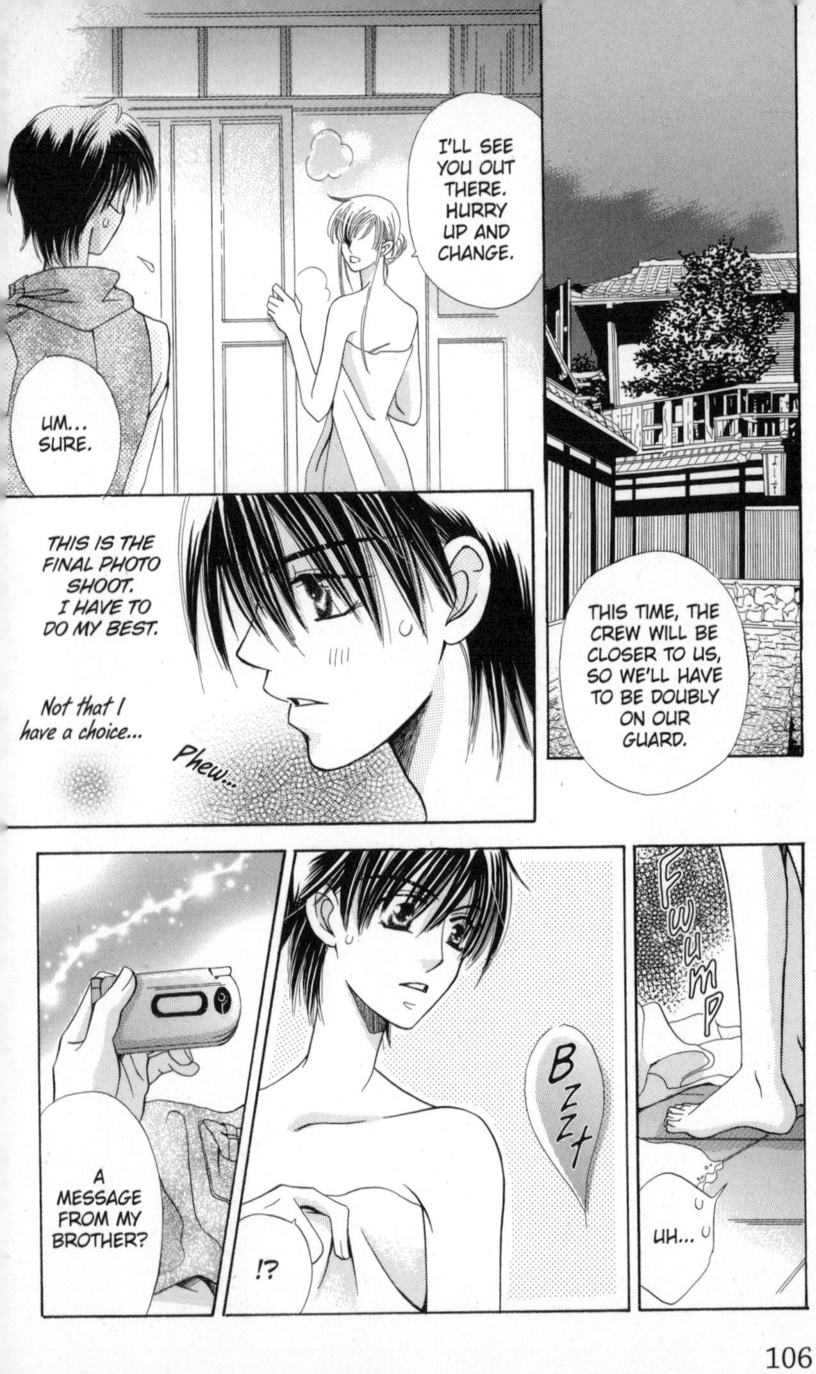
THIS TIME, THE CREW WILL BE CLOSER TO US, SO WE'LL HAVE TO BE DOUBLY ON OUR GUARD.
I'LL SEE YOU OUT THERE. HURRY UP AND CHANGE.
UM... SURE.
THIS IS THE FINAL PHOTO SHOOT. I HAVE TO DO MY BEST.
Not that I have a choice...
Phew...
FWUMP
UH...
BZZT
!?
A MESSAGE FROM MY BROTHER?

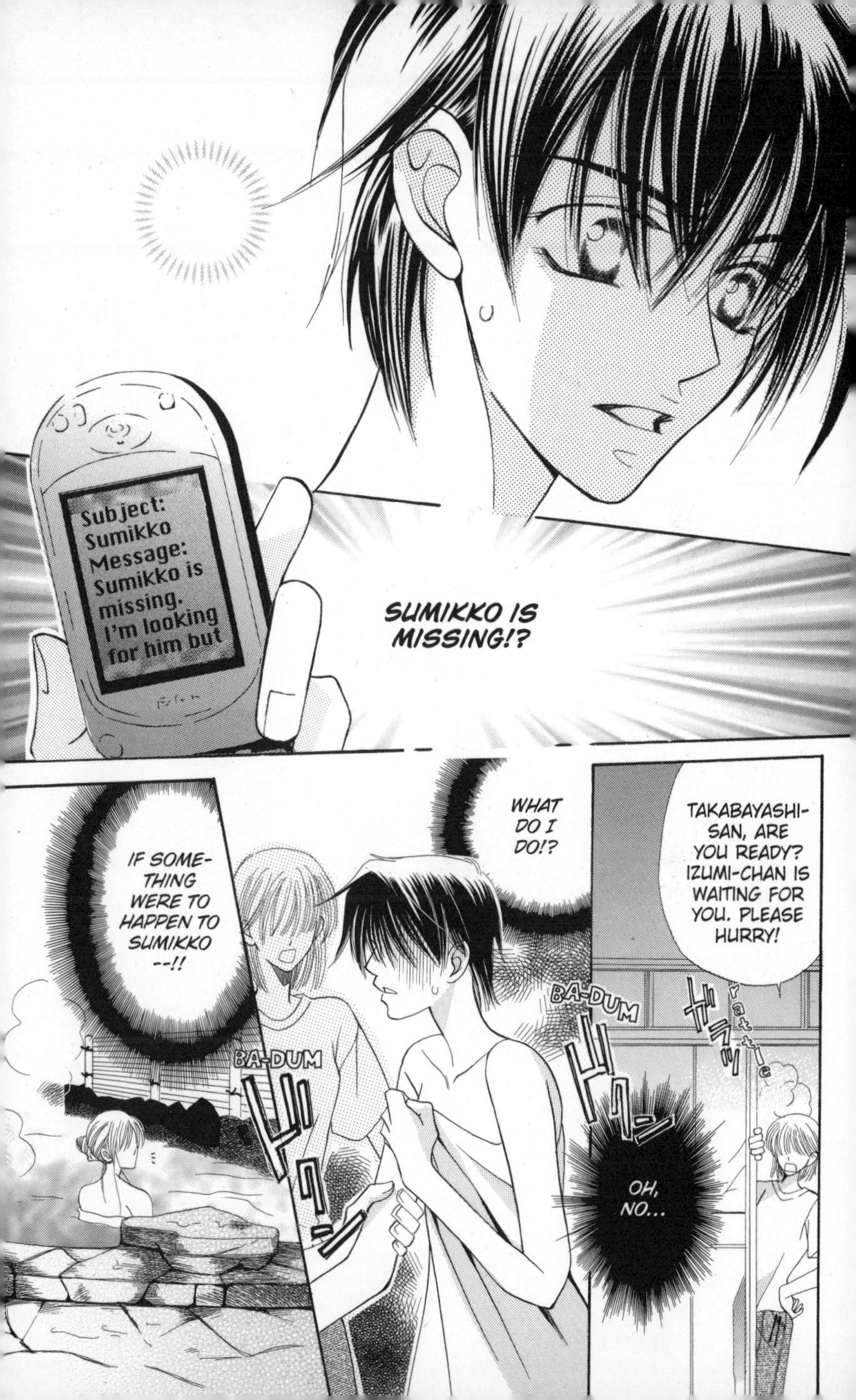
Subject: Sumikko
Message: Sumikko is missing. I'm looking for him but
SUMIKKO IS MISSING!?
TAKABAYASHI-SAN, ARE YOU READY? IZUMI-CHAN IS WAITING FOR YOU. PLEASE HURRY!
rattle
WHAT DO I DO!?
BA-DUM
OH, NO...
IF SOMETHING WERE TO HAPPEN TO SUMIKKO --!!
BA-DUM

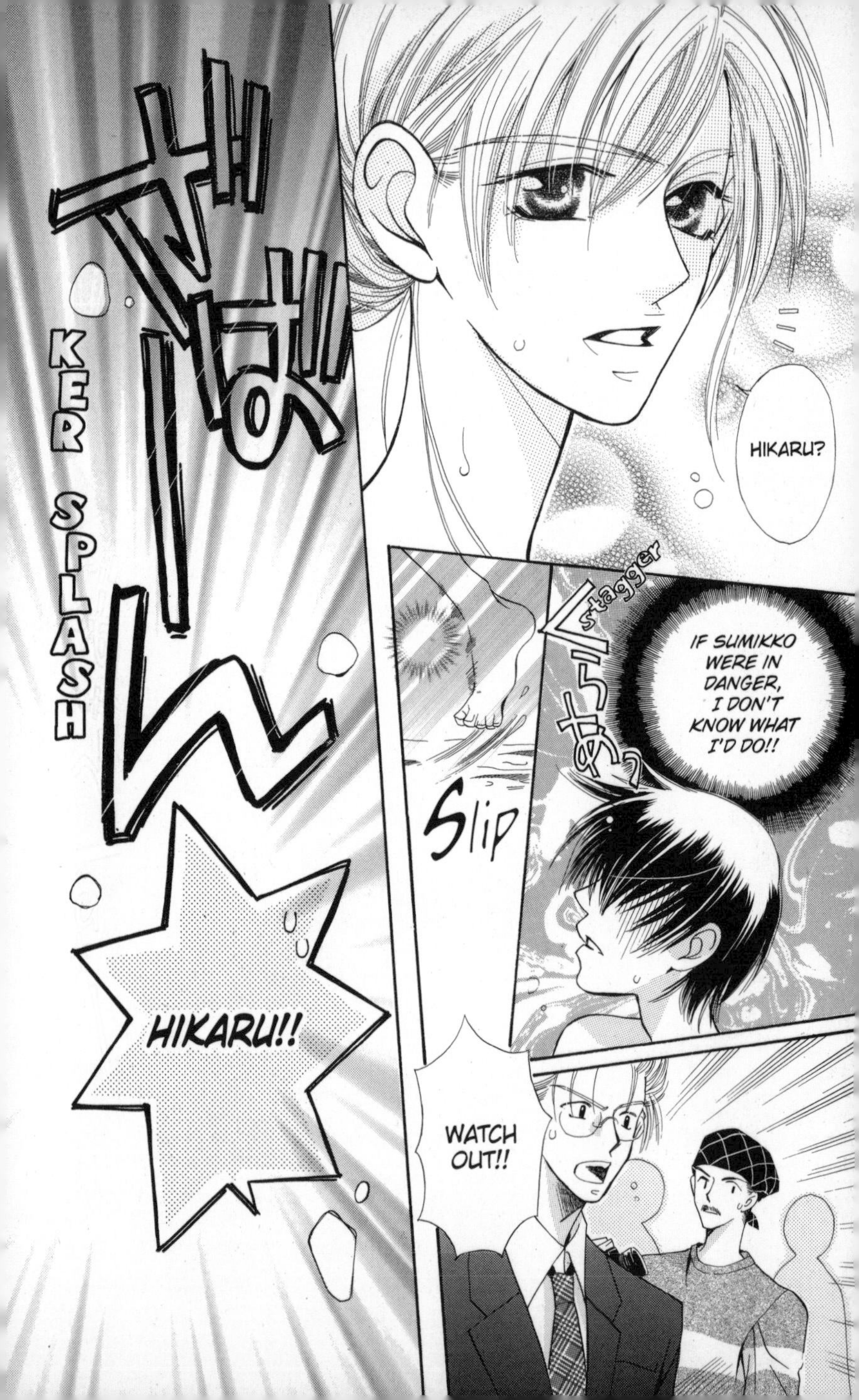
HIKARU?
stagger
IF SUMIKKO WERE IN DANGER, I DON'T KNOW WHAT I'D DO!!
Slip
WATCH OUT!!
KER SPLASH
HIKARU!!

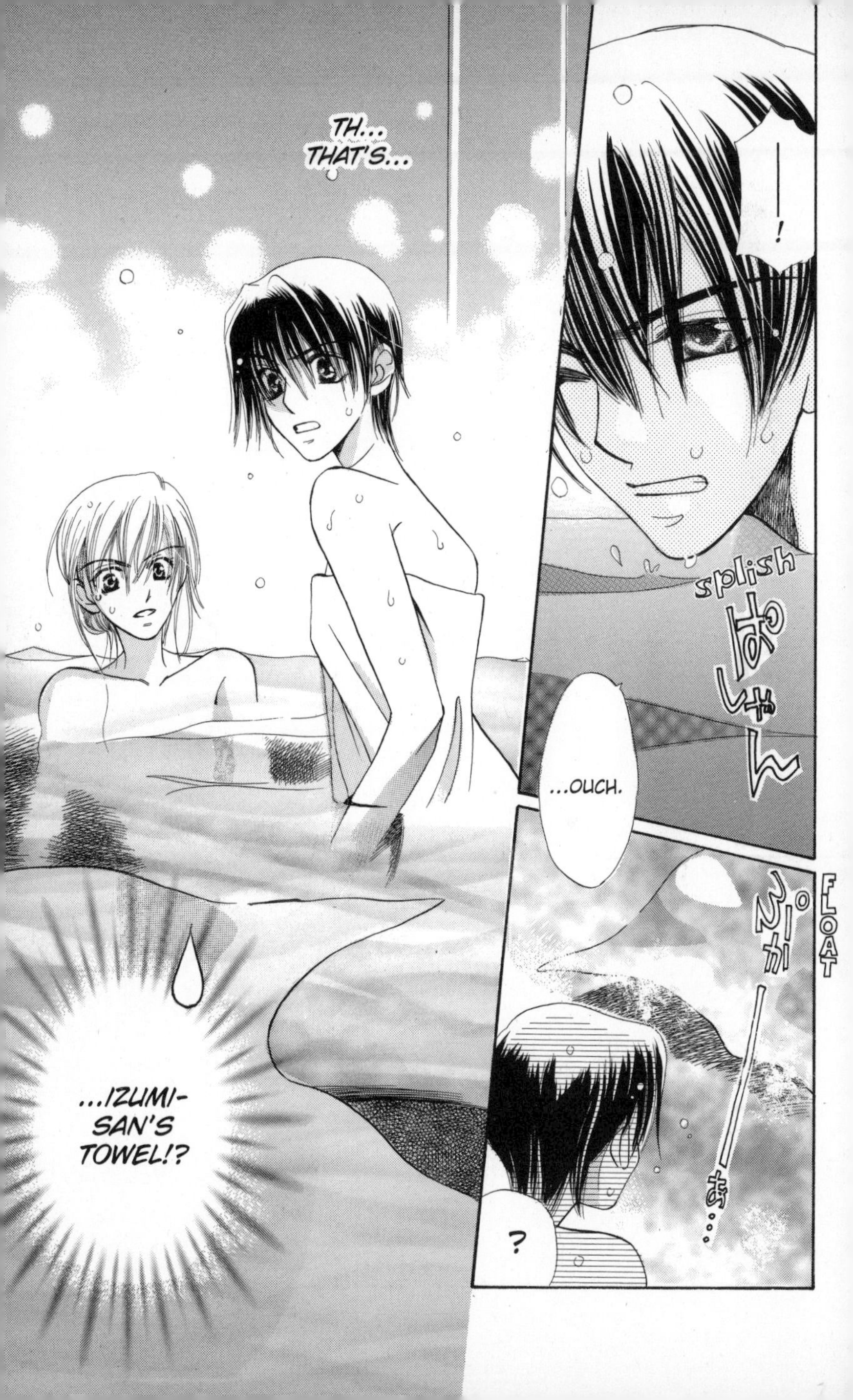
—!
splish
ぱしゃん
...OUCH.
FLOAT
?
TH... THAT'S...
...IZUMI-SAN'S TOWEL!?

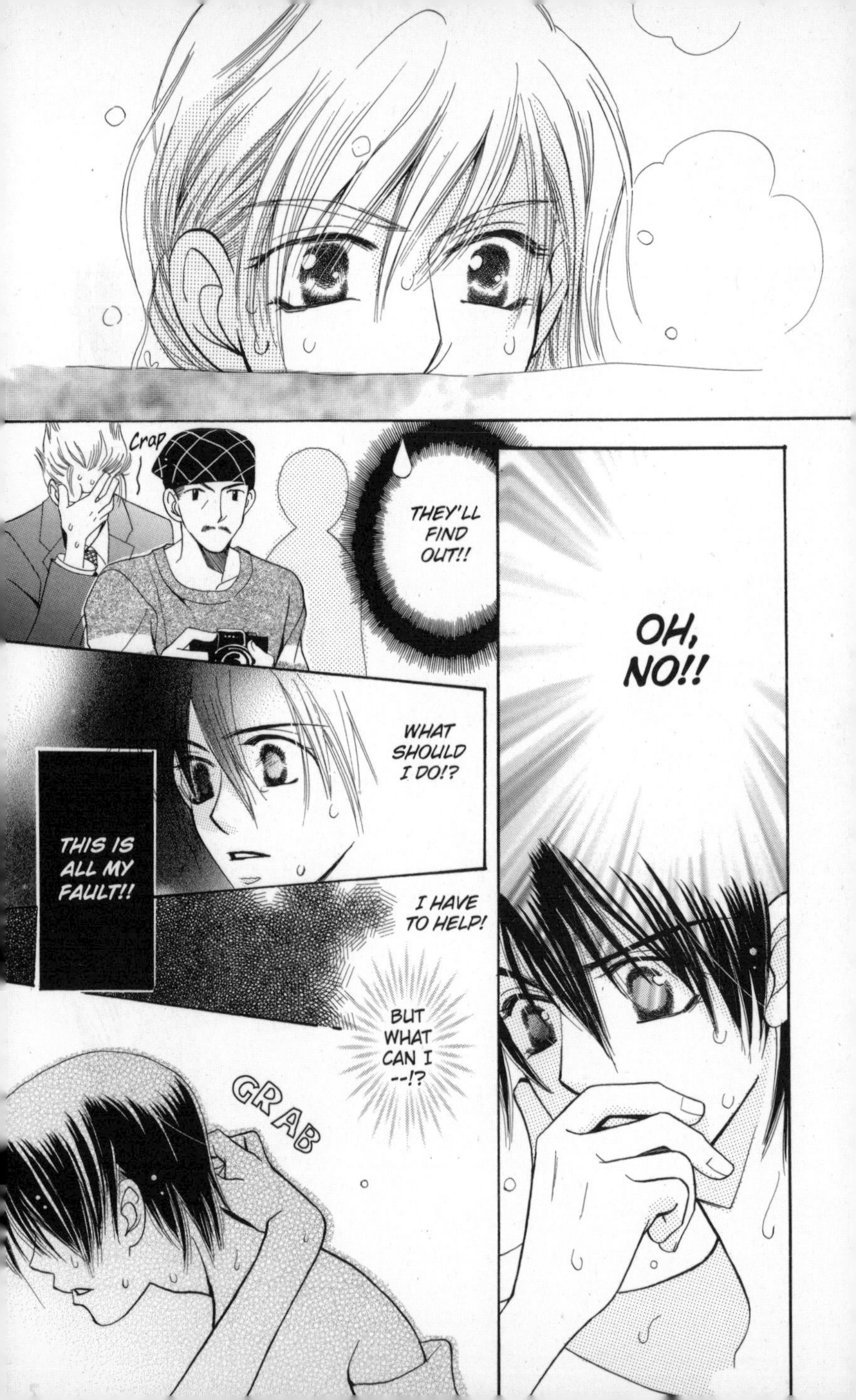
OH, NO!!
THEY'LL FIND OUT!!
Crap
WHAT SHOULD I DO!?
THIS IS ALL MY FAULT!!
I HAVE TO HELP!
BUT WHAT CAN I --!?
GRAB

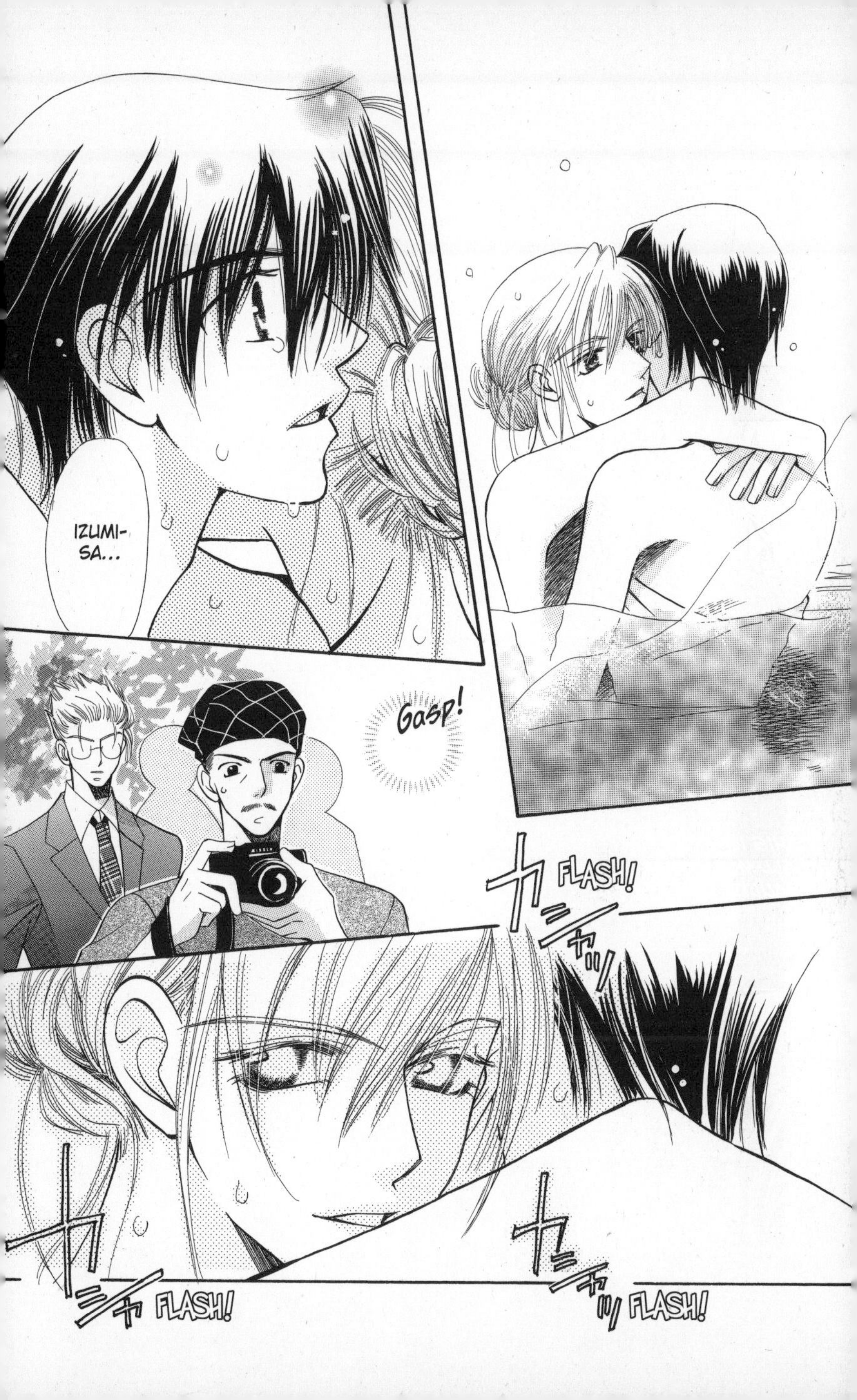
IZUMI-SA...
Gasp!
FLASH!
FLASH!
FLASH!

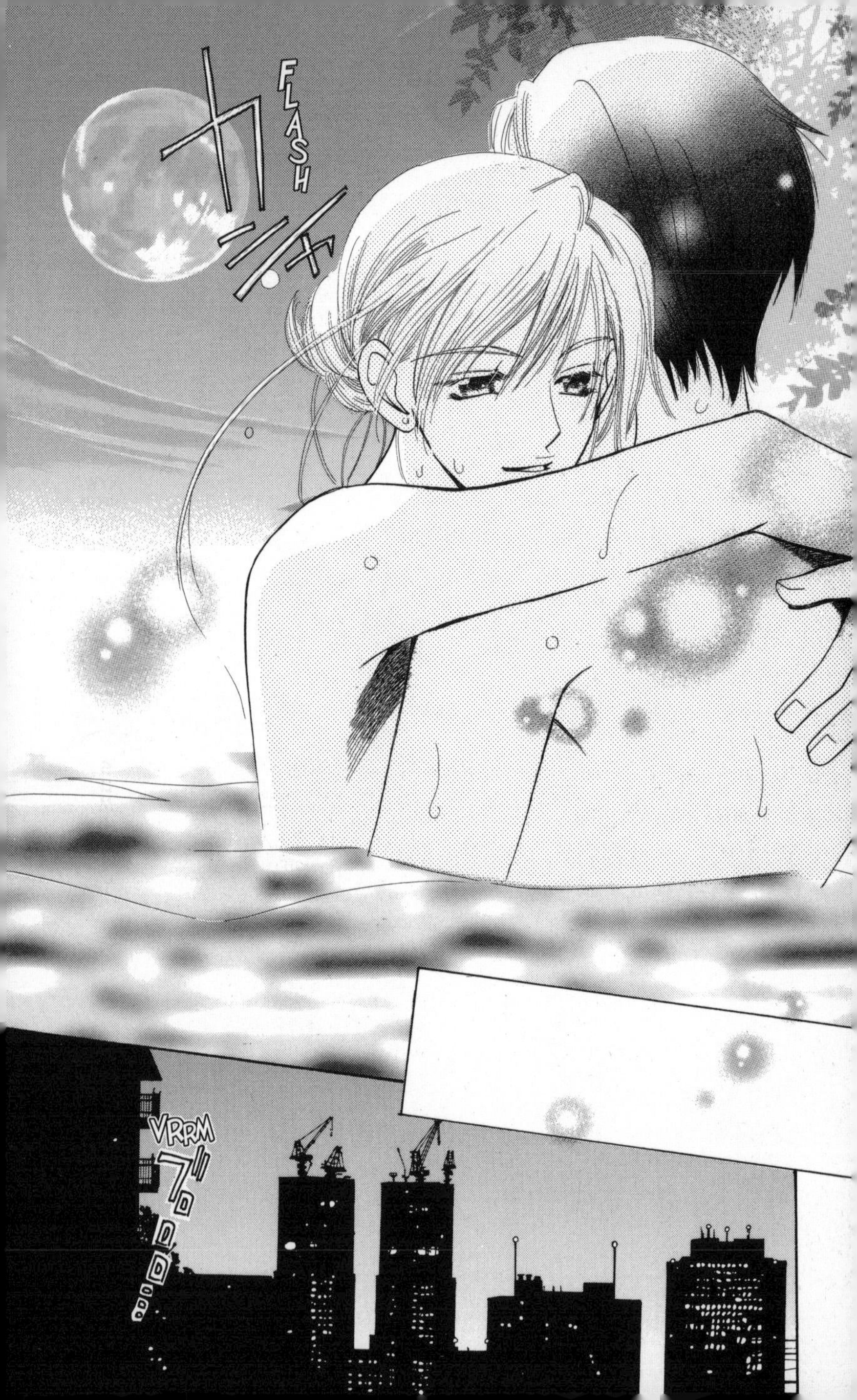
FLASH
VRRM

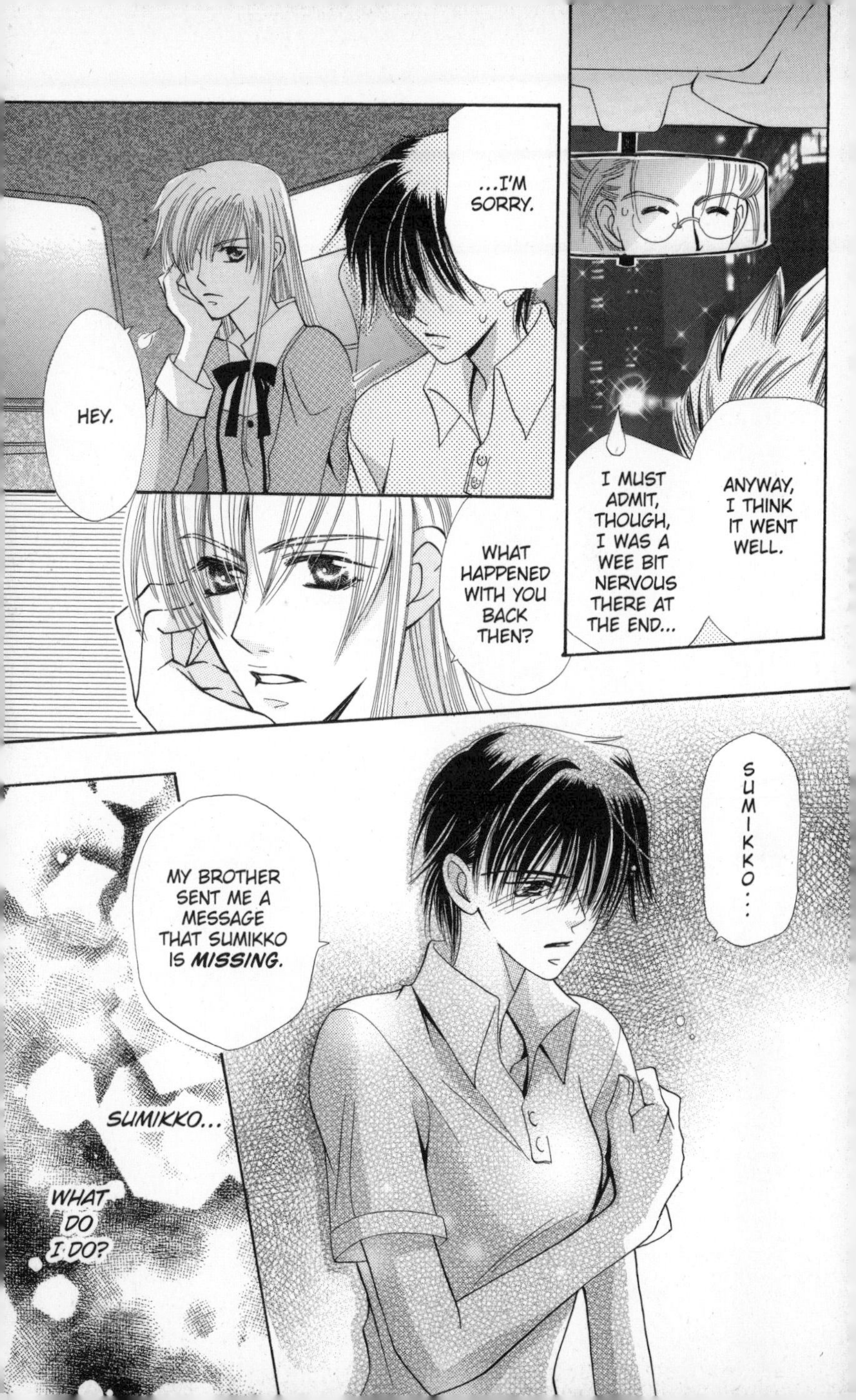
ANYWAY, I THINK IT WENT WELL.
I MUST ADMIT, THOUGH, I WAS A WEE BIT NERVOUS THERE AT THE END...
...I'M SORRY.
HEY.
WHAT HAPPENED WITH YOU BACK THEN?
SUMIKKO...
MY BROTHER SENT ME A MESSAGE THAT SUMIKKO IS MISSING.
SUMIKKO...
WHAT DO I DO?

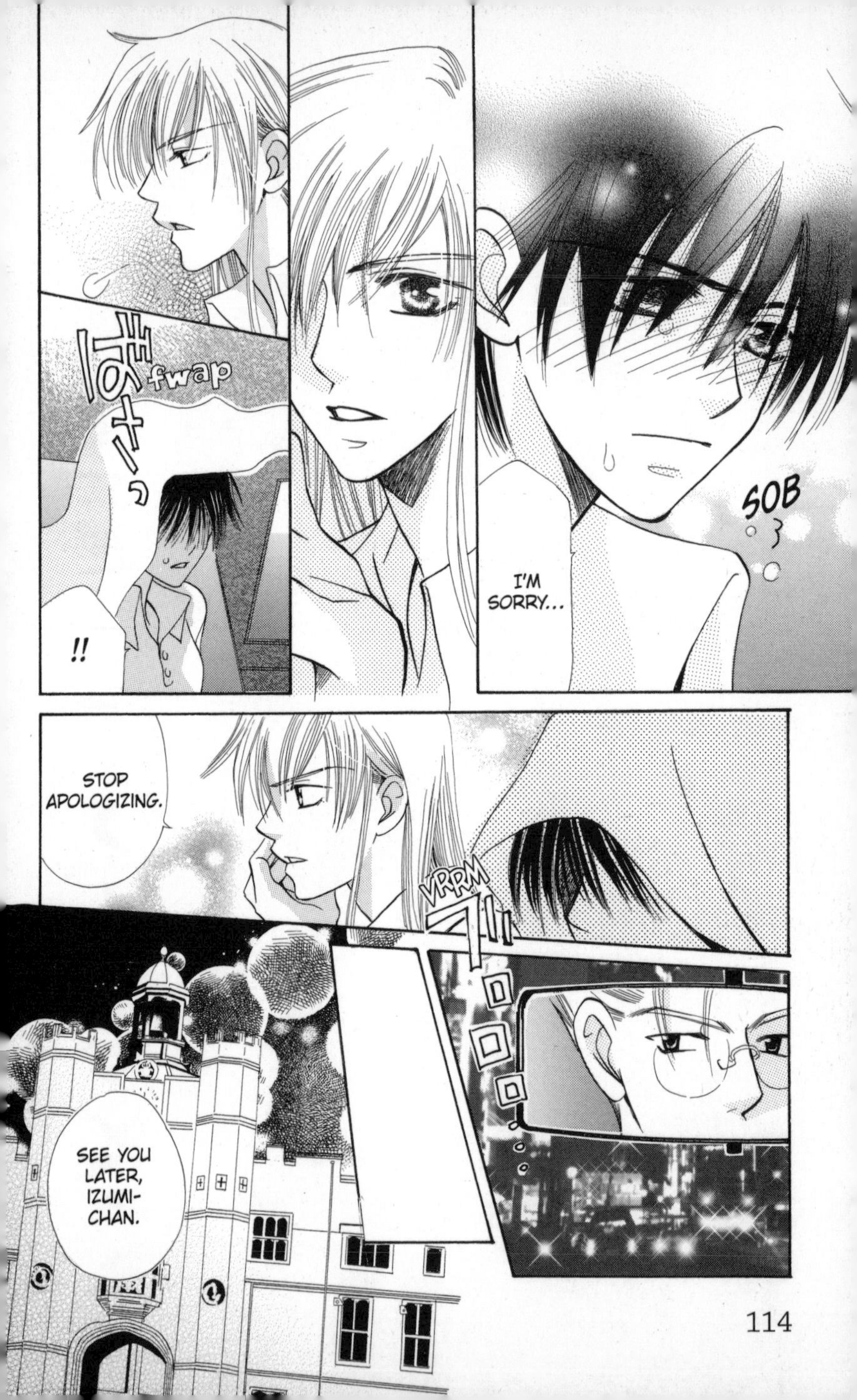
SOB
I'M SORRY...
fwap
!!
STOP APOLOGIZING.
VRRM
SEE YOU LATER, IZUMI-CHAN.

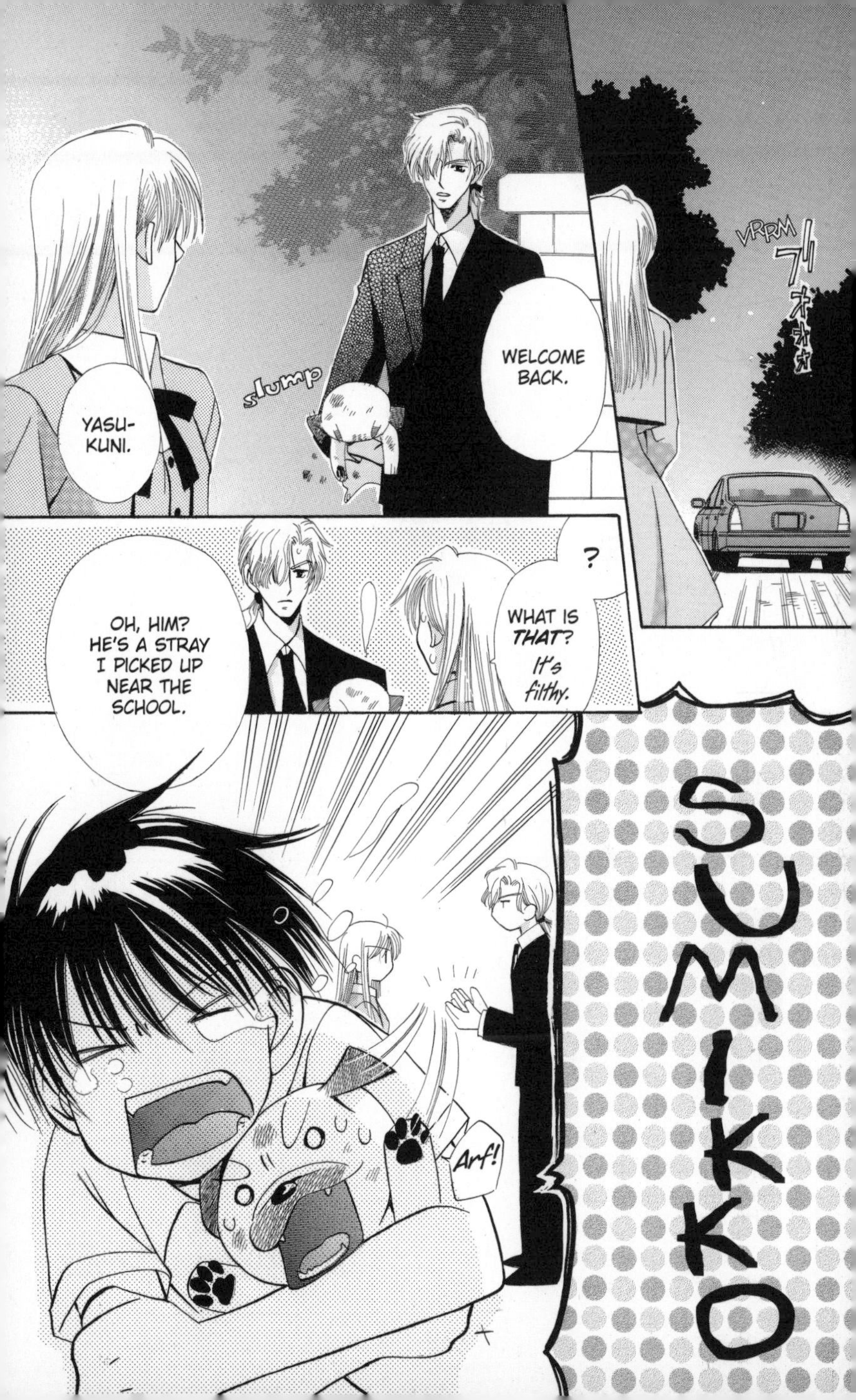
VRRM
WELCOME BACK.
slump
YASU-KUNI.
?
WHAT IS *THAT*? It's filthy.
OH, HIM? HE'S A STRAY I PICKED UP NEAR THE SCHOOL.
SUMIKKO
Arf!

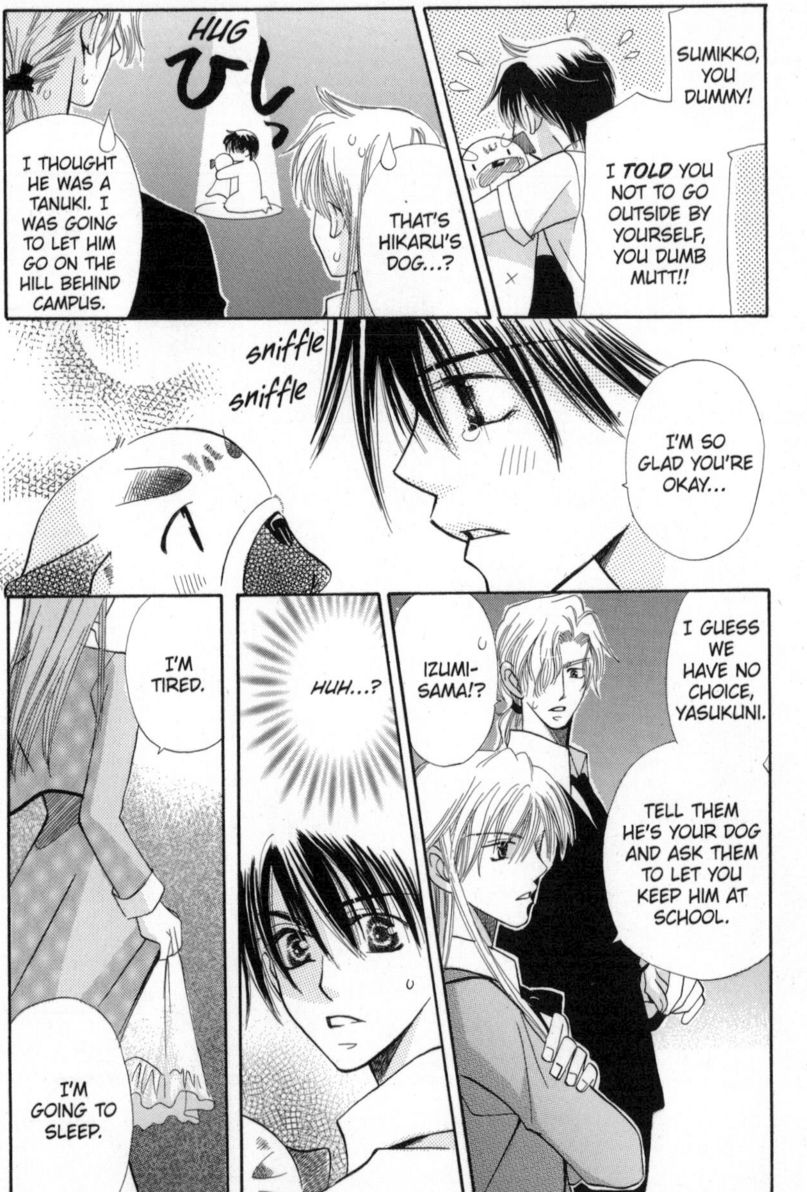
SUMIKKO, YOU DUMMY!
I **TOLD** YOU NOT TO GO OUTSIDE BY YOURSELF, YOU DUMB MUTT!!
HUG
ひし
THAT'S HIKARU'S DOG...?
I THOUGHT HE WAS A TANUKI. I WAS GOING TO LET HIM GO ON THE HILL BEHIND CAMPUS.
sniffle
sniffle
I'M SO GLAD YOU'RE OKAY...
I GUESS WE HAVE NO CHOICE, YASUKUNI.
IZUMI-SAMA!?
TELL THEM HE'S YOUR DOG AND ASK THEM TO LET YOU KEEP HIM AT SCHOOL.
HUH...?
I'M TIRED.
I'M GOING TO SLEEP.

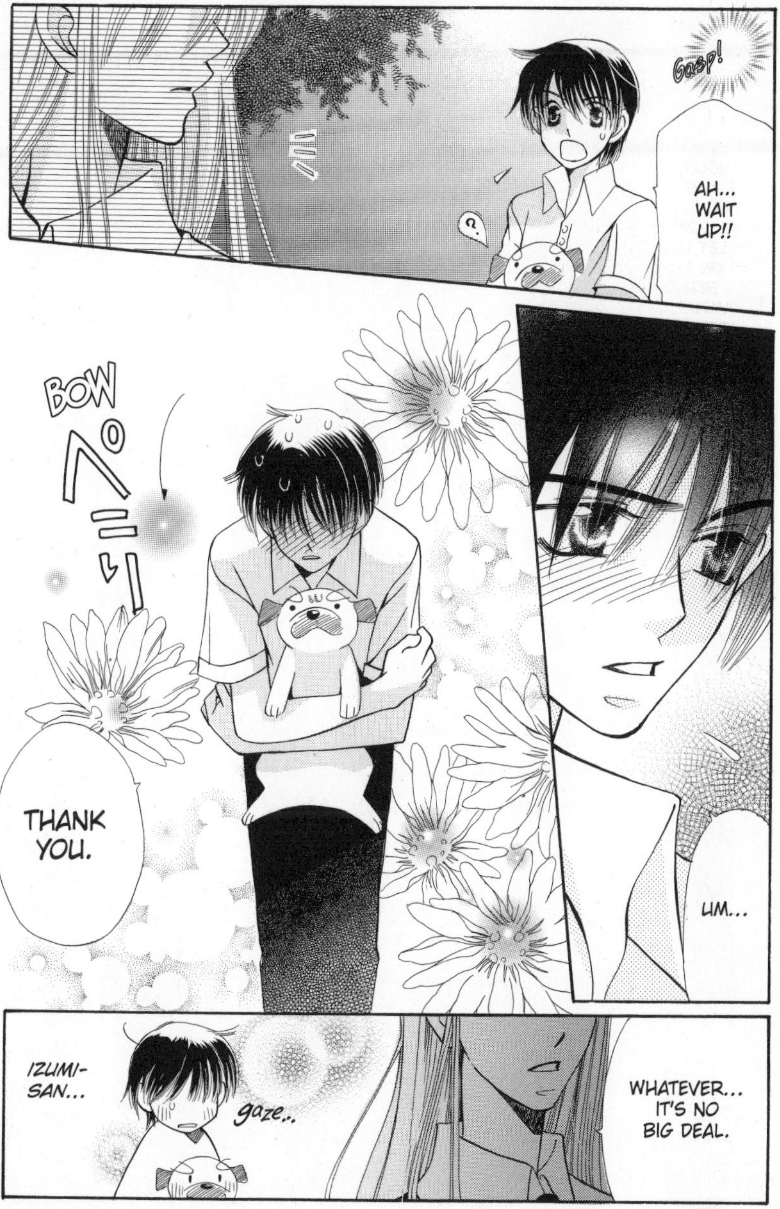
Gasp!
AH... WAIT UP!!
UM...
BOW
THANK YOU.
WHATEVER... IT'S NO BIG DEAL.
gaze..
IZUMI-SAN...

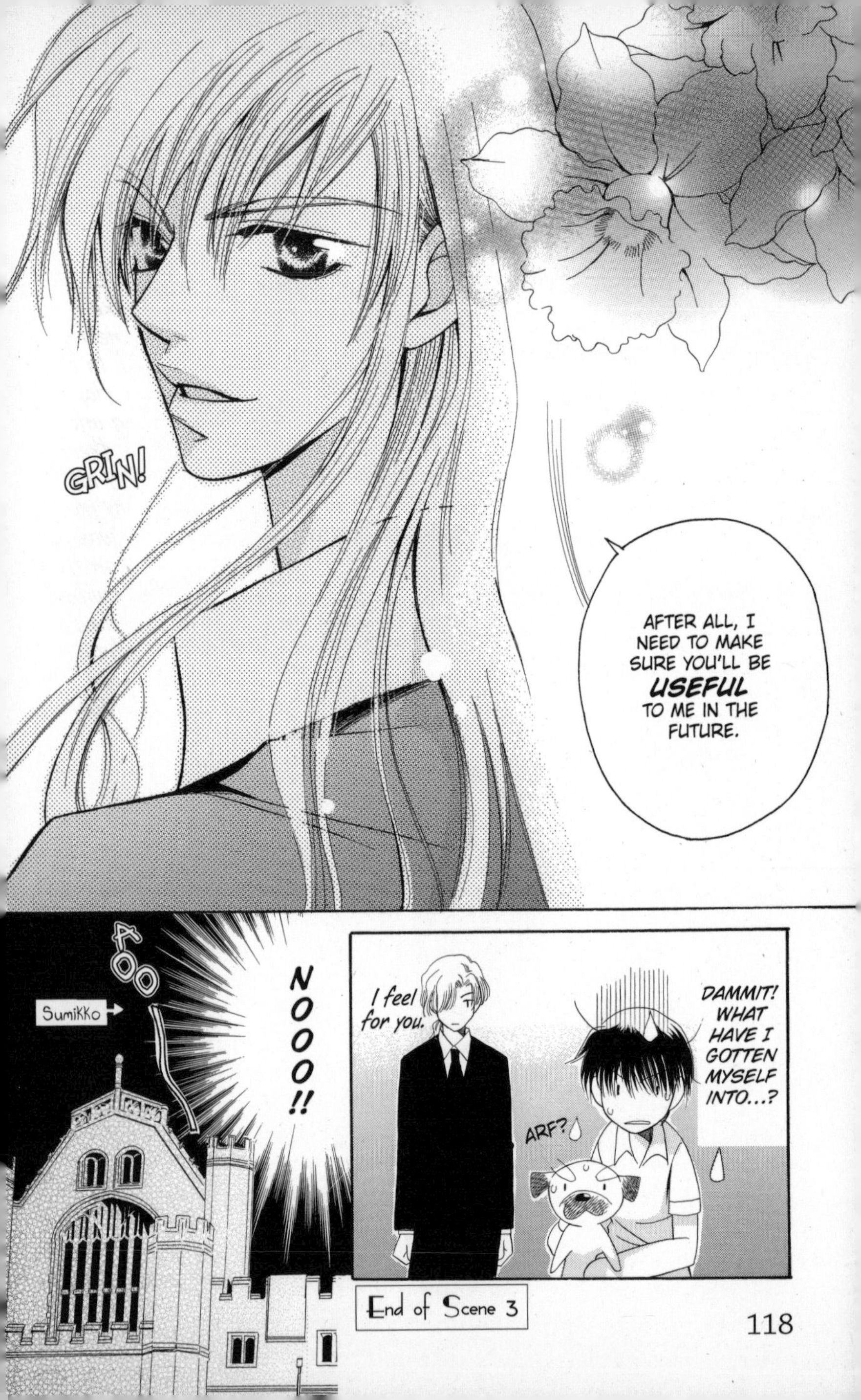
AFTER ALL, I NEED TO MAKE SURE YOU'LL BE **USEFUL** TO ME IN THE FUTURE.
GRIN!
DAMMIT! WHAT HAVE I GOTTEN MYSELF INTO...?
I feel for you.
ARF?
NOOOO!!
AOO
Sumikko

End of Scene 3

Cats and Me

I like dogs. I also like cats, but cats don't seem to like me very much. I now have a new member in my household. In the photograph on the cover flap, you can see Molly looking into a basket. It's no baby in there, though—that's Reggie, my new kitten. On my birthday, my mother rescued Reggie when he was being attacked by crows on the street. Reggie is a tabby with a coat that almost looks like a tiger's. He has a very strong personality. I sincerely hope that he'll get along with Molly when he gets older.

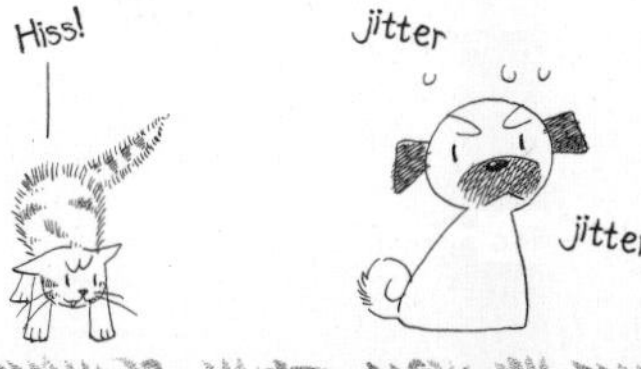
Hiss!
jitter
jitter

I try to make sure Molly doesn't get jealous as I raise Reggie, but it's not easy...

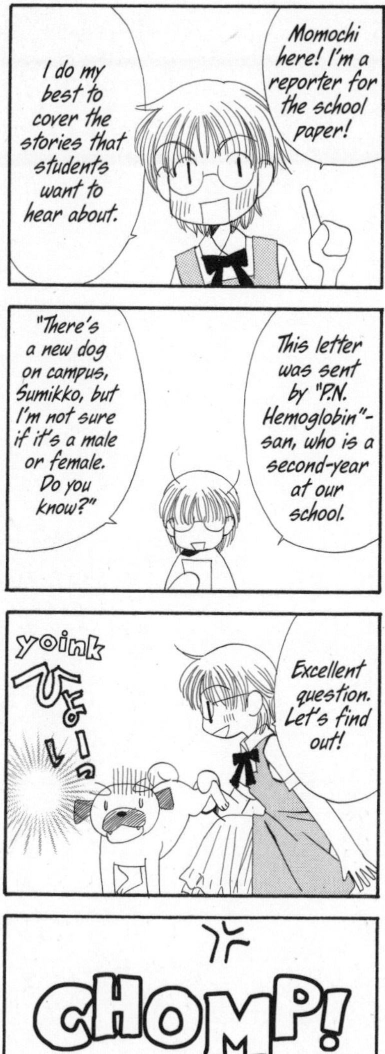
Momochi here! I'm a reporter for the school paper!
I do my best to cover the stories that students want to hear about.
This letter was sent by "P.N. Hemoglobin"-san, who is a second-year at our school.
"There's a new dog on campus, Sumikko, but I'm not sure if it's a male or female. Do you know?"
Excellent question. Let's find out!
yoink
CHOMP!

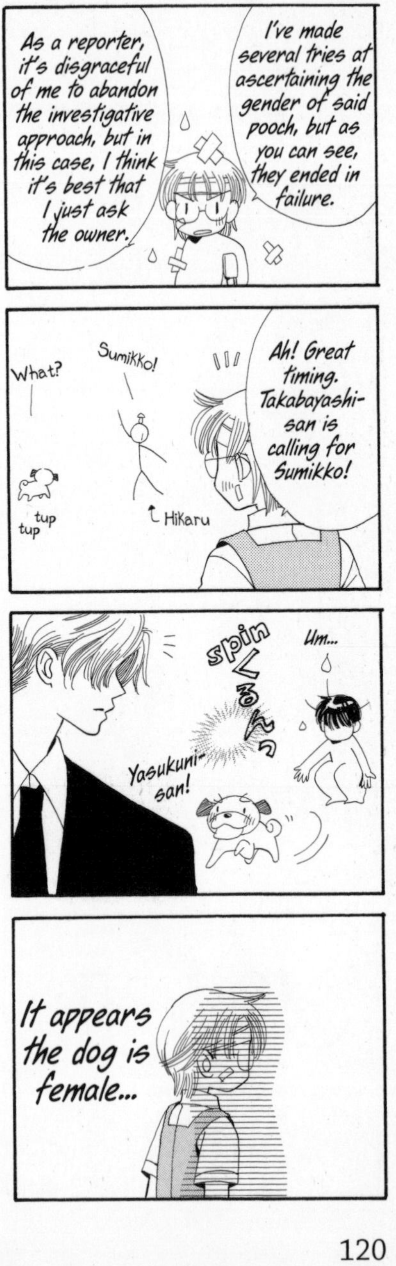
I've made several tries at ascertaining the gender of said pooch, but as you can see, they ended in failure.
As a reporter, it's disgraceful of me to abandon the investigative approach, but in this case, I think it's best that I just ask the owner.
Ah! Great timing. Takabayashi-san is calling for Sumikko!
Sumikko!
What?
tup tup
Hikaru
Um...
spin くるん
Yasukuni-san!
It appears the dog is female...

I MAY OWN A PUG, BUT PLEASE DON'T CALL MY DOG SUMIKKO. -LAUGH-

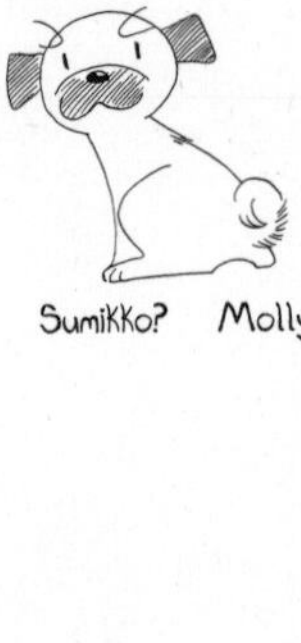
Sumikko?
Molly?

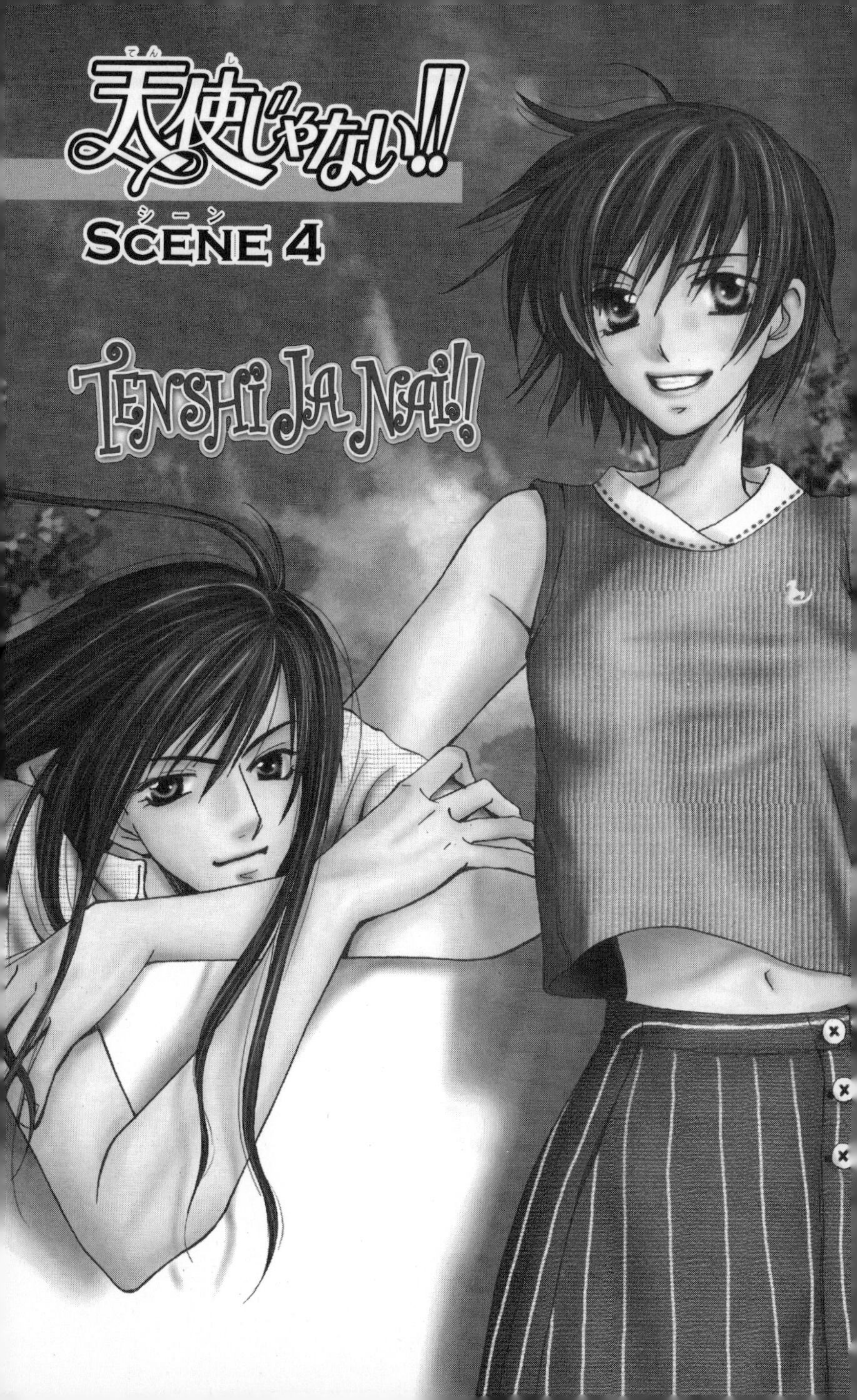
天使じゃない!!
SCENE 4
TENSHI JA NAI!!

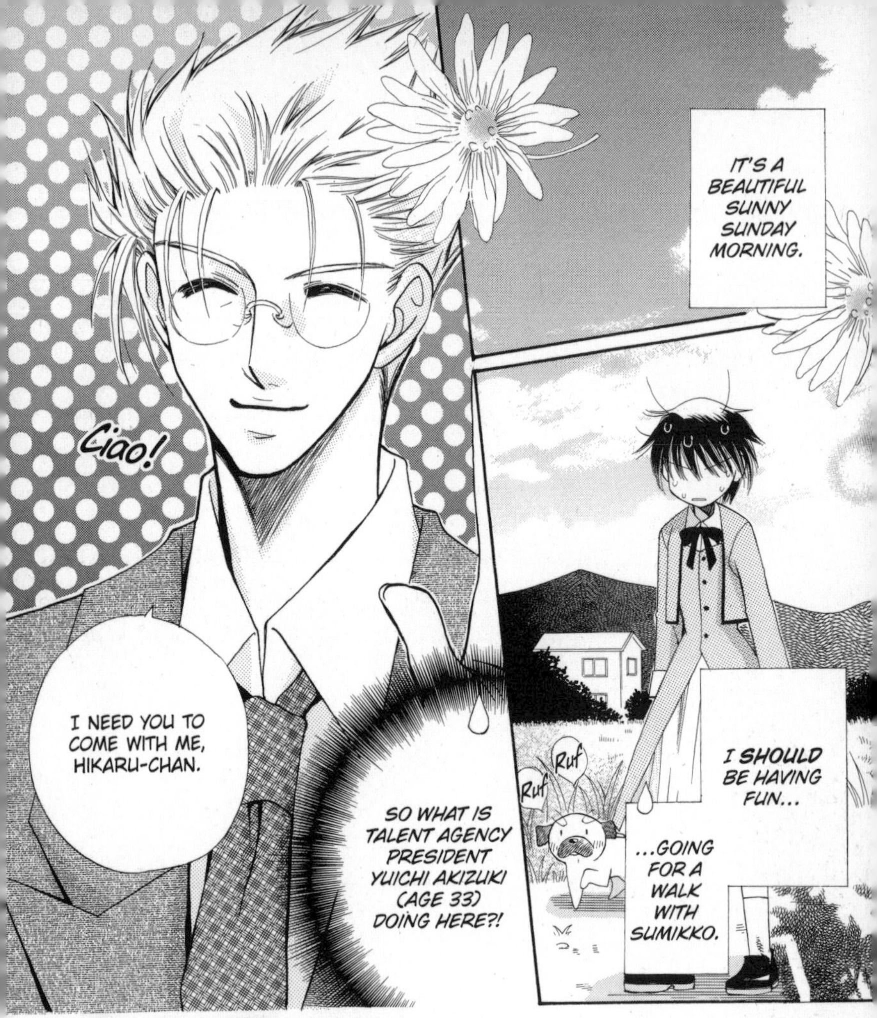
IT'S A BEAUTIFUL SUNNY SUNDAY MORNING.
I SHOULD BE HAVING FUN...
...GOING FOR A WALK WITH SUMIKKO.
Ruf
Ruf
Ciao!
I NEED YOU TO COME WITH ME, HIKARU-CHAN.
SO WHAT IS TALENT AGENCY PRESIDENT YUICHI AKIZUKI (AGE 33) DOING HERE?!

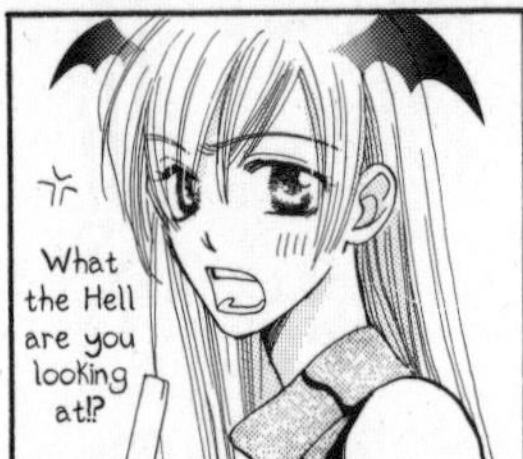
What the Hell are you looking at!?

Izumi Kido (Age 15)
Birthday: April 1
Blood type: B
Idol-type.
He lives a double life. Sexual preference is unknown. He has beautiful looks and a strong personality. Hardly opens up to anyone.
He may hurt you if you're not careful.

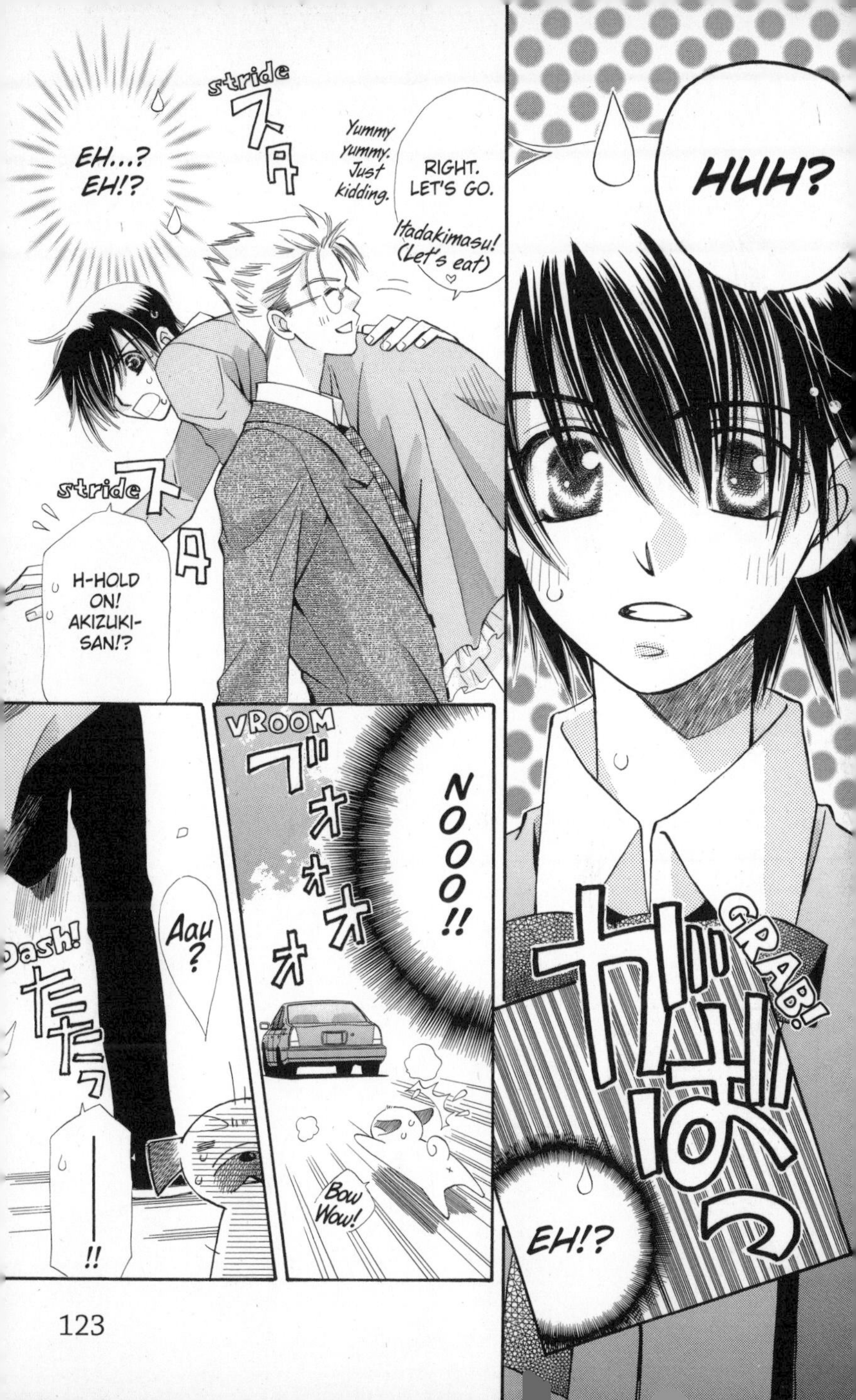
HUH?
GRAB!
EH!?
RIGHT. LET'S GO.
Itadakimasu! (Let's eat)
Yummy yummy. Just kidding.
stride
EH...? EH!?
stride
H-HOLD ON! AKIZUKI-SAN!?
VROOM
NOOOO!!
Bow Wow!
Aau?
Dash!
——!!

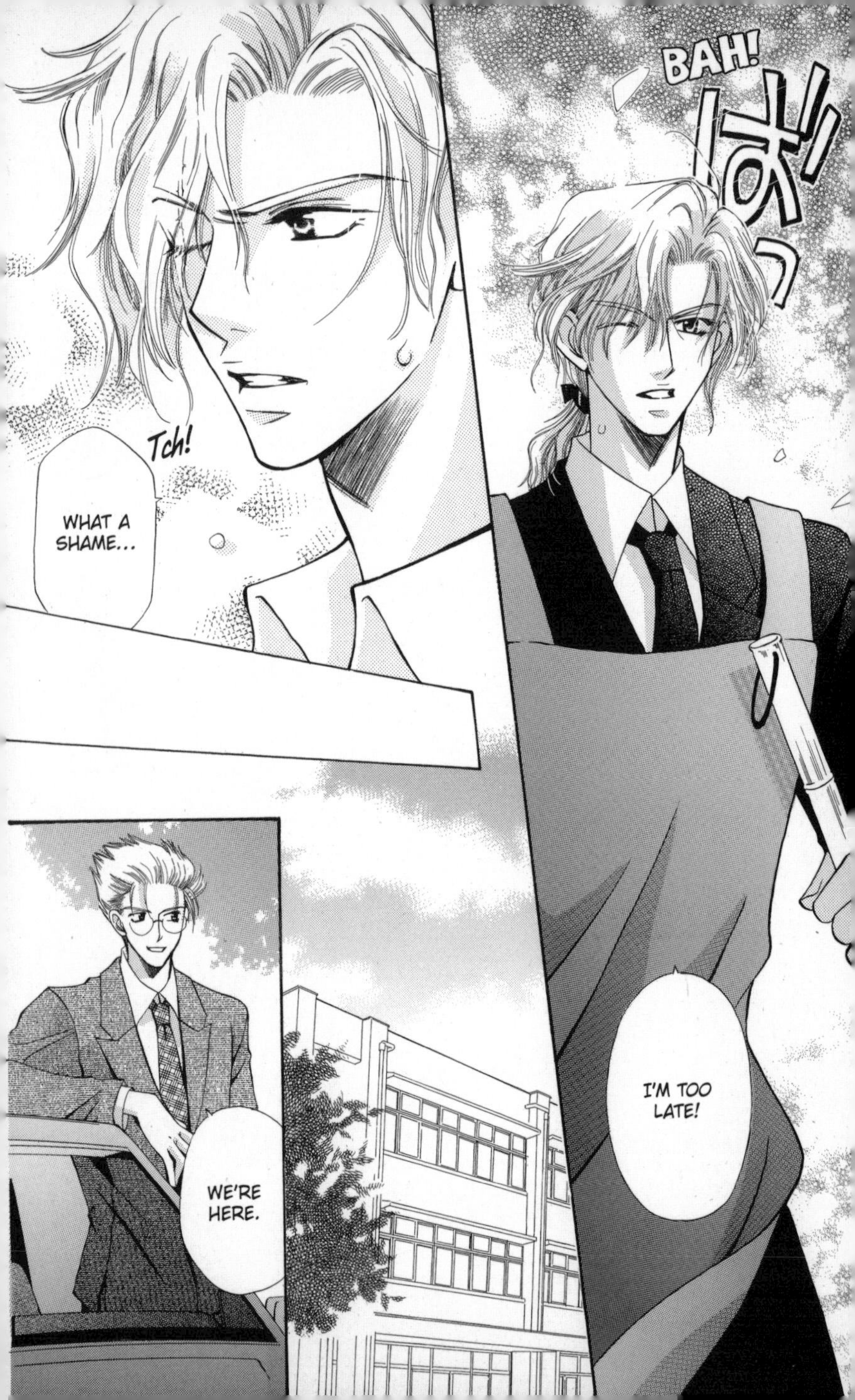
BAH!
ばっ
I'M TOO LATE!
Tch!
WHAT A SHAME...
WE'RE HERE.

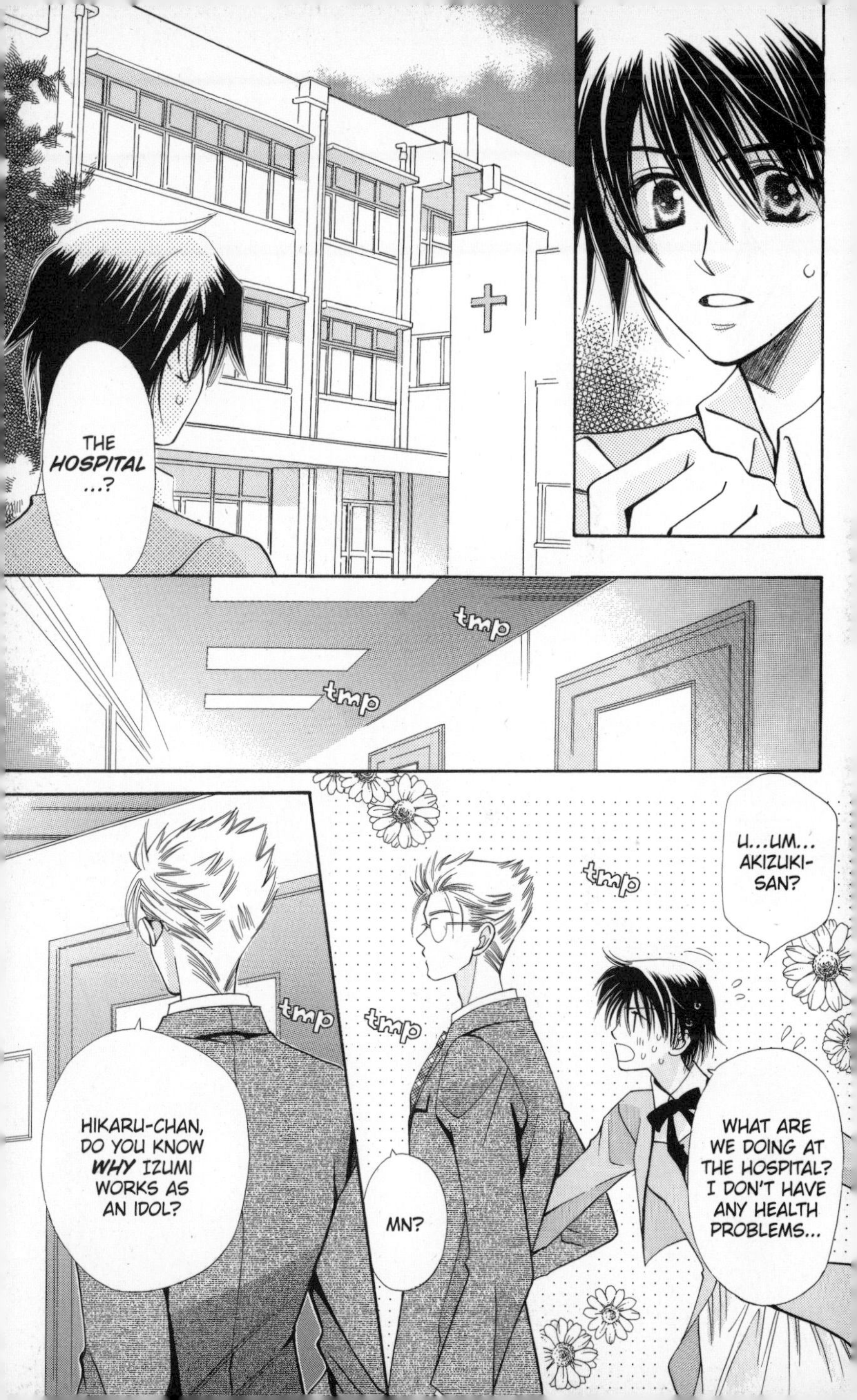
THE HOSPITAL ...?
tmp
tmp
U...UM... AKIZUKI-SAN?
tmp
WHAT ARE WE DOING AT THE HOSPITAL? I DON'T HAVE ANY HEALTH PROBLEMS...
tmp
tmp
MN?
HIKARU-CHAN, DO YOU KNOW WHY IZUMI WORKS AS AN IDOL?

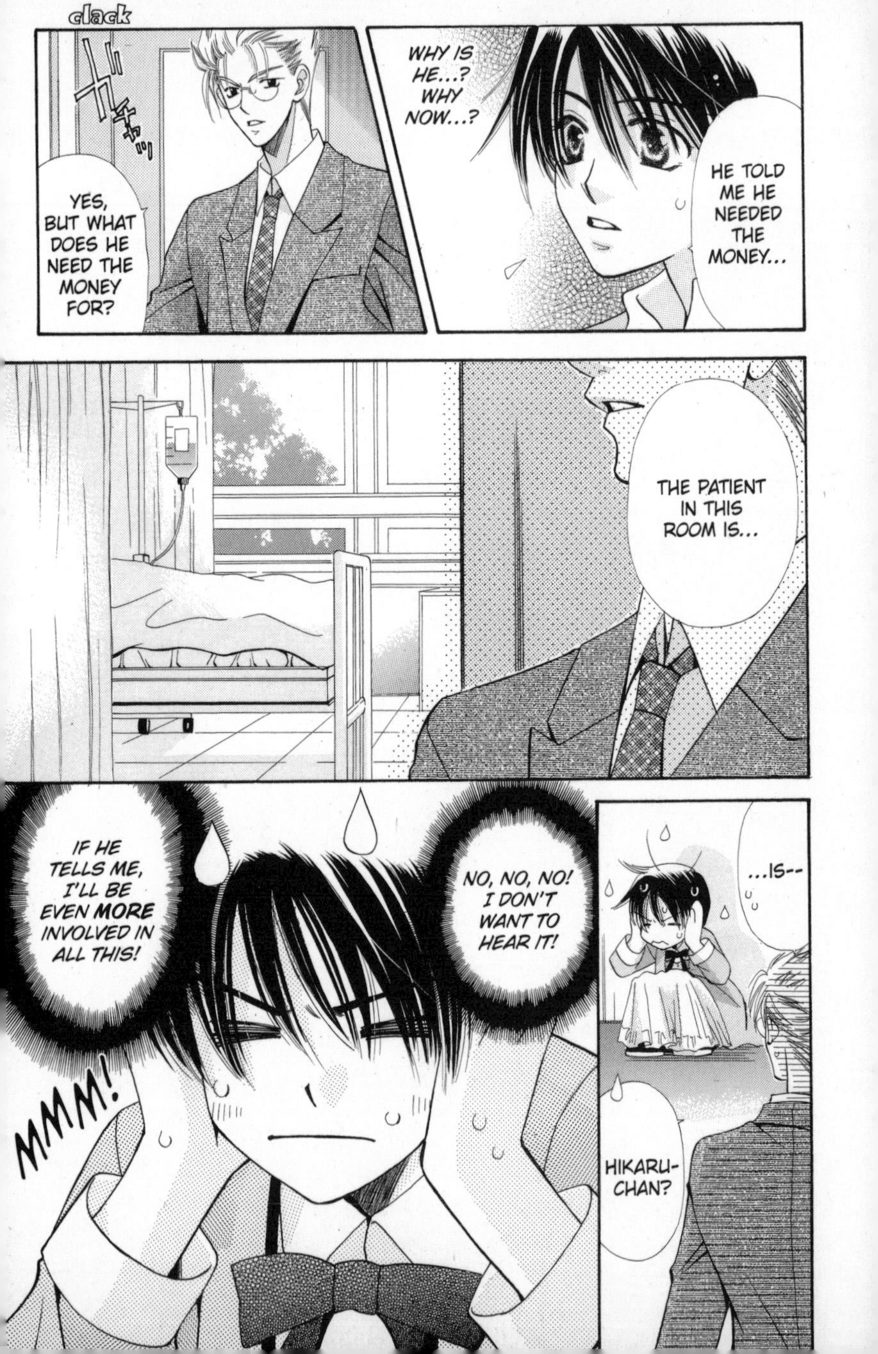
HE TOLD ME HE NEEDED THE MONEY...
WHY IS HE...? WHY NOW...?
clack
YES, BUT WHAT DOES HE NEED THE MONEY FOR?
THE PATIENT IN THIS ROOM IS...
...IS--
HIKARU-CHAN?
NO, NO, NO! I DON'T WANT TO HEAR IT!
IF HE TELLS ME, I'LL BE EVEN MORE INVOLVED IN ALL THIS!
MMM!

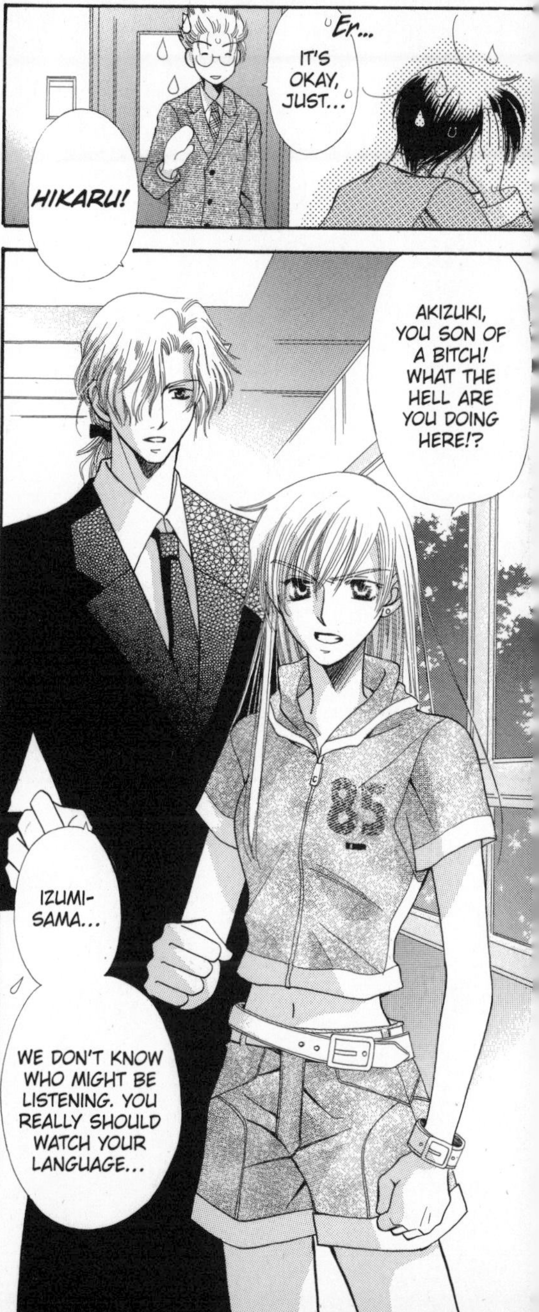
Er...
IT'S OKAY, JUST...
HIKARU!
AKIZUKI, YOU SON OF A BITCH! WHAT THE HELL ARE YOU DOING HERE!?
IZUMI-SAMA...
WE DON'T KNOW WHO MIGHT BE LISTENING. YOU REALLY SHOULD WATCH YOUR LANGUAGE...

My Favorite Things Part 2

Lately--no, for a while now--

I've been crazy about my pile blanket!

Actually, I would love to have pile sheets and pile pillow cases. But...[sob] because my pile blanket is getting worn out on the gauze side, the fibers are starting to fall out. This is my favorite blanket and I'm afraid of buying a new one. If I can, I want to replace it with exactly the same model. That's my plan...

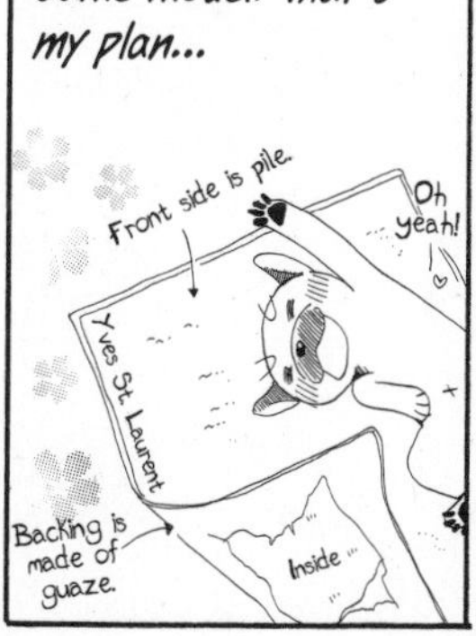
Front side is pile.
Oh yeah!
Yves St Laurent
Backing is made of guaze.
Inside

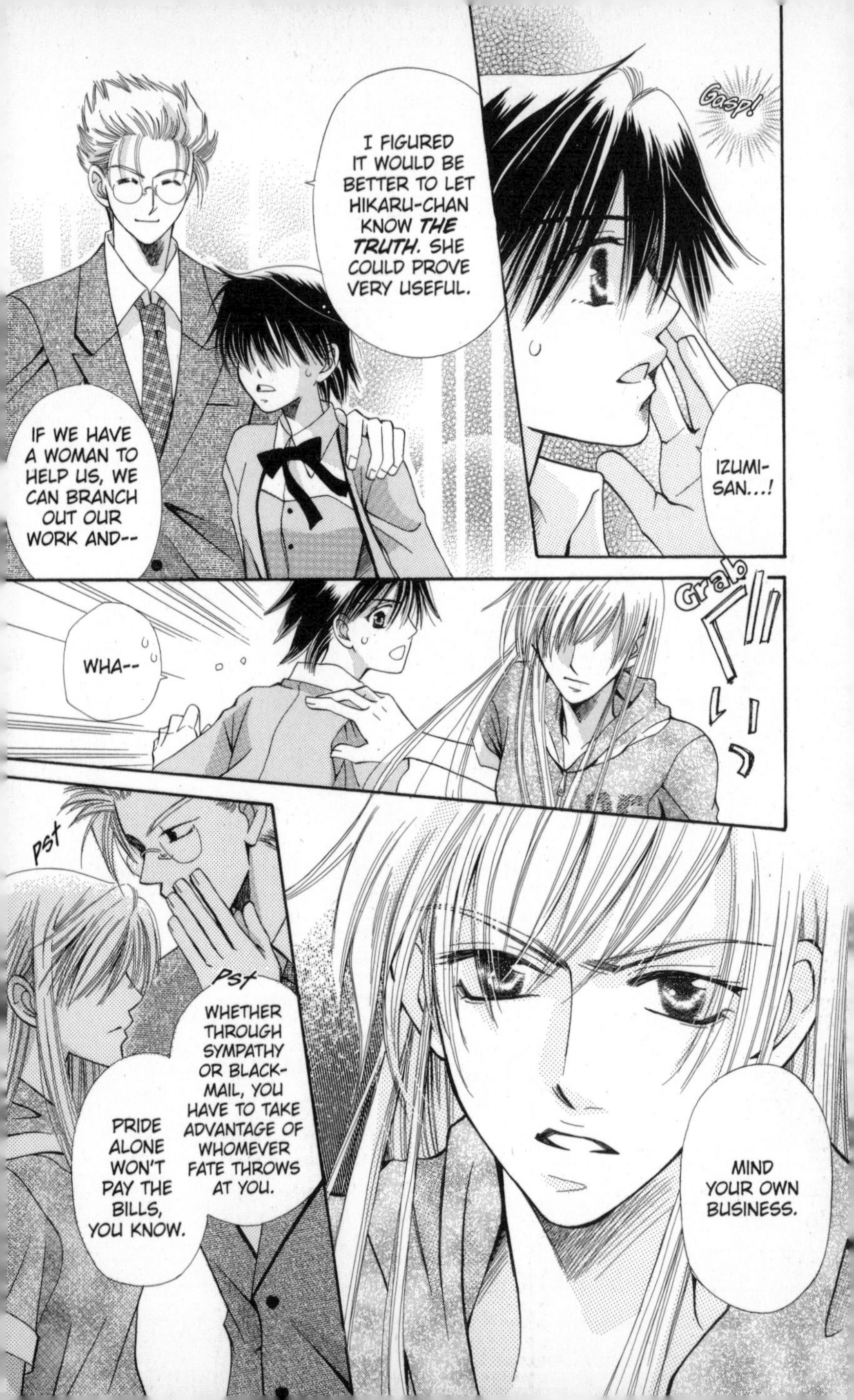
I FIGURED IT WOULD BE BETTER TO LET HIKARU-CHAN KNOW *THE TRUTH*. SHE COULD PROVE VERY USEFUL.
IF WE HAVE A WOMAN TO HELP US, WE CAN BRANCH OUT OUR WORK AND--
Gasp!
IZUMI-SAN...!
WHA--
Grab
pst
pst
WHETHER THROUGH SYMPATHY OR BLACK-MAIL, YOU HAVE TO TAKE ADVANTAGE OF WHOMEVER FATE THROWS AT YOU.
PRIDE ALONE WON'T PAY THE BILLS, YOU KNOW.
MIND YOUR OWN BUSINESS.

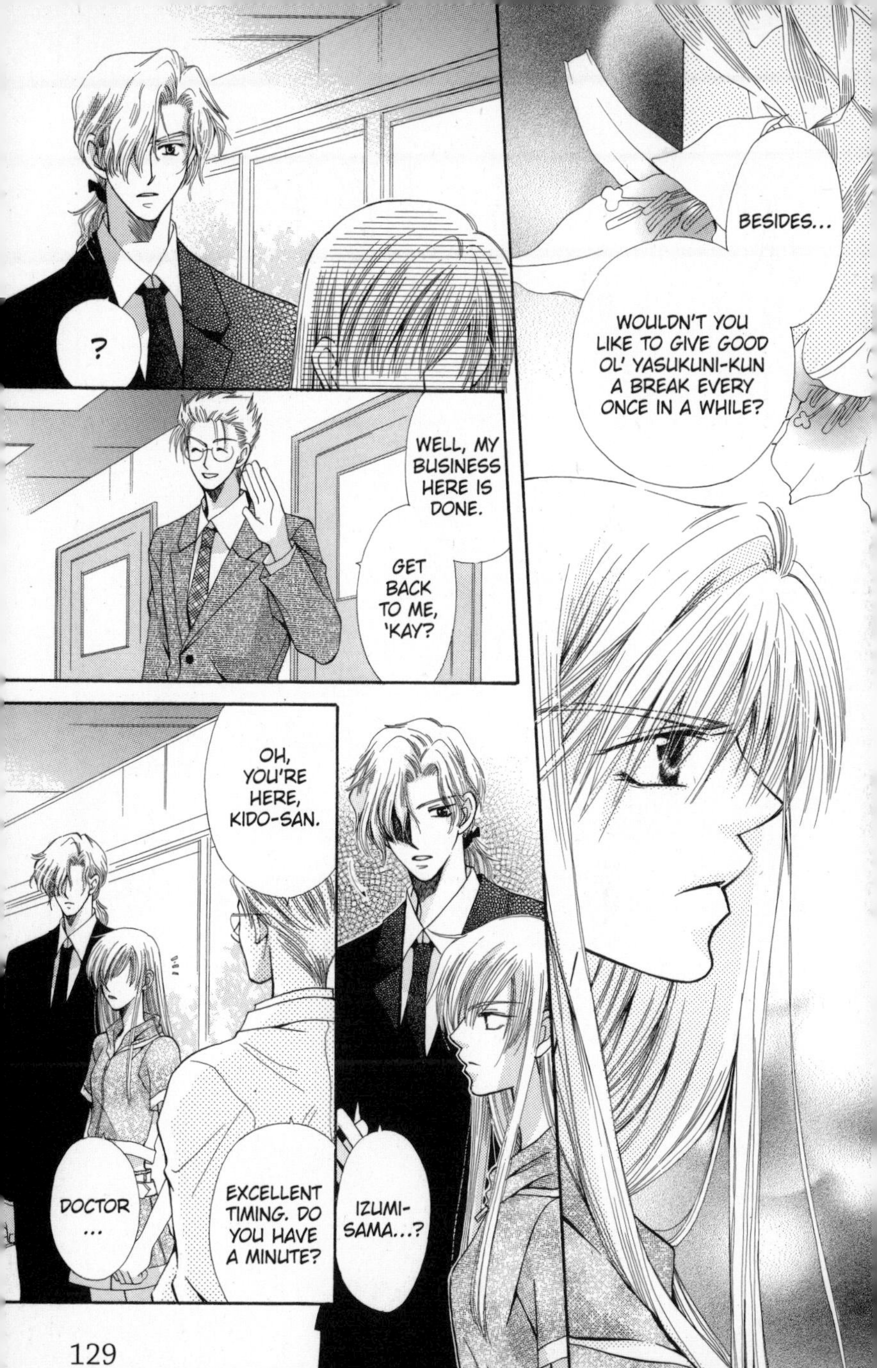
BESIDES...
WOULDN'T YOU LIKE TO GIVE GOOD OL' YASUKUNI-KUN A BREAK EVERY ONCE IN A WHILE?
?
WELL, MY BUSINESS HERE IS DONE.
GET BACK TO ME, 'KAY?
OH, YOU'RE HERE, KIDO-SAN.
IZUMI-SAMA...?
EXCELLENT TIMING. DO YOU HAVE A MINUTE?
DOCTOR ...

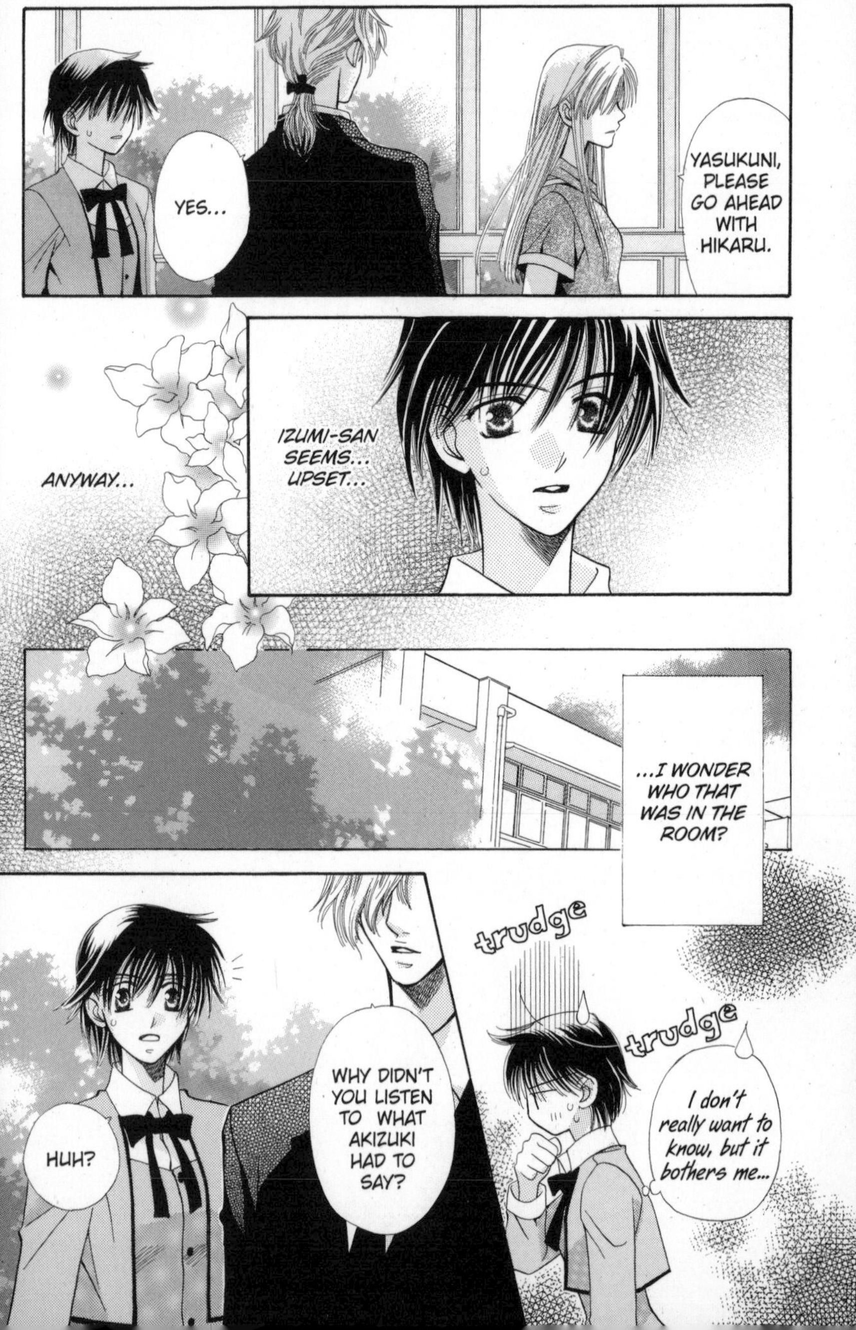
YASUKUNI, PLEASE GO AHEAD WITH HIKARU.
YES...
IZUMI-SAN SEEMS... UPSET...
ANYWAY...
...I WONDER WHO THAT WAS IN THE ROOM?
trudge
trudge
I don't really want to know, but it bothers me...
WHY DIDN'T YOU LISTEN TO WHAT AKIZUKI HAD TO SAY?
HUH?

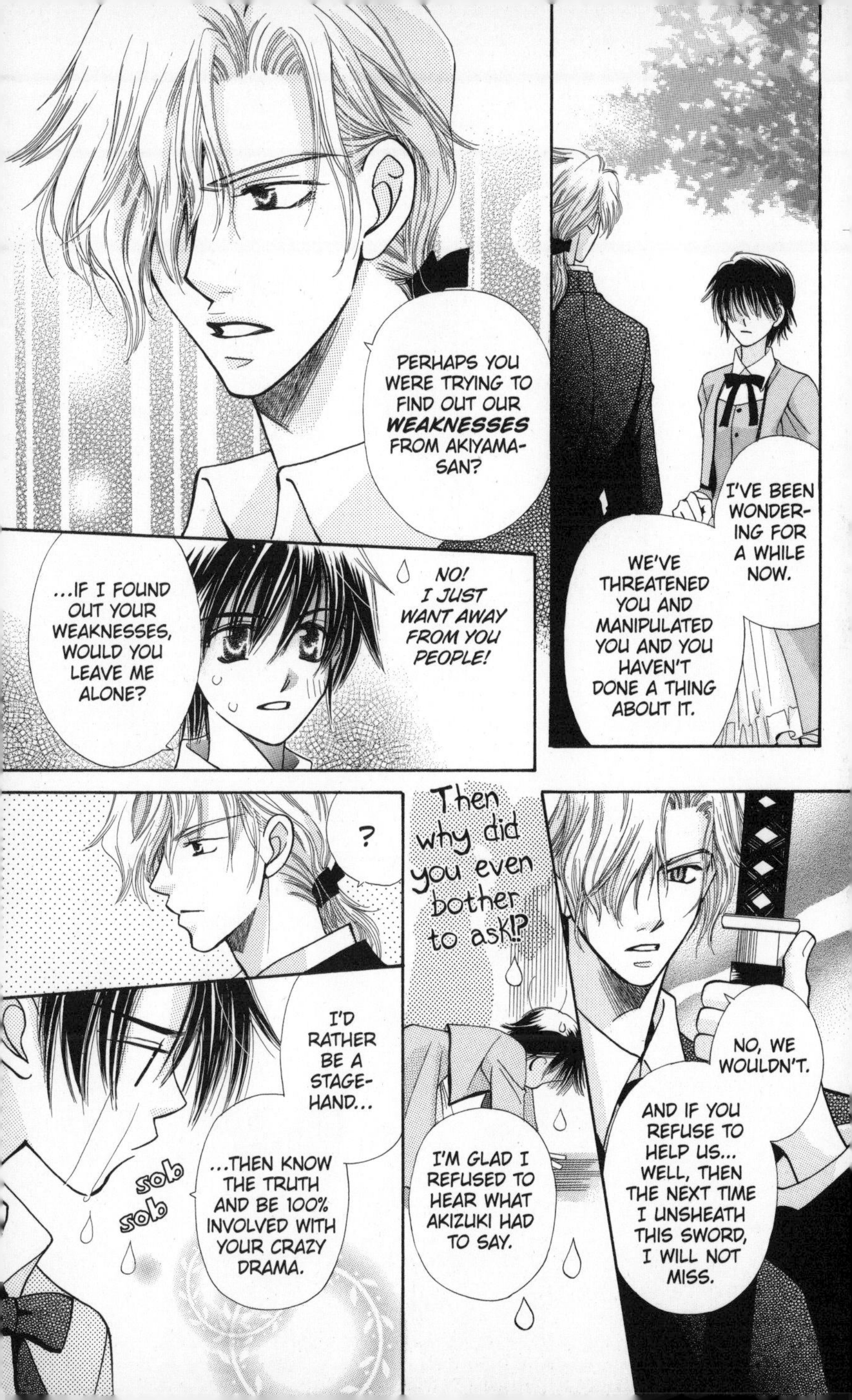
I'VE BEEN WONDERING FOR A WHILE NOW.
WE'VE THREATENED YOU AND MANIPULATED YOU AND YOU HAVEN'T DONE A THING ABOUT IT.
PERHAPS YOU WERE TRYING TO FIND OUT OUR WEAKNESSES FROM AKIYAMA-SAN?
NO! I JUST WANT AWAY FROM YOU PEOPLE!
...IF I FOUND OUT YOUR WEAKNESSES, WOULD YOU LEAVE ME ALONE?
NO, WE WOULDN'T.
AND IF YOU REFUSE TO HELP US... WELL, THEN THE NEXT TIME I UNSHEATH THIS SWORD, I WILL NOT MISS.
I'M GLAD I REFUSED TO HEAR WHAT AKIZUKI HAD TO SAY.
Then why did you even bother to ask!?
?
I'D RATHER BE A STAGE-HAND...
...THEN KNOW THE TRUTH AND BE 100% INVOLVED WITH YOUR CRAZY DRAMA.
sob sob

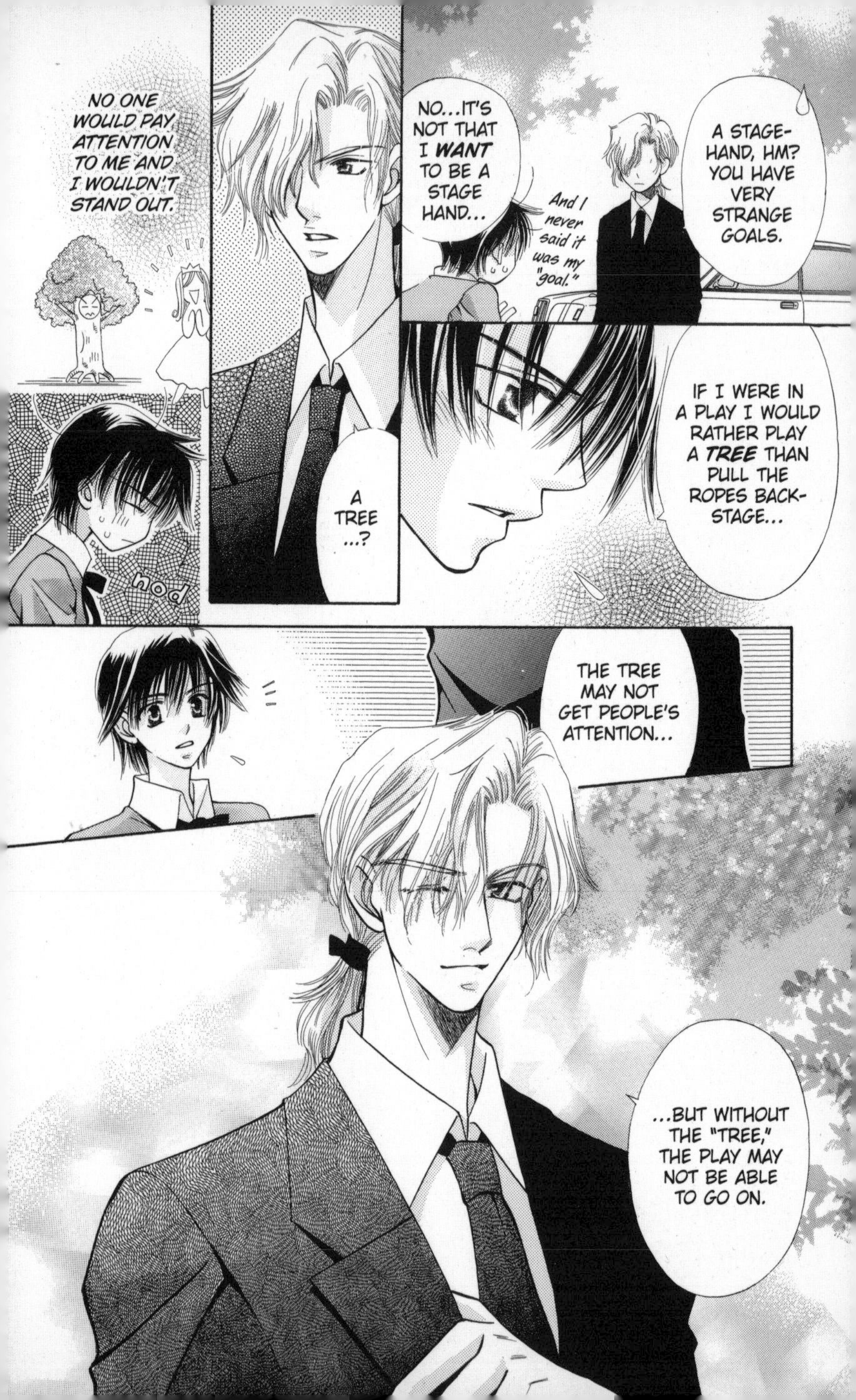

A STAGE-HAND, HM? YOU HAVE VERY STRANGE GOALS.
NO...IT'S NOT THAT I WANT TO BE A STAGE HAND...
And I never said it was my "goal."
IF I WERE IN A PLAY I WOULD RATHER PLAY A TREE THAN PULL THE ROPES BACK-STAGE...
A TREE ...?
NO ONE WOULD PAY ATTENTION TO ME AND I WOULDN'T STAND OUT.
nod
THE TREE MAY NOT GET PEOPLE'S ATTENTION...
...BUT WITHOUT THE "TREE," THE PLAY MAY NOT BE ABLE TO GO ON.

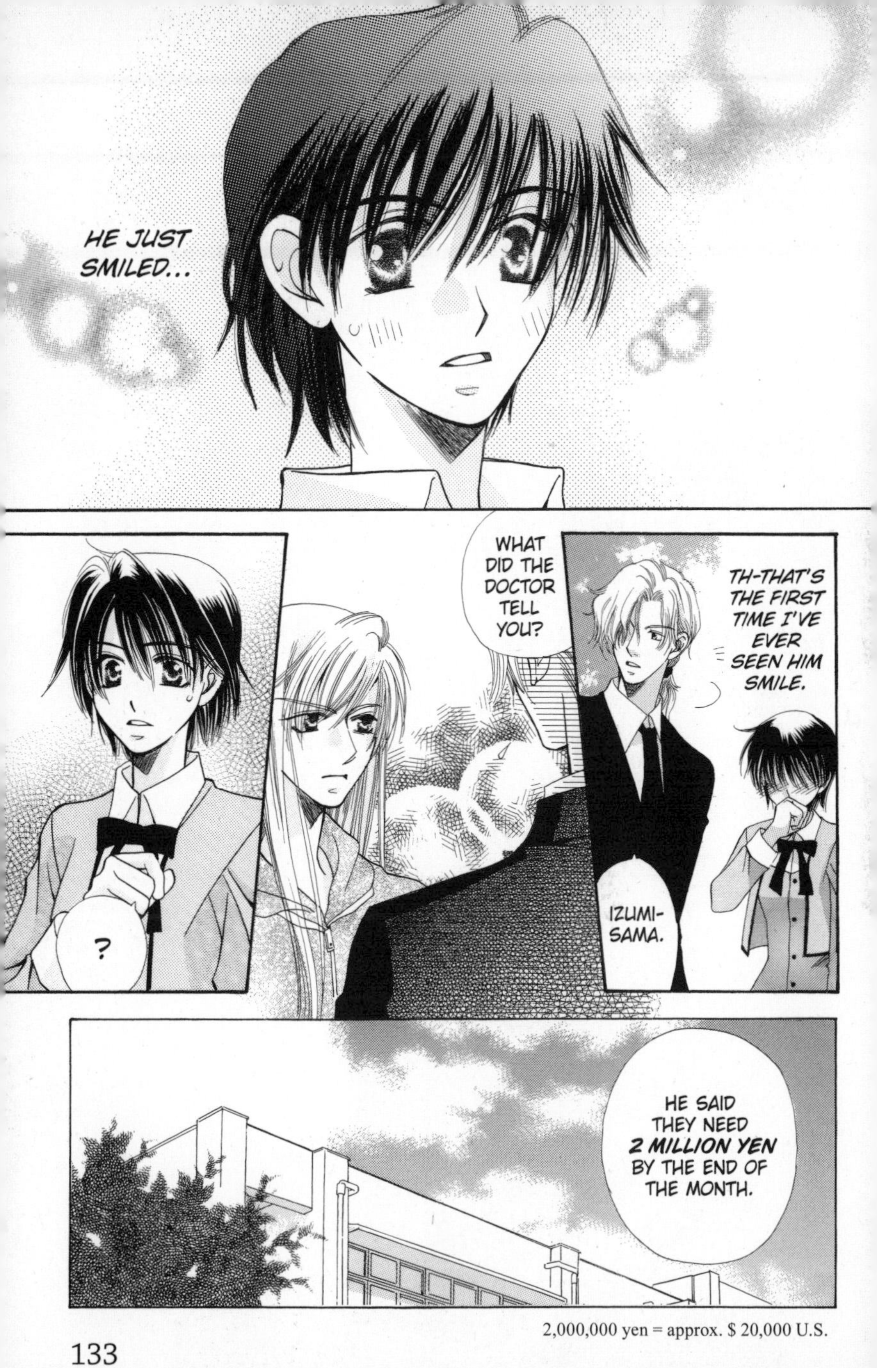
HE JUST SMILED...
TH-THAT'S THE FIRST TIME I'VE EVER SEEN HIM SMILE.
IZUMI-SAMA.
WHAT DID THE DOCTOR TELL YOU?
?
HE SAID THEY NEED **2 MILLION YEN** BY THE END OF THE MONTH.

2,000,000 yen = approx. $ 20,000 U.S.

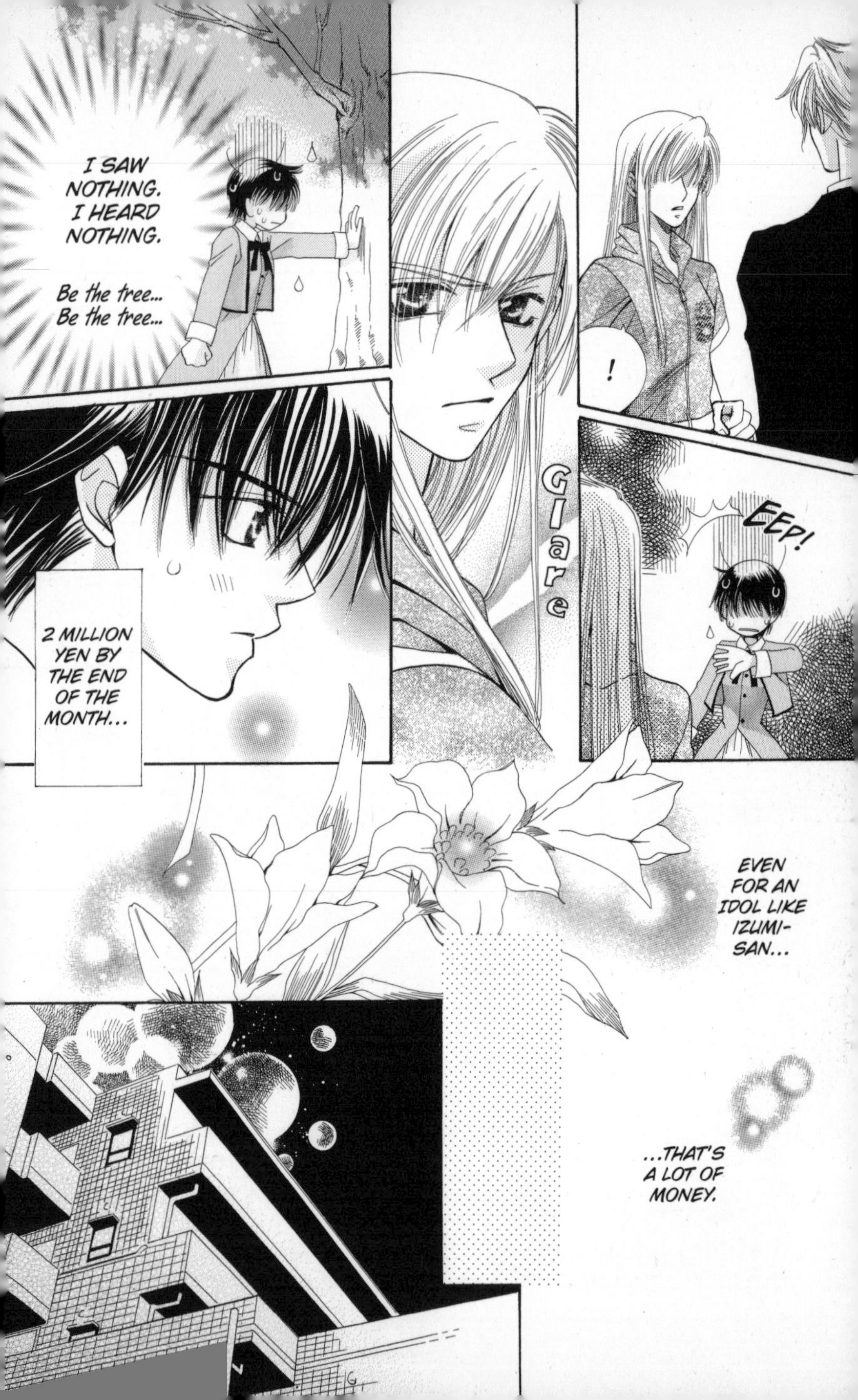
!
EEP!
Glare
I SAW NOTHING. I HEARD NOTHING.
Be the tree... Be the tree...
2 MILLION YEN BY THE END OF THE MONTH...
EVEN FOR AN IDOL LIKE IZUMI-SAN...
...THAT'S A LOT OF MONEY.

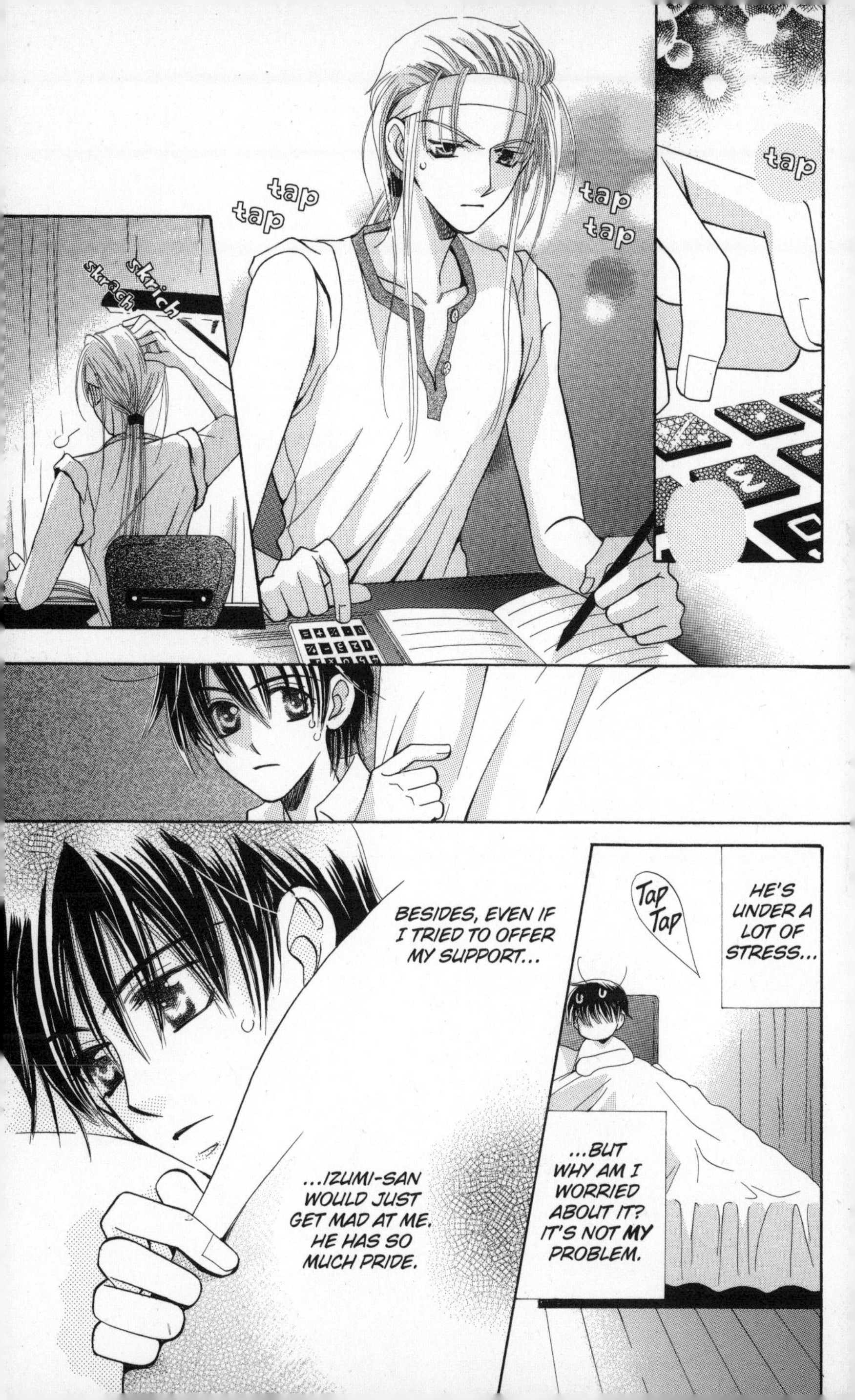

tap
tap tap
tap tap
skrich skrach
HE'S UNDER A LOT OF STRESS...
Tap Tap
...BUT WHY AM I WORRIED ABOUT IT? IT'S NOT **MY** PROBLEM.
BESIDES, EVEN IF I TRIED TO OFFER MY SUPPORT...
...IZUMI-SAN WOULD JUST GET MAD AT ME. HE HAS SO MUCH PRIDE.

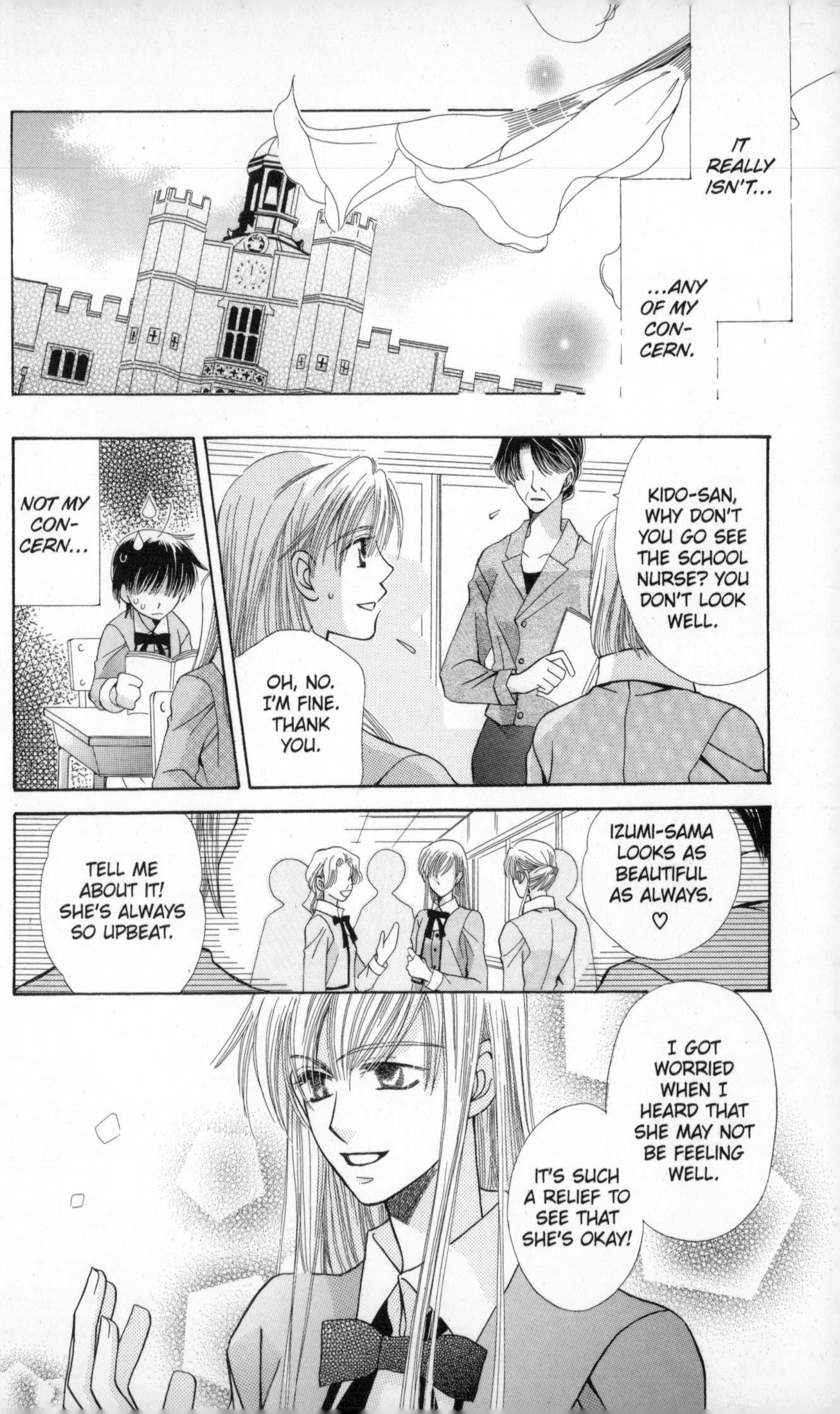
IT REALLY ISN'T...
...ANY OF MY CONCERN.
KIDO-SAN, WHY DON'T YOU GO SEE THE SCHOOL NURSE? YOU DON'T LOOK WELL.
OH, NO. I'M FINE. THANK YOU.
NOT MY CONCERN...
IZUMI-SAMA LOOKS AS BEAUTIFUL AS ALWAYS. ♡
TELL ME ABOUT IT! SHE'S ALWAYS SO UPBEAT.
I GOT WORRIED WHEN I HEARD THAT SHE MAY NOT BE FEELING WELL.
IT'S SUCH A RELIEF TO SEE THAT SHE'S OKAY!

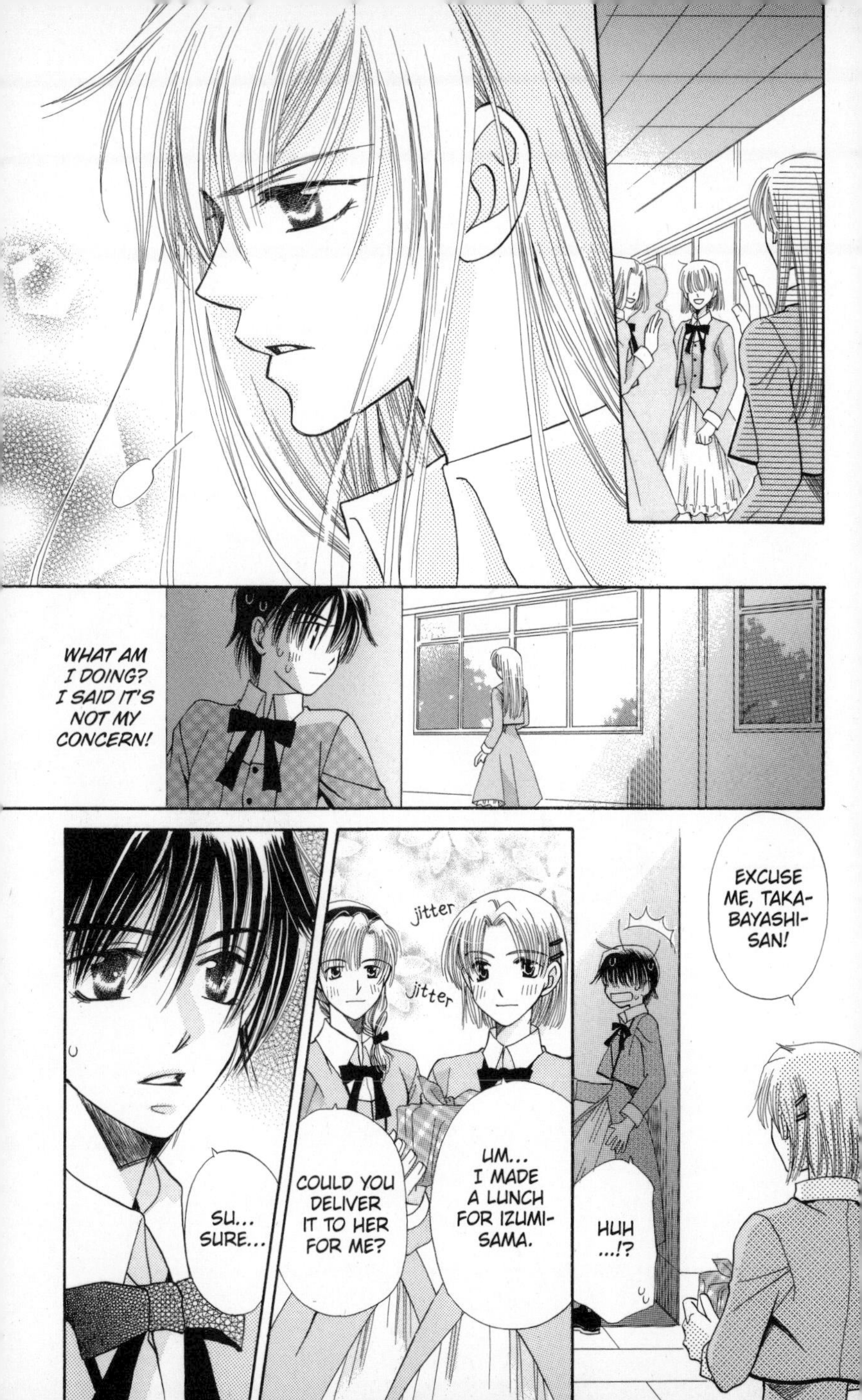
WHAT AM I DOING? I SAID IT'S NOT MY CONCERN!
EXCUSE ME, TAKA-BAYASHI-SAN!
HUH ...!?
UM... I MADE A LUNCH FOR IZUMI-SAMA.
jitter
jitter
COULD YOU DELIVER IT TO HER FOR ME?
SU... SURE...

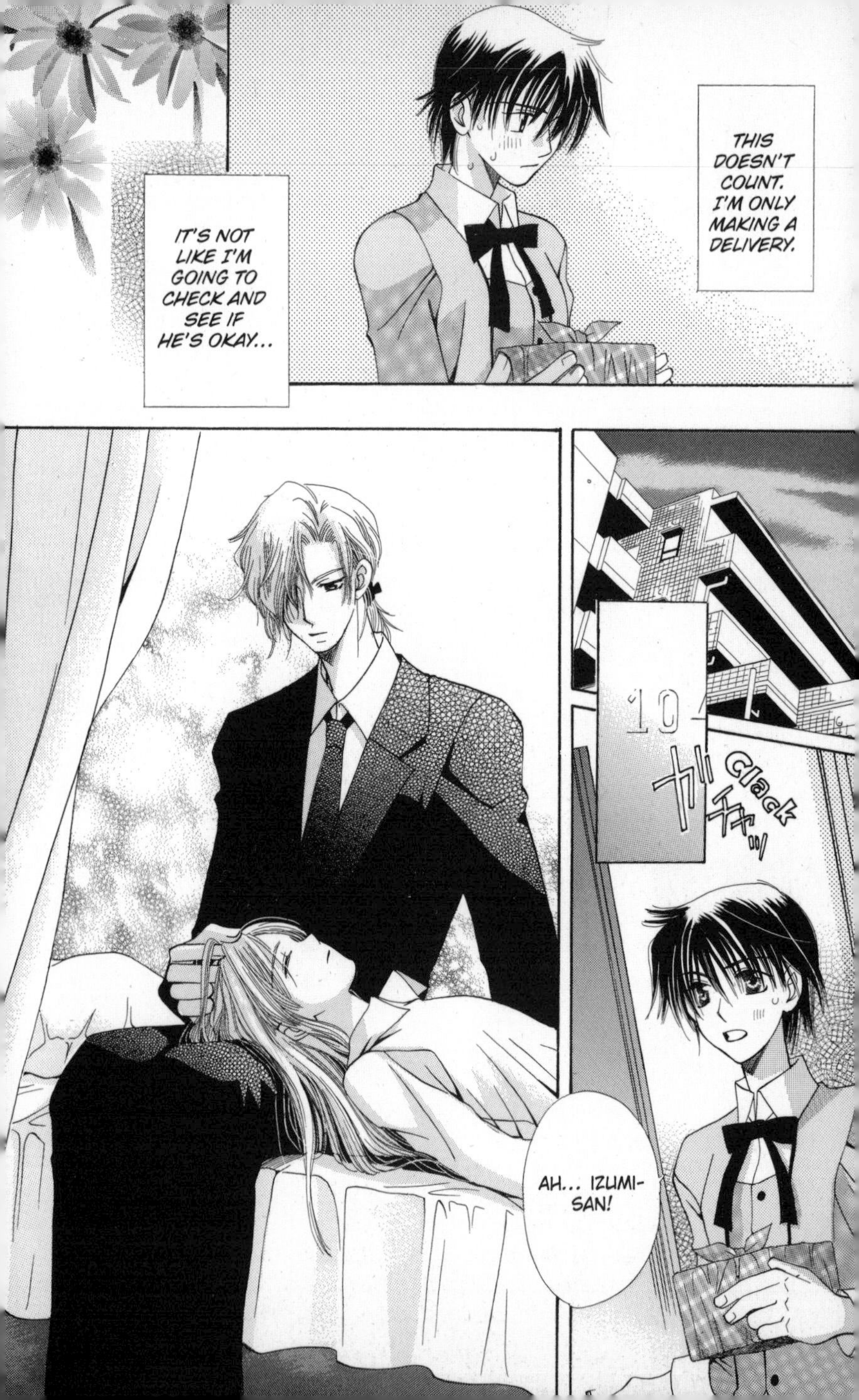
THIS DOESN'T COUNT. I'M ONLY MAKING A DELIVERY.
IT'S NOT LIKE I'M GOING TO CHECK AND SEE IF HE'S OKAY...
Clack
AH... IZUMI-SAN!

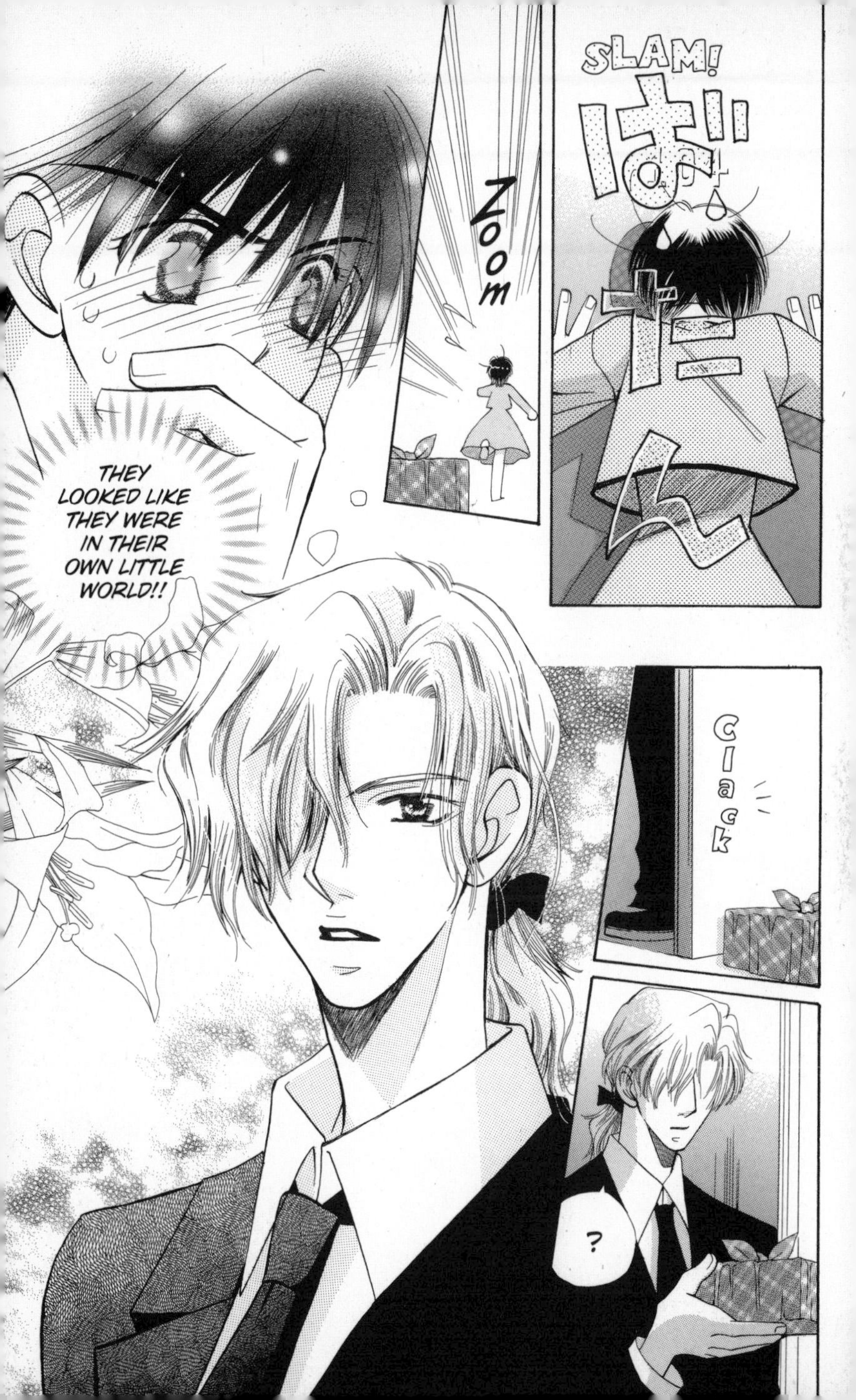
SLAM!
Zoom
THEY LOOKED LIKE THEY WERE IN THEIR OWN LITTLE WORLD!!
Clack
?

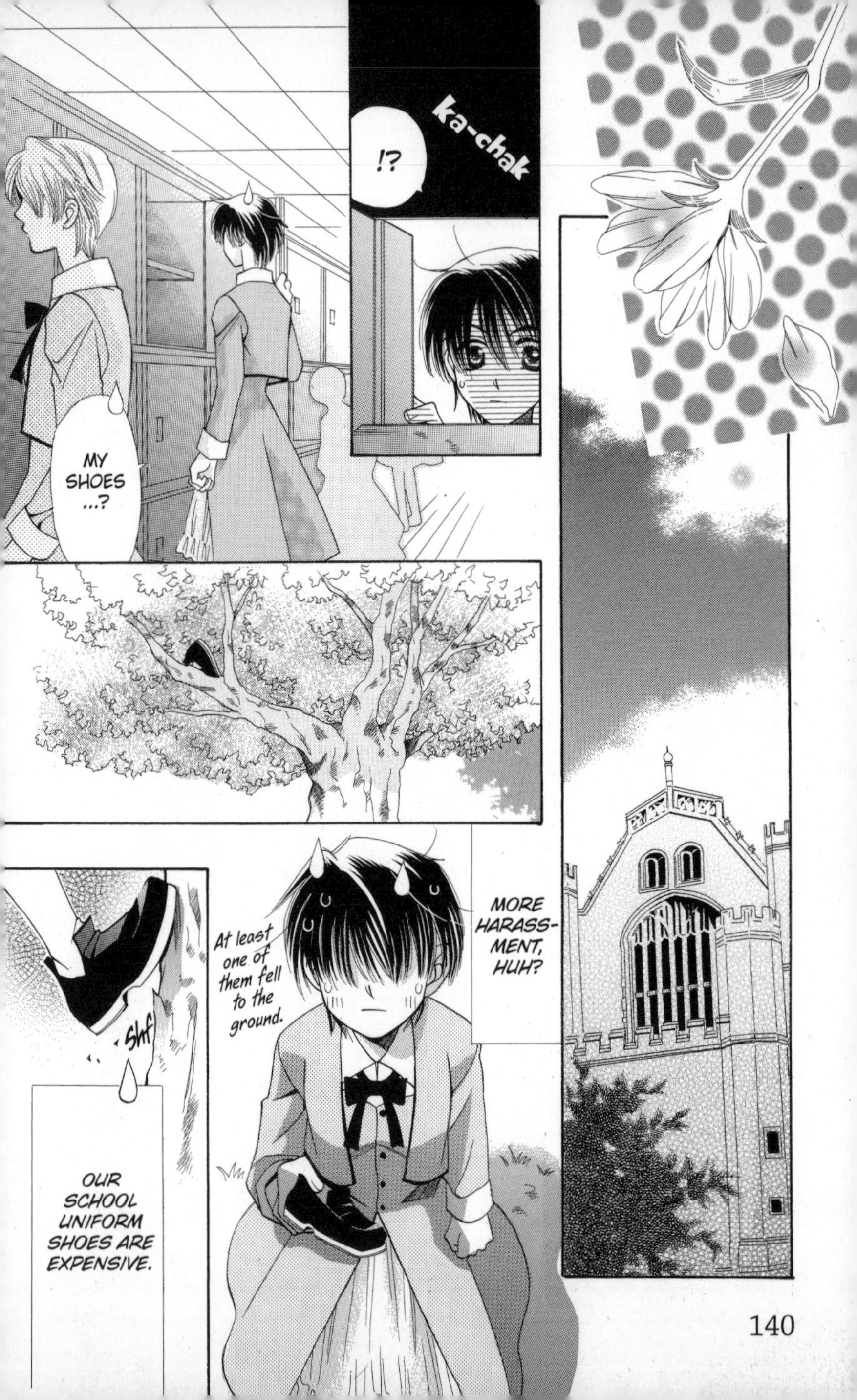
ka-chak
!?
MY SHOES ...?
MORE HARASS-MENT, HUH?
At least one of them fell to the ground.
Shf
OUR SCHOOL UNIFORM SHOES ARE EXPENSIVE.

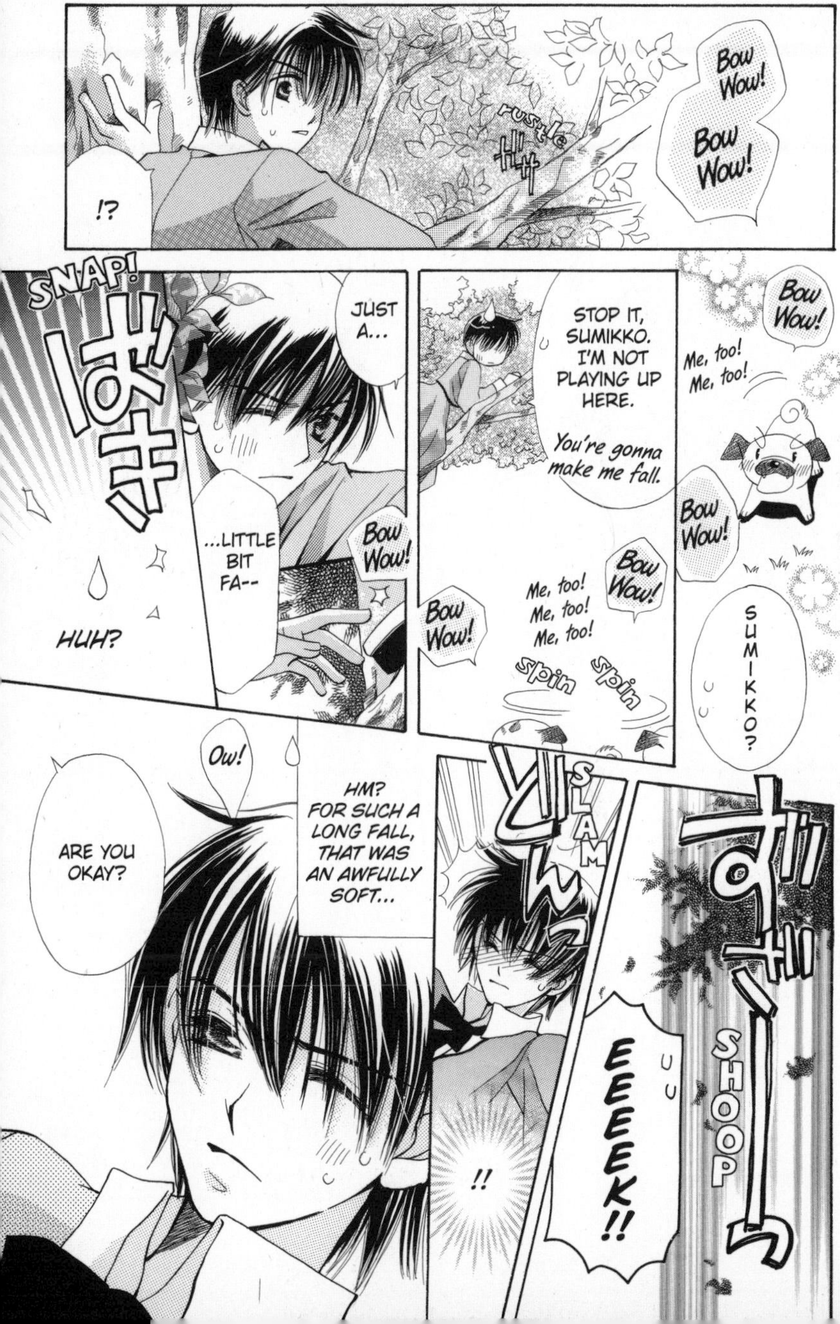
Bow Wow!
Bow Wow!
rustle
!?
Bow Wow!
Me, too! Me, too!
Bow Wow!
SUMIKKO?
STOP IT, SUMIKKO. I'M NOT PLAYING UP HERE.
You're gonna make me fall.
Bow Wow!
Me, too! Me, too! Me, too!
Bow Wow!
spin
spin
JUST A...
...LITTLE BIT FA--
Bow Wow!
SNAP!
HUH?
SHOOP
EEEEEK!!
SLAM
!!
HM? FOR SUCH A LONG FALL, THAT WAS AN AWFULLY SOFT...
Ow!
ARE YOU OKAY?

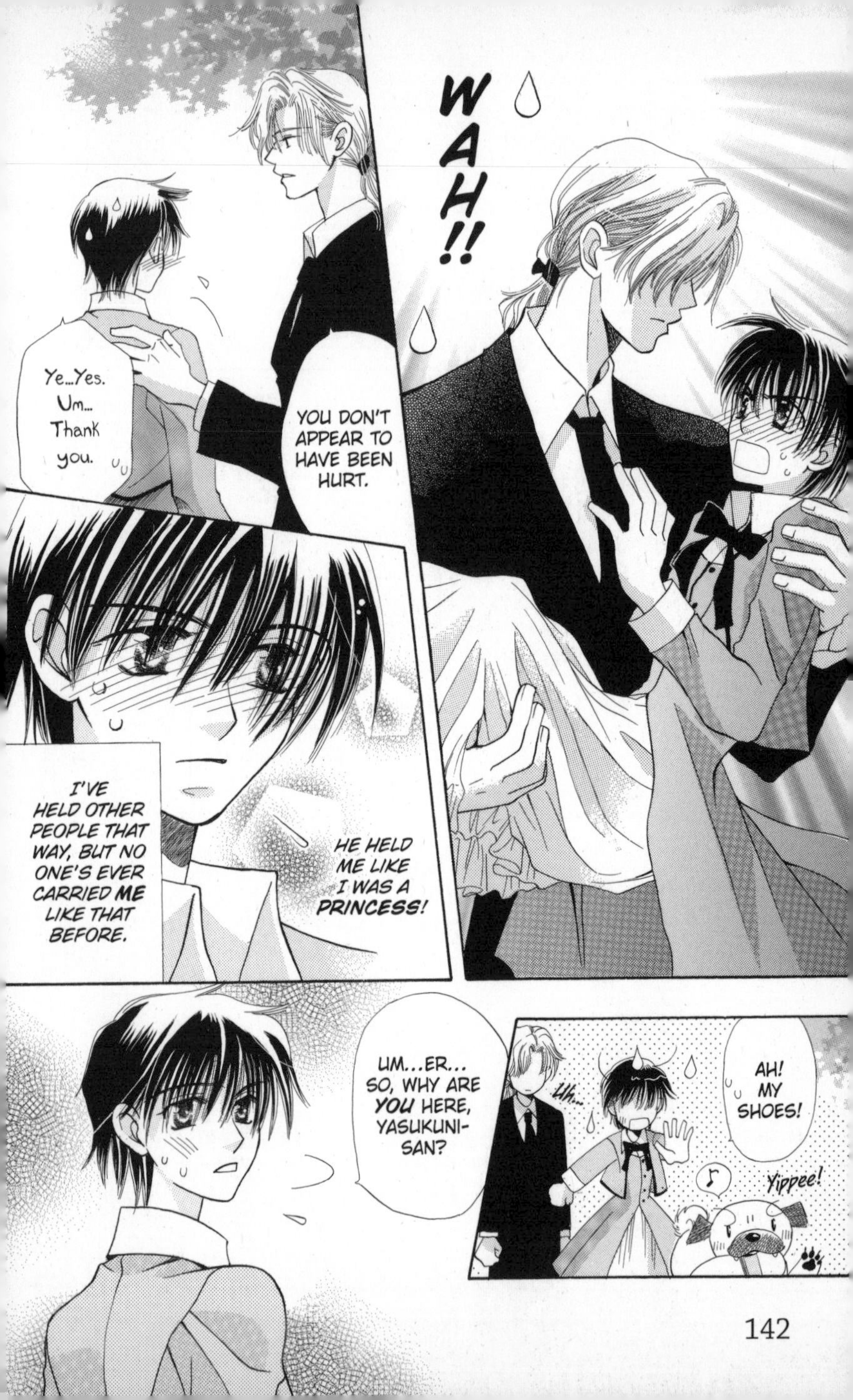
WAH!!
YOU DON'T APPEAR TO HAVE BEEN HURT.
Ye...Yes. Um... Thank you.
HE HELD ME LIKE I WAS A PRINCESS!
I'VE HELD OTHER PEOPLE THAT WAY, BUT NO ONE'S EVER CARRIED ME LIKE THAT BEFORE.
AH! MY SHOES!
Yippee!
Uh...
UM...ER... SO, WHY ARE YOU HERE, YASUKUNI-SAN?

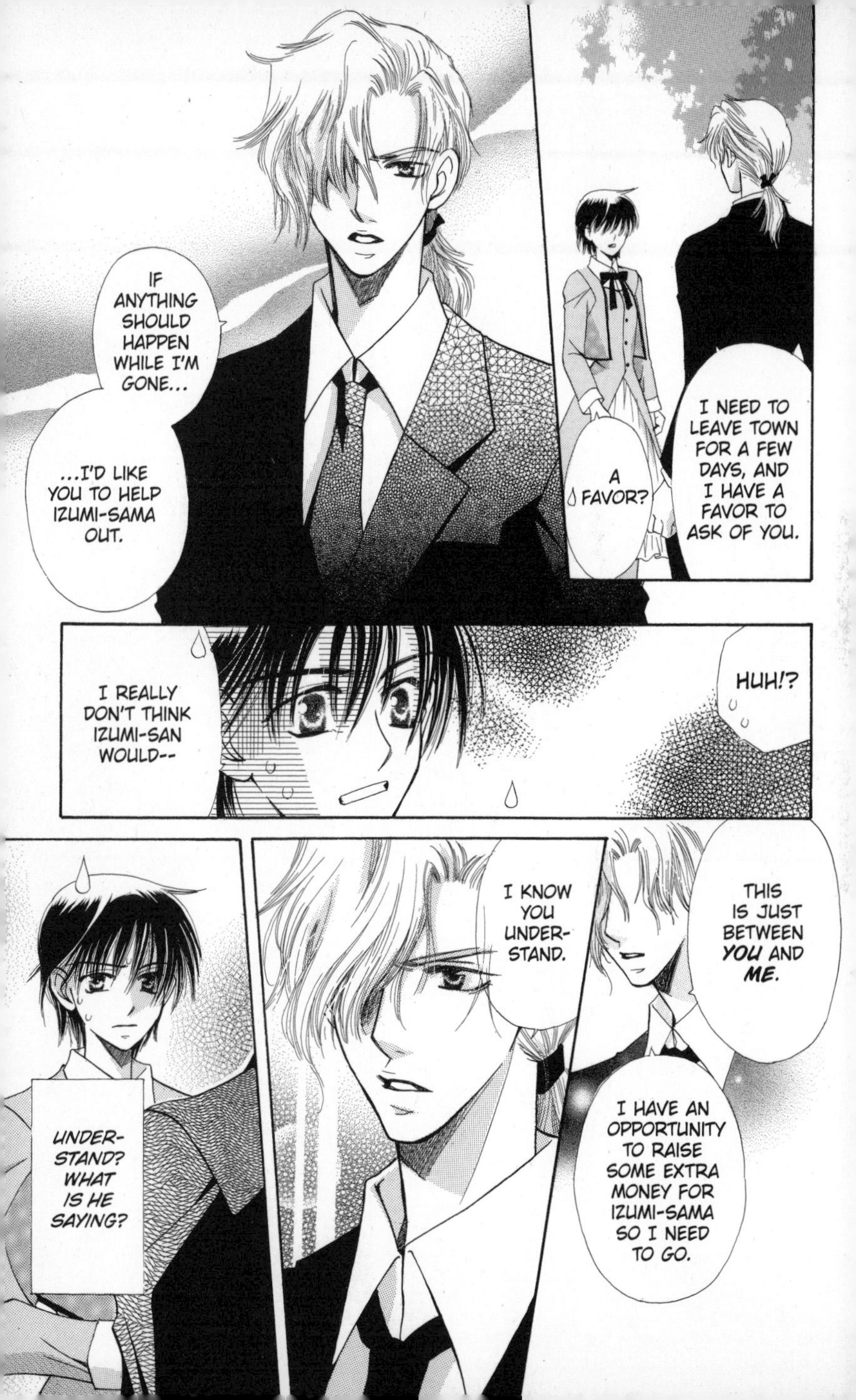
I NEED TO LEAVE TOWN FOR A FEW DAYS, AND I HAVE A FAVOR TO ASK OF YOU.
A FAVOR?
IF ANYTHING SHOULD HAPPEN WHILE I'M GONE...
...I'D LIKE YOU TO HELP IZUMI-SAMA OUT.
HUH!?
I REALLY DON'T THINK IZUMI-SAN WOULD--
THIS IS JUST BETWEEN YOU AND ME.
I HAVE AN OPPORTUNITY TO RAISE SOME EXTRA MONEY FOR IZUMI-SAMA SO I NEED TO GO.
I KNOW YOU UNDER-STAND.
UNDER-STAND? WHAT IS HE SAYING?

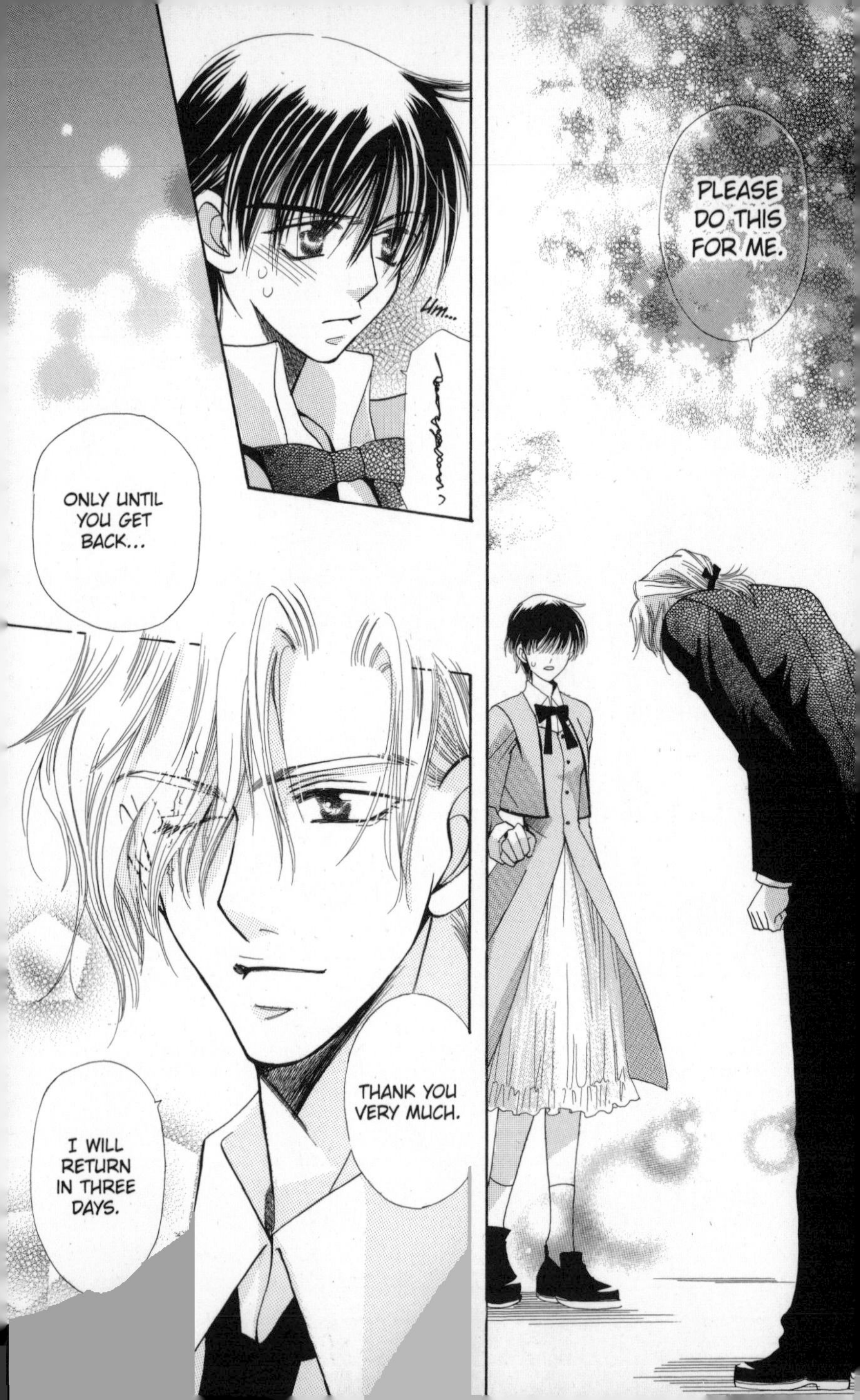
PLEASE DO THIS FOR ME.
Um...
ONLY UNTIL YOU GET BACK...
THANK YOU VERY MUCH.
I WILL RETURN IN THREE DAYS.

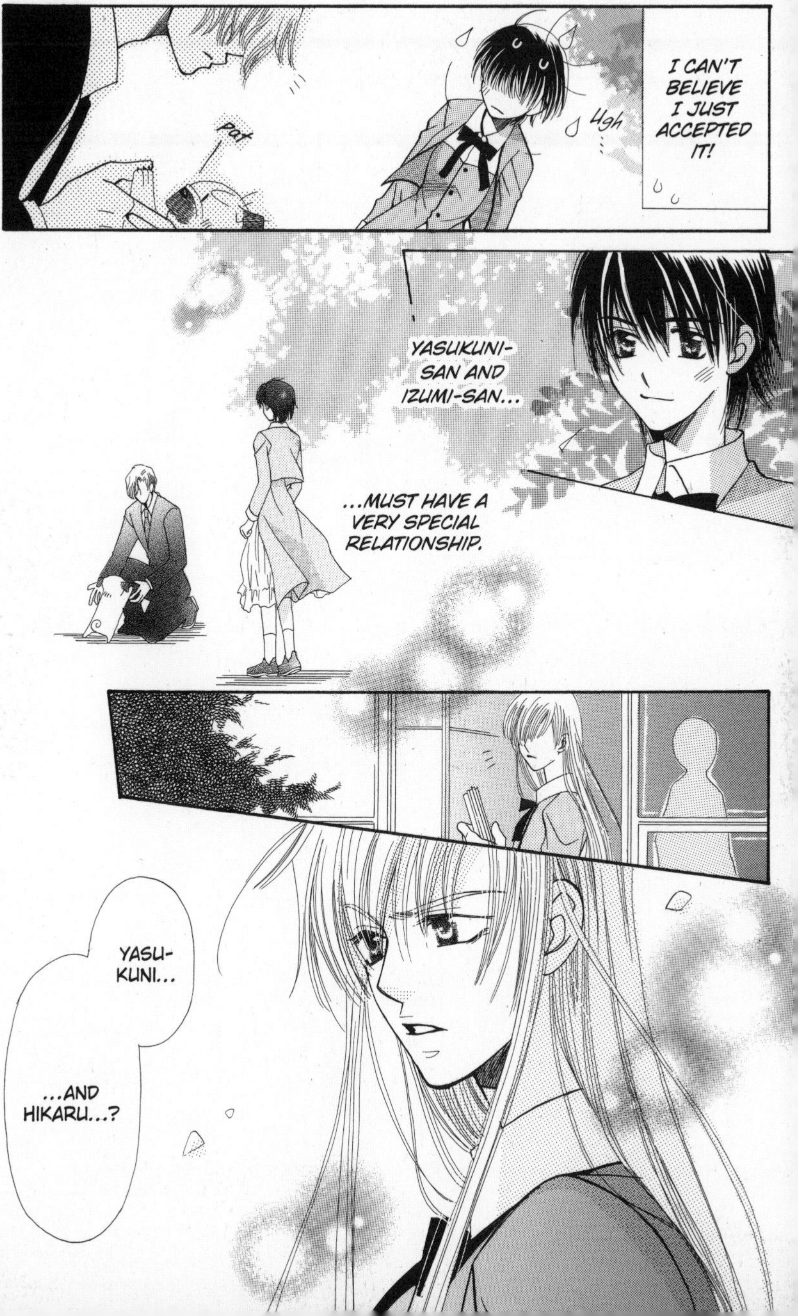
I CAN'T BELIEVE I JUST ACCEPTED IT!
Ugh
Pat
YASUKUNI-SAN AND IZUMI-SAN...
...MUST HAVE A VERY SPECIAL RELATIONSHIP.
YASU-KUNI...
...AND HIKARU...?

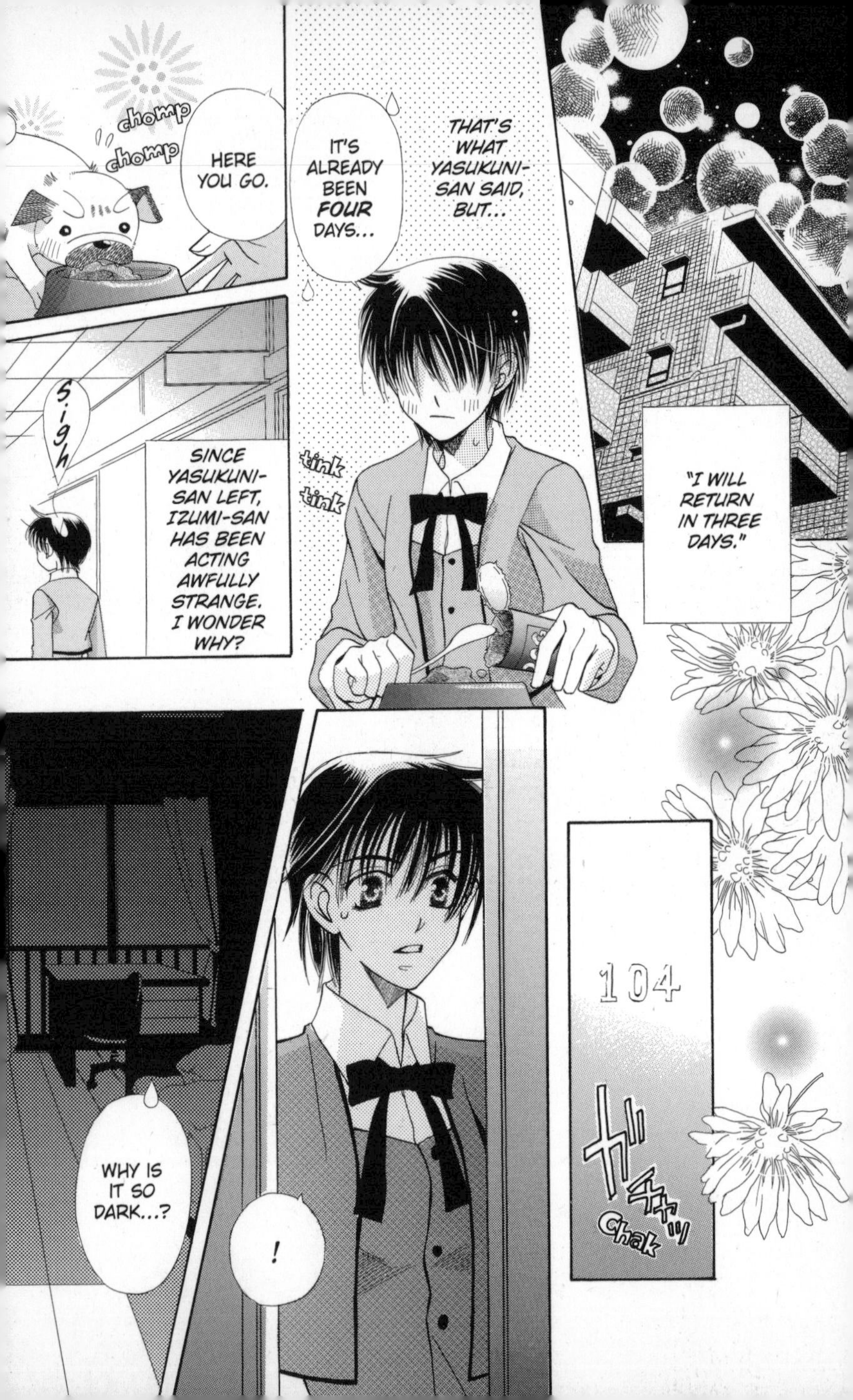
"I WILL RETURN IN THREE DAYS."
THAT'S WHAT YASUKUNI-SAN SAID, BUT...
IT'S ALREADY BEEN **FOUR** DAYS...
tink
tink
chomp
chomp
HERE YOU GO.
Sigh
SINCE YASUKUNI-SAN LEFT, IZUMI-SAN HAS BEEN ACTING AWFULLY STRANGE. I WONDER WHY?
104
ガチャッ
Chak
!
WHY IS IT SO DARK...?

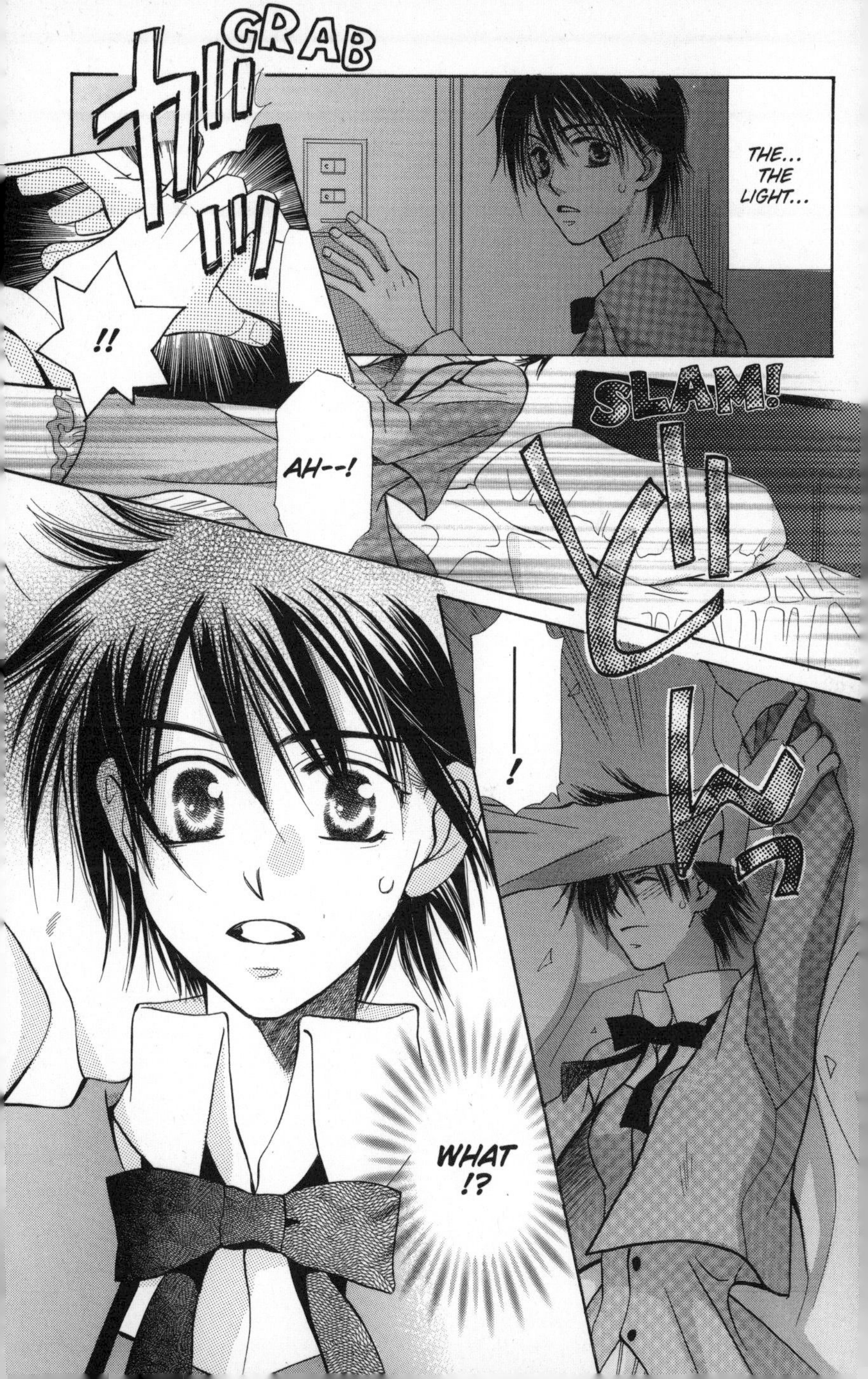
THE... THE LIGHT...
GRAB
!!
SLAM!
AH--!
—!
WHAT!?

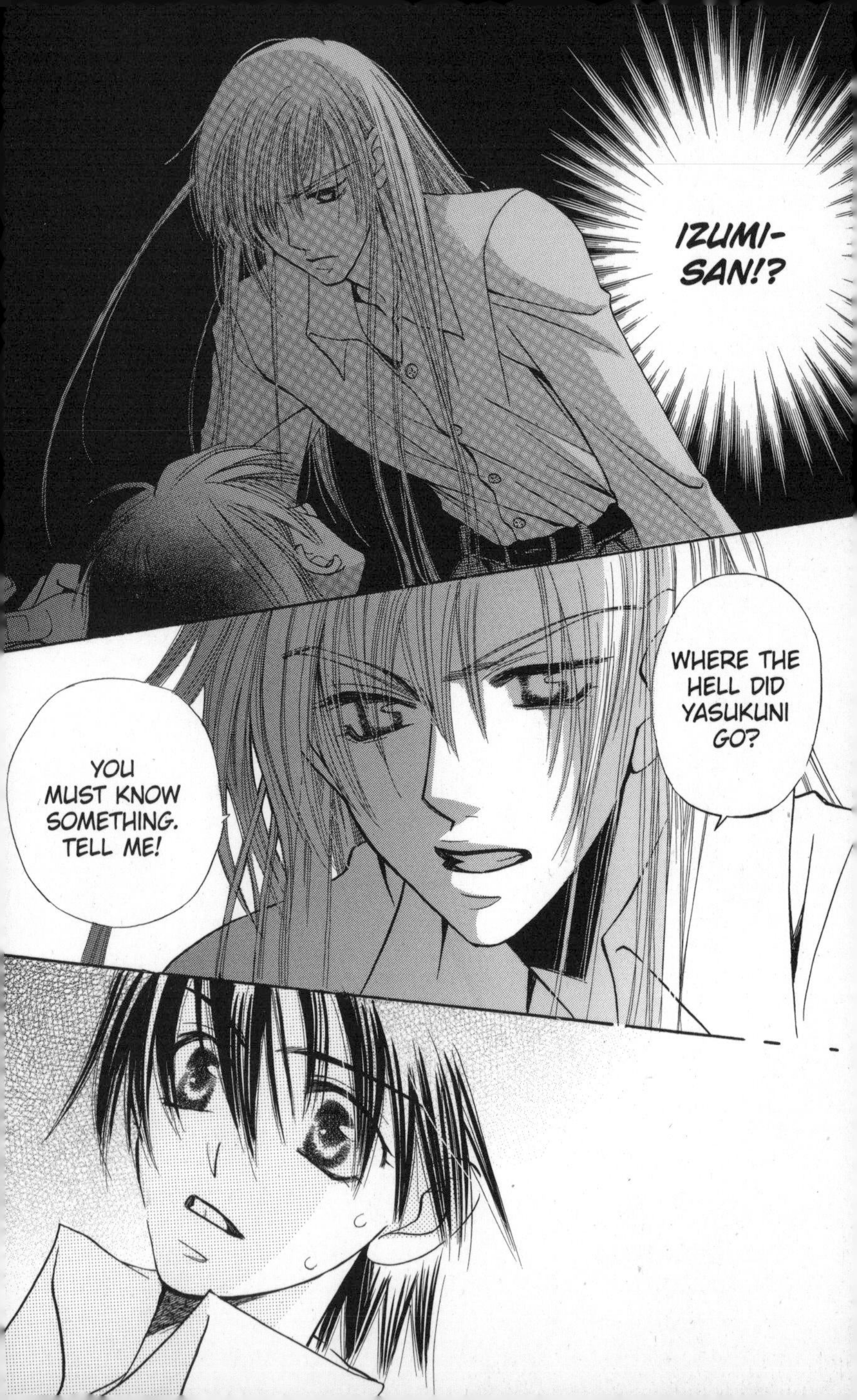
IZUMI-SAN!?
WHERE THE HELL DID YASUKUNI GO?
YOU MUST KNOW SOMETHING. TELL ME!

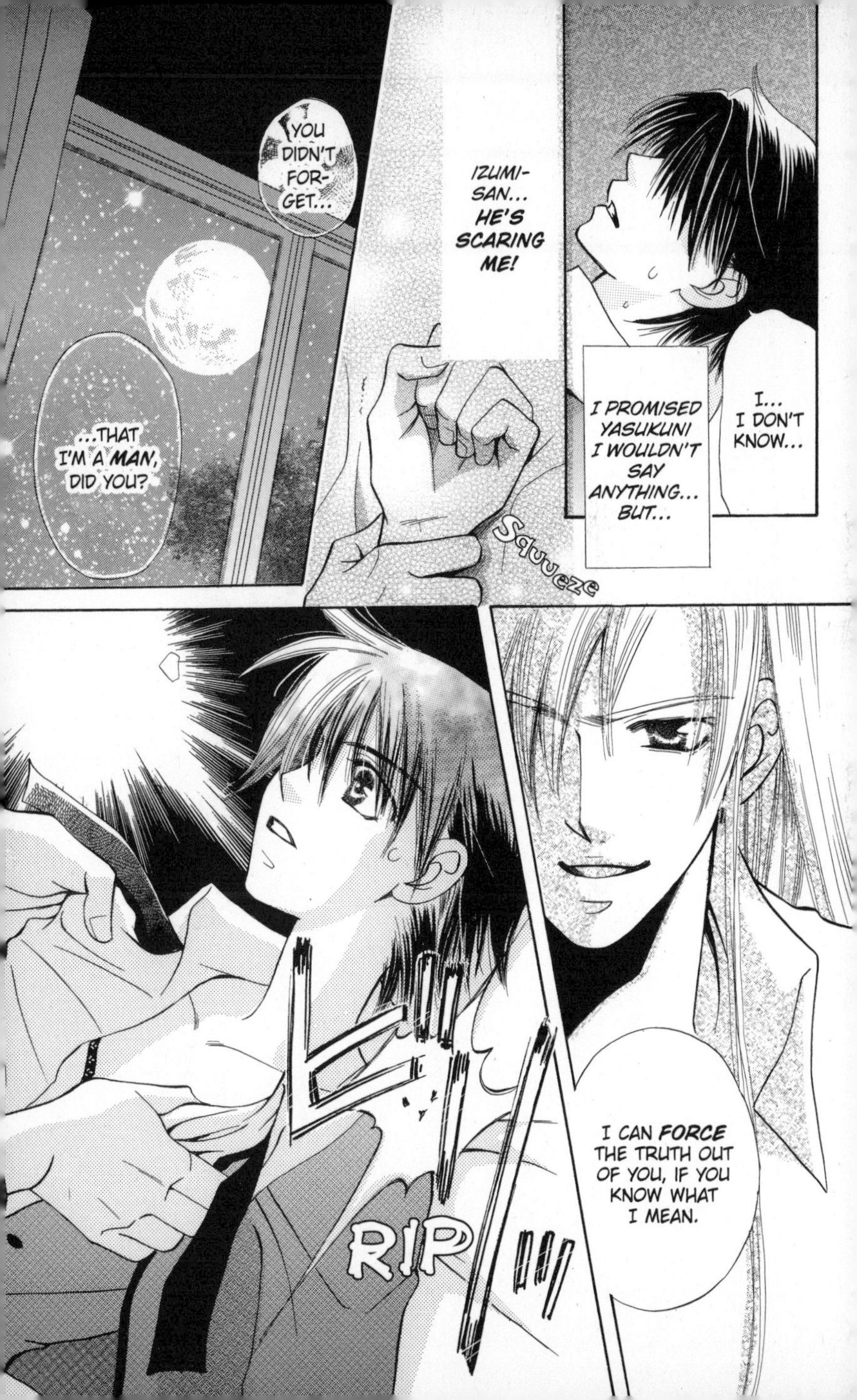
I... I DON'T KNOW...
I PROMISED YASUKUNI I WOULDN'T SAY ANYTHING... BUT...
IZUMI-SAN... **HE'S SCARING ME!**
Squueze
YOU DIDN'T FOR-GET...
...THAT I'M A *MAN*, DID YOU?
I CAN **FORCE** THE TRUTH OUT OF YOU, IF YOU KNOW WHAT I MEAN.
RIP

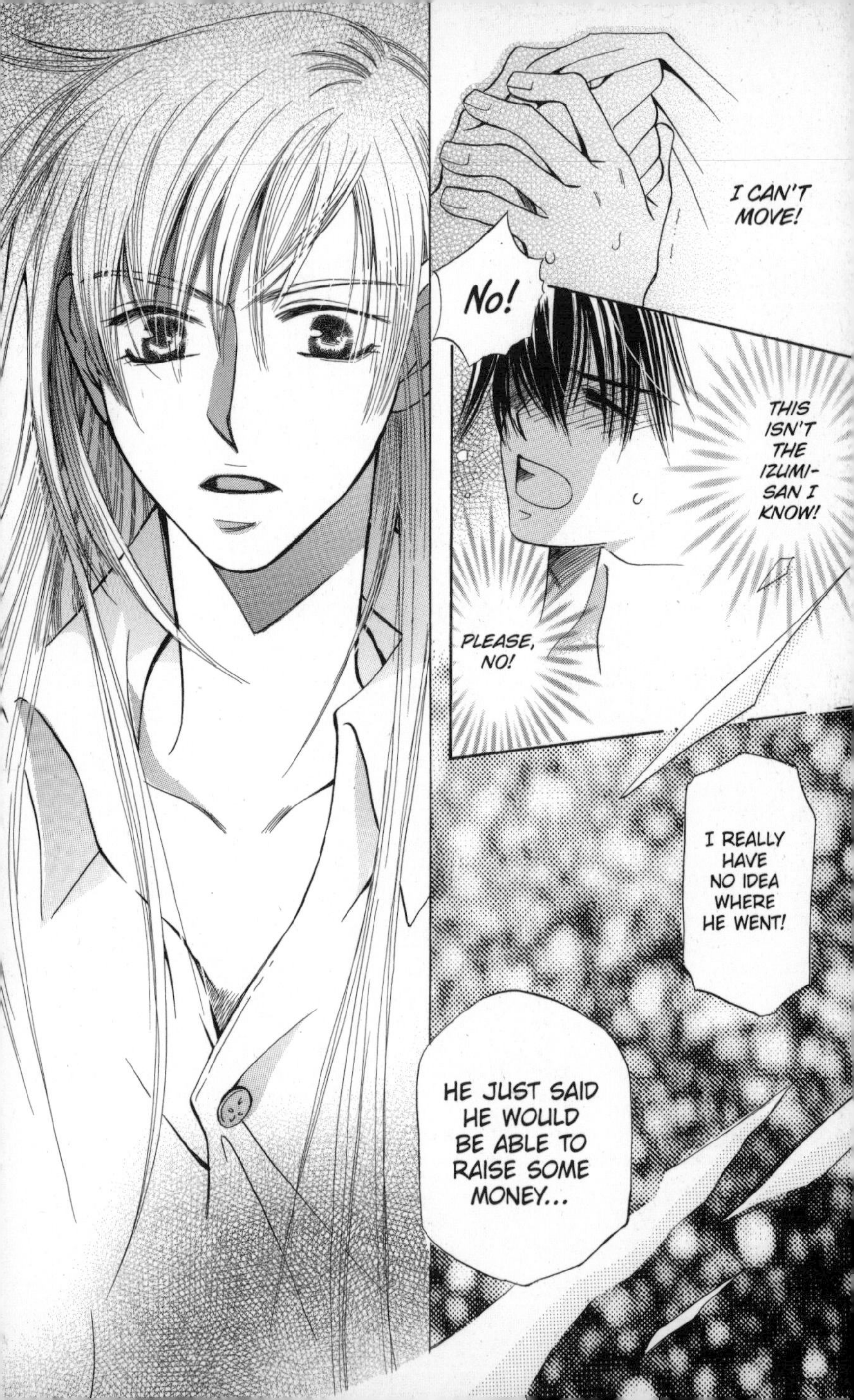
I CAN'T MOVE!
No!
THIS ISN'T THE IZUMI-SAN I KNOW!
PLEASE, NO!
I REALLY HAVE NO IDEA WHERE HE WENT!
HE JUST SAID HE WOULD BE ABLE TO RAISE SOME MONEY...

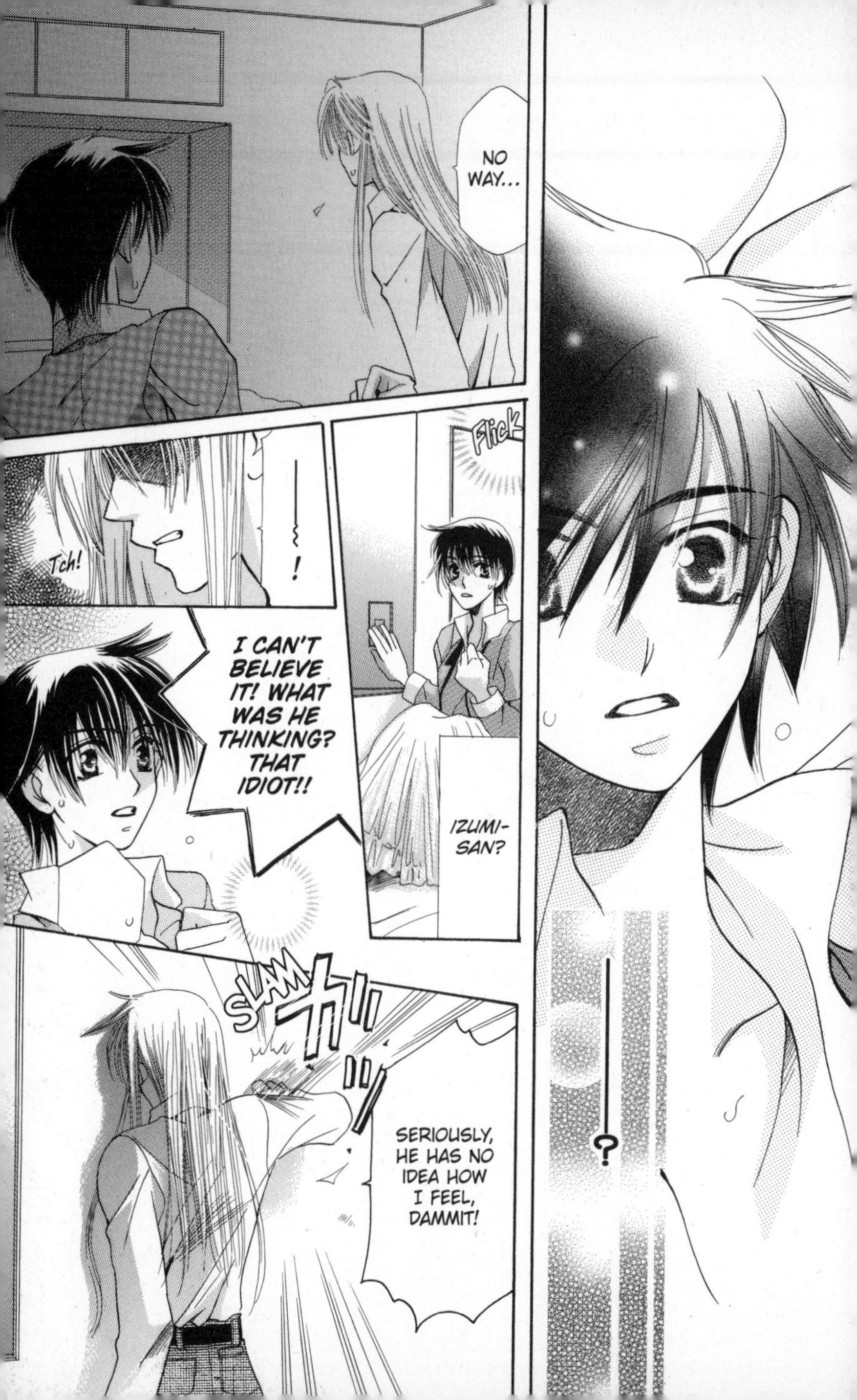
—?
NO WAY...
Flick
IZUMI-SAN?
Tch!
—!
I CAN'T BELIEVE IT! WHAT WAS HE THINKING? THAT IDIOT!!
SLAM
SERIOUSLY, HE HAS NO IDEA HOW I FEEL, DAMMIT!

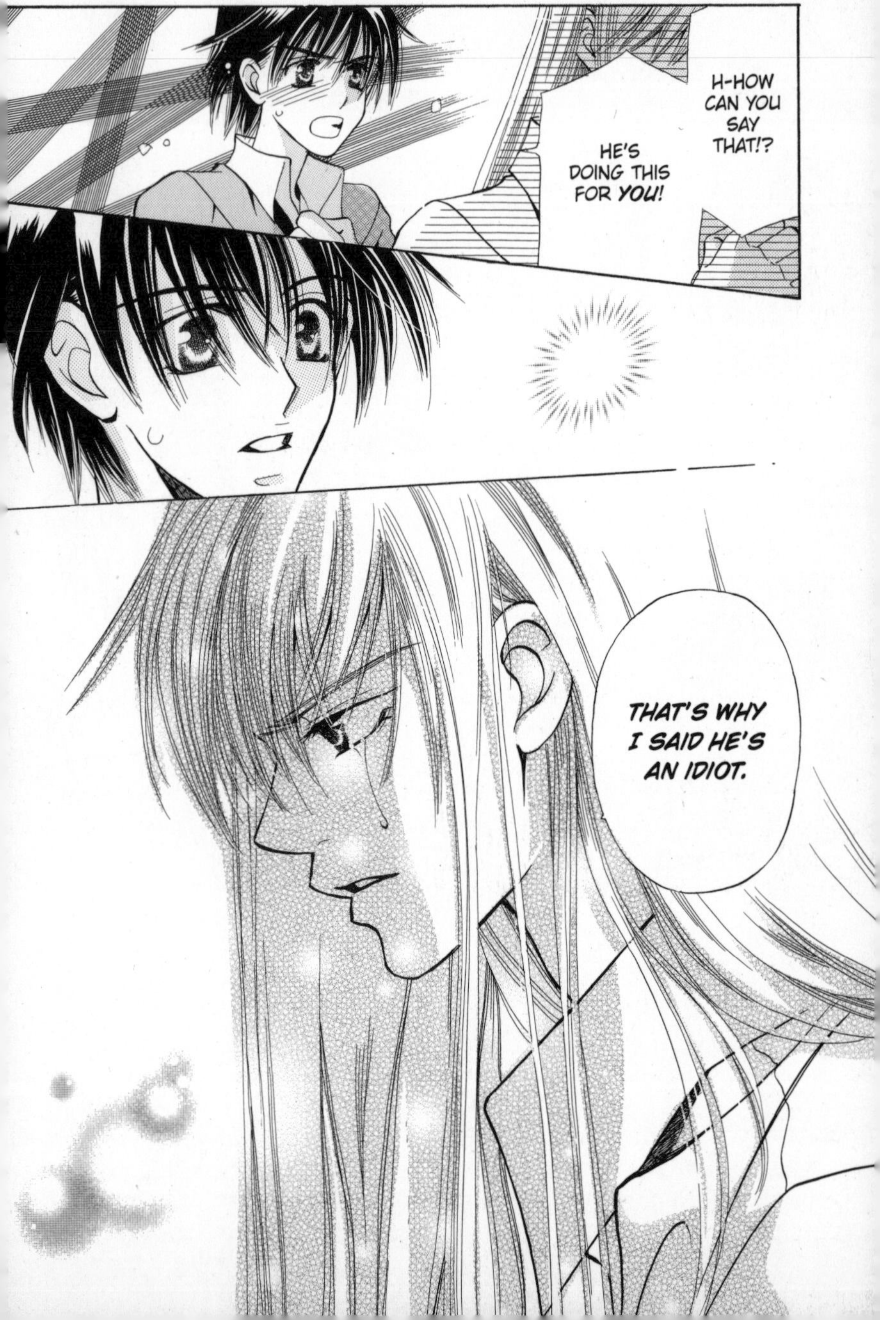
H-HOW CAN YOU SAY THAT!?
HE'S DOING THIS FOR *YOU!*
THAT'S WHY I SAID HE'S AN IDIOT.

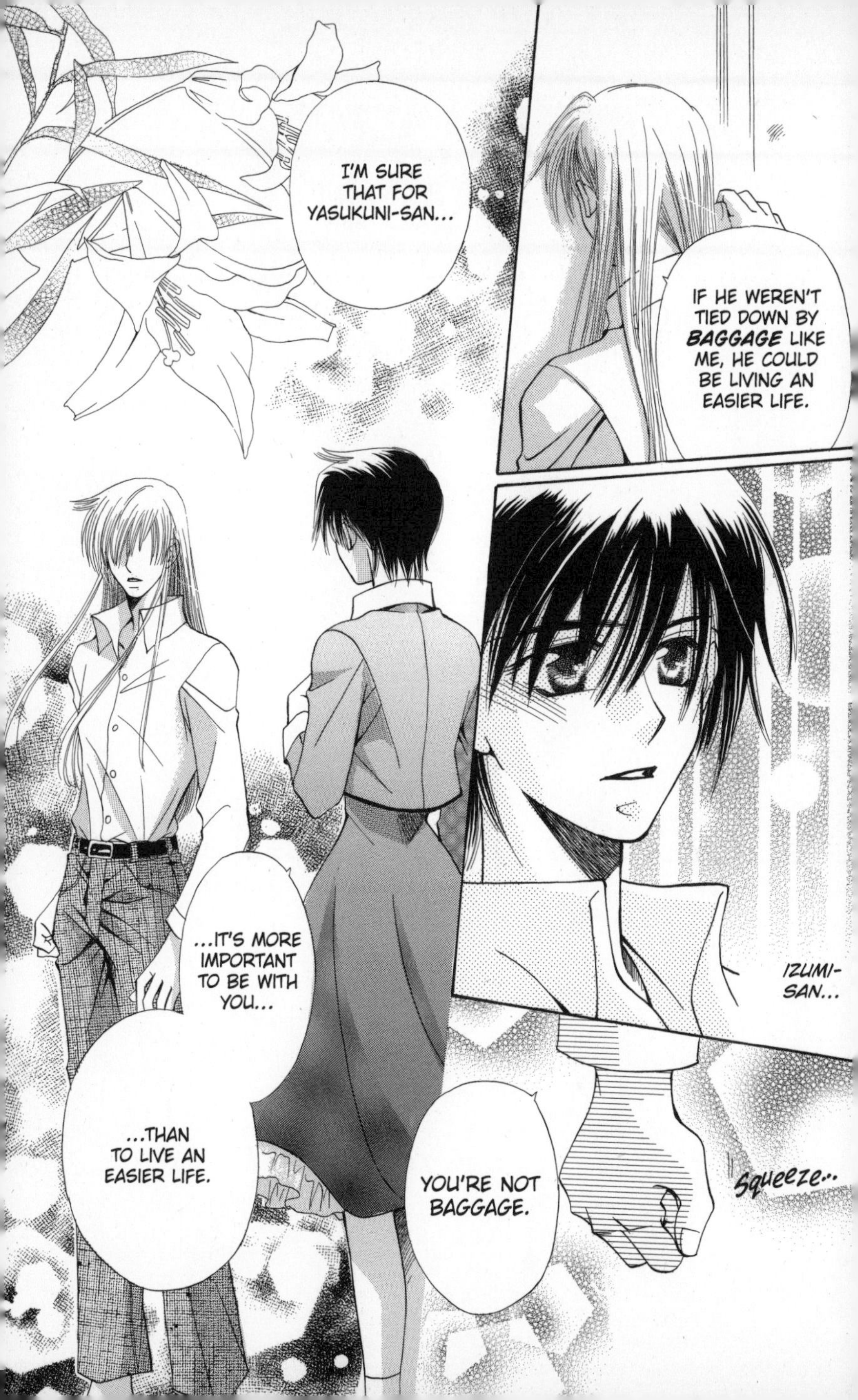
IF HE WEREN'T TIED DOWN BY **BAGGAGE** LIKE ME, HE COULD BE LIVING AN EASIER LIFE.
IZUMI-SAN...
Squeeze...
YOU'RE NOT BAGGAGE.
I'M SURE THAT FOR YASUKUNI-SAN...
...IT'S MORE IMPORTANT TO BE WITH YOU...
...THAN TO LIVE AN EASIER LIFE.

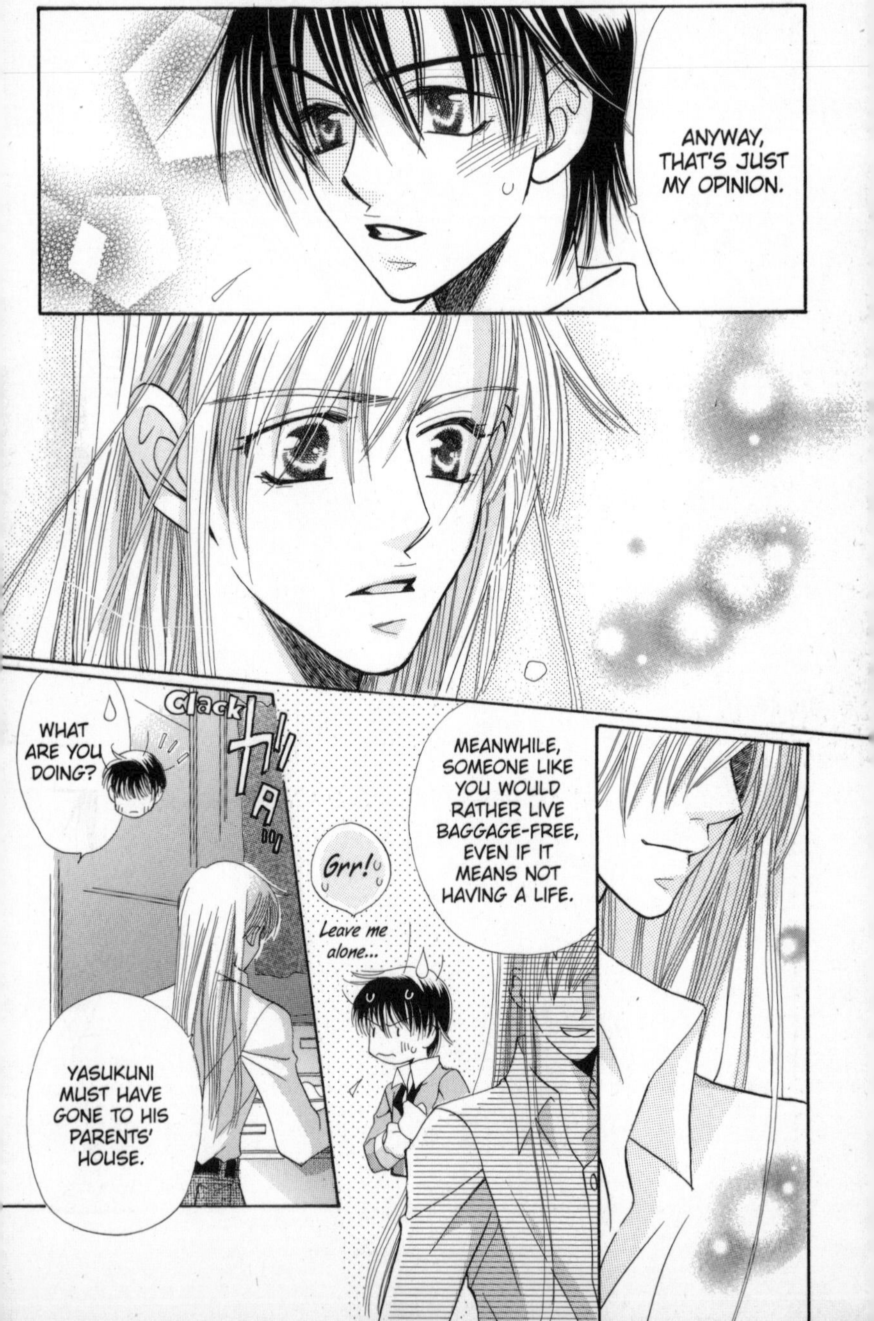
ANYWAY, THAT'S JUST MY OPINION.
MEANWHILE, SOMEONE LIKE YOU WOULD RATHER LIVE BAGGAGE-FREE, EVEN IF IT MEANS NOT HAVING A LIFE.
Grr!
Leave me alone...
Clack
WHAT ARE YOU DOING?
YASUKUNI MUST HAVE GONE TO HIS PARENTS' HOUSE.

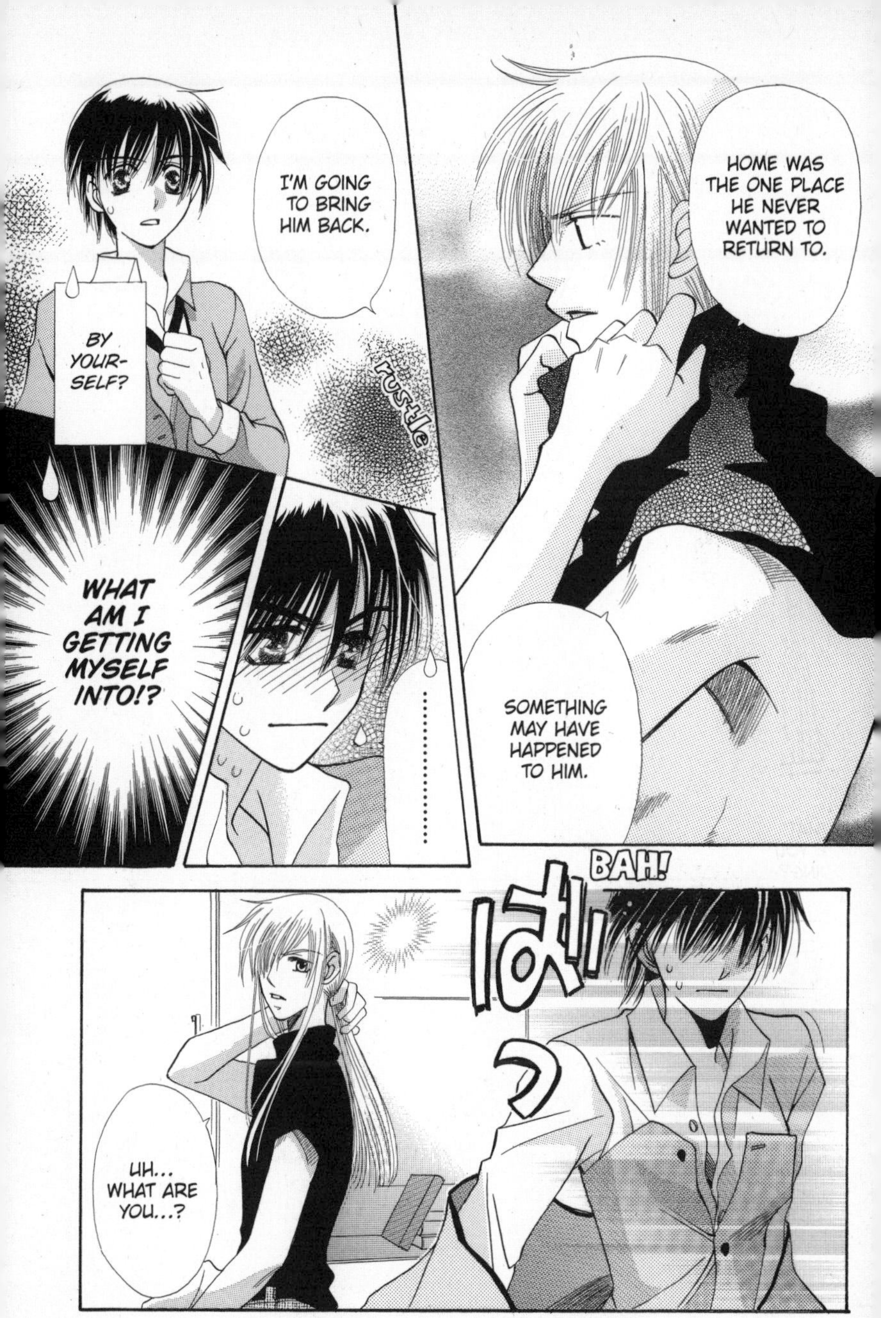
HOME WAS THE ONE PLACE HE NEVER WANTED TO RETURN TO.
SOMETHING MAY HAVE HAPPENED TO HIM.
I'M GOING TO BRING HIM BACK.
BY YOURSELF?
rustle
......
WHAT AM I GETTING MYSELF INTO!?
BAH!
は!っ
UH... WHAT ARE YOU...?

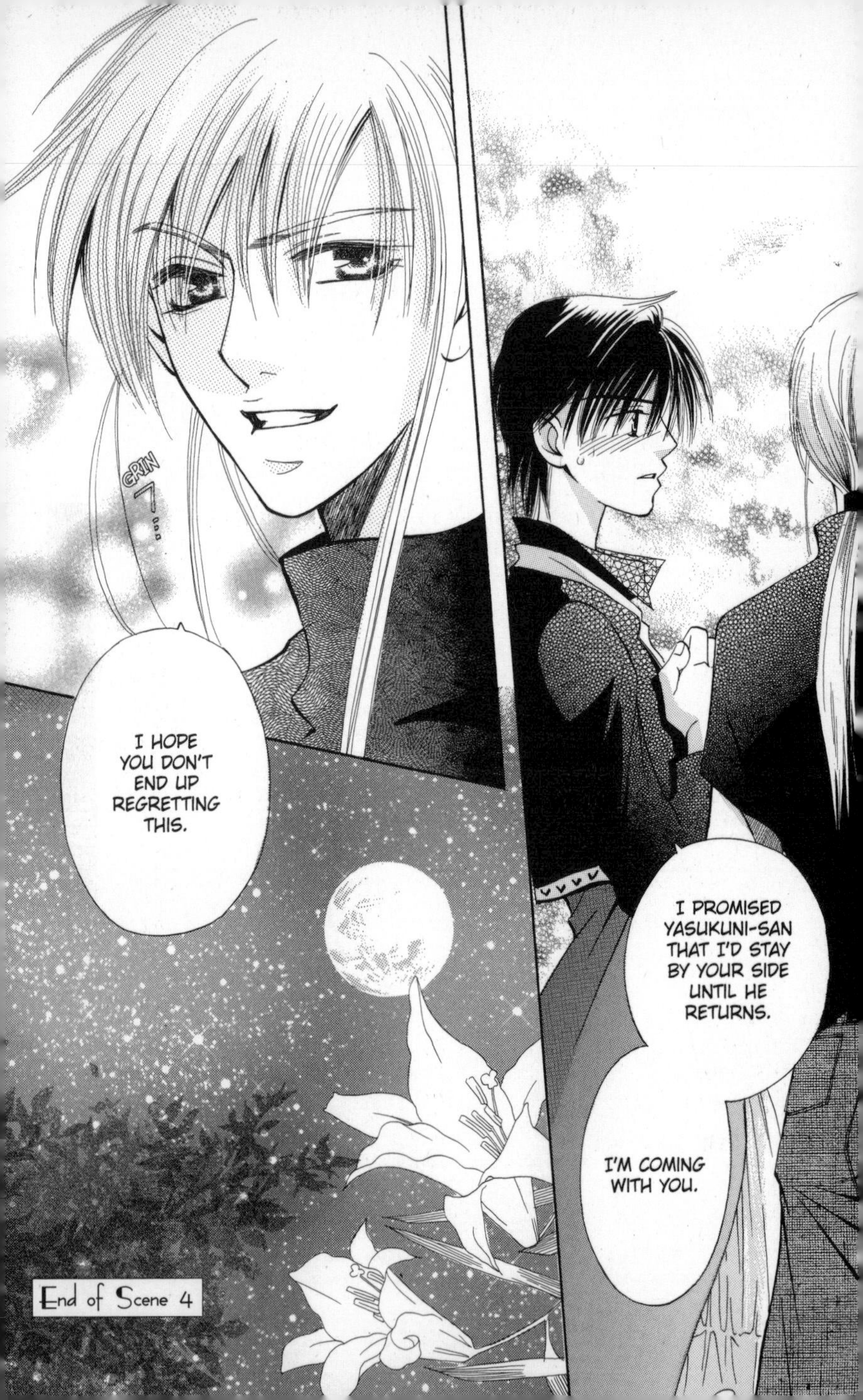
I PROMISED YASUKUNI-SAN THAT I'D STAY BY YOUR SIDE UNTIL HE RETURNS.
I'M COMING WITH YOU.
GRIN
I HOPE YOU DON'T END UP REGRETTING THIS.
End of Scene 4

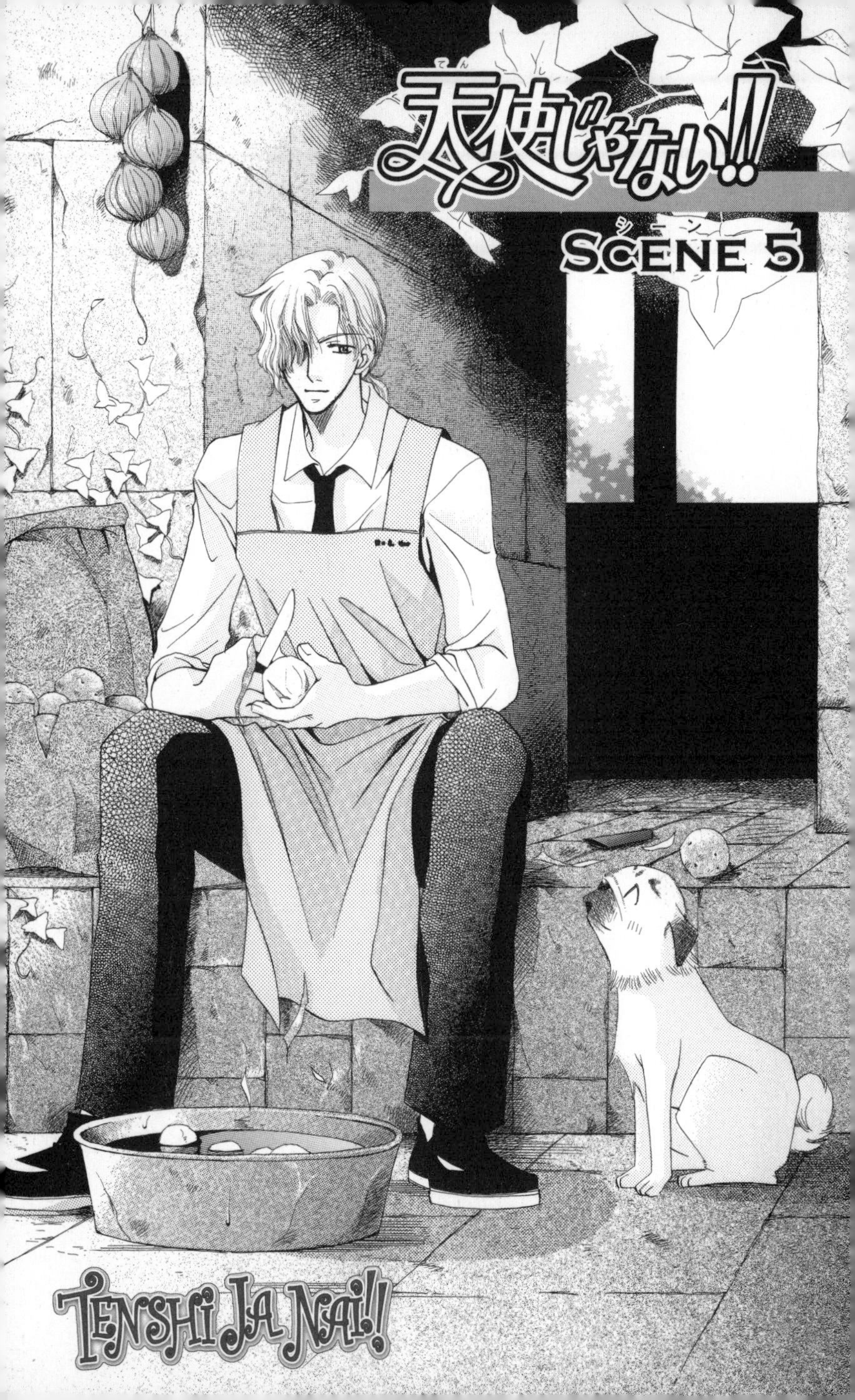
天使じゃない!!
SCENE 5
TENSHI JA NAI!!

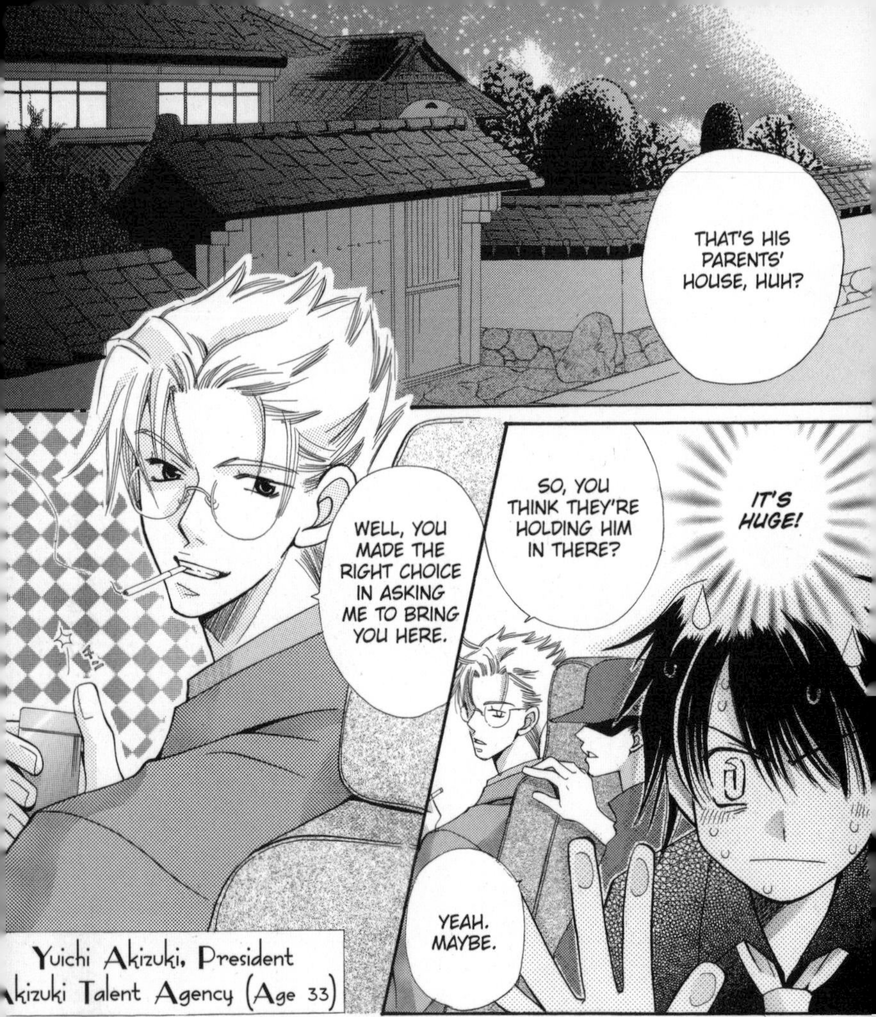
THAT'S HIS PARENTS' HOUSE, HUH?
IT'S HUGE!
SO, YOU THINK THEY'RE HOLDING HIM IN THERE?
YEAH. MAYBE.
WELL, YOU MADE THE RIGHT CHOICE IN ASKING ME TO BRING YOU HERE.
Yuichi Akizuki, President
Akizuki Talent Agency (Age 33)

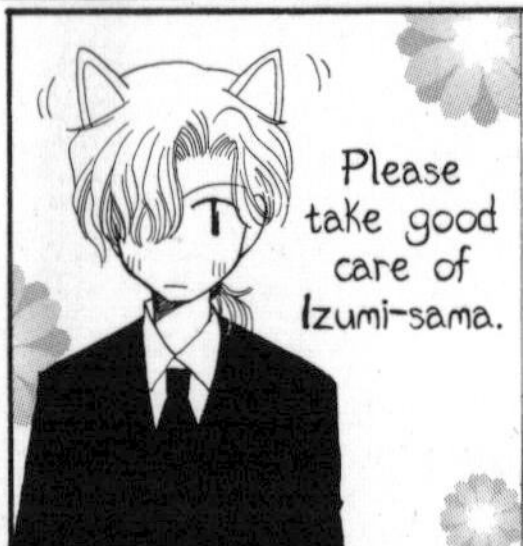
Please take good care of Izumi-sama.

Yasukuni Inukai (Age 23)
Birthday: July 7
Blood type: AB
Dog-type
He's Izumi Kido's guard dog. Don't be fooled by his gentle Golden Retriever looks. His true character is that of a lone wolf. And when it comes to Izumi, he can be savage as a pit bull.

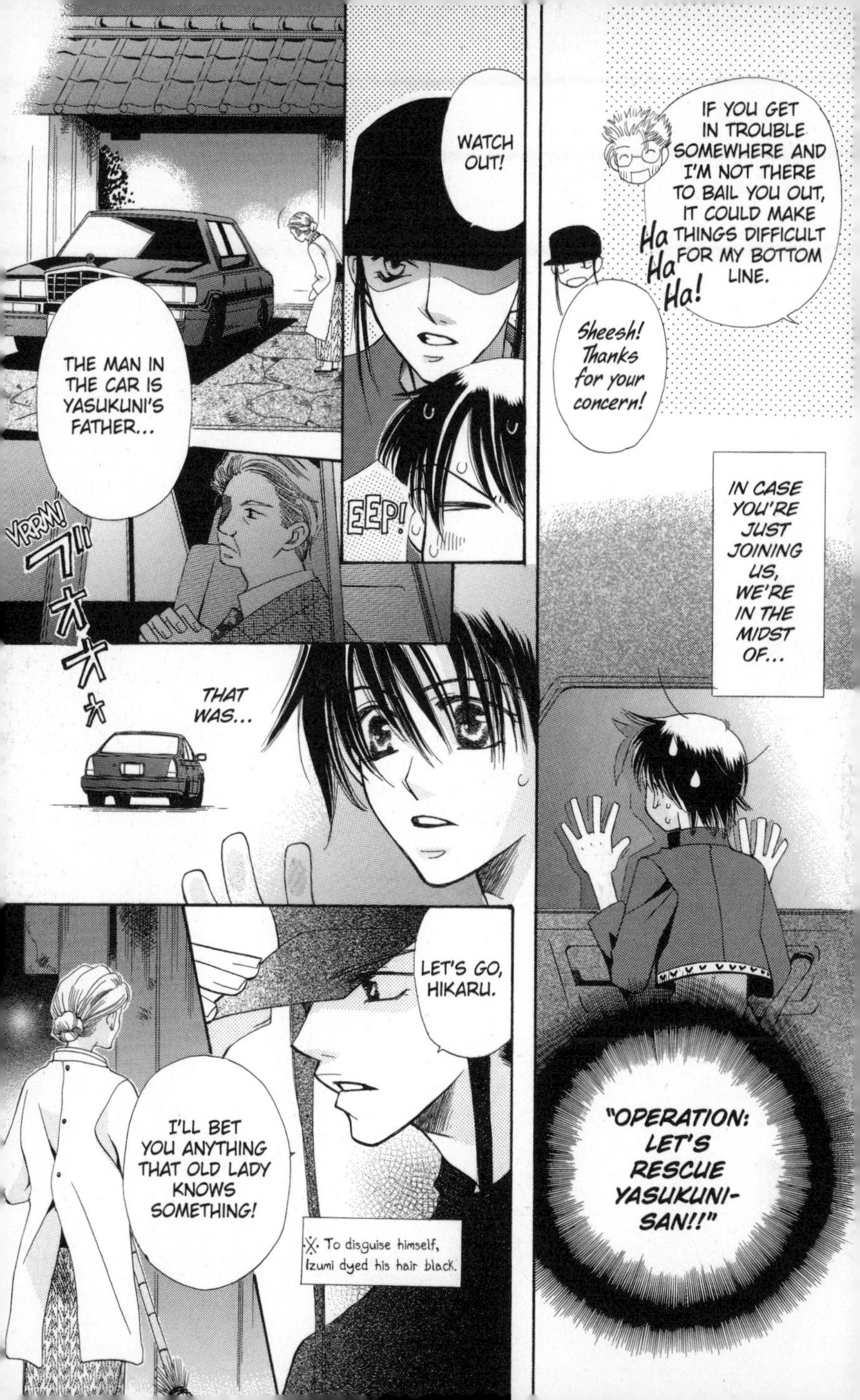
IF YOU GET IN TROUBLE SOMEWHERE AND I'M NOT THERE TO BAIL YOU OUT, IT COULD MAKE THINGS DIFFICULT FOR MY BOTTOM LINE.
Ha Ha Ha!
Sheesh! Thanks for your concern!
IN CASE YOU'RE JUST JOINING US, WE'RE IN THE MIDST OF...
"OPERATION: LET'S RESCUE YASUKUNI-SAN!!"
WATCH OUT!
EEP!
THE MAN IN THE CAR IS YASUKUNI'S FATHER...
VRRM!
ブォォォォ
THAT WAS...
LET'S GO, HIKARU.
I'LL BET YOU ANYTHING THAT OLD LADY KNOWS SOMETHING!
※ To disguise himself, Izumi dyed his hair black.

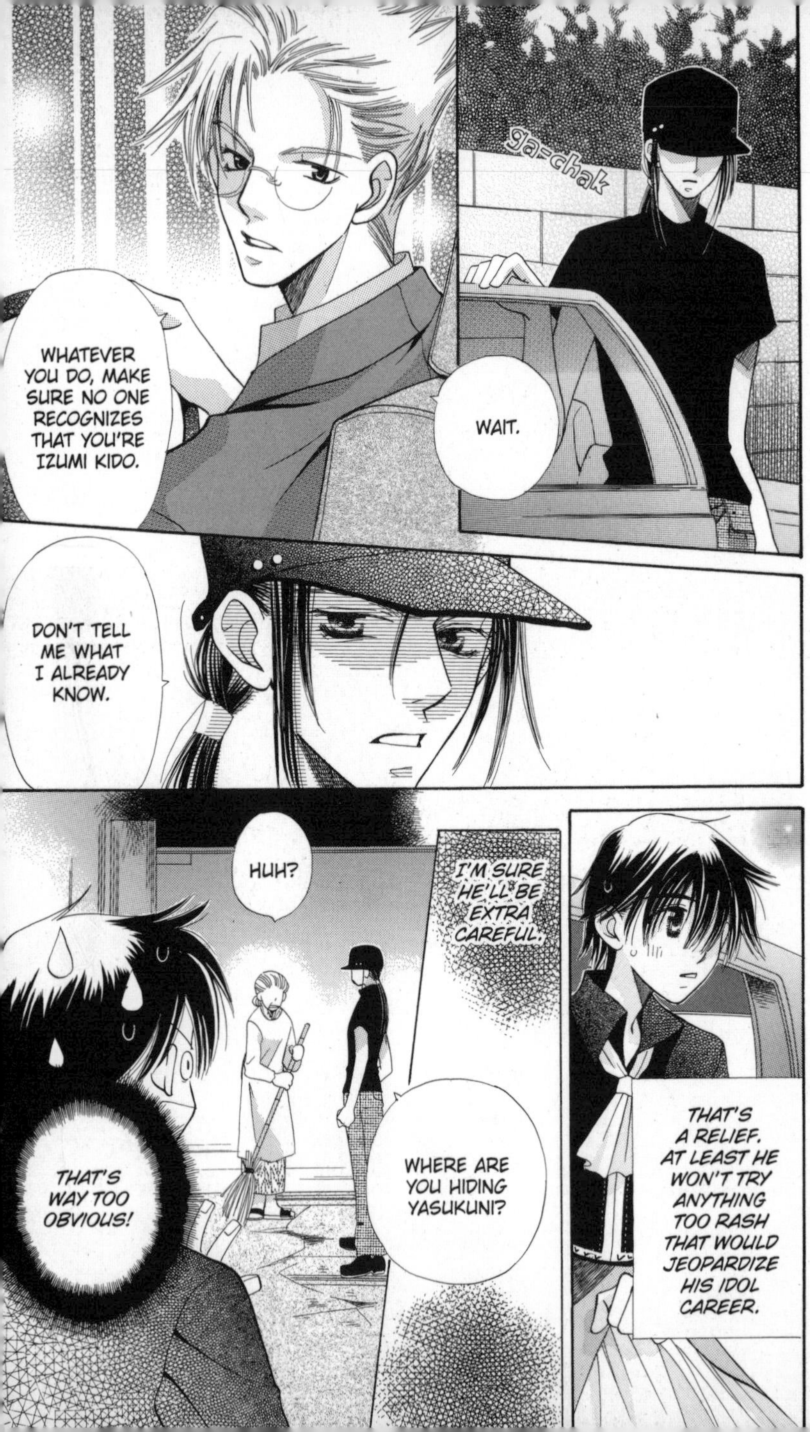
ga-chak
WAIT.
WHATEVER YOU DO, MAKE SURE NO ONE RECOGNIZES THAT YOU'RE IZUMI KIDO.
DON'T TELL ME WHAT I ALREADY KNOW.
I'M SURE HE'LL BE EXTRA CAREFUL.
THAT'S A RELIEF. AT LEAST HE WON'T TRY ANYTHING TOO RASH THAT WOULD JEOPARDIZE HIS IDOL CAREER.
WHERE ARE YOU HIDING YASUKUNI?
HUH?
THAT'S WAY TOO OBVIOUS!

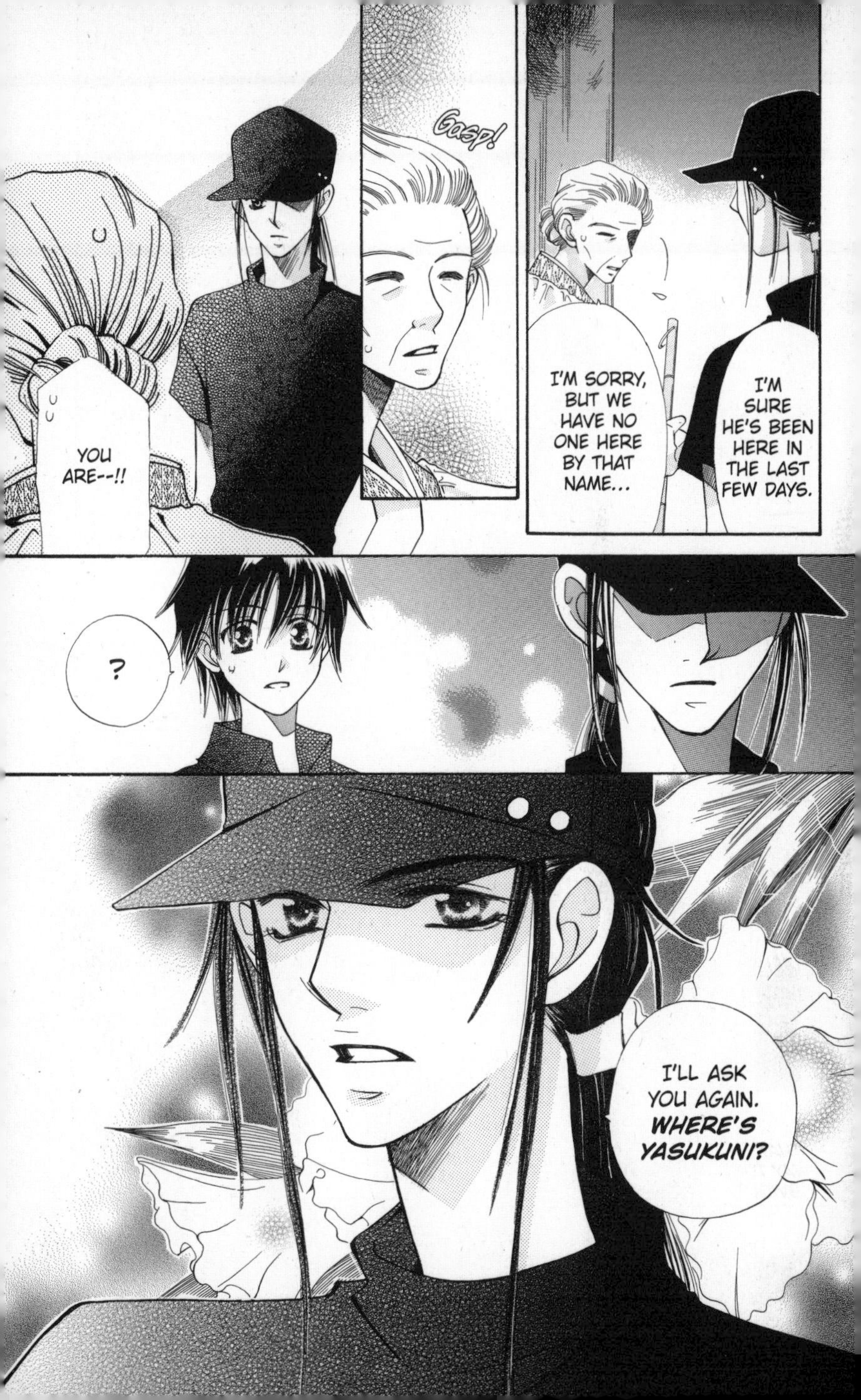
I'M SURE HE'S BEEN HERE IN THE LAST FEW DAYS.
I'M SORRY, BUT WE HAVE NO ONE HERE BY THAT NAME...
Gasp!
YOU ARE--!!
?
I'LL ASK YOU AGAIN. **WHERE'S YASUKUNI?**

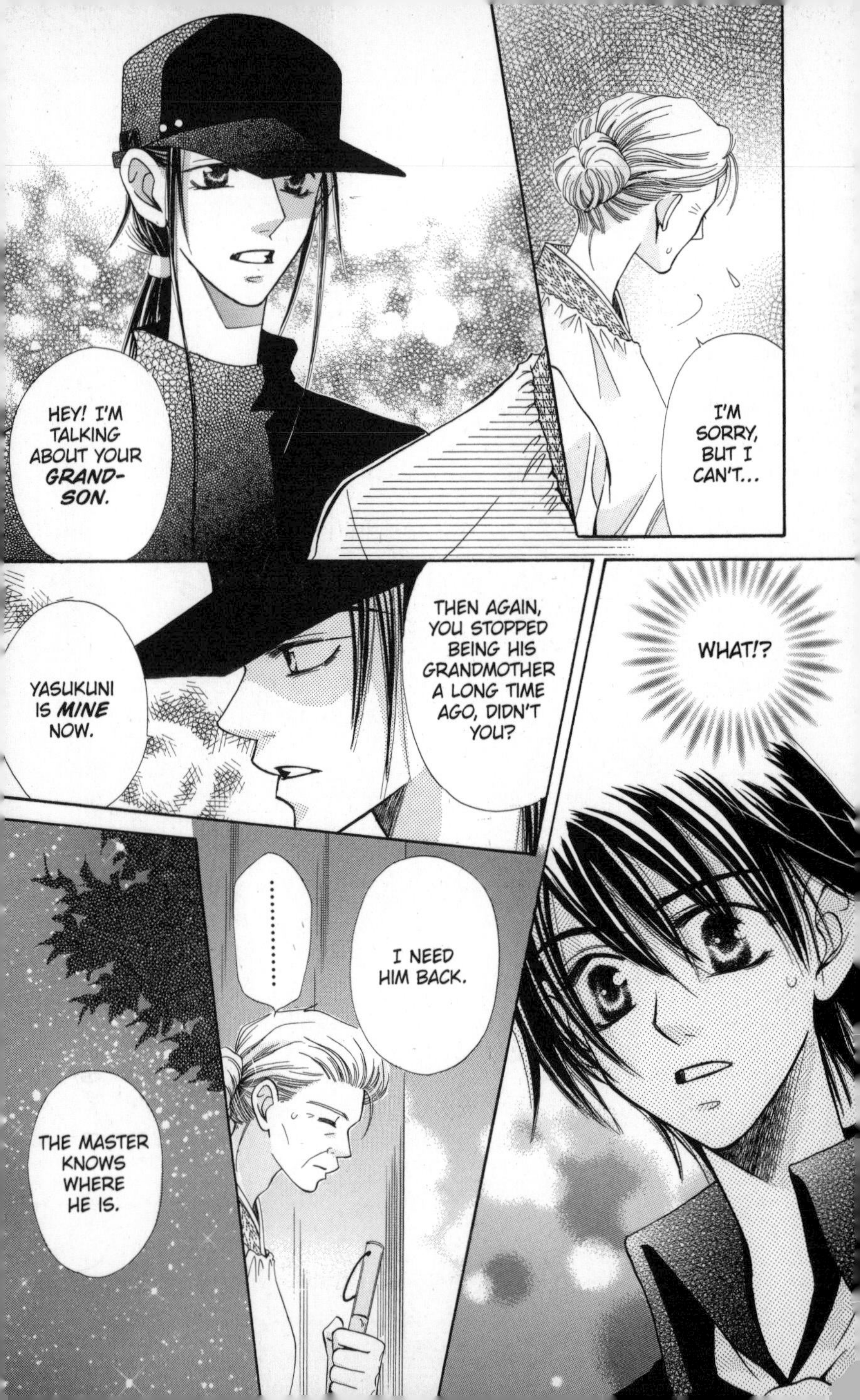
I'M SORRY, BUT I CAN'T...
HEY! I'M TALKING ABOUT YOUR *GRANDSON.*
WHAT!?
THEN AGAIN, YOU STOPPED BEING HIS GRANDMOTHER A LONG TIME AGO, DIDN'T YOU?
YASUKUNI IS *MINE* NOW.
I NEED HIM BACK.
....
THE MASTER KNOWS WHERE HE IS.

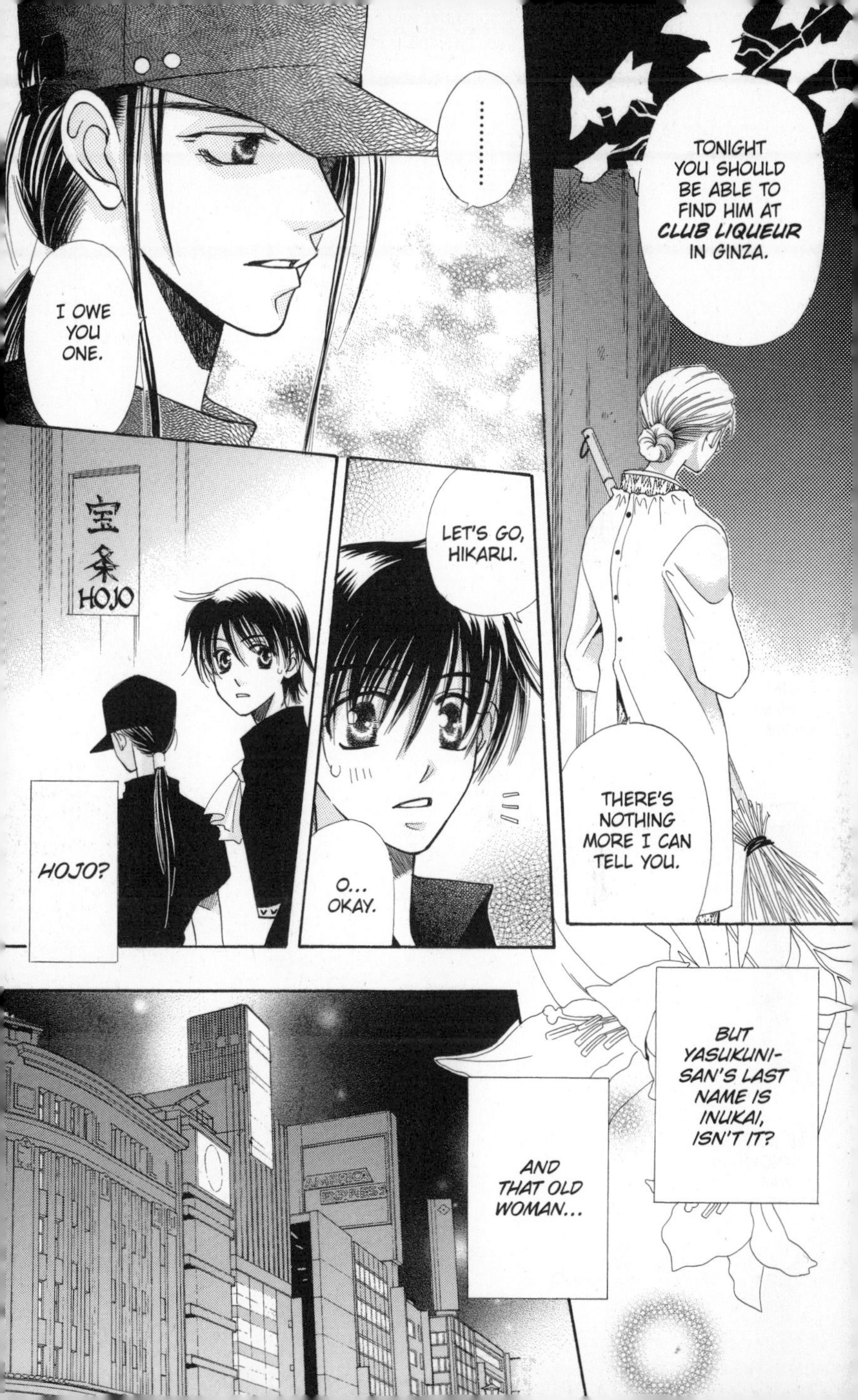
TONIGHT YOU SHOULD BE ABLE TO FIND HIM AT ***CLUB LIQUEUR*** IN GINZA.
THERE'S NOTHING MORE I CAN TELL YOU.
......
I OWE YOU ONE.
LET'S GO, HIKARU.
O... OKAY.
宝条
HOJO
HOJO?
BUT YASUKUNI-SAN'S LAST NAME IS INUKAI, ISN'T IT?
AND THAT OLD WOMAN...

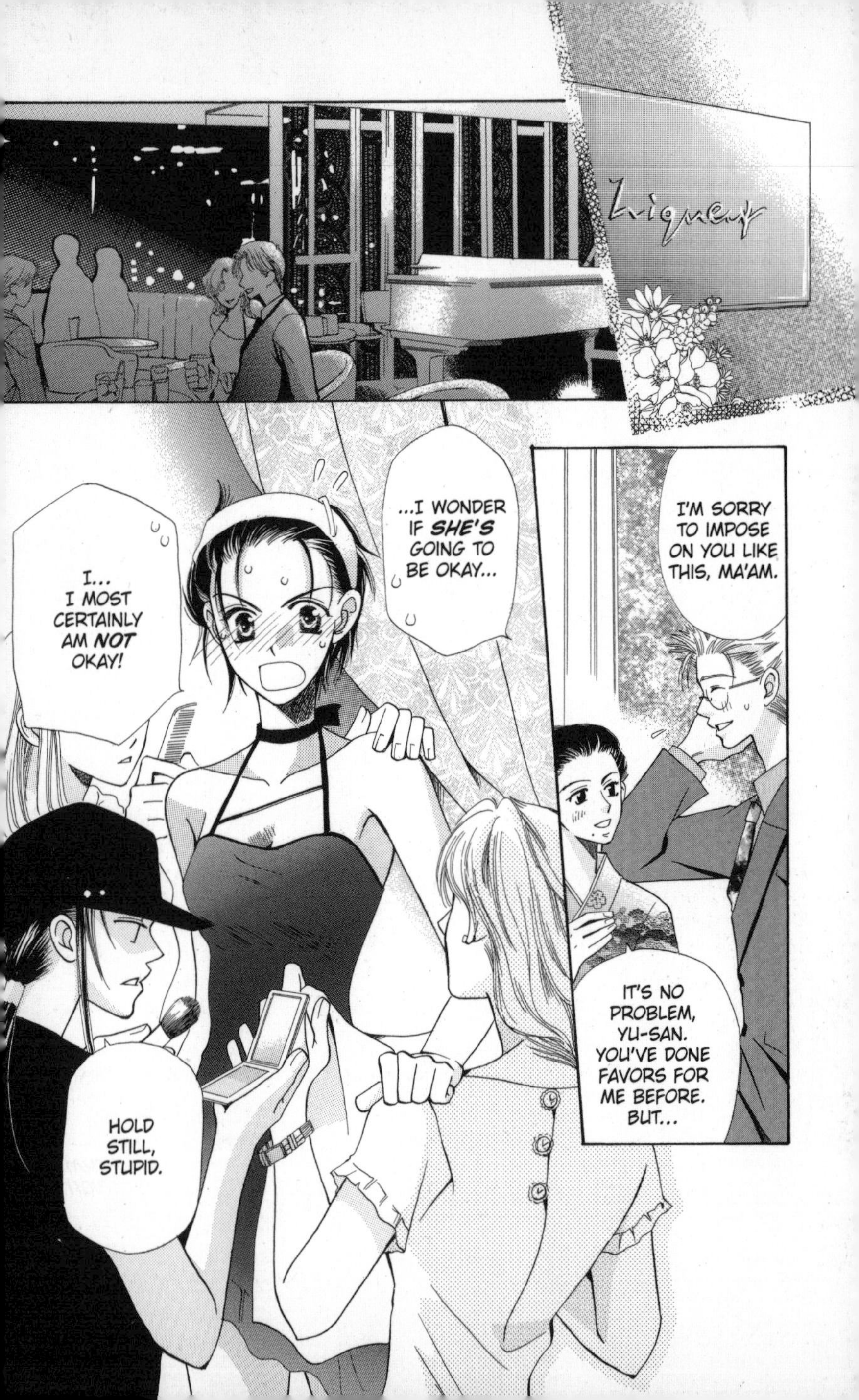
I'M SORRY TO IMPOSE ON YOU LIKE THIS, MA'AM.
IT'S NO PROBLEM, YU-SAN. YOU'VE DONE FAVORS FOR ME BEFORE. BUT...
...I WONDER IF ***SHE'S*** GOING TO BE OKAY...
I... I MOST CERTAINLY AM ***NOT*** OKAY!
HOLD STILL, STUPID.

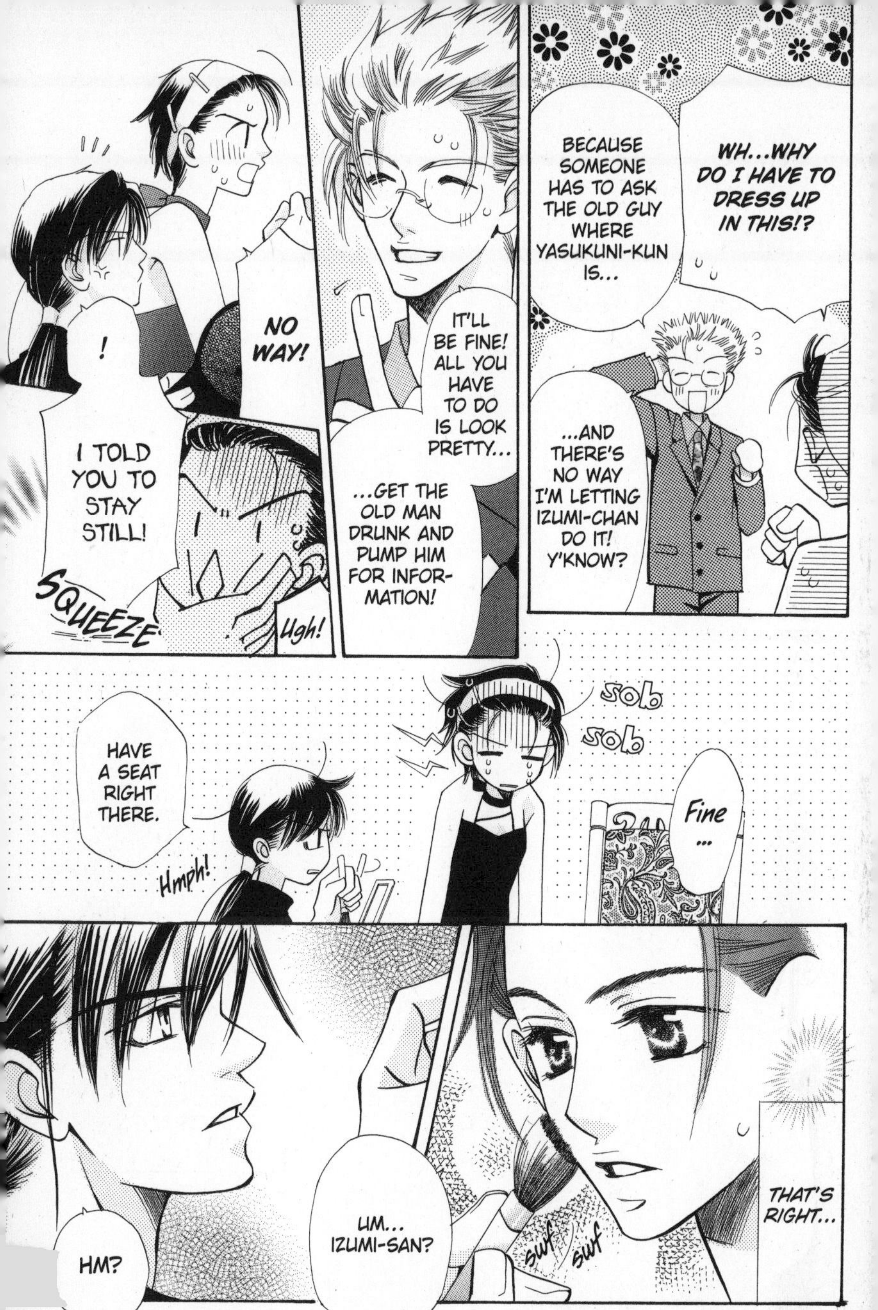
WH...WHY DO I HAVE TO DRESS UP IN THIS!?
BECAUSE SOMEONE HAS TO ASK THE OLD GUY WHERE YASUKUNI-KUN IS...
...AND THERE'S NO WAY I'M LETTING IZUMI-CHAN DO IT! Y'KNOW?
IT'LL BE FINE! ALL YOU HAVE TO DO IS LOOK PRETTY...
...GET THE OLD MAN DRUNK AND PUMP HIM FOR INFOR-MATION!
NO WAY!
!
I TOLD YOU TO STAY STILL!
Ugh!
SQUEEZE
sob
sob
Fine ...
HAVE A SEAT RIGHT THERE.
Hmph!
THAT'S RIGHT...
swf
swf
UM... IZUMI-SAN?
HM?

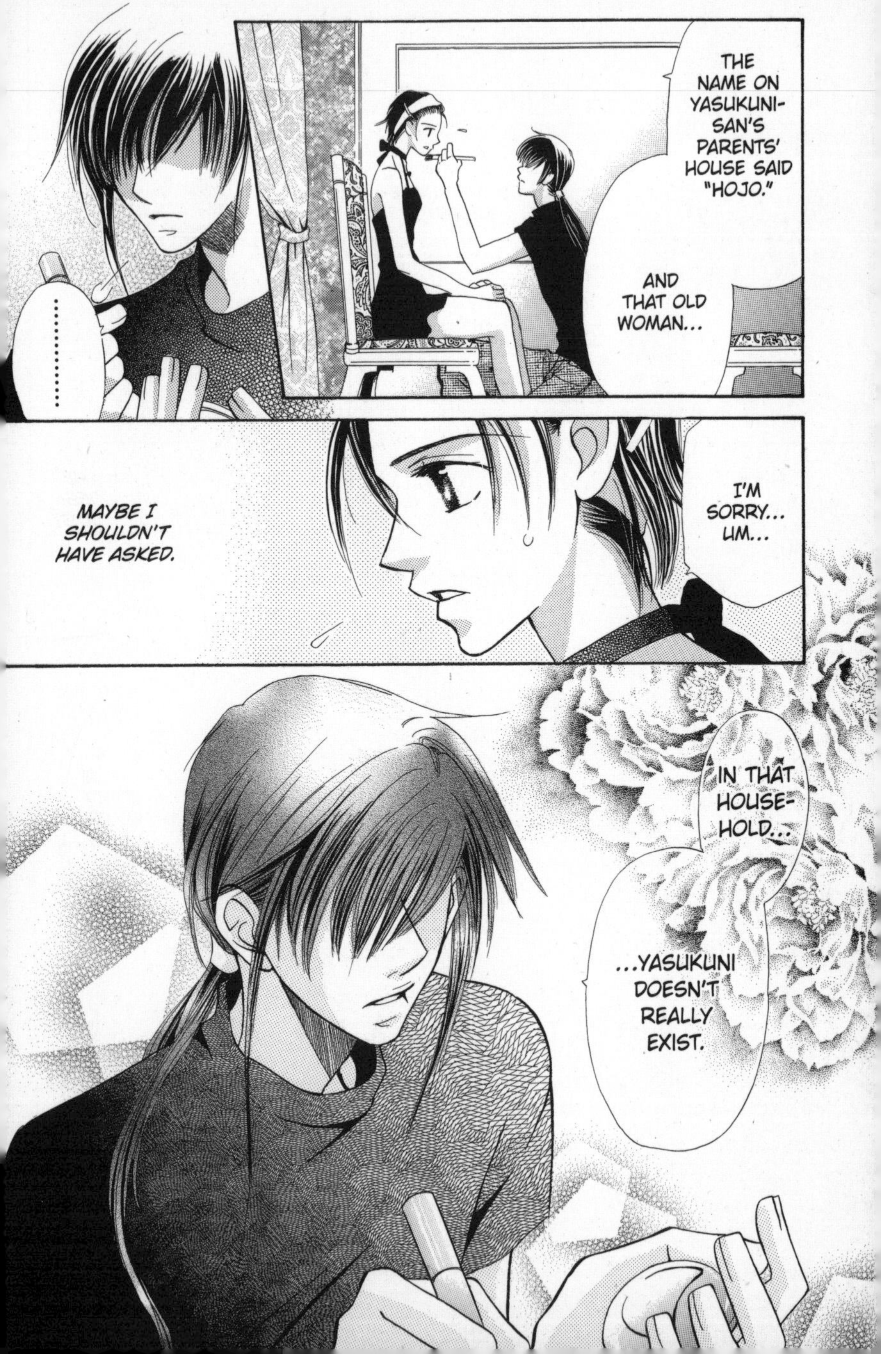
THE NAME ON YASUKUNI-SAN'S PARENTS' HOUSE SAID "HOJO."
AND THAT OLD WOMAN...
......
I'M SORRY... UM...
MAYBE I SHOULDN'T HAVE ASKED.
IN THAT HOUSEHOLD...
...YASUKUNI DOESN'T REALLY EXIST.

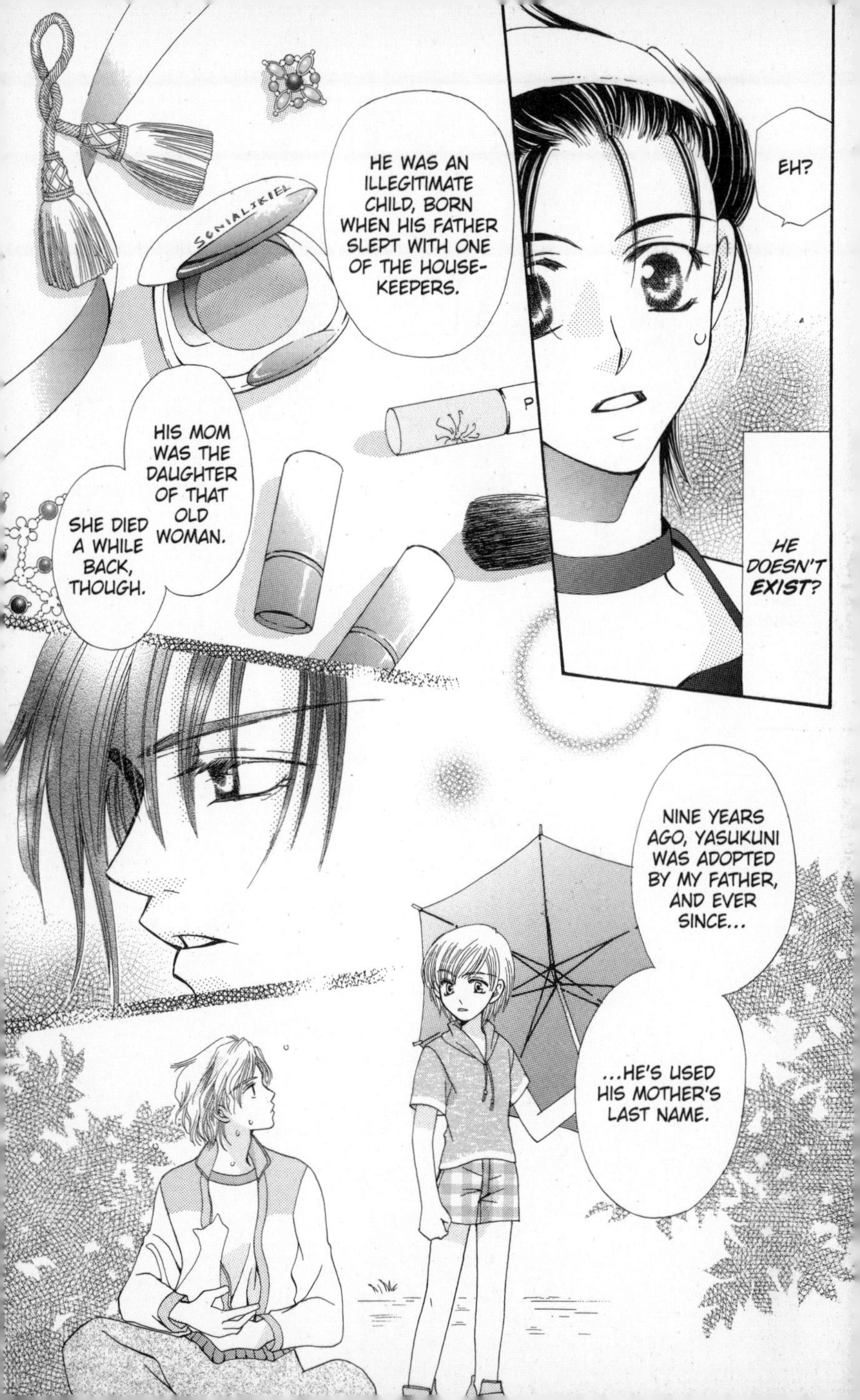
EH?
HE DOESN'T EXIST?
HE WAS AN ILLEGITIMATE CHILD, BORN WHEN HIS FATHER SLEPT WITH ONE OF THE HOUSE-KEEPERS.
HIS MOM WAS THE DAUGHTER OF THAT OLD WOMAN.
SHE DIED A WHILE BACK, THOUGH.
NINE YEARS AGO, YASUKUNI WAS ADOPTED BY MY FATHER, AND EVER SINCE...
...HE'S USED HIS MOTHER'S LAST NAME.

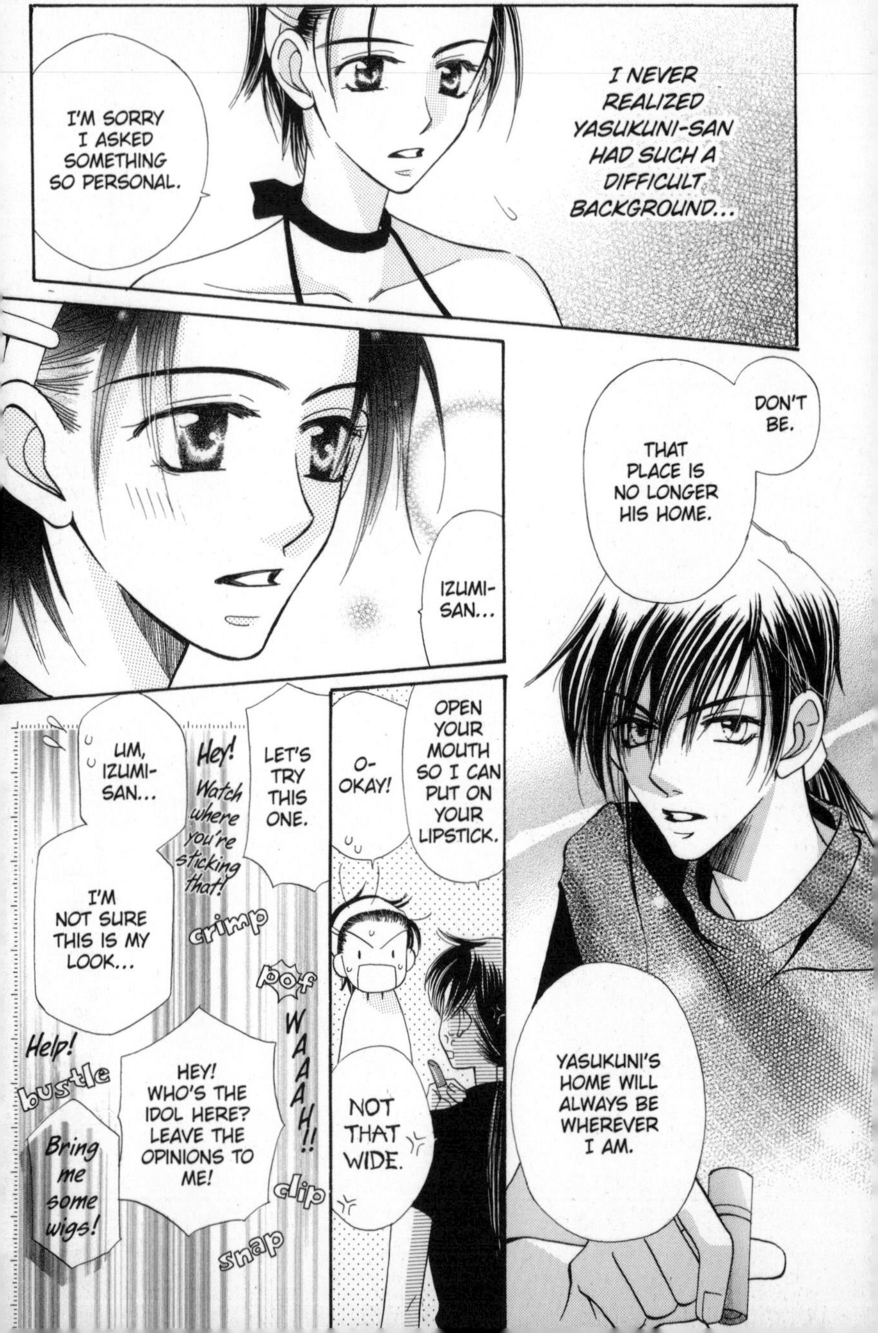
I NEVER REALIZED YASUKUNI-SAN HAD SUCH A DIFFICULT BACKGROUND...
I'M SORRY I ASKED SOMETHING SO PERSONAL.
DON'T BE.
THAT PLACE IS NO LONGER HIS HOME.
YASUKUNI'S HOME WILL ALWAYS BE WHEREVER I AM.
IZUMI-SAN...
OPEN YOUR MOUTH SO I CAN PUT ON YOUR LIPSTICK.
O-OKAY!
pof
WAAAAH!!
NOT THAT WIDE.
clip
LET'S TRY THIS ONE.
Hey! Watch where you're sticking that!
UM, IZUMI-SAN...
crimp
I'M NOT SURE THIS IS MY LOOK...
HEY! WHO'S THE IDOL HERE? LEAVE THE OPINIONS TO ME!
Help!
bustle
Bring me some wigs!
snap

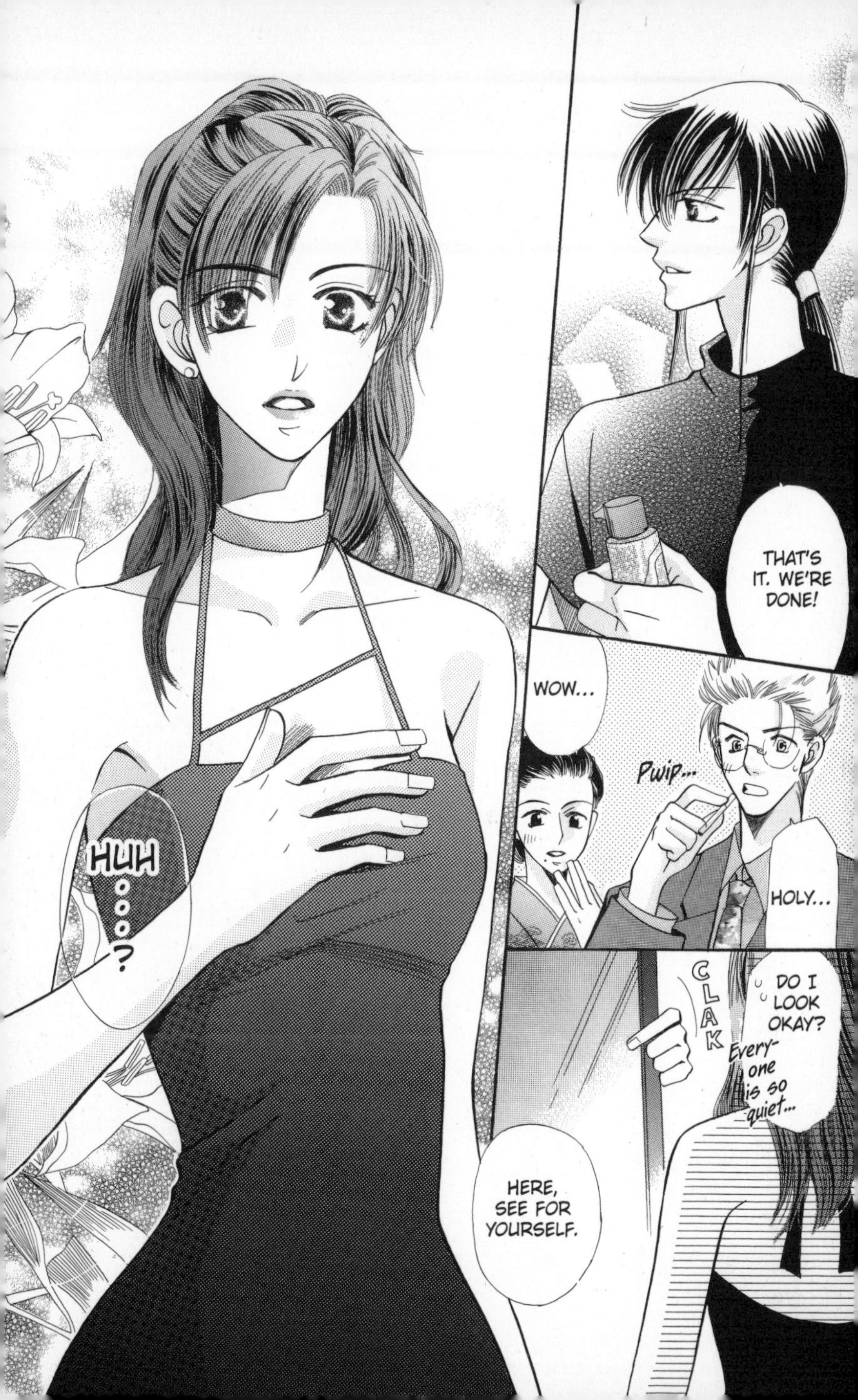
THAT'S IT. WE'RE DONE!
WOW...
Pwip...
HOLY...
DO I LOOK OKAY?
CLAK
Every-one is so quiet...
HERE, SEE FOR YOURSELF.
HUH....?

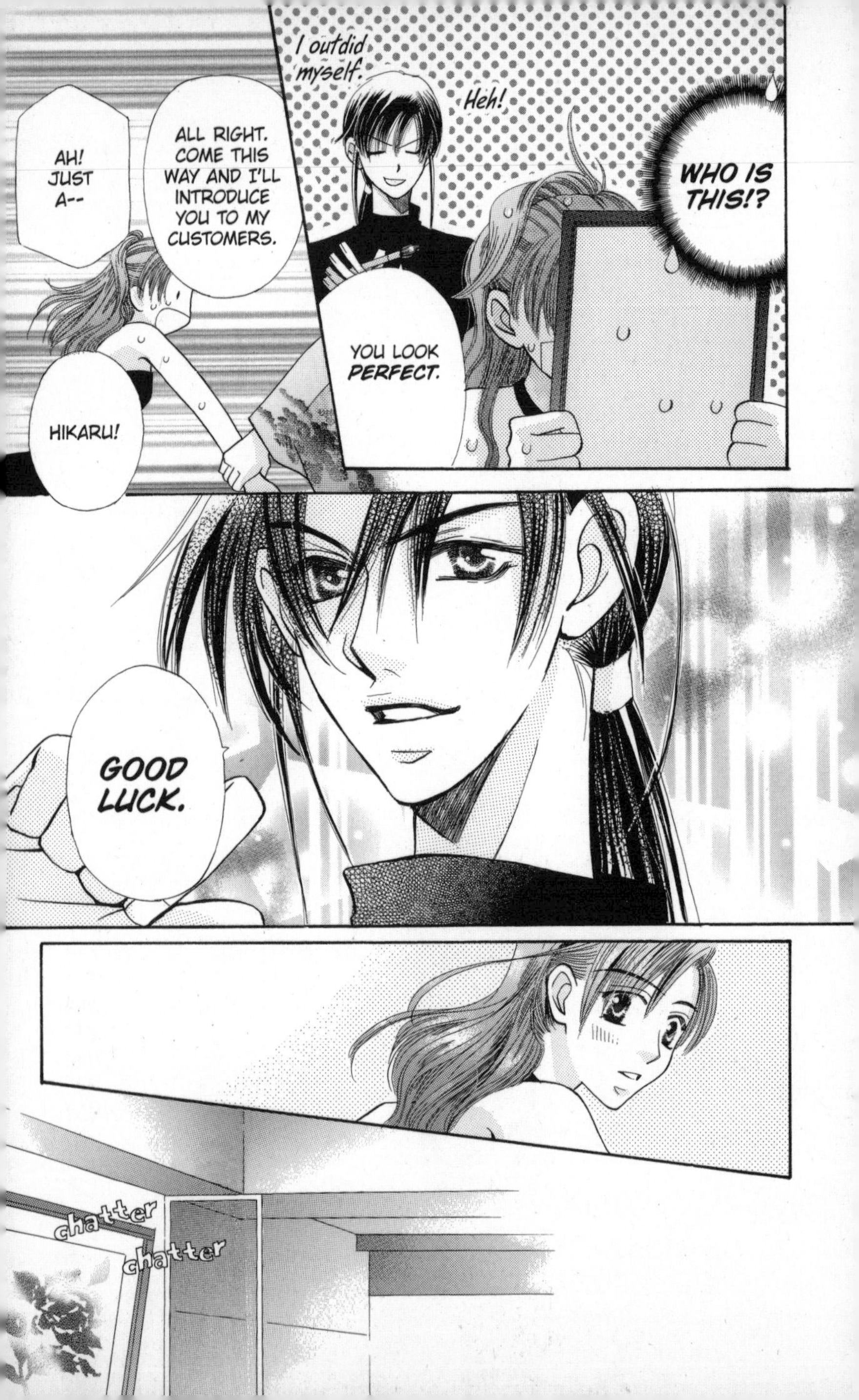
I outdid myself.
Heh!
WHO IS THIS!?
YOU LOOK PERFECT.
ALL RIGHT. COME THIS WAY AND I'LL INTRODUCE YOU TO MY CUSTOMERS.
AH! JUST A--
HIKARU!
GOOD LUCK.
chatter
chatter

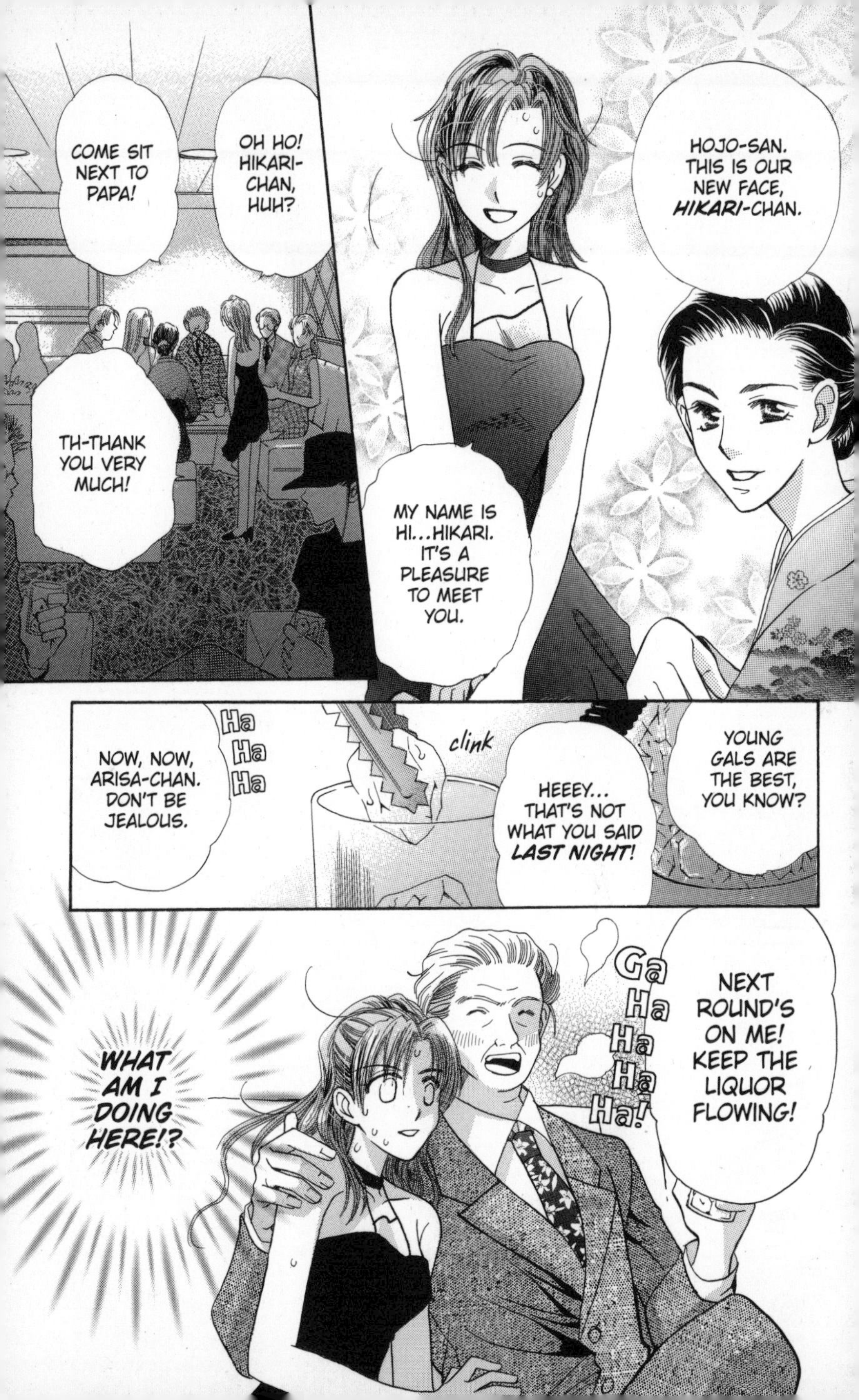
HOJO-SAN. THIS IS OUR NEW FACE, HIKARI-CHAN.
MY NAME IS HI...HIKARI. IT'S A PLEASURE TO MEET YOU.
OH HO! HIKARI-CHAN, HUH?
COME SIT NEXT TO PAPA!
TH-THANK YOU VERY MUCH!
YOUNG GALS ARE THE BEST, YOU KNOW?
HEEEY... THAT'S NOT WHAT YOU SAID LAST NIGHT!
clink
Ha Ha Ha
NOW, NOW, ARISA-CHAN. DON'T BE JEALOUS.
NEXT ROUND'S ON ME! KEEP THE LIQUOR FLOWING!
Ga Ha Ha Ha Ha!
WHAT AM I DOING HERE!?

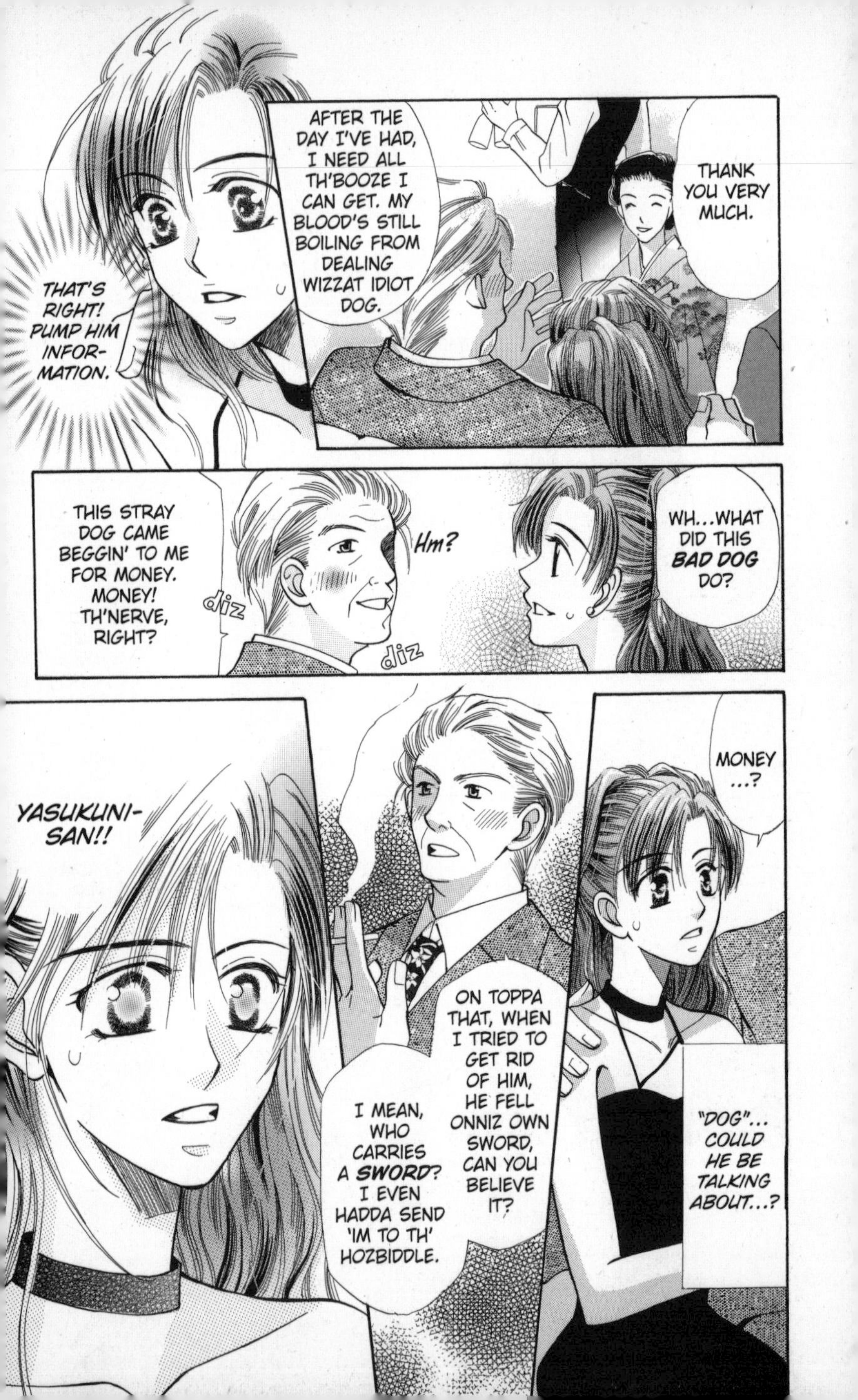
THANK YOU VERY MUCH.
AFTER THE DAY I'VE HAD, I NEED ALL TH'BOOZE I CAN GET. MY BLOOD'S STILL BOILING FROM DEALING WIZZAT IDIOT DOG.
THAT'S RIGHT! PUMP HIM INFORMATION.
WH...WHAT DID THIS BAD DOG DO?
Hm?
THIS STRAY DOG CAME BEGGIN' TO ME FOR MONEY. MONEY! TH'NERVE, RIGHT?
diz
diz
MONEY ...?
"DOG"... COULD HE BE TALKING ABOUT...?
ON TOPPA THAT, WHEN I TRIED TO GET RID OF HIM, HE FELL ONNIZ OWN SWORD, CAN YOU BELIEVE IT?
I MEAN, WHO CARRIES A SWORD? I EVEN HADDA SEND 'IM TO TH' HOZBIDDLE.
YASUKUNI-SAN!!

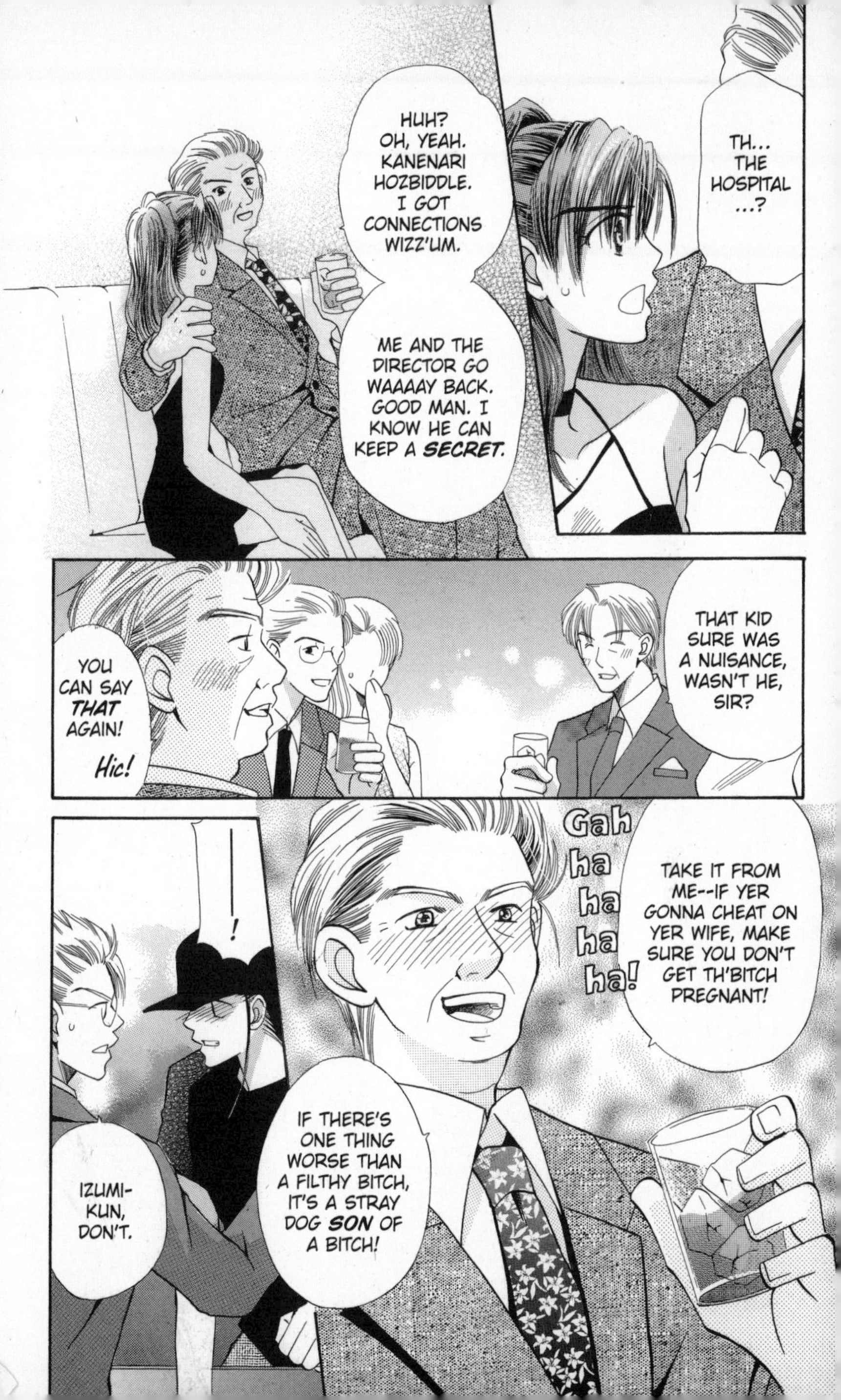
TH... THE HOSPITAL ...?
HUH? OH, YEAH. KANENARI HOZBIDDLE. I GOT CONNECTIONS WIZZ'UM.
ME AND THE DIRECTOR GO WAAAAY BACK. GOOD MAN. I KNOW HE CAN KEEP A ***SECRET.***
THAT KID SURE WAS A NUISANCE, WASN'T HE, SIR?
YOU CAN SAY ***THAT*** AGAIN!
Hic!
TAKE IT FROM ME--IF YER GONNA CHEAT ON YER WIFE, MAKE SURE YOU DON'T GET TH'BITCH PREGNANT!
Gah ha ha ha ha!
—!
IF THERE'S ONE THING WORSE THAN A FILTHY BITCH, IT'S A STRAY DOG ***SON*** OF A BITCH!
IZUMI-KUN, DON'T.

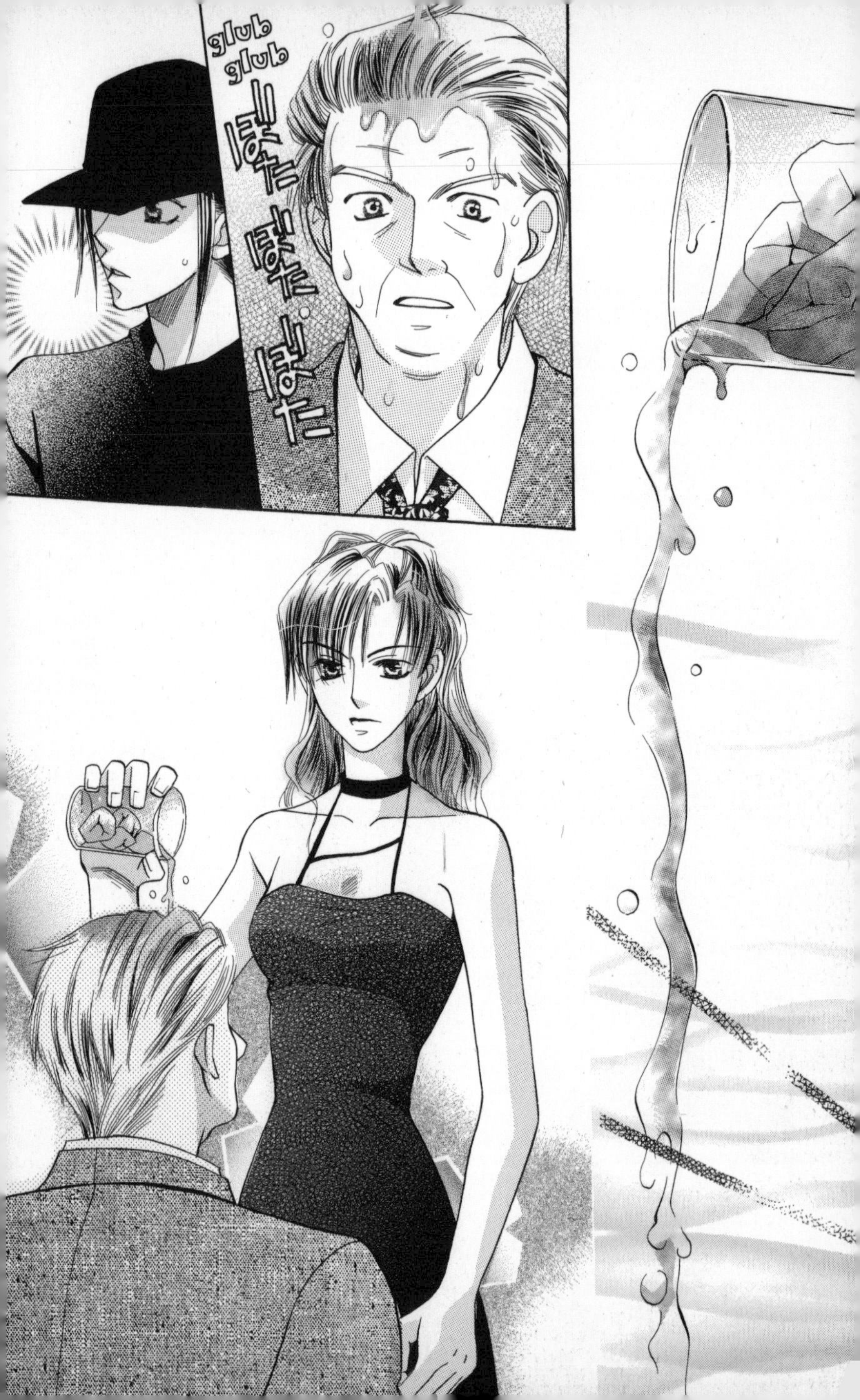
glub
glub
ぽたぽたぽた

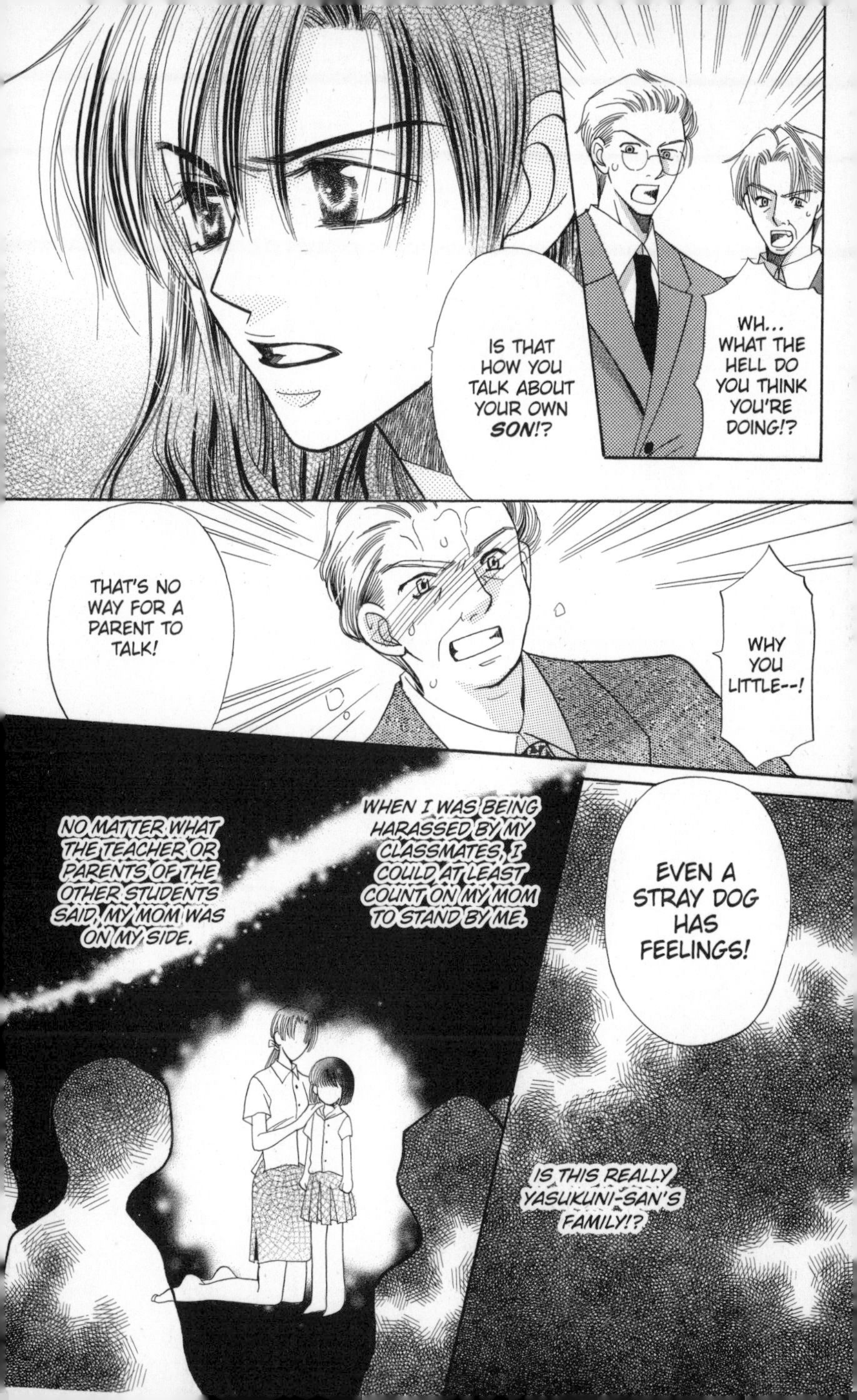
WH... WHAT THE HELL DO YOU THINK YOU'RE DOING!?
IS THAT HOW YOU TALK ABOUT YOUR OWN ***SON***!?
WHY YOU LITTLE--!
THAT'S NO WAY FOR A PARENT TO TALK!
EVEN A STRAY DOG HAS FEELINGS!
IS THIS REALLY YASUKUNI-SAN'S FAMILY!?
WHEN I WAS BEING HARASSED BY MY CLASSMATES, I COULD AT LEAST COUNT ON MY MOM TO STAND BY ME.
NO MATTER WHAT THE TEACHER OR PARENTS OF THE OTHER STUDENTS SAID, MY MOM WAS ON MY SIDE.

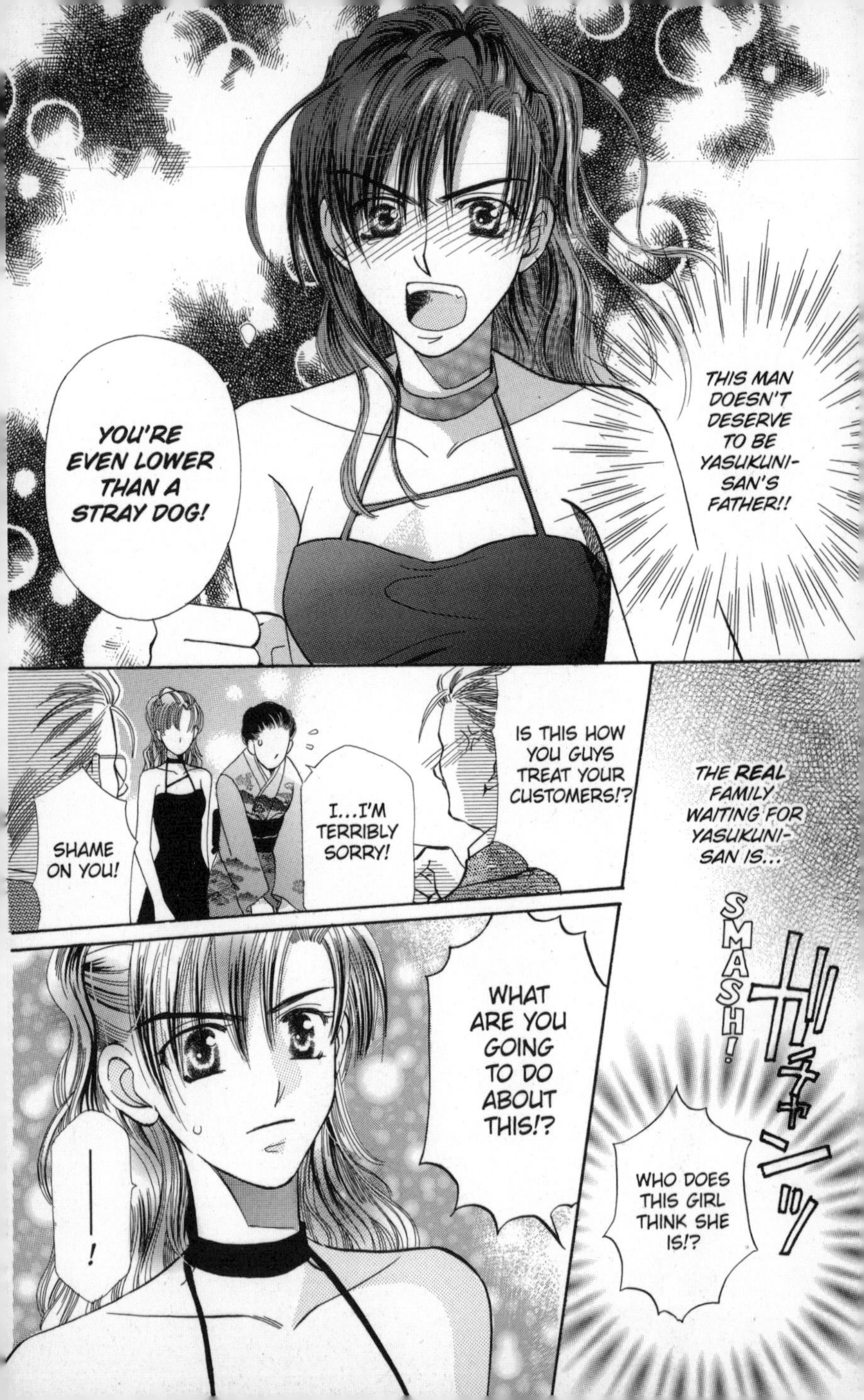
THIS MAN DOESN'T DESERVE TO BE YASUKUNI-SAN'S FATHER!!
YOU'RE EVEN LOWER THAN A STRAY DOG!
THE REAL FAMILY WAITING FOR YASUKUNI-SAN IS...
IS THIS HOW YOU GUYS TREAT YOUR CUSTOMERS!?
I...I'M TERRIBLY SORRY!
SHAME ON YOU!
SMASH!
ガチャーン
WHO DOES THIS GIRL THINK SHE IS!?
WHAT ARE YOU GOING TO DO ABOUT THIS!?
—!

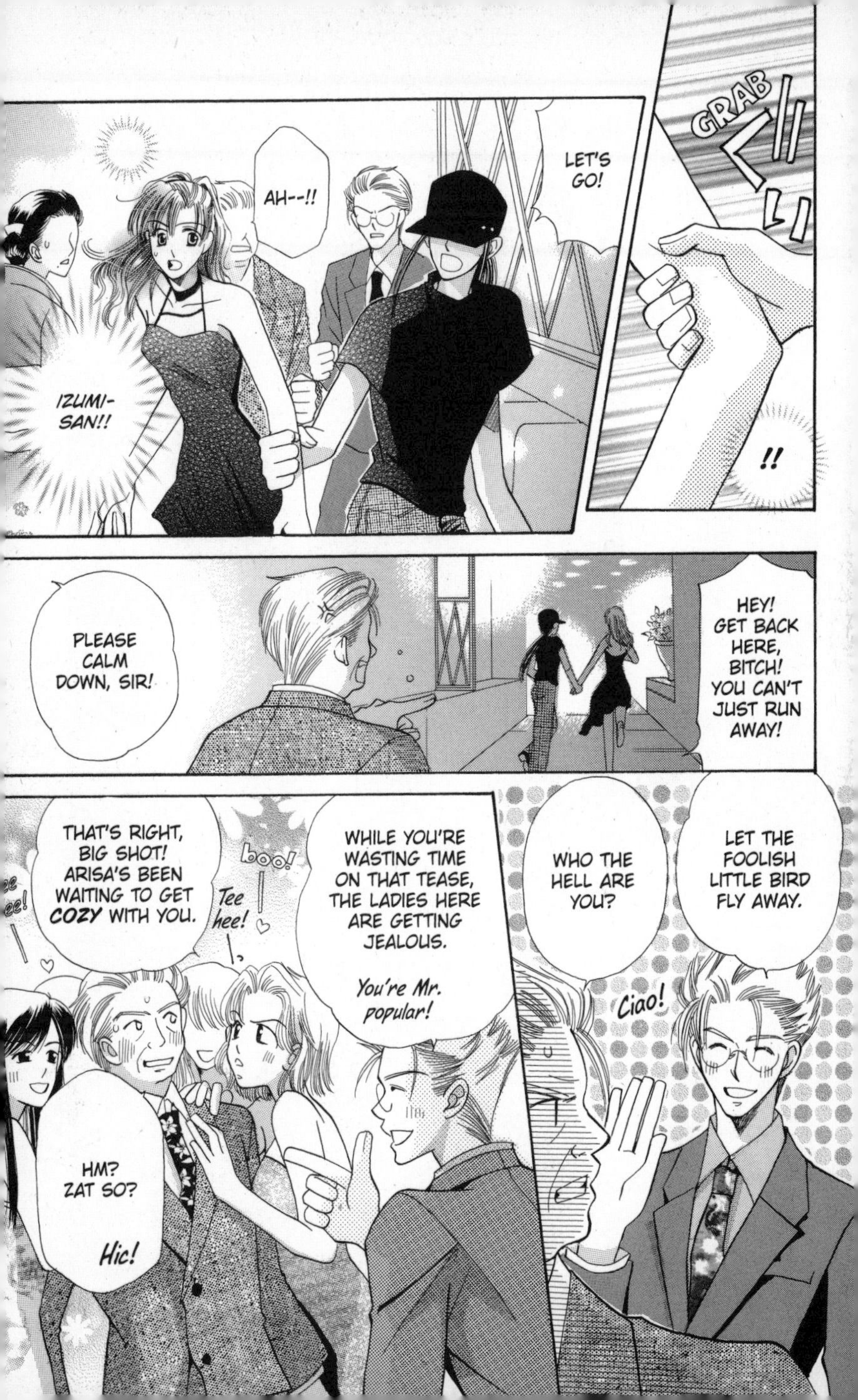

GRAB
!!
LET'S GO!
AH--!!
IZUMI-SAN!!
HEY! GET BACK HERE, BITCH! YOU CAN'T JUST RUN AWAY!
PLEASE CALM DOWN, SIR!
LET THE FOOLISH LITTLE BIRD FLY AWAY.
Ciao!
WHO THE HELL ARE YOU?
WHILE YOU'RE WASTING TIME ON THAT TEASE, THE LADIES HERE ARE GETTING JEALOUS.
You're Mr. popular!
boo!
Tee hee!
THAT'S RIGHT, BIG SHOT! ARISA'S BEEN WAITING TO GET **COZY** WITH YOU.
HM? ZAT SO?
Hic!

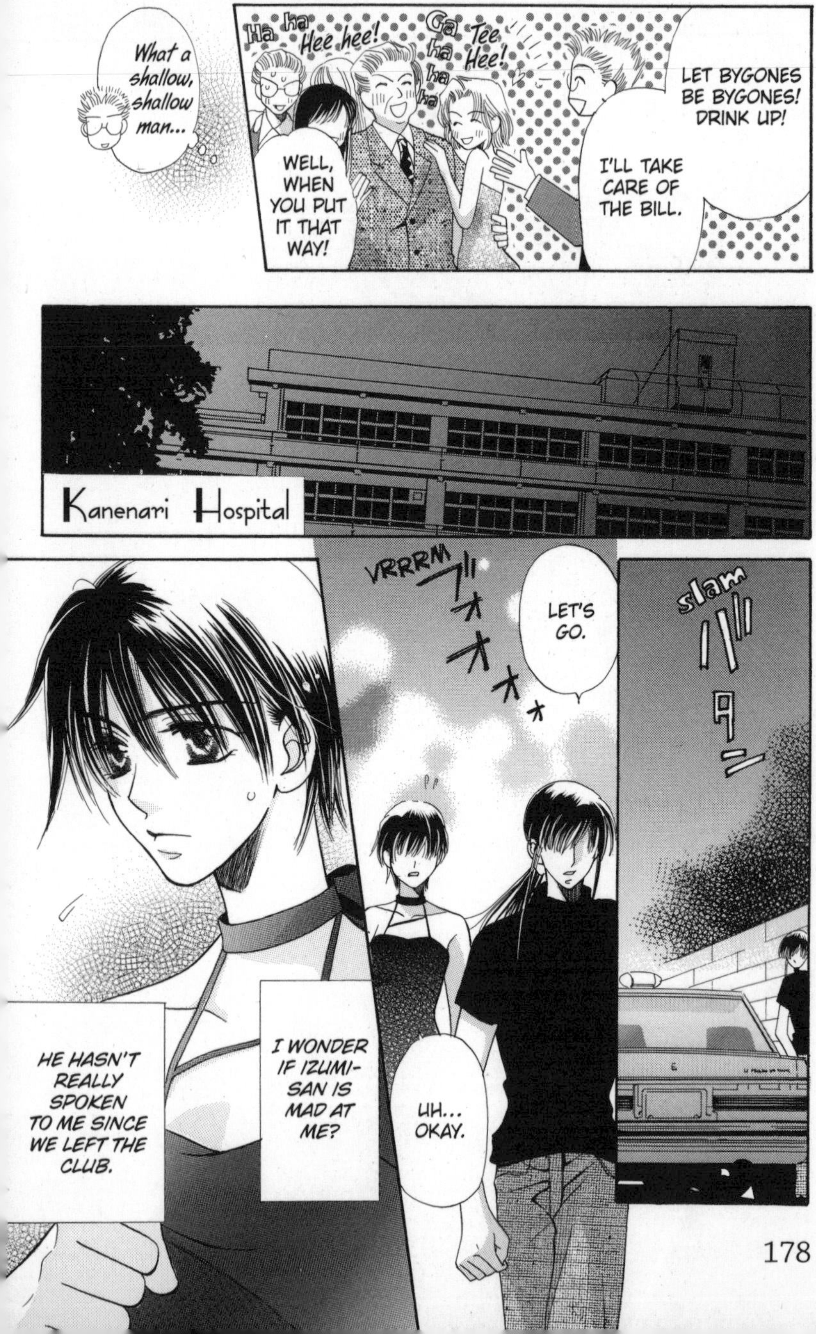

LET BYGONES BE BYGONES! DRINK UP!
I'LL TAKE CARE OF THE BILL.
Tee Hee!
Ga ha ha ha
Hee hee!
Ha ha
WELL, WHEN YOU PUT IT THAT WAY!
What a shallow, shallow man...
Kanenari Hospital
slam
LET'S GO.
VRRRM
UH... OKAY.
I WONDER IF IZUMI-SAN IS MAD AT ME?
HE HASN'T REALLY SPOKEN TO ME SINCE WE LEFT THE CLUB.

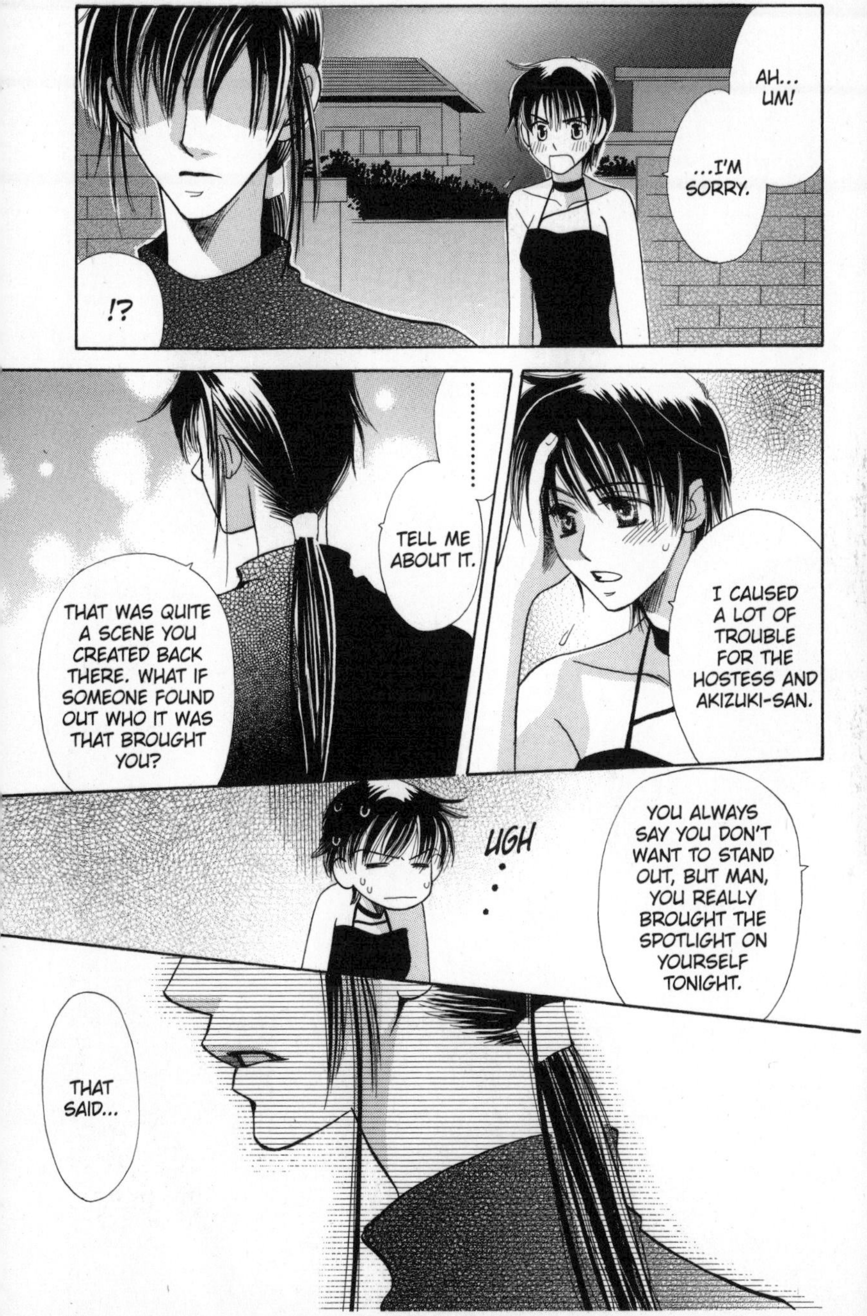
AH... UM!
...I'M SORRY.
!?
I CAUSED A LOT OF TROUBLE FOR THE HOSTESS AND AKIZUKI-SAN.
......
TELL ME ABOUT IT.
THAT WAS QUITE A SCENE YOU CREATED BACK THERE. WHAT IF SOMEONE FOUND OUT WHO IT WAS THAT BROUGHT YOU?
YOU ALWAYS SAY YOU DON'T WANT TO STAND OUT, BUT MAN, YOU REALLY BROUGHT THE SPOTLIGHT ON YOURSELF TONIGHT.
UGH
THAT SAID...

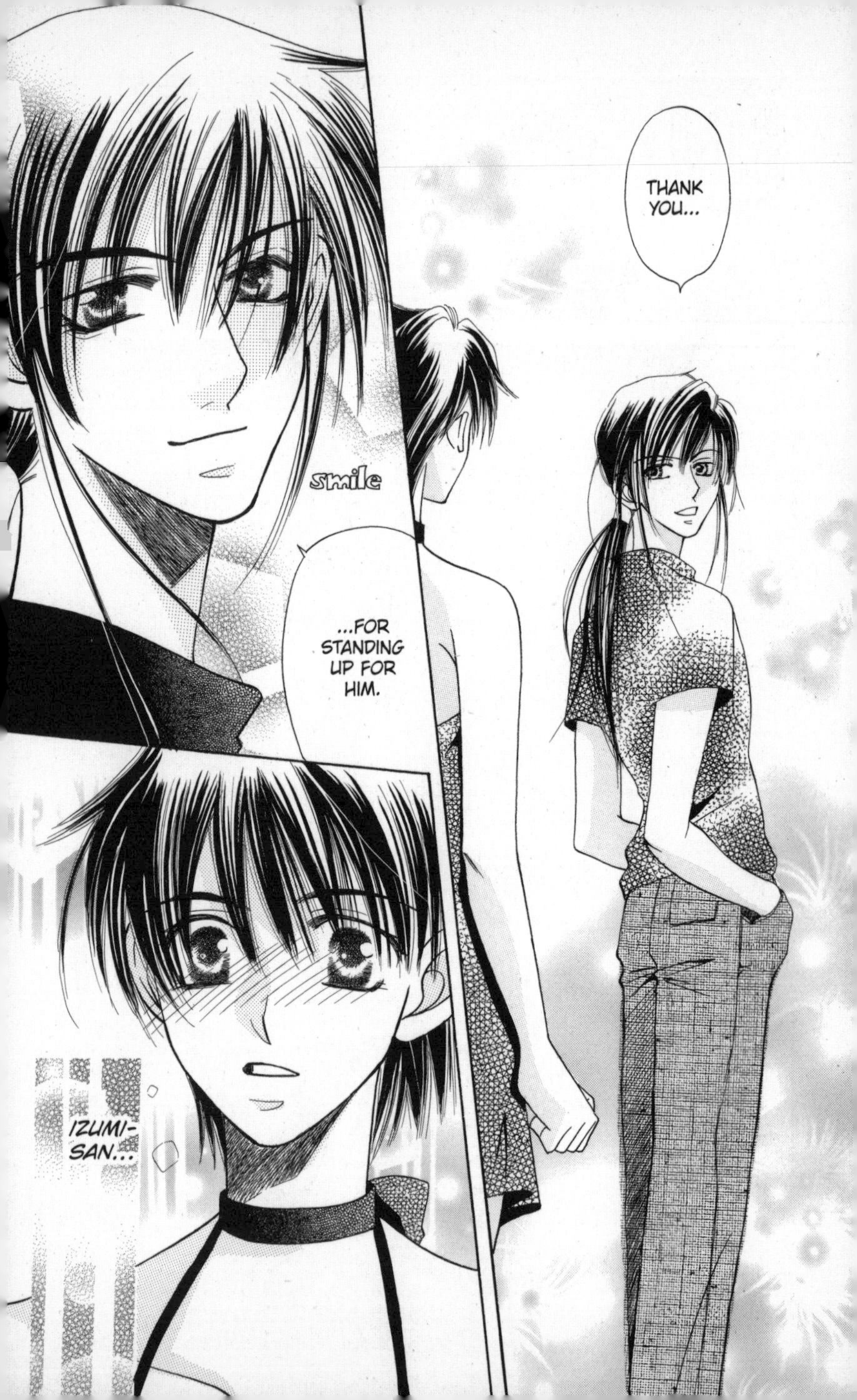
THANK YOU...
...FOR STANDING UP FOR HIM.
smile
IZUMI-SAN...

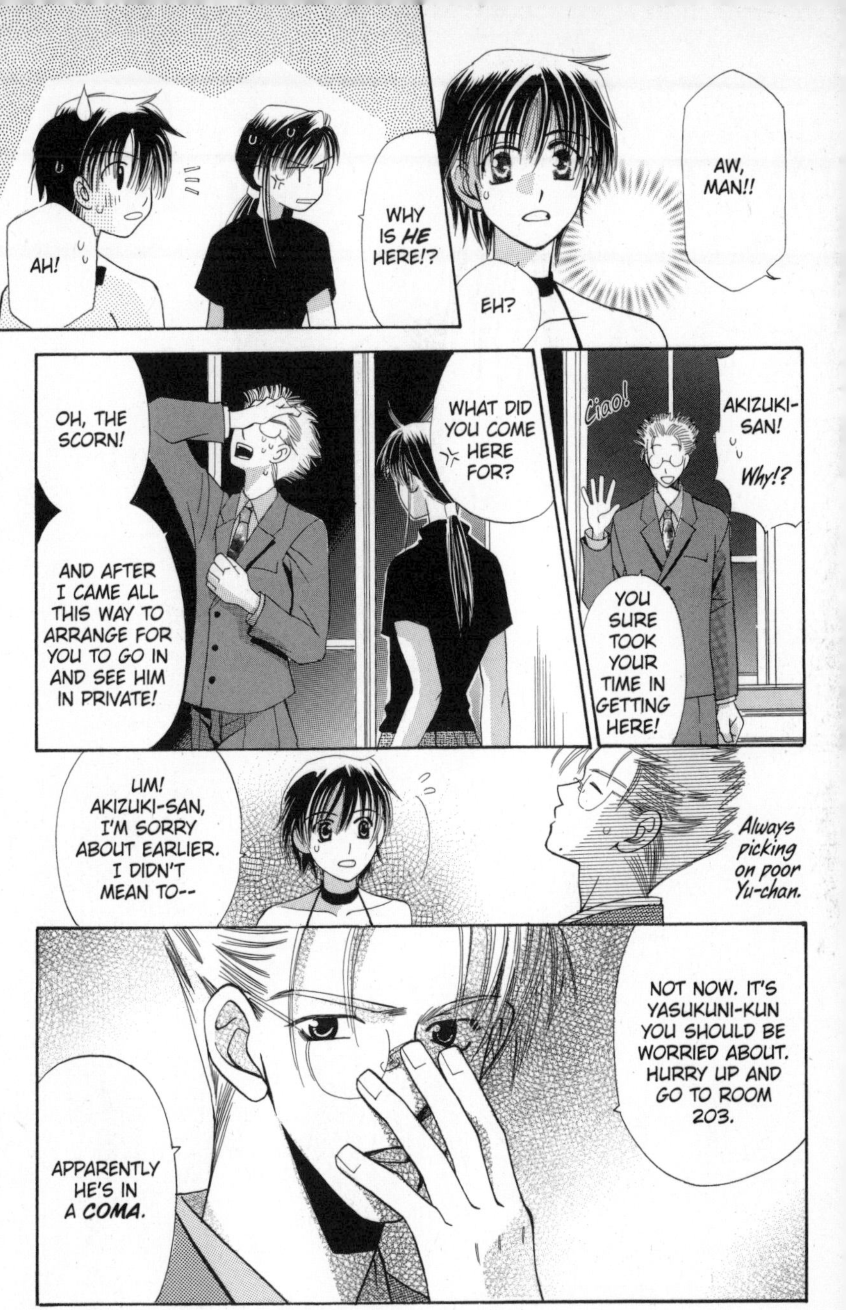
AW, MAN!!
EH?
WHY IS *HE* HERE!?
AH!
AKIZUKI-SAN!
Why!?
Ciao!
YOU SURE TOOK YOUR TIME IN GETTING HERE!
WHAT DID YOU COME HERE FOR?
OH, THE SCORN!
AND AFTER I CAME ALL THIS WAY TO ARRANGE FOR YOU TO GO IN AND SEE HIM IN PRIVATE!
Always picking on poor Yu-chan.
UM! AKIZUKI-SAN, I'M SORRY ABOUT EARLIER. I DIDN'T MEAN TO--
NOT NOW. IT'S YASUKUNI-KUN YOU SHOULD BE WORRIED ABOUT. HURRY UP AND GO TO ROOM 203.
APPARENTLY HE'S IN A *COMA*.

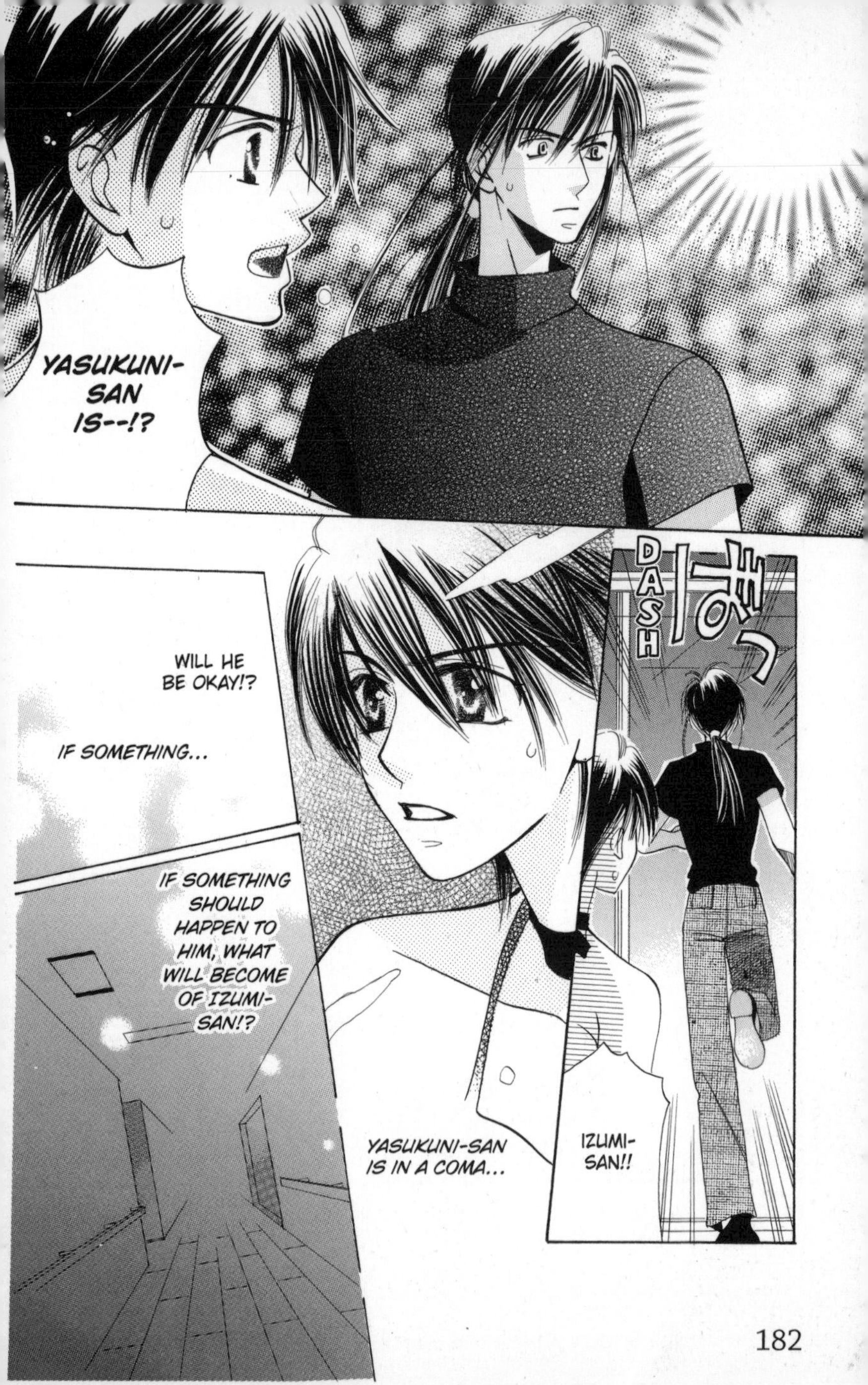
YASUKUNI-SAN IS--!?
DASH
IZUMI-SAN!!
YASUKUNI-SAN IS IN A COMA...
WILL HE BE OKAY!?
IF SOMETHING...
IF SOMETHING SHOULD HAPPEN TO HIM, WHAT WILL BECOME OF IZUMI-SAN!?

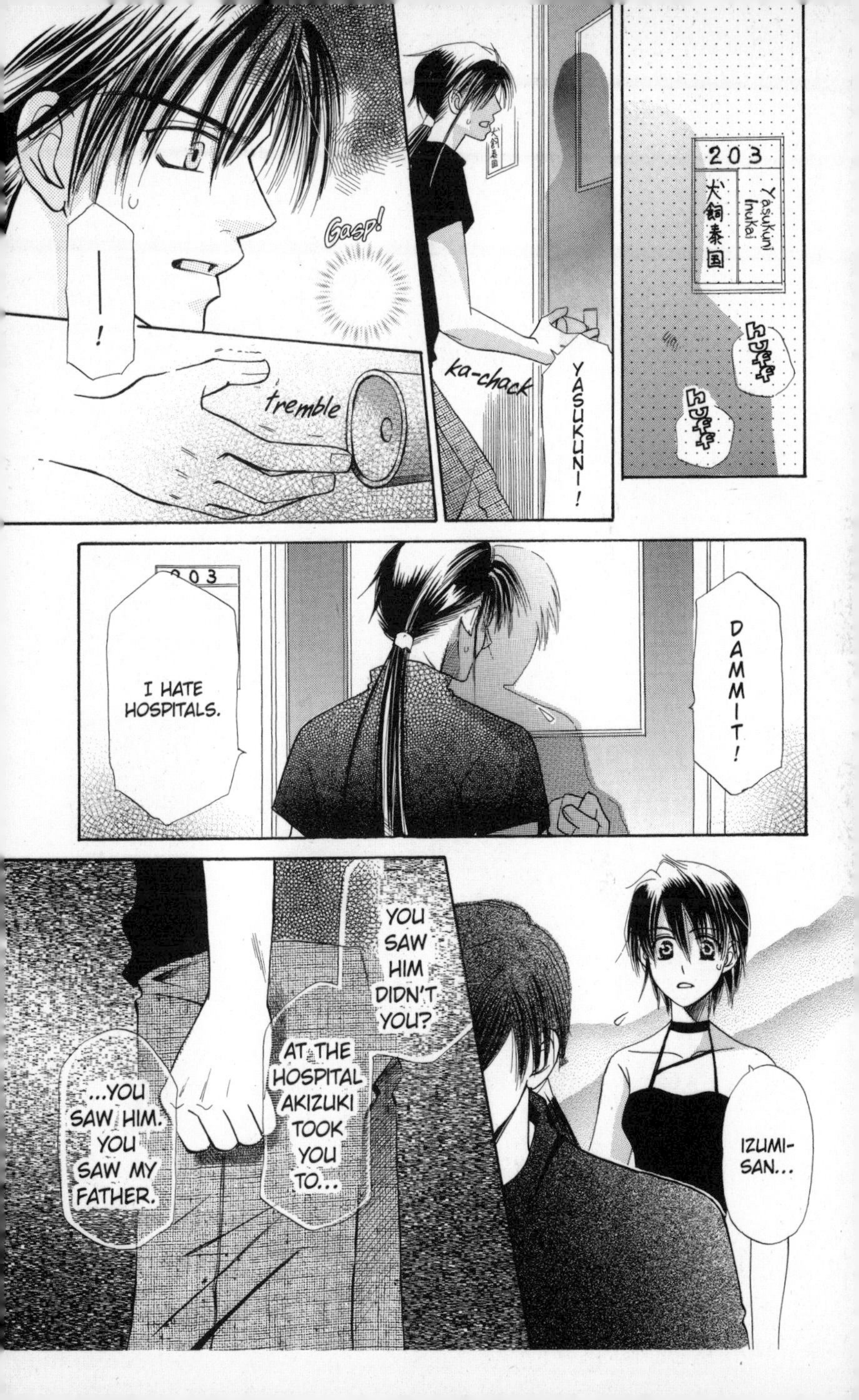
203
犬飼泰国
Yasukuni Inukai
huff
huff
YASUKUNI!
ka-chack
Gasp!
—!
tremble
DAMMIT!
203
I HATE HOSPITALS.
IZUMI-SAN...
YOU SAW HIM DIDN'T YOU?
AT THE HOSPITAL AKIZUKI TOOK YOU TO...
...YOU SAW HIM. YOU SAW MY FATHER.

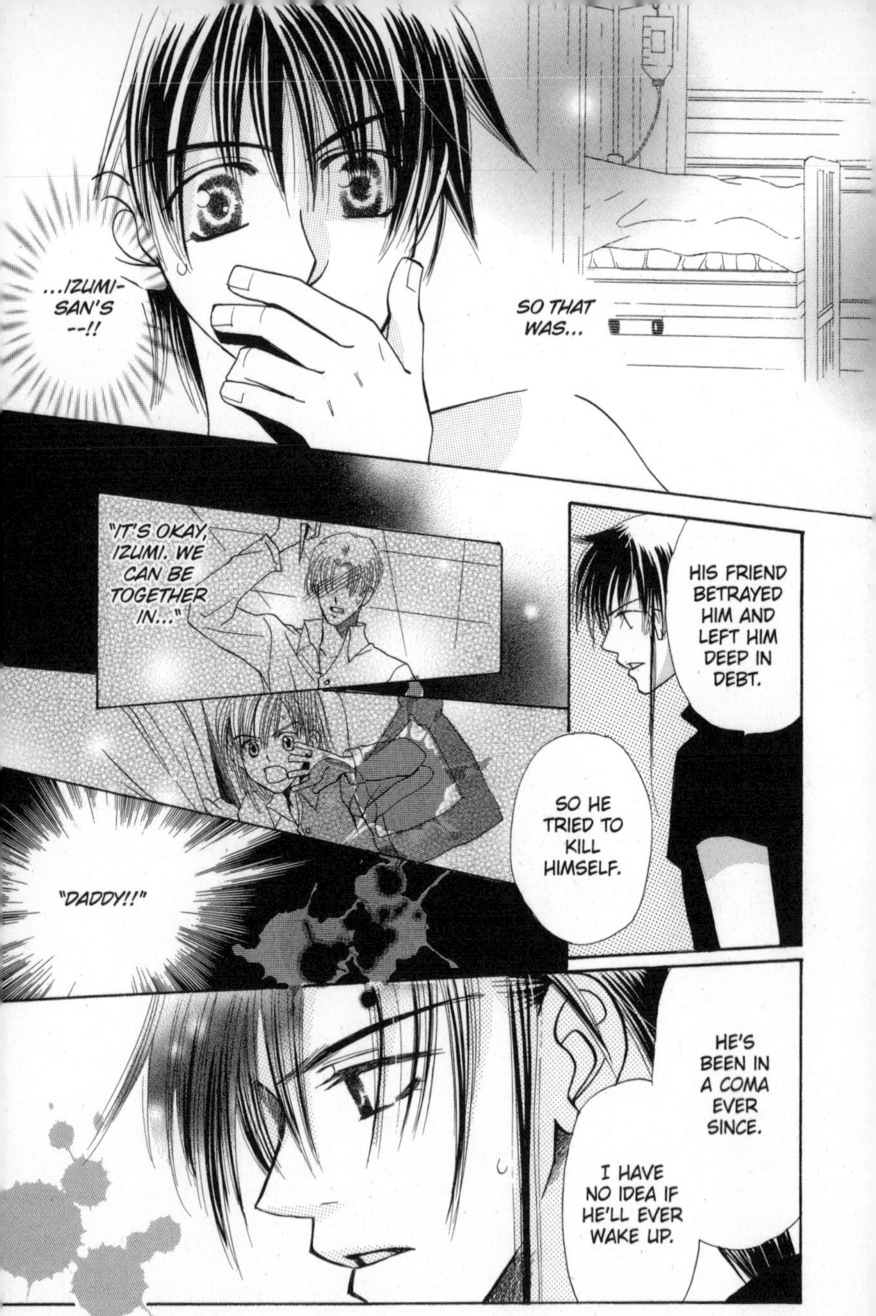
SO THAT WAS...
...IZUMI-SAN'S --!!
HIS FRIEND BETRAYED HIM AND LEFT HIM DEEP IN DEBT.
SO HE TRIED TO KILL HIMSELF.
"IT'S OKAY, IZUMI. WE CAN BE TOGETHER IN..."
"DADDY!!"
HE'S BEEN IN A COMA EVER SINCE.
I HAVE NO IDEA IF HE'LL EVER WAKE UP.

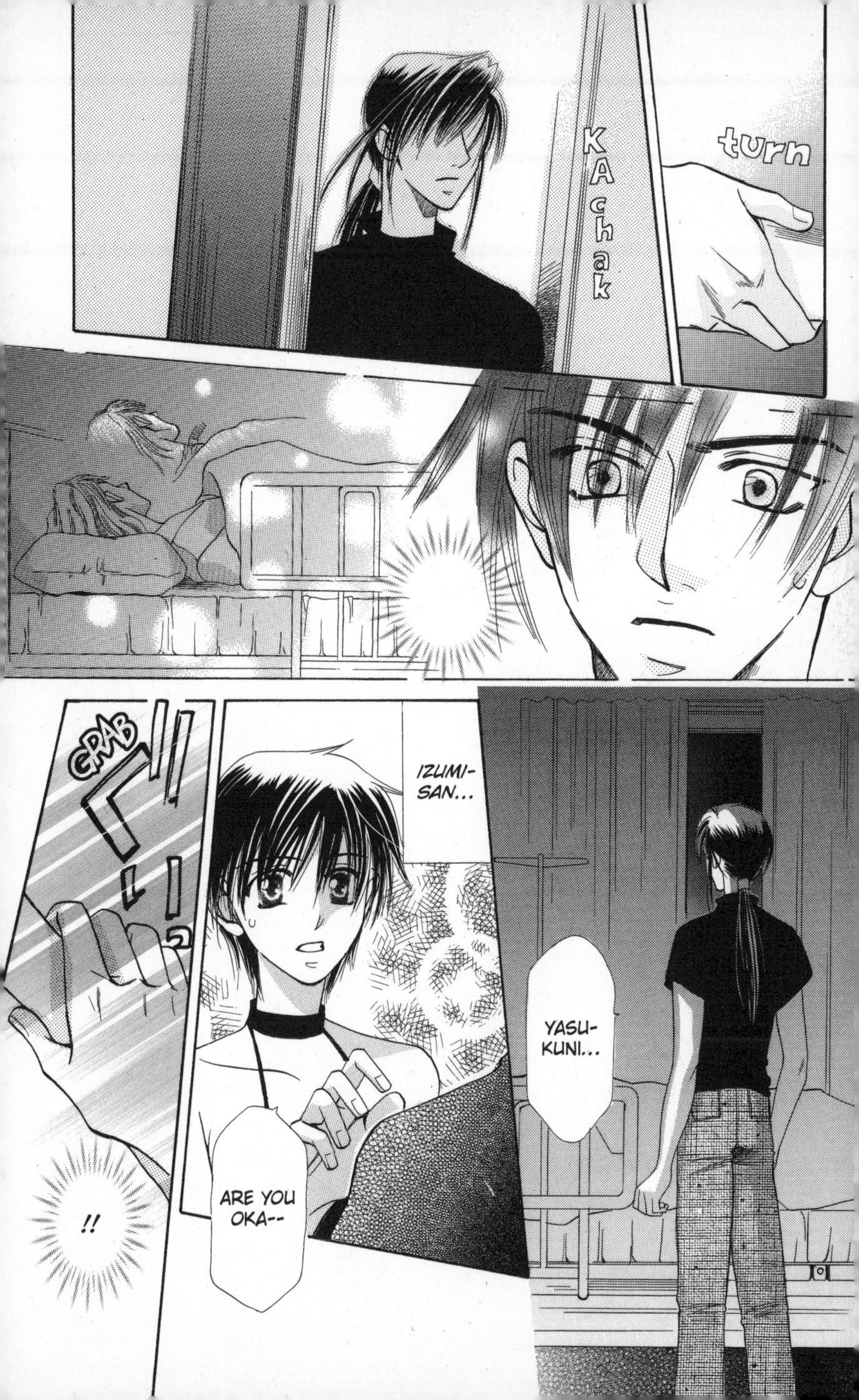
turn
KAchak
YASU-KUNI...
IZUMI-SAN...
ARE YOU OKA--
GRAB
!!

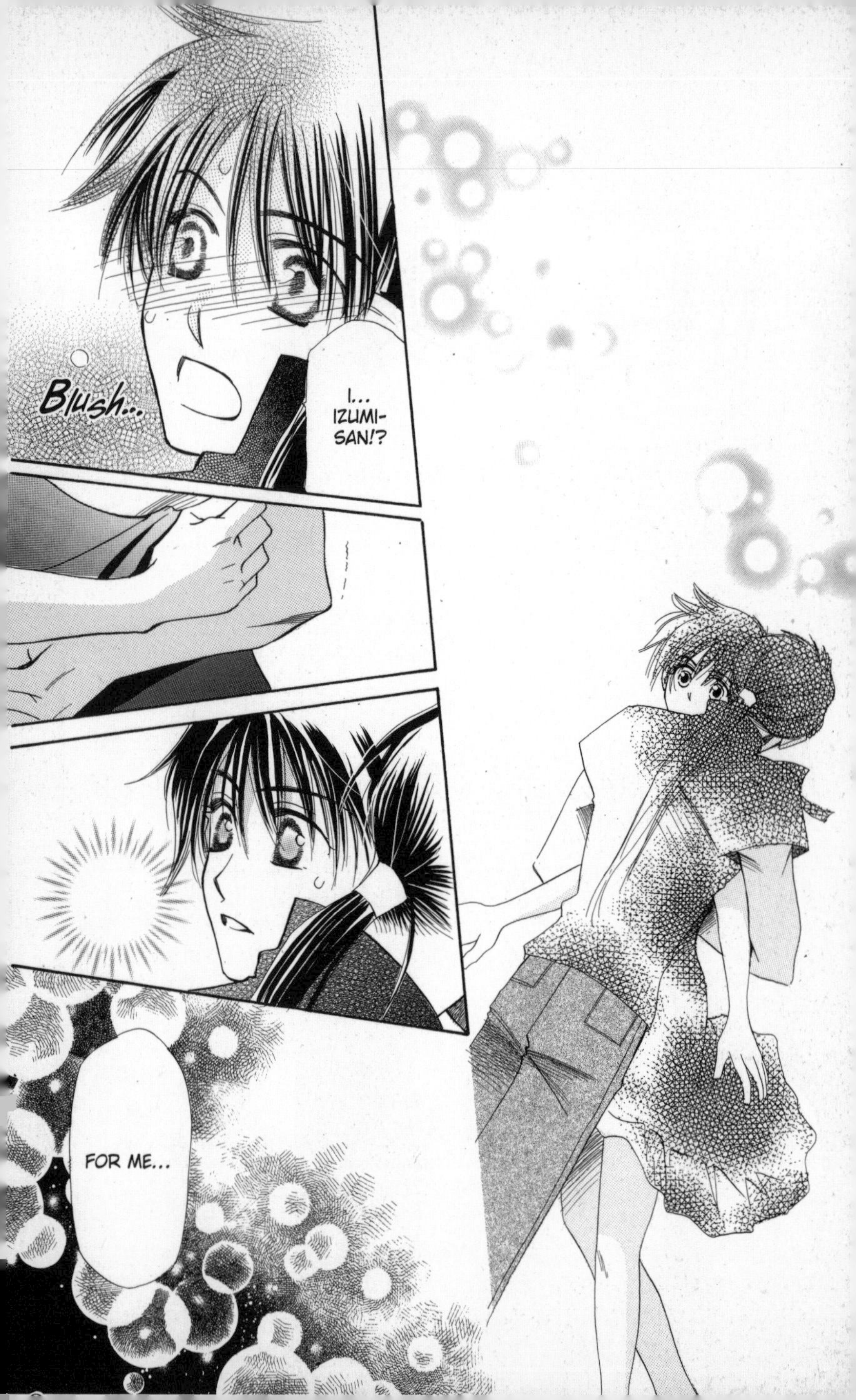
Blush...
I... IZUMI-SAN!?
FOR ME...

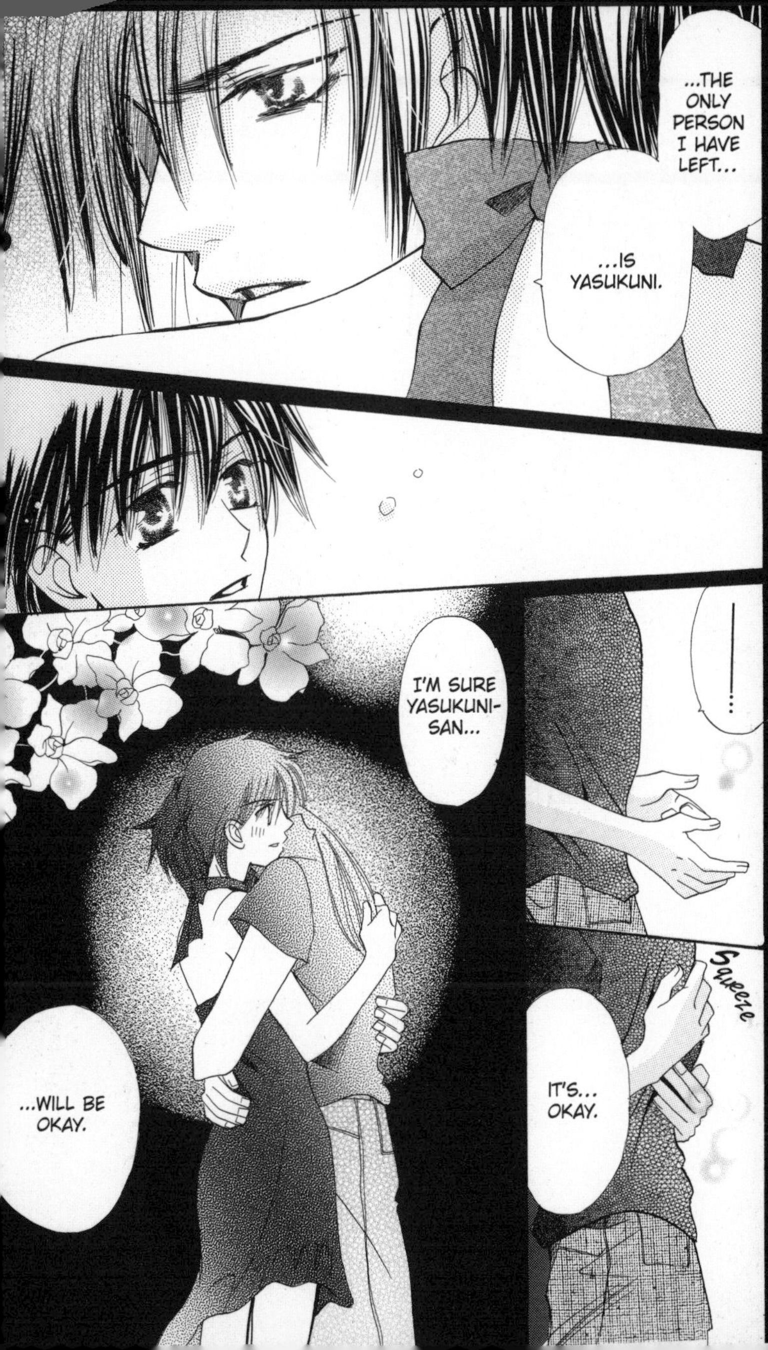
...THE ONLY PERSON I HAVE LEFT...
...IS YASUKUNI.
Squeeze
IT'S... OKAY.
I'M SURE YASUKUNI-SAN...
...WILL BE OKAY.

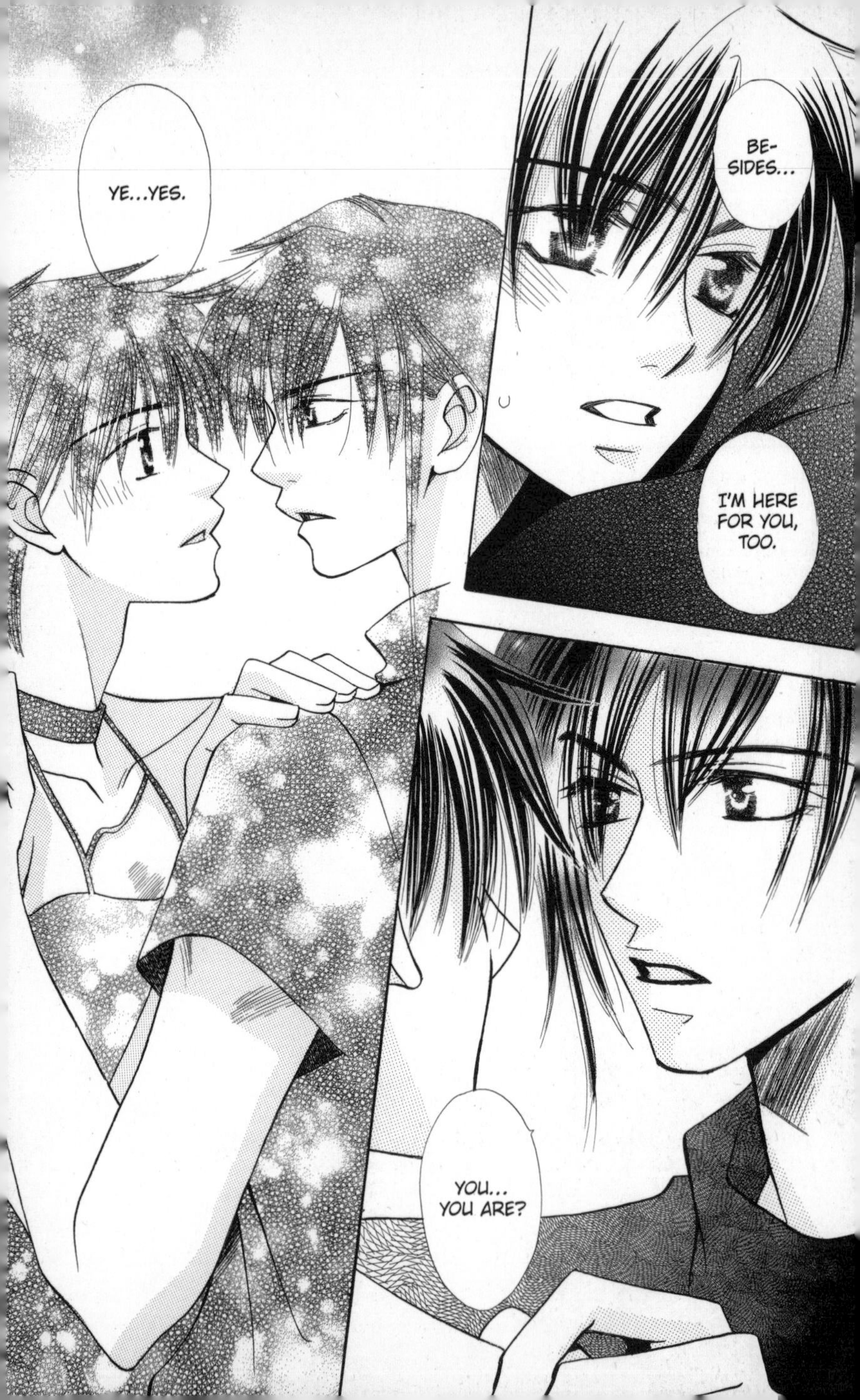
BE-SIDES...
I'M HERE FOR YOU, TOO.
YOU... YOU ARE?
YE...YES.

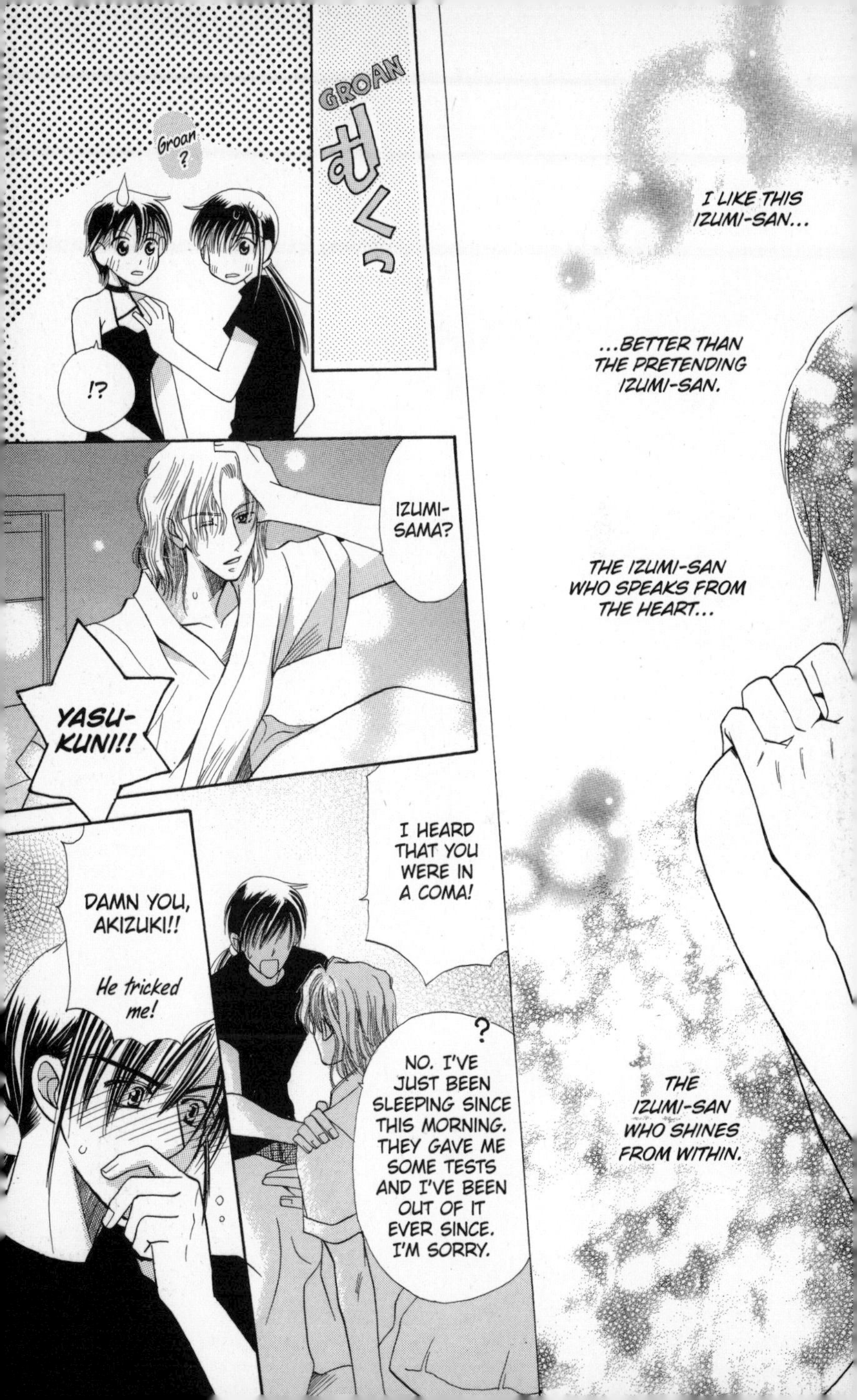
I LIKE THIS IZUMI-SAN...
...BETTER THAN THE PRETENDING IZUMI-SAN.
THE IZUMI-SAN WHO SPEAKS FROM THE HEART...
THE IZUMI-SAN WHO SHINES FROM WITHIN.
GROAN
むくっ
Groan ?
!?
IZUMI-SAMA?
YASU-KUNI!!
I HEARD THAT YOU WERE IN A COMA!
DAMN YOU, AKIZUKI!!
He tricked me!
?
NO. I'VE JUST BEEN SLEEPING SINCE THIS MORNING. THEY GAVE ME SOME TESTS AND I'VE BEEN OUT OF IT EVER SINCE. I'M SORRY.

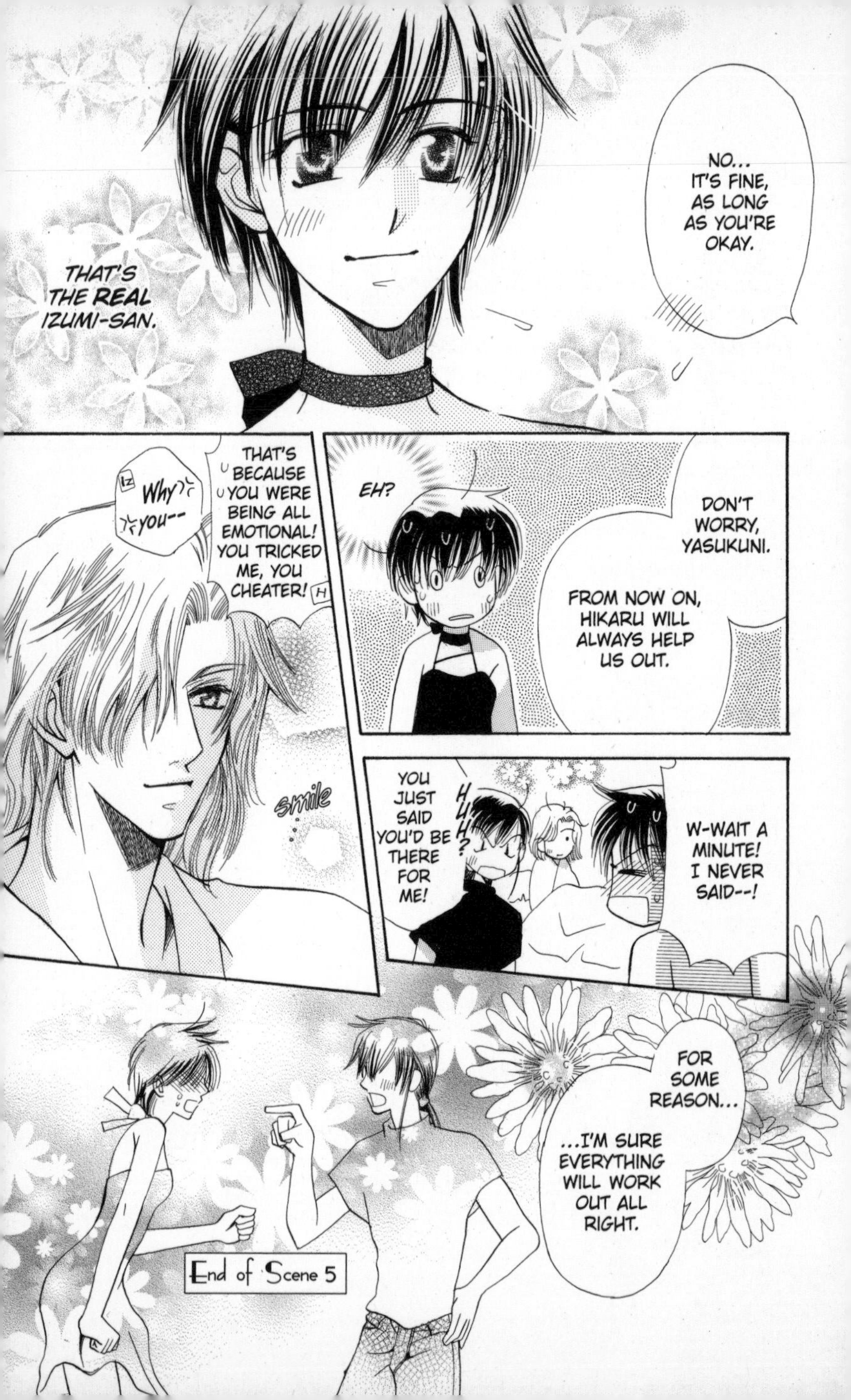
NO... IT'S FINE, AS LONG AS YOU'RE OKAY.
THAT'S THE REAL IZUMI-SAN.
DON'T WORRY, YASUKUNI.
FROM NOW ON, HIKARU WILL ALWAYS HELP US OUT.
EH?
W-WAIT A MINUTE! I NEVER SAID--!
HUH?
YOU JUST SAID YOU'D BE THERE FOR ME!
THAT'S BECAUSE YOU WERE BEING ALL EMOTIONAL! YOU TRICKED ME, YOU CHEATER!
Why you--
smile
FOR SOME REASON...
...I'M SURE EVERYTHING WILL WORK OUT ALL RIGHT.
End of Scene 5

An Afterward?

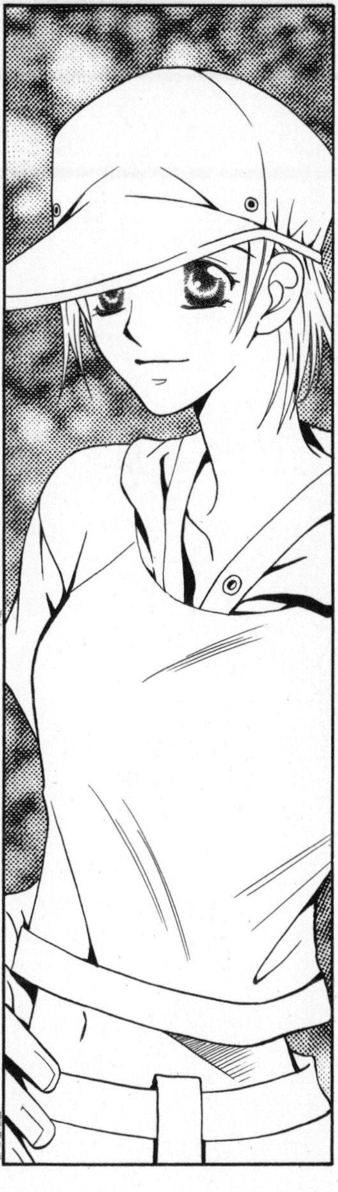

Thank you for reading Tenshi ja Nai!! vol 1! Did you like it? (ba-dum ba-dum) I'm so anxious (ba-dum ba-dum) to find out if a volume 2 will be released! There are so many issues to worry about, can you blame me for being nervous!? (ba-dum ba-dum). Whether or not people like the plot... Whether they will accept the title... Not to mention that my deadlines are getting close. No wonder I have more gray hair now!

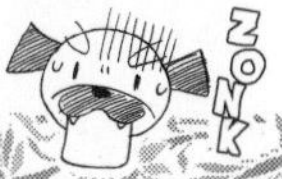
ZONK

Ohh...This isn't right. Not at all! I swore I wouldn't cry! How terrible. I will not cry until my work is done! At any rate, I, more than anyone else, am really hoping (laugh) that I will see you again in volume 2.

See you again soon!

2003. 7.20

Takako Shigematsu

Special thanks

Everyone who read my book.

My assistants, Hariguchi-san and Kashiwabara-san.

My dear pets Molly and Reggie.

My supportive family and friends.

My editor, Kijima-san.

Many, many thanks!
2003. 7.19

TENSHI JA NAI!!

I'm No Angel!

Like what you read?
Please send your feedback,
your fan art and letters to:

Go! Media Entertainment, LLC
5737 Kanan Rd., #591
Agoura Hills, CA 91301

See you again!

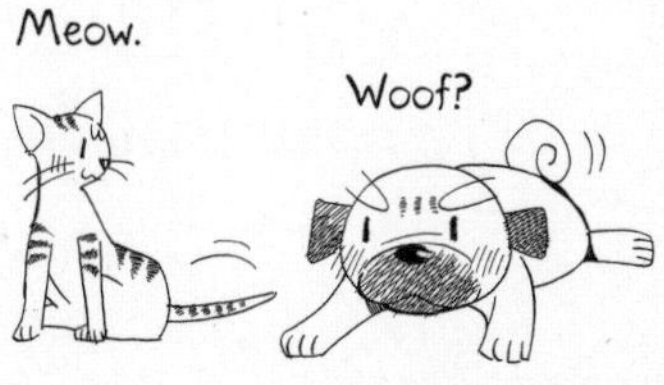
Meow.
Woof?

In the next volume of

TENSHI JA NAI!!

I'm No Angel!

a **SCHOOLGIRL CRUSH**
transforms into
FORBIDDEN LUST!

Will Hikaru give in to
the ultimate temptation!?

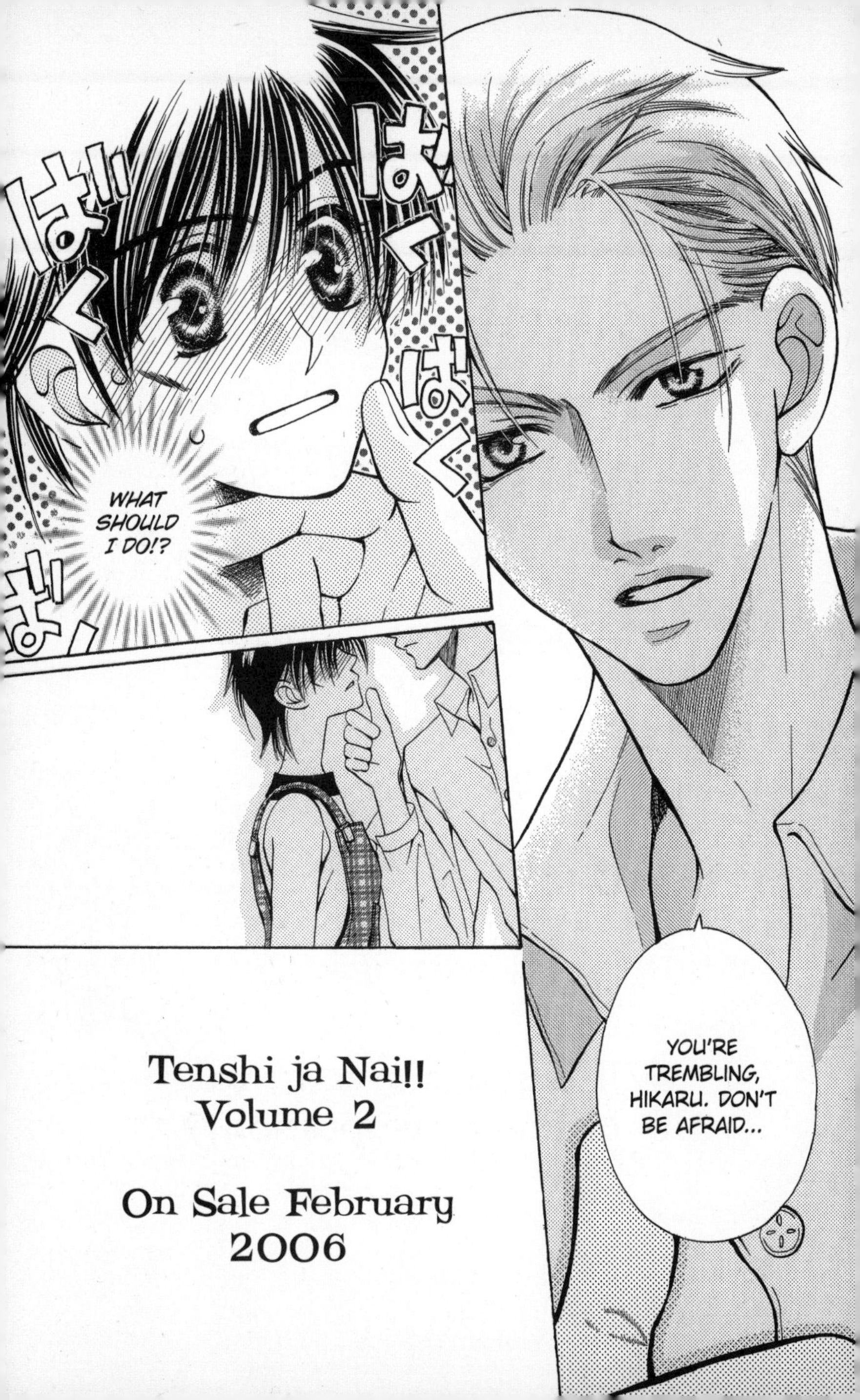
YOU'RE TREMBLING, HIKARU. DON'T BE AFRAID...
WHAT SHOULD I DO!?
Tenshi ja Nai!!
Volume 2
On Sale February 2006

If you enjoyed this book,
check out these other
great Manga available
now from Go! Comi...

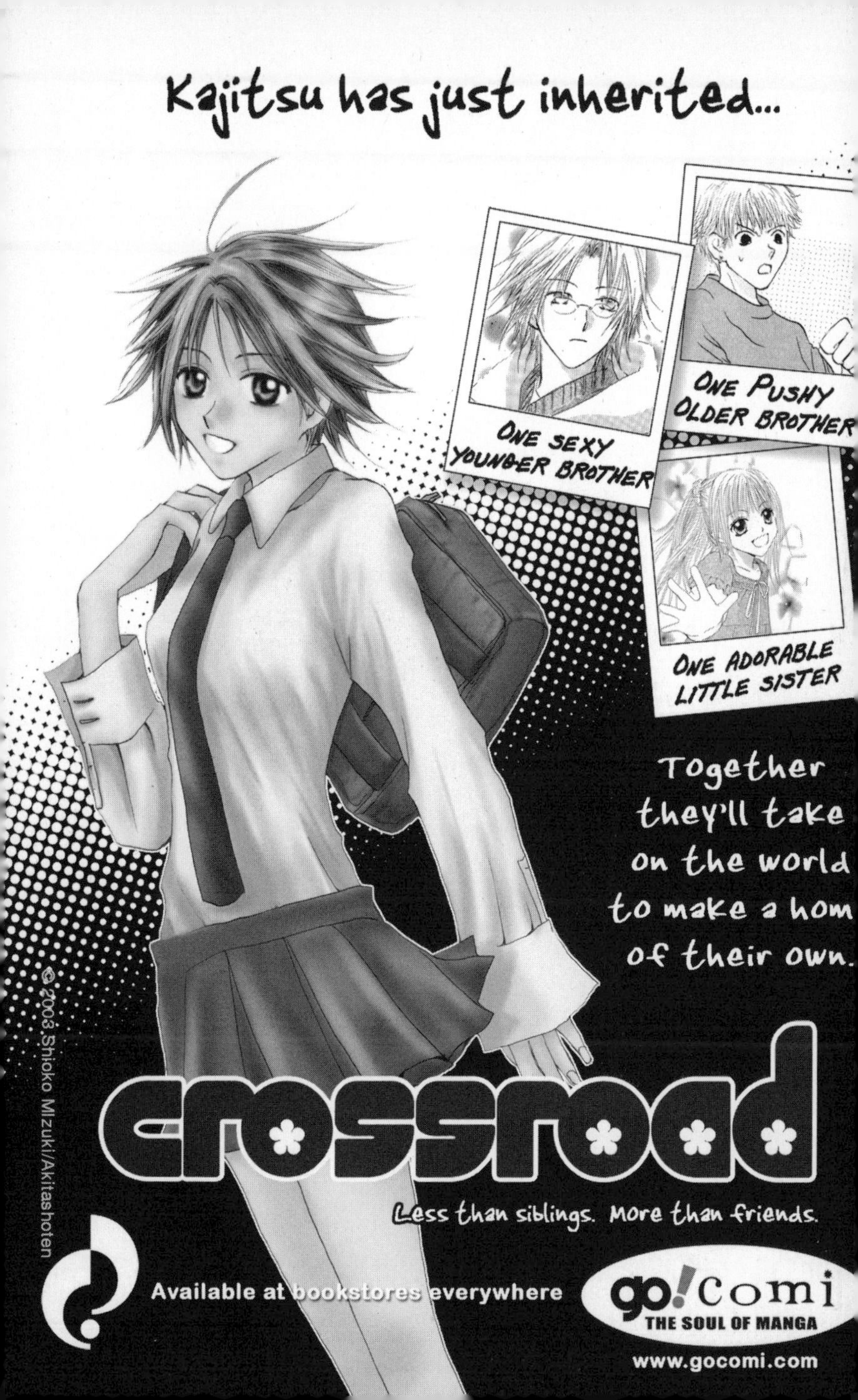
Kajitsu has just inherited...
ONE SEXY YOUNGER BROTHER
ONE PUSHY OLDER BROTHER
ONE ADORABLE LITTLE SISTER
Together they'll take on the world to make a hom of their own.
© 2003 Shioko Mizuki/Akitashoten
crossroad
Less than siblings. More than friends.
Available at bookstores everywhere
go!comi
THE SOUL OF MANGA
www.gocomi.com

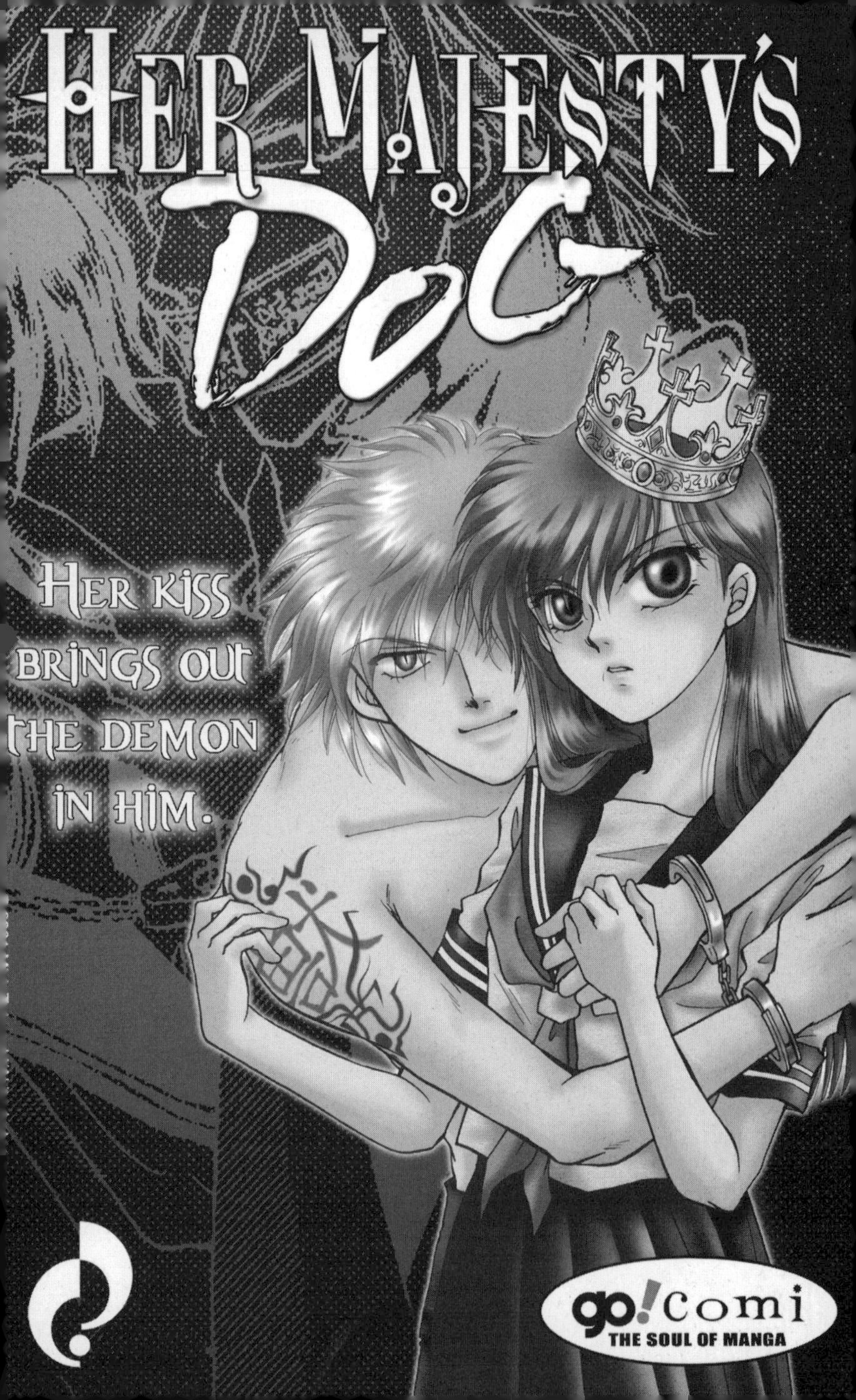
HER MAJESTY'S DOG
HER KISS BRINGS OUT THE DEMON IN HIM.
go! comi
THE SOUL OF MANGA

INNOCENT.

PURE.

BEAUTIFUL.

DAMNED.

Cantarella

© 2001 You Higuri/Akitashoten

A DARK FANTASY
INSPIRED BY THE LIFE OF CESARE BORGIA
WROUGHT BY THE HAND OF YOU HIGURI
IN A SIGNATURE EDITION FROM GO! COMI

Author's Note

Volume 1 is Finally Here!
Thanks to all of my fans for making
this happen! In order to support my
new family member, I'm looking forward
to working harder! The photo above is
of my beloved dog, Molly, who is looking
after our new family member. (laugh)

-Takako Shigematsu

Visit Shigematsu-sensei online at
http://www5b.biglobe.ne.jp/~taka_s/